THE STRATEGIC PLANNING MANAGEMENT READER

LIAM FAHEY

Associate Professor, Management Policy
Boston University

PRENTICE HALL
Englewood Cliffs, New Jersey 07632

LIBRARY OF CONGRESS
Library of Congress Cataloging-in-Publication Data

The Strategic planning management reader / [edited by] Liam Fahey.
    p.   cm.
    "Readings and case applications . . . are drawn from Strategic
planning management"—Introd.
    Includes index.
    ISBN 0-13-851759-2
    1. Corporate planning—Case studies.   2. Strategic planning—Case
studies.   I. Fahey, Liam.   II. Strategic planning
management.
HD30.28.S7344 1989
658.4'012'0926—dc19   88-25237
                                                       CIP

Editorial/production supervision: York Production Services
Interior design: York Production Services
Manufacturing buyer: Ed O'Dougherty

 ©1989 by Prentice-Hall, Inc.
A division of Simon & Schuster
Englewood Cliffs, New Jersey 07632

Printed in the United States of America

10   9   8   7   6   5   4   3   2   1

ISBN 0-13-851759-2

Prentice-Hall International (UK) Limited, *London*
Prentice-Hall of Australia Pty. Limited, *Sydney*
Prentice-Hall Canada Inc., *Toronto*
Prentice-Hall Hispanoamericana, S.A., *Mexico*
Prentice-Hall of India Private Limited, *New Delhi*
Prentice-Hall of Japan, Inc., *Tokyo*
Prentice-Hall of Southeast Asia Pte. Ltd., *Singapore*
Editora Prentice-Hall do Brasil, Ltda., *Rio de Janeiro*

■ CONTENTS ■

PART

1

STRATEGIC MANAGEMENT: MANAGING STRATEGIC CHANGE

CHAPTER 1 STRATEGY: CREATING AND MANAGING CHANGE 1

The Strategy Revolution *Lewis J. Perelman* 1
Strategic Planning: Enhancing Strategic Innovation *Robert Markus* 6

CHAPTER 2 STRATEGY: CREATING AND SUSTAINING COMPETITIVE ADVANTAGE 12

Finding A Theme: The Problem of Business Definition *Stephen Burnett* 12
Discovering Your Firm's Strongest Competitive Advantages *Liam Fahey* 18
How Long Can You Sustain A Competitive Advantage? *Ian C. MacMillan* 23
To Build or Not to Build: The Market-Share Question *V. K. Narayanan* 27
Strategic Signaling: Convincing Competitors You Mean It *Colin Camerer* 32

PART
2

ANALYSIS INPUTS TO STRATEGY MAKING

CHAPTER 3   MACROENVIRONMENTAL ANALYSIS   38

Understanding the Macroenvironment: A Framework for Analysis *Liam Fahey*   38

Integrating Macroenvironmental Analysis into Strategy Analysis: Some Problems *Liam Fahey*   43

How the Broader Environment Can Shape Industry Elements *V. K. Narayanan*   47

CHAPTER 4   INDUSTRY AND COMPETITIVE ANALYSIS   52

COMPETITIVE ANALYSIS   52

Competitive Analysis: Understanding Winners and Losers *William F. Rothschild*   52

Application in Strategic Management: Identifying Potential New Industry Entrants *Liam Fahey*   57

COMPETITOR ANALYSIS   61

Evaluating A Competitor's Product Strategy *William E. Rothschild*   61

Understanding Your Competitor's Functional Strategies *Robert M. Fifer*   68

Understanding Competitors Through Financial Analysis *Robert M. Fifer*   72

Understanding Your Competitor's "Personality" *Robert M. Fifer*   76

CUSTOMER ANALYSIS   81

Understanding Your Customers Through Market Audits *Michael Freehill*   81

Application in Strategic Management: Understanding Your Customers *Liam Fahey*   86

SUPPLIER ANALYSIS   90

Managing Suppliers: The Strategic Implications *Albert W. Isenman*   90

Supplier Analysis: The Supplier Perspective *Liam Fahey*   95

ANALYSIS OF STRATEGIC ALLIANCES   102

Strategic Alliances: A New Competitive Force *Jan Herring*   102

Securing Competitive Edge Through Strategic Information System Alliances *Charles Wiseman*   108

CHAPTER 5　ORGANIZATIONAL ANALYSIS　113

Building Distinctive Competences Into Competitive Advantages *Liam Fahey and H. Kurt Christensen*　113

Evaluating Your Costs Strategically *Frank T. Paine and Leonard J. Tischler*　118

CHAPTER 6　MANAGING MACROENVIRONMENTAL, INDUSTRY, AND ORGANIZATIONAL ANALYSIS　124

Managing Macroenvironmental Analysis: Organizational Prerequisites *V. K. Narayanan*　124

Building Competitive Analysis Into Your Planning Process *Craig W. Moore*　129

Application in Strategic Management: Building A Competitor Analysis System *Liam Fahey*　136

Application in Strategic Management: Don't Let Data Collection Bog Down Your Strategic Analysis *Liam Fahey*　141

PART
3
STRATEGY IN DIFFERENT CONTEXTS

CHAPTER 7　STRATEGY UNDER DIFFERENT ENVIRONMENTAL CONDITIONS: FITTING STRATEGY TO THE MARKET AND INDUSTRY CONTEXT　145

Strategies for Stagnant Businesses *Joel A. Dysart*　145

Strategies for Small-Share Firms in Mature Markets *Stanley F. Stasch and John L. Ward*　151

Entry Strategies in Emerging Markets *Teri Louden*　156

Strategies for Business Turnarounds *Charles W. Hofer*　164

Avoiding Some Pitfalls in Cost Leadership Strategies *Raphael Amit and Chaim Fershtman*　173

CHAPTER 8　BUSINESS-LEVEL STRATEGY: ATTACKING COMPETITORS　178

Frontal Strategies: Attacking Competitors *Liam Fahey*　178

Flanking Strategies: Competition by Avoidance *Liam Fahey*　181

Encirclement Strategy: Attacking Competitors by Surrounding Them *Liam Fahey*　185

Bypass Strategy: Attacking by Surpassing Competitors *Liam Fahey*   189

Guerrilla Strategy: The "Hit-and-Run" Attack *Liam Fahey*   194

Application in Strategic Management: Choosing a Flanking Strategy: Some Questions *Liam Fahey*   197

Application in Strategic Management: Developing a Bypass Strategy: Some Considerations *Liam Fahey*   201

CHAPTER 9 CORPORATE-LEVEL STRATEGY: SOME DECISION CONTEXTS 206

The Strategic Management of First Diversification: A New Perspective *Charles W. Hofer and James J. Chrisman*   206

The Strategic Management of First Diversification: A New Perspective *Charles W. Hofer and James J. Chrisman*   214

Managing Divestiture Effectively *Marilyn Taylor*   219

Application in Strategic Management: Problems in Managing a Divestment Decision *Liam Fahey*   229

PART

4

THE MAKING OF STRATEGIC DECISIONS

CHAPTER 10 THE PHASES OF STRATEGIC DECISIONS 234

Strategic Problems: How to Identify Them *Marjorie A. Lyles*   234

Identifying and Generating Strategic Alternatives *Kenneth Hatten and Mary Louise Hatten*   239

Evaluating Alternative Strategies *George Day*   250

CHAPTER 11 THE POLITICS OF STRATEGIC DECISION MAKING: MANAGING INTERNAL AND EXTERNAL STAKEHOLDERS 255

Sustaining Your Political Position in Strategy Making *Warren K. Schilit*   255

Building Support for Your Strategy by Communicating Your Plans *Frank M. Corrado*   260

Application in Strategic Management: Building Support for New Ventures *Liam Fahey*   265

PART
5

IMPLEMENTING STRATEGY:
TRANSFORMING STRATEGY INTO ACTION

CHAPTER 12 IMPLEMENTING STRATEGY: UNDERSTANDING THE ORGANIZATIONAL CONTEXT 270

Putting Your Strategy Into Action *L. J. Bourgeois III and David R. Brodwin* 270

CHAPTER 13 IMPLEMENTING STRATEGY: MONITORING ACTION PROGRAMS 283

Deciding If You're on the Right Track: How to Monitor Your Strategy *Donald W. Collier* 283

Strategy Monitoring in Multi-Business Companies *Donald W. Collier* 286

Application in Strategic Management: Testing Your Plan of Action *Liam Fahey* 290

PART
6

EXECUTING STRATEGIC MANAGEMENT:
BUILDING THE STRATEGIC ORGANIZATION
TO FORMULATE AND IMPLEMENT STRATEGY

CHAPTER 14 BUILDING THE STRATEGIC ORGANIZATION: INITIATING AN ORGANIZATIONAL THRUST THROUGH STRATEGIC PLANNING SYSTEMS 295

Launching a Strategic Planning System *Donna Williamson* 295

Launching Strategic Planning in a Small, Closely Held Business *Joel A. Dysart* 305

How the CEO Can Help Strategic Planning Get Off the Ground *John R. Gaulding* 311

Application in Strategic Management: A Planning System That Went Awry: Learning From Failure *Liam Fahey* 315

CHAPTER 15 BUILDING THE STRATEGIC ORGANIZATION: MANAGING THE PLANNING PROCESS 320

Before Planning, Let Managers Know What They're in For *Robert A. Vecchiotti* 320
Keep Your Planning Alive *R. T. Lenz and Marjorie A. Lyles* 325
Less Is More: How Less Formal Planning Can Be Best *Andrew Thomas* 331

CHAPTER 16 BUILDING THE STRATEGIC ORGANIZATION: CREATING AND SUSTAINING STRATEGIC THINKING 337

How to Avoid Being Straightjacketed by Your Managers' Frames of Reference *Paul Shrivastava* 337

Techniques for Imaginative Strategic Thinking *James F. Bandrowski* 346

Scenarios: A Means to Avoiding Strategic "Groupthink" *Samuel M. Felton, Robert E. Kelley, and Ian H. Wilson* 352

CHAPTER 17 SUSTAINING THE STRATEGIC ORGANIZATION: IDENTIFYING AND MANAGING ISSUES 357

Issues Management: The Issue of Definition *John Mahon* 357

Issues Management: Two Approaches *Liam Fahey* 365

Application in Strategic Management: Issues Management: How One Firm Does It *Liam Fahey* 369

Application in Strategic Management: Resolve Strategic Issues via Your Own Planning Conference *Liam Fahey* 371

PART
7

FORMULATING AND IMPLEMENTING STRATEGY: LINKING STRATEGY TO FUNCTIONAL AREAS

CHAPTER 18 STRATEGY AND R&D 377

Adapting Your R&D Strategies to the "Product Life-Cycle" *H. Kurt Christensen* 377

CHAPTER 19 STRATEGY AND MANUFACTURING 382

Making Operating Decisions Strategic *Elwood S. Buffa* 382

Positioning the Production System—A Key Element in Manufacturing Strategy *Elwood S. Buffa* 387

CHAPTER 20 STRATEGY AND MARKETING 396

Strategy and Marketing: Design As Competitive Advantage *Philip Kotler and G. Alexander Roth* 396

Developing Pricing Strategies in an Uncertain Environment *Dan Nimer* 401

CHAPTER 21 STRATEGY AND FINANCE 407

Planning "Right on the Money": Capital Budgeting That Pays Off *Frances E. Baird* 407

CHAPTER 22 STRATEGY AND INFORMATION SYSTEMS 412

Information Systems for Competitive Advantage: Planning Implementation *Nick Rackoff, Walter A. Ullrich, and Charles Wiseman* 412

CHAPTER 23 STRATEGY AND HUMAN RESOURCES 421

Linking Strategic Planning and Human Resource Planning *David Ulrich* 421

■ ACKNOWLEDGMENTS ■

Kathryn Sederberg, Commerce Communications, Inc, deserves a special word of thanks for granting me permission to publish these articles in the form of a book. I also want to thank Albert Nader for prevailing upon me to get involved with *Strategic Planning Management* when it was only a glimmer in his prescient eyes and Barbara Powell for her careful and courteous attention to the many details involved in keeping the publication running smoothly.

Finally, this book is dedicated to Elizabeth A. Friskey who served as the associate editor of *Strategic Planning Management* for a longer period of time than she may care to remember. Beth's ability to transform manuscripts that were sometimes loosely structured and often excessively lengthy into intelligible, insightful and pithy articles never ceased to amaze me. Beth always maintained her wit, poise and enthusiasm despite persistent deadlines, the frequent vagaries of authors and the constant necessity to juggle her own hectic schedule.

■ INTRODUCTION ■

All the readings and case applications contained in this book are drawn from *Strategic Planning Management*. I cofounded *SPM* in late 1982, and served as its editor from January, 1983, until December, 1986. The journal provides short, pithy, easy-to-read articles on all aspects of strategic planning and management. Its readership consists of practicing managers and academics interested in the practice of creating and executing business strategies.

The articles have been chosen and organized to cover the key domains in the strategic management literature. The following paragraphs provide a brief synopsis of the scope and content of each of the book's seven parts.

PART 1: AN INTRODUCTION TO STRATEGIC MANAGEMENT

Strategic management can be viewed as the management or coalignment of strategy and operations. Strategy revolves around two issues: which businesses or product-markets to compete in, and how to compete in them. Operations involves management of the internal workings of the organization—the functional areas such as R&D, marketing, manufacturing, human resources, finance/accounting, procurement, and engineering.

The essence of the articles in Part 1 is that strategy is about change. Strategy both causes change and is the product of change.

The internal change that must occur within an organization to facilitate the development and execution of strategies that are likely to cause change in the marketplace is a dominant theme in the articles in Chapter 1 by Lewis Perelman and Robert Markus. They emphasize that strategic change and operational change do not flow easily from what often passes for strategic planning or strategic management. Key concepts such as strategic planning, resource allocation, long-range planning, short-range planning, and results measurement must be clearly understood if the confused thinking about strategic management so prevalent in many organizations is to be eliminated.

The integrating theme in the articles in Chapter 2 is that the essence of strategy as rivalry among competitors is the creation of change in the form of competitive advantage. It is the marketplace test of the innovative strategic thinking the articles in Chapter 1 deem so necessary; if strategy is to result in superior performance (compared with competitors), it must create sustainable competitive advantage.

Stephen Burnett argues that superior business definitions will yield stronger and more enduring competitive advantages. Chapter 2 also provides an analysis framework for identifying specific competitive advantages, to be used once a firm has a working understanding of its business definition. The linkage to business definition should be clear from some of the questions posed: What is the product-market? What advantages are desired and why? How do they compare with competitors' offerings? Ian MacMillan reminds us that competitors are neither asleep nor stupid: they too can create change and thus overcome others' competitive advantages. Thus, firms must understand current and potential competitive dynamics if they hope to keep ahead of competitors. V. K. Narayanan demonstrates that competitive-advantage issues reside at the heart of most questions about what level of market share firms should strive to attain. Colin Camerer provides a convincing argument that if a firm is to sustain its competitive advantages it must be able to signal effectively to its competitors.

PART 2: ANALYSIS INPUTS TO STRATEGY MAKING

Creating and managing strategic change, the focus of Part 1, does not and can not occur in a vacuum. It must take place within the context of an understanding of both the environment surrounding the organization and how the organization relates to its environment. In other words, before an organization can decide what strategies it should pursue, it must analyze both its environment and itself.

Environmental analysis is typically divided into industry analysis and macroenvironmental analysis—that is, analysis of the environment surrounding the industry. Chapter 3 addresses macroenvironmental analysis. Unfortunately, the macroenvironment is often underemphasized and poorly conceptualized in many strategic management texts. The macroenvironment is defined as consisting of the social environment (which includes demographics, lifestyles, and social values), the economy, technology, and the political/regulatory milieu. My two articles provide a framework for analyzing the macroenvironment, and identify a number of difficulties that organizations have encountered in integrating macroenvironmental analysis into strategy analysis. The importance of understanding the macroenvironment is clearly evident in V.K. Narayanan's article, which shows many different ways in which the macroenvironment affects the dominant structural elements within an industry.

Chapter 4 provides an overview of industry analysis. It illustrates the importance of a thorough understanding of competitors, customers, suppliers, and alliances among these entities as key inputs to strategy development and execution. Each article shows what analysis is important and why it is important, and provides extensive illustrations of how to conduct the analysis.

Chapter 5 provides an overview of some key issues in analyzing the organization. It suggests that an assessment of the organization's distinctive competences (that is, what the organization does better than its competitors) is an insightful means of linking organizational analysis and competitive advantage. Frank Paine and Leonard Tischler emphasize the need to take a strategic perspective in identifying and evaluating the organization's cost structure.

A premise underlying many of the articles in this book is that strategic analysis (and the thinking associated with it) doesn't just happen of its own accord; it must be managed. Chapter 6 therefore examines some of the issues involved in managing macroenvironmental, industrial, and organizational analysis.

PART 3: STRATEGY IN DIFFERENT CONTEXTS

The central theme of Part 3 is that strategy is inherently conditional—that is, the choice of strategy is always dependent on the environmental conditions confronting the organization. No single strategy will succeed under all environmental conditions.

Each of the articles in Chapter 7 illustrates the need to fit strategy to the environment and to the organization. Each specifies types of strategic behaviors best suited to different configurations of environmental circumstances. The articles address many of the environmental and organizational elements discussed in Part 2: social, economic, technological, and political change; competitor, supplier, and customer elements of industry change; as well as the history, resources, characteristics, and limitations of the organization itself.

Chapter 8 refines further the need to fit strategy to environmental and organizational conditions. It is examined in the context of competitive rivalry, in which competitors attack each other directly and indirectly. Using the language of military strategy, this series of articles identifies the industrial, macroenvironmental, and organizational conditions under which an organization should seek to frontally attack competitors (compete head-to-head against them), flank competitors (avoid taking them on directly), encircle competitors (surround them by providing greater numbers of product offerings and going after a greater variety of customer segments), bypass competitors (surpass them by providing the next generation of products or going after a different geographic customer segment), or adopting a guerrilla attack (launch a quick strike and then retreat). These are quite distinct strategies: they involve distinct actions, and are intended to realize very different goals. If the conditions that facilitate each strategy type are not present, the competitive results are likely to be unfortunate, if not disastrous.

Corporate-level strategies are not immune to environmental and organizational conditions. The success of corporate-level decisions involving acquisitions, mergers, divestitures, and business-unit spin-offs are also greatly affected by change in environmental and organizational conditions. Charles Hofer and James Chrisman drive home this point in Chapter 9 when they discuss the importance of understanding the nature of the industry into which a firm diversifies: because it is often quite different than the parent industry, firms frequently encounter severe problems in their first attempt to diversify.

PART 4: THE MAKING OF STRATEGIC DECISIONS

Although organizations may sometimes get lucky, strategic change that results in superior business performance doesn't just happen. Strategic change that results in sustained competitive advantage is more likely the consequence of specific decisions. Thus, how organizations make "strategic" decisions is central to understanding why some organizations win and others lose in the competitive arena.

Chapter 10 details three critical phases in the making of individual strategic decisions. Marjorie Lyles documents how decision problems or contexts are identified; Kenneth and Mary Louise Hatten detail how alternatives can be identified and generated; and George Day describes how alternatives should be evaluated. Each of these phases critically affects the decision that is ultimately made. (Implementing the chosen alternatives is, of course, the next phase in strategic decision making and is the subject of Part 5.)

In reading these articles it will become apparent again that assessing and anticipating environmental and organizational change is unavoidable in strategic decision making. For example, Marjorie Lyles notes that examination of the environment frequently leads to the detection of strategic "problems" long before they become apparent either in the organization's performance or in industry change, and George Day clearly illustrates how the outputs of an assessment of the environment and the organization are pivotal in evaluating strategy alternatives.

However, strategic decision making is not simply an analytical exercise. It takes place within the give-and-take that is organizational life. Thus, organizational politics can shape—sometimes dramatically—what problems or opportunities are addressed, what alternatives are developed, and how they are evaluated.

Chapter 11 thus examines the political context of strategic decision making. Politics may be broadly defined as the way in which individuals wield power and influence over each other within an organization, and how the organization wields power and influence over external entities. Warren Schilit identifies a number of ways that individuals or an organizational subunit can build and sustain their political power base in the process of strategic decision making and how the exercise of politics can affect various aspects of decision making. Frank Corrado argues that an organization needs to develop a program of activities to communicate its strategies to relevant external audiences such as consumer and environmental groups, governmental agencies, and suppliers, and to internal audiences such as unions and managers at different levels of the organization. These articles suggest that political behavior, rather than disruptive and divisive behavior (as it is often portrayed in the popular and business press), actually facilitates the development and execution of strategy.

PART 5: IMPLEMENTING STRATEGY: TRANSFORMING STRATEGY INTO ACTION

Making decisions, of course, is not enough; they must be executed. Historically, the strategic management literature has drawn a sharp divide between strategy formulation and strategy implementation. Implementation is viewed as following formulation in a neat, logical, sequential process. However, an emerging viewpoint, buttressed in research exploring how organizations actually establish and execute strategy, indicates that formulation and implementation are much more the same sides of the same coin rather than sequential activities. The articles in Part 4—as well as many others in this book—illustrate the many ways in which the formulation of strategy (that is, diagnosing the strategic context, generating and developing strategy alternatives, evaluating alternatives, and choosing among them) and the implementation of strategy are inextricably intertwined.

One view of the evolution of how organizations have approached strategy implementation is contained in the article by Jay Bourgeois and David Brodwin. Based on a study of the management practices of a variety of companies, they categorize approaches to strategy implementation into five basic models or descriptions. Each model clearly reflects a different relationship between strategy formulation and strategy implementation. The CEO role is also quite different depending on which model is used. The discussion of these five distinct ways to implement strategy point to the importance of building a "strategic organization," the focus of Part 6.

Irrespective of whatever strategy implementation model or framework is preferred by any given organization, any broad strategic thrust, such as building a market share as aggressively as possible, and its specific action programs must be monitored. As noted by Donald Collier, "carrying out strategy is like racing a yacht. You can't simply chart your course, point in the desired direction, and assume you'll beat everyone to the finish line." He identifies the two things that must always be monitored: whether the company is actually executing the plan, and whether the action programs or tactics are still desirable in light of changing circumstances. Each of these points reinforces key themes already noted in the introductions to previous parts of the book and in many individual articles: strategy execution must always be tracked and reevaluated against inevitable environmental and organizational change.

PART 6: EXECUTING STRATEGIC MANAGEMENT: BUILDING THE STRATEGIC ORGANIZATION TO FORMULATE AND IMPLEMENT STRATEGY

Increasingly, academics, consultants, and practitioners concerned with the execution of strategic management have begun to assert that organizations must become "strategic" if winning strategies are to be successfully designed and implemented. While there is not a generally accepted single conception of what a strategic organization is or what makes an organization strategic, a number of the characteristics of a strategic organization are frequently noted: widespread commitment within the organization to creating and sustaining competitive advantage (the focus of Part 1); systematic, comprehensive environmental and organizational analysis to identify opportunities (the focus of Part 2); involvement of all layers of the organization in strategic decision making (the focus of Part 4) and strategy implementation (the focus of Part 5).

Part 6 addresses a set of distinct though related approaches to building a strategic organization. It draws on the experiences of many organizations that have endeavored to become more strategic in their behavior and orientation.

In Chapter 14, Donna Williamson and Joel Dysart provide a good overview of what a strategic planning system entails, and what is involved in getting a planning system off the ground in a large multidivisional corporation and in a small, closely held firm.

Once some type of strategic planning or analysis system is instituted, it must be managed. The articles in Chapter 15 identify a variety of methods that organizations have developed to manage the planning process.

A strategic planning and analysis system is only as good as the quality of the strategic thinking that it fosters. There is always the danger that the organizational processes inherent in strategic planning systems will degenerate into mere routines: managers go through the motions of doing strategy analysis, but the analysis is devoid of serious and reflective thinking. The articles in

Chapter 16 lay out a wide variety of ways in which organizations can generate critical thinking in all phases of strategy development and implementation.

Chapter 17 offers some articles on issues management, one specific approach to strategic analysis that has emerged in the past few years as a significant means to make organizations more strategic. It requires managers to identify and assess the key issues confronting (or likely to confront) their organization, and to determine what actions they should take pertaining to these issues. Thus, issues management provides an opportunity for managers to come together to consider problems, opportunities, and events of strategic importance to the organization—in short, to engage in strategic thinking.

PART 7: FORMULATING AND IMPLEMENTING STRATEGY: LINKING STRATEGY TO FUNCTIONAL AREAS

Many of the articles in this book have noted the need to build analytical and organizational bridges between strategy as an organization-wide phenomenon and the activities that are involved in the functional "trenches" within the organization. Much of the analysis inputs to strategy development come from the functional areas: R&D, manufacturing, marketing, finance and accounting, information systems, and human resources. Moreover, the functional areas, working in conjunction with each other, ultimately must assume responsibility for implementing strategy.

It is important to remember that functional area managers must understand the organization's strategy before they can muster their unit's support behind it. Strategy researchers have often noted that unless functional area managers concur with the broad thrust and details of the organization's strategy, they are likely, at best, to give it only grudging support, and at worst may sabotage it. The last point, of course, argues strongly for the involvement of functional area managers in setting strategic direction and ironing out the details of individual strategies—a theme that is evident in many articles in Parts 4, 5, and 6.

The intent of the articles in Part 7, therefore, is to identify and illustrate how an organization's strategy and key functional areas are interrelated. A central theme in these articles is the contribution that individual functional areas can make to attaining and sustaining competitive advantage. For example, in Chapter 18 H Kurt Christensen shows how R&D can provide competitive advantage across the stages of the product life-cycle, and in Chapter 22 Nick Rackoff, Walter Ullrich, and Charles Wiseman illustrate how a number of firms have used information systems to generate sustainable competitive advantage.

A related emphasis is that in many organizations a new perspective may need to be brought to bear on management of the functional areas if they are to facilitate and contribute to sustaining competitive advantage. Day-to-day manufacturing decisions are not usually thought to be strategic, yet many decisions, although they may be relatively unimportant in the broad sweep of strategy, can be made in a strategic way, adding up to the implementation of a conscious manufacturing contribution to the organization's overall business strategy.

Implicitly, these articles reinforce the fact that no functional area can or should be treated as an island unto itself. Each functional area can play a significant part in every aspect of strategic management discussed in each Chapter of this book.

CHAPTER

—1—

STRATEGY: CREATING AND MANAGING CHANGE

∎

□

THE STRATEGY REVOLUTION
LEWIS J. PERELMAN

The strategy revolution is marked by a shift in focus from "hard" to "soft"—that is, away from "hard" data, rational analysis, and singleminded pursuit of the bottom line, and toward such "soft" dimensions of management as goals, philosophy, culture, organization, systems, creativity, innovation, and motivation.

Similarly, the old concept of "strategy" as a static document in a black notebook, generated by an often thoughtless planning ritual, is being replaced by a new vision of strategy as management *thinking* and total organizational *performance*.

Based on a number of years of professional experience in strategic management, I recommend the following five essential steps for corporations that want to be leaders in strategic performance. There are examples of each of these steps being practiced in American companies today. But *superior* strategy requires all these steps to be carried out in a coherent approach, and I know no examples where that is yet being done.

1. UNDERSTAND THE MEANING OF "STRATEGY"

Important business strategy needs are often unmet because executives get distracted by tactical activities which are misleadingly labelled "strategic." It is, therefore, important to know what we mean by "strategy."

Strategic Planning Management, January, 1984; Commerce Communications, Inc.

Strategy literally refers to the decisions made by a military general, or similar top manager. In essence, strategy is the line decision-maker's consciousness of the implications of each competitive decision. Strategy is ideas—intentions (what do we want to do and to achieve), perceptions (what are the *relevant* facts), and expectations (the "what if" questions).

At best, planning may help you to organize the execution of strategy, but the rigidities of formal planning systems also have been known to stifle the creativity and flexibility that superior strategic performance requires. For example, the vice-president for planning of a major electronics company, which recently abandoned a consumer product line that had lost half a billion dollars, admitted that the company's planning had failed because of "the tendency to substitute mechanics for thought," resulting in a process of "strategy by cookbook."

The critical fact to understand about "strategic planning" (which I have never seen stated clearly in any text on the subject) is this: *no strategic plan has ever been implemented.* Anyone who ever tried to adhere to a prefabricated "strategic plan" in war, politics, poker, business, or any other competitive game suffered disaster. "Strategic plan" really is a contradiction in terms. Plans are most useful under conditions that are predictable and controllable. Strategy is essential precisely because the events of a competitive battle are always, to some extent, unpredictable and uncontrollable. The importance of strategy increases as the feasibility of planning decreases. Also, while planning is highly concerned with analysis of data, strategy is mainly concerned with creation of ideas—that is, patterns and meanings.

If you try to define the ideal strategy for creating a new business or entering a new market, environmental changes will continually invalidate the assumptions on which your plans are based. Competent competitors, who know that surprise is the most effective strategic weapon, will go out of their way to do what you least expect. Customers will behave "irrationally." The plan will be compromised by internal politicking; subordinates will be insubordinate. And on, and on.

Such disruptive events, commonly referred to as strategic problems, cannot be "solved" like algebra problems. Instead, they must be addressed as *issues* to be managed—the desired result is not an ideal solution, but some resolution that at least allows you to make continued progress toward your strategic goals.

2. MANAGE ISSUES

Superior strategic performance requires getting away from the annual ritual of concocting an ideal "plan," and instead developing a proactive, flexible, day-to-day process for managing strategic issues. "Issues management" is being practiced in a growing number of corporations. Although corporations are devising substantially different ways of establishing an issues management process, the most effective approaches reflect at least the following three characteristics;

Business intelligence.   The American headquarters office of a major Japanese electronics company has been described as an "anthill of intelligence activity." A Defense Department consultant estimates that Japanese electronic firms have some 1,500 software experts deployed in the U.S., spending up to $30 million a year, primarily to gather intelligence about American computer technology. The same expert estimates that 35–40% of the baseline data required to develop Japanese VLSI semiconductor chips came from such intelligence operations.

Few American companies take the intelligence process as seriously as do their foreign competitors. The corporate planning department of a Fortune 500 company I know had a staff of 20 people receiving over 220 periodicals a month, yet had no process for systematically scanning, analyzing, consolidating, and reporting the strategic information in this resource to responsible decision-makers. In this company, millions of dollars and thousands of people-hours were being invested in reading, professional seminars, conferences, sales reports, market research, and so forth. Yet only a few percent of the potential intelligence value of all this activity was actually used.

Teamwork.   Information is useless if it is not digested and integrated into the consciousness of decisionmakers. Teamwork helps reduce information overload. Teamwork also helps sharpen pattern recognition, and therefore issue definition, by subjecting business intelligence to a variety of perspectives and thinking styles. For example, one corporation has created an issue team to answer the question of what technological capabilities the firm should possess to remain dominant in its industry.

Teamwork is really essential to getting the full strategic benefit of issues management. Critical strategic issues almost always cut across the boundaries that define professional fields and organizational units. Superior performance requires a holistic view of corporate strategy which can only emerge from an interdisciplinary or interdepartmental approach.

Line responsibility.   Issues must be managed by line managers, not by an academic department of staff "issues managers." Staff or consultants can provide technical expertise, but the process should remain in the hands of line people and centered ultimately on the CEO.

3. MANAGE "TELEMATICS"

Telematics—the marriage of computer and communications technology—is transforming the structure and function of our whole economy, including corporate management.

Nobody yet knows exactly how to capture the full benefits of these powerful tools, but it is clear that enormous strategic advantage will accrue to those companies that lead the way. A leading oil services company is using computerized production scheduling and parts-inventory records to enable plant managers to decide quickly whether to fill an emergency order for the company's specialized oil drilling equipment.

If you wait for the perfect system, you will be accepting a permanent and growing competitive disadvantage. Leading organizations will learn to coevolve with the technology.

The important requirement here is to make this development a collaborative effort of computer experts, communications experts, industrial psychologists, organization developers, human resource specialists, and managers themselves. You will need to establish a multidisciplinary team, calling on consultants if needed. The whole program should be directed by a forceful line manager who will report to the CEO.

4. CREATE A STRATEGIC ORGANIZATION

Though "corporate culture" is currently a hot management topic, many managers still seem not to realize that superior strategic performance, in relation to the external environment, requires a "strategic" internal organization, including structure, systems, human resources, values, goals, and so forth.

Creating a strategic organization is a complex task, but let me suggest three fundamental requirements.

Clear line responsibility.   "Implementation" has become a key buzzword in recent strategy articles, because top managers are coming to realize that having an elegant strategy on paper is useless if the organization cannot carry out the actions it demands for success. The simple fact is that line people are not effective in carrying out a strategy that they do not "own," and they feel ownership only of what they have created themselves.

You should make it explicit and forcefully clear that strategy is a line responsibility which should be shared broadly (to encourage the sense of "ownership"), but must not be delegated to those who lack decisionmaking authority.

A lean staff and/or consultants may be used to support the process generating and implementing strategy, but the essential work—thinking, deciding, acting—must be retained by line management.

Flat, broad, and lean structure.   In the turbulent business environment that will persist for decades to come, strategic advantage will be commanded by those companies that are most flexible and adaptive to change. Hierarchical bureaucracies are doomed. Superior strategic performance requires a flat, broad structure—few levels in the "chain of command," broad "span of control," and human-scale business units (500 employees seems about the optimum size).

The overhead burden of sprawling staff, once a necessary evil of governing a large organization, has been made an unnecessary evil thanks to telematic technology. One desktop computer with good software, and the right kind of communications system, can provide the line manager with far greater support to analyze and execute decisions than do dozens of staff and middle managers.

Participatory strategic management. A growing number of American corporations are encouraging employee participation in operational management through such devices as "Quality Circles." Few companies yet have grasped the necessity of broadening participation in strategic decisionmaking.

We need a more powerful process than just the usual "open door" or suggestion box, i.e., the use of "Strategic Circles" which could provide companies with an effective mechanism for broadened participation in strategic management.

5. MANAGE THINKING

It should be evident that the quality of corporate strategy is limited by the quality of the thinking that creates it. Though "strategic thinking" long has been a popular catch phrase, we are just beginning to learn how much we really can do to manage and cultivate this most critical resource. This is a complex task, but again let me offer a few simple suggestions.

First, learn as much as you can about the intellectual capabilities of your company's people. People vary not only in their level of "IQ," but in their knowledge, interests, experience, values, and thinking "styles." No one human can be a perfect thinker about all problems; it pays to learn what your organization's mental strengths and "blind spots" are.

Second, develop opportunities to expand your collective cognitive skills. There are a surprising number of workshops, seminars, books and other training resources available to cultivate creativity, innovation, imagination, intuition, logic, and other problem-solving skills.

Finally, develop your intellectual support network of individuals with powerful minds and provocative ideas to leaven the thinking of your own people. Bring them in to reason with—not just talk at—your folks and keep them involved over a sufficient period of time for them to get to know your goals and values.

CONCLUSION

These things are happening in many companies today. But, to be a leader in the strategy revolution, you need to pursue them all in a consistent, integrated program: keep a clear focus on what "strategy" really means; move toward flexible issues management and away from planning rituals; take full advantage of the power of emerging telematic technologies; make your total organization an effective strategic weapon; and make a conscious effort to expand and use your uniquely human capacity for creative thinking.

□

STRATEGIC PLANNING: ENHANCING STRATEGIC INNOVATION

ROBERT MARKUS

Every organization needs to take an occasional "time-out" to reflect upon some fundamental questions about itself. Too many firms only do so in the face of a performance downturn, or worse, impending disaster.

Strategy issues should be at the heart of these questions. In this article, I want to address three key questions which I believe will help you to considerably improve the strategic capability of your organization:

1. Does what passes for strategic planning in your organization really have a strategic element?
2. What are the dominant assumptions about strategy and strategic thinking in your organization?
3. Is your organization doing the things that seem to facilitate and spur strategic entrepreneurialism and innovation?

COMPONENTS OF THE STRATEGIC MANAGEMENT PROCESS

Before dealing with the above questions, I have found it useful to identify and define what I believe are the five key interrelated components in strategic management: strategic planning; resource allocation; long range planning; short range planning; and results measurement.

Strategic planning addresses two questions: what are we as an organization and where are we going? Stated differently, what businesses are we in or want to be in? It is a participative process—the facts, discussions, feelings and results from the involvement of Senior Management should determine the answers to these questions. It is a key part and first step of subsequent planning.

Resource allocation is budgeting to decide who gets how much of what resources. Resources might include dollars, people, and equipment, not only for core business operations but for new ventures.

Strategic Planning Management, October, 1984; Commerce Communications, Inc.

Long range planning, as distinct from strategy planning, is an extrapolation of the past or a projection of current operations into the future, suggesting how the organization might get to where it wants to be. It addresses two questions: how will we operate long term and what tactics will we use? It relies heavily on experience and recorded data.

Short range planning focuses on operational decision making. It involves choosing actions after defining and analyzing problems and opportunities within the scope of a twelve month time frame. "How do we operate now?" is its driving question.

Results measurement, including follow-up monitoring against your financial control reports and qualitative objectives, indicates how you performed against plan.

The failure to clearly distinguish between these elements is a major reason for much of the confused thinking about strategic management and much of the operational difficulties experienced in practicing it. This is particularly evident in the widespread construal of long range planning for strategic planning.

DISTINGUISHING BETWEEN LONG RANGE AND STRATEGIC PLANNING

It can not be overemphasized that long range planning is *not* strategic planning. In fact, long range planning (as defined above) may be detrimental to strategic thinking. The following are some of the critical distinctions between long range planning and strategic planning:

1. As practiced in many firms, long range planning is a *projection* from the present or an extrapolation from the past. In other words, it takes off from where you have been or where you are now.

   Strategic planning on the other hand, builds on anticipated future trends, data and assumptions. It is premised upon alternative futures.

2. Long range planning tends to be *bottom up* rather than top down planning. It is largely done down in the bowels of the organization rather than at its apex.

   True strategic planning resides at the top levels of the organization. It feeds and informs long range planning at the lower levels.

3. Long range planning is generally dangerously *optimistic*. In the absence of alternative views of the future, it is easy to suppress the undesirable and promote the favorable.

   Strategic planning assesses worst case, best case and other real world scenarios. It forces some degree of realism. It can not, of course, guarantee level-headed assessment or eliminate all biases.

4. Long range planning is really the *consolidation* and compromise of individual subunit plans.

Strategic planning is intended to provide a clear and precise overall company focus or direction.

5. Long range planning merely extends *short range* planning because:
    a. Attention is given to the next twelve months, due to compensation policies, bonus considerations, stockholder pressure, etc.
    b. Business evaluation systems emphasize here and now. Managers are not evaluated on long term results, but on short term failures.
    c. Planning beyond the next year is less precise.
    d. If the current year does not meet expectations, there is always next year to make adjustments. How often have you heard that?

6. Long range plans frequently become non-strategic, because they are fundamentally based on *numerical assumptions.* Numbers tend to drive long range plans.

    Strategic plans, however, tend to be driven by ideas. Assumptions about the future are critical. They are much more qualitative in nature.

7. Long range plans are inflexible, despite the loose-leaf format in which they are put together. They are filed and seldom referred to.

Strategic thinking should be an everyday process, carried around in your head. It is forward thinking, opportunistic oriented, forcing you and others in the organization to continually ask, "What is relevant to long run and operational actions?" It provides for constant refreshing and updating.

These distinctions between long range and strategic planning will help you to focus upon that which is truly strategic. However, there are a number of assumptions that are frequently made about strategic planning and thinking that work against your organization becoming more strategic.

FALLACIOUS ASSUMPTIONS ABOUT STRATEGY

Six common but false assumptions about strategy and strategic planning are worth noting:

1. A very prevalant and dangerous assumption is that if the top management team works together, they *all agree* on where they are going and they *share* the same concept and vision of their company. The contrary is much more often true.

    Most executives have a very *fuzzy* understanding of where their company is heading. They tend to focus on operations not strategy. Much of this arises because executives, in such areas as MIS, marketing, finance, manufacturing, engineering, research, etc., reflect different views based on the disciplines of their earlier training and management development.

2. The assumption is often made that the top executive or management team is driving and controlling the company's destiny.

   You simply cannot assume that the top executive group has unlimited discretion to chart the firm's destiny. There are just too many uncontrollable factors in the firm's environment.

   This assumption may also collapse for internal reasons. Where is top management spending its time? Research suggests that 90-95% is on operations and only 5-10% is on strategy. This must be brought into better balance, particularly by managers who hold senior level positions.

3. You may falsely assume that since you have long term plans, i.e., greater than twelve months, they are strategic.

   The existence of plans does not make them strategic. Strategy is driven by vision and direction, not time. Some immediate decisions are strategic. It is where you are going. Strategy is the shape of the future.

4. A dangerous assumption about strategy is that since you are organized effectively, your organization will take you where you want to go.

   You can not assume that your organization's structure is right for your strategy. It is much more likely that your organization may be too restrictive, have too many layers, too many policies and procedures to support your strategy. You will probably have to organize, or reorganize, your organization after you have set your vision and strategy for the future.

5. Do not assume that your corporate strategy is sound because your strategic business units have clear and good strategies and direction.

   You need corporate strategy first, in order to guide the strategic business units, so that they can properly support the desired corporate direction. The converse is dangerous—strategic business units may be directing the corporation inappropriately because they do not have the proper overall vision from the top.

6. Another dangerous assumption about strategy is that if things are going well now, you will think about planning your strategy when, and only if, you get into trouble.

   When all's well, you should do your best strategic thinking, in order to sustain and improve your competitive position. The luxury of success affords a golden opportunity to think strategically. When you are in trouble, you generally think operationally, not strategically.

Strategy relates to the *risks* of business and their subsequent *rewards.* When your organization is in trouble, you take fewer risks, although the need for a clear strategy for survival may be required. If you don't have a clear strategic focus, you will miss opportunities when the economy or your market niche is strong.

FACILITATING STRATEGIC INNOVATION

Reflection upon the distinctions between long range planning and strategic planning, and the assumptions underlying strategy and strategic thinking in your organization, will tell you a lot about your organization. This knowledge is necessary before you can move to make your organization be more strategic as well as integrating the strategic and the operational. But what actions should you take?

There are eight key steps that most organizations seem to follow as they try to encourage and facilitate strategic entrepreneurialism and innovation.

1. Adopt the right mentality.

    An organization must create a mentality—attitude, philosophy, culture, call it what you will—that accepts and nourishes strategic thinking. Let people in your organization know what strategic thinking is—and what it is not. Avail of every opportunity to push others to develop their own strategic thinking and to share it.

2. Decentralize and allow bottom up input, creativity and innovation.

    The right mentality is not enough. You must push the capacity to make strategic decisions down into the organization. The top executives simply can't do it all; they are dependent on those further down in the organization to throw up opportunities and the strategies to exploit them.

3. Be willing to experiment.

    Strategic thinking must be translated into action. Not just action, but innovative actions. Your organization must be willing to experiment, to try new ideas, to do things differently. Individuals should be encouraged to do so.

4. Make lists of ideas and review them regularly.

    Innovative ideas can come from anywhere, inside or outside of the organization. These ideas need to be captured and tested. Organizations that manifest a high degree of entrepreneurial activity seem to do a very good job of building "idea banks" and assessing their strategic relevance. Without the "right mentality" and a willingness to experiment, this is much less likely to happen.

5. Create a plan for the innovative project.

    Ideas must be given shape and fashioned into experiments. They can not remain on the shelf. One way to get them off the ground is to have someone develop a plan to transform the ideas into a project—a plan of action. The plan is not embedded in stone but is largely a basis for furthering thinking and action.

6. Allocate authority and accountability.

    To effect strategic innovation you have no choice but to "put someone in charge" and hold them accountable. Idea and project champions will come forward. The trick is to harness their energy and creativity by giving them authority and responsibility. They then do the experimenting and push the project through the organization.

7. Organize a separate experimental unit without bureaucracy.

Entrepreneurial and innovative activity clashes head-on with the structure, systems, controls and procedures in most organizations. In short, experimenting flies in the face of the organization. One way a number of strategically innovative firms have overcome this problem is by creating relatively autonomous units that are not subject to the organization's normal bureaucratic rules. This gives individuals the institutional freedom to engage in strategic thinking and to experiment.

8. Communicate innovative projects to all levels.

Finally, successful organizations provide the opportunity for all levels and units to contribute to innovative activity. It is not seen as the prerogative of any one group. Ideas and projects, therefore, need to be communicated throughout the organization and channels established for receiving feedback. You will probably be surprised by the insights and critical capacities that this process can unlease in your organization.

CONCLUSION

Strategic management involves both creative thinking and innovative actions. Both are necessary. The purpose of this article is to help you focus upon some key questions that will aid you to creatively think about strategic management in your organization and some actions that will spur you toward innovative strategies.

Creative thinking and innovative actions are often hampered by adherence to the fallacious assumptions discussed in this article. The eight steps outlined above, that have facilitated strategic entrepreneurialism in many corporations, help provide the means to avoid succumbing to these fallacious assumptions.

CHAPTER

—2—

STRATEGY: CREATING AND SUSTAINING COMPETITIVE ADVANTAGE

■

□

FINDING A THEME: THE PROBLEM OF BUSINESS DEFINITION

STEPHEN BURNETT

BUSINESS DEFINITION DEFINED

- What business are we really in?
- What is our mission?
- What is our philosophy of growth?
- How should we conceive of ourselves?
- How should we be centered? By markets? Technology? Customer needs?

All of these questions refer to the search for a central thrust, an underlying theme that guides strategic decision-making.

Take, for example, a company that has defined its business as "the protection of people's hearing from noise." What kinds of strategy choices might flow from this definition? Here are four diverse examples of products and services for various markets that would be consistent with this definition:

1. Ear plugs and ear protectors for chain-saw operators, gun enthusiasts, workers on assembly lines;

Strategic Planning Management, October, 1983; Commerce Communications, Inc.

2. hearing-testing and record-keeping services for employers subject to OSHA noise standards;
3. noise abatement materials and coatings for heavy machinery.

Not all hearing protection products would be appropriate for this company. The company would not, for example, market its earplugs to swimmers, unless the firm's business definition was expanded to "the protection of hearing from any threat," not just from noise. Still, the focus in noise protection alone is broad enough to yield multiple market strategies, manufacturing technologies, and competitors—all related to the protection of hearing from noise. Simply put, business definition is a question of strategy linkages.

WHY BE CONCERNED WITH BUSINESS DEFINITION?

Warnings about the importance of defining your business are hardly new. Nearly two decades ago, Theodore Levitt admonished us, in the *Harvard Business Review,* to avoid "marketing myopia"—which was, in fact, a suggestion to link strategy in terms of fairly broad customer needs.

A major benefit of defining a business in terms of customers' needs is that it helps sensitize management to potential competition from technological substitutes. Federal Express, for example, defined its business three years ago as "handling random, planned emergencies." Originally, air freight was the only mechanism that they used to meet this need. But now Federal is developing an electronic mail service, because in some cases electronic mail can handle "random, unplanned emergencies" more effectively than air freight. Electronic mail is totally consistent with Federal's definition.

Defining your business requires more than a casual effort. It should be an explicit and thoughtful, long-range planning decision. After all, how you define your business determines the environments in which you will operate: who your customers' competitors, and suppliers are, or will be.

Superior business definitions will yield stronger and more enduring competitive advantages. In addition, your business definition will determine all possible avenues of expansion and contraction. In short, it tells management where to look for logical growth and retrenchment.

HOW BUSINESS DEFINITION AFFECTS PERFORMANCE: A CASE HISTORY

The experience of Polaroid in the past decade is a good example of how business definition determines relevant environmental forces, competitive advantage, and growth/contraction avenues. Published statements by founder Edwin Land, in the early 1970s, suggest that Polaroid defined its business as:

"perfecting and marketing instant photography to satisfy social needs (e.g., affection, humor, companionability) of more affluent U.S. and West European families."

Given this assumed definition, what was the nature of the environment in which Polaroid could and did operate? The economy and the population were both growing strongly in the 1950s and 1960s, and both of these environmental trends were favorable to camera sales and, therefore, to Polaroid's definition.

These trends did not go unnoticed by Polaroid management. The $20 Swinger camera, introduced in 1965, was positioned as a gift for teenagers at exactly the time that many baby-boomers were reaching their early teens. The fit of Polaroid's definition with its environment in the 1950s and 1960s was excellent.

But, Polaroid's definition does not fit as well with the environment of the 1970s and 1980s. While their earlier definition emphasized affluence, families, and instant photography, society is now characterized by an aging population, fewer children, more single-parent households, stagnant economic conditions, and strong international competition.

Consequently, Polaroid appears to be changing its definition. According to the company's 1982 annual report, the definition is being broadened to include professional photographers, businesses (e.g., instant cameras for computer graphics), and medical organizations (e.g., instant cameras for ultrasound equipment).

In the context of the 1970s and beyond, Polaroid's earlier definition provided both competitive advantages and disadvantages. Their reliance on a single technology (Land's instant photography) made Polaroid vulnerable to rival ways of satisfying social needs of affluent families. Videotape cameras, video games, and rapid film-developing services are examples.

On the other hand, Polaroid's tight focus on perfecting a single and patentable technology acted as an entry barrier. With the notable exception of Kodak, few competitors could and still can emulate the performance of Polaroid's instant cameras.

To understand how business definition affects growth, think about how Polaroid could grow without changing its definition. Only two avenues were open. One was to persuade more people to buy instant cameras by targeting new consumer segments and increasing international penetration. The other was to get camera-owners to replace their equipment by creating obsolescence through continuous technological advancements.

Given that the market for instant cameras matured quickly, Polaroid's definition placed a tremendous burden on R&D. For continued growth they needed breakthrough advancements, such as the SX-70 camera (which Polaroid introduced in 1972). As a technology grows older, major innovations become more and more difficult to achieve. Edwin Land precisely summarized the growth avenues available to Polaroid under its earlier definition, when he said that the only thing that keeps Polaroid alive is its brilliance.

MAKING THE DEFINITION DECISION

Like most strategic management issues, the question of how to define your business is far easier to raise than to answer. If a local pub defined its business as "worldwide entertainment," for example, how useful would the definition be? The avenues of growth available with such a definition are almost unlimited, and most are beyond the scope of what a pub could do.

A business' definition cannot, then, be so broad as to be meaningless. At the same time, it cannot be so narrow that there are few opportunities for growth.

Choosing a sound definition for your organization requires several insights. In general, plenty of creativity and conceptual thinking are mandatory, of course. More specifically, the following ideas should be helpful.

1. *Understand the key dimensions of your business.* An understanding of the dimensions along which a business could be defined, and how business definitions can differ, are prerequisites for selecting a definition. Drawing upon ideas from Derek Abell, *Defining the Business,* (Prentice-Hall 1980), and Hans Thorelli, *Strategy + Structure = Performance,* (Indiana Press, 1977), a business may be defined along four dimensions, which serve as the underlying themes to strategy decisions:
   - *customer groups served*—who the business markets to;
   - *customer needs satisfied*—the specific customer needs the business attempts to satisfy;
   - *technologies utilized*—how the business satisfies these needs;
   - *functions performed*—degree of vertical integration desired.

   It is easy to illustrate these four dimensions of business definitions by returning to the case of Polaroid in the early 1970s. They served affluent U.S. and West European families, satisfied social needs, utilized the technology of instant photography, and performed the functions of developing and marketing the product.

   There is also a time dimension to a business' definition, reflecting the fact that definitions can and often should change. Polaroid's current definition requires them to perform more functions (i e., become more vertically integrated) and to serve a greater variety of customer groups. Polaroid's technological dimension, however, remains narrowly focused on instant photography.

2. *Definition scope.* The major question in selecting a definition is always how broadly or narrowly the business will be defined along each of the four dimensions or themes. This is often called the scope or breadth of the definition and refers to the variety and number of customers served, needs satisfied, technologies used, and functions performed. An organization may define its business in a variety of ways: broadly along all four dimensions; narrowly along four; broadly on two; narrowly on two; etc.

TABLE 2-1   Broad vs. Narrow Definitions
Some Examples for a Safety Hearing—
Protection Company

Definition A

(broadly defined along all four dimensions)

Customers	Consumers and workers, worldwide
Needs	Safety
Technologies	Personal products (e.g., earplugs, aprons, safety shoes, etc.) Education and training, testing services, filtering devices, noise abatement materials
Functions	Basic and applied R&D, manufacturing of products and component parts, direct marketing and service

Definition B

(narrowly defined along all four dimensions)

Customers	World-class swimmers
Needs	Protection of hearing from water
Technologies	Disposable earplugs
Functions	Marketing through wholesalers

3. *Evaluating definitions.* Armed with the knowledge that business definitions should include four dimensions that may each vary in its scope or breadth, the question now is how to evaluate which definition is best. As with most strategy decisions, the logical starting point is to consider the status quo: your organization's current definition. Articulating your current definition sounds easy; but it may be difficult to determine exactly which customer groups you are serving, and which of their needs are being satisfied.

Once you have identified your organization's current definition as a reference point, the next step is to broaden and narrow it incrementally along each of the four dimensions. The following questions, adapted from Abell's *Defining the Business* (1980), should be addressed with each incremental change.

    a. *Would customers benefit measurably if the firm defines each dimension broadly or narrowly?* The point of this question is to identify definitions that will satisfy customers more effectively and, therefore, yield competitive advantages. For example, in many industrial machinery markets, small, unsophisticated companies are often influenced by the purchase decisions of larger, more experienced customers. A definition that spans both customer groups, large and small, would benefit smaller companies by simplifying their decision process and increasing confidence in the machinery.

    b. *How will the organization's cost structure change as the definition is broadened and narrowed along each dimension?* The search here is for a cost advantage, in addition to a customer satisfaction advantage. The cost implications of broadening and narrowing your definition are complex, making it difficult to offer you specific rules-of-thumb.

Definitions that target multiple needs (broad customer-need scope) of a limited number of customer groups (narrow customer-group scope) are thought to provide marketing cost economies. Marketing research tends to be less costly, new products are introduced to existing customers, and umbrella advertising and branding are often possible.

   c. *As the definition is broadened along each dimension, what skills and resources will be required to compete effectively?* How dissimilar are these skills and resources? Does the organization have them? Can they be acquired? At what cost?

Within reason, broad definitions are attractive. They encourage innovation, provide ample and flexible growth opportunities, and often help the company become less vulnerable to competitive attacks from new technologies and direct competitors.

These benefits have a price, unfortunately, which is the cost and complexity of embracing numerous markets, product technologies, and manufacturing processes. At some point, management's attention, plus the organization's skills and resources, become too tightly stretched over too many diverse tasks.

One approach to tempering the appeal of breadth is to define the scope narrowly along at least one or perhaps even two dimensions. Kodak, for example, serves many needs of numerous consumer and industrial markets with a high degree of vertical integration. Yet, many of its products and services tend to be related to photography (e.g., cameras, film, film processing, chemicals, and plastics).

THE IDEAL DEFINITION

To sum it all up, an ideal business definition will possess the following characteristics. First, it will explicitly address all four dimensions of the business. If you neglect to define one dimension, it is as if you are specifying unlimited breadth on that dimension.

Second, it manages to be simultaneously broad and narrow. The definitions should help encourage growth while avoiding resource and skill overextension.

Third, it is flexible. The definition should not lock you into a restrictive role but, rather, should guide your evolution. You should be able to incrementally change one or more dimension without completely going out of one business and entering another.

Fourth, it will allow the firm to do a superior job at satisfying customer needs. Simultaneously, it helps the firm develop comparative advantages so it can satisfy customer needs at costs equal to or lower than those of competitors.

Finally, the ideal definition will provide ample growth opportunities, yet it specifically directs growth towards areas attractive to the organization now and in the future.

□

DISCOVERING YOUR FIRM'S STRONGEST COMPETITIVE ADVANTAGES

LIAM FAHEY

Executives planning their strategy are a little like high school freshmen athletes choosing a sport. One determinant of their long-run success is whether they choose to compete where their assets will give them a natural advantage. From then on, they can focus on which talents to develop to excel in that game.

Discovering which of their assets can yield the greatest rewards at the least cost has enabled successful firms to take advantage of market niches, to adapt to changing market conditions, and to find new ways to market their products. It's not easy to identify the strongest potential advantage. It requires that a management team undertake a thorough assessment of its strengths, limitations, and opportunities in the marketplace.

WHAT IS A COMPETITIVE ADVANTAGE?

By "competitive advantage" we mean anything that favorably distinguishes a firm or its product from those of its competitors in the eyes of its customers or end-users. From this perspective, such alleged competitive strengths as a modern manufacturing plant, larger R&D capability or greater financial resources are not necessarily competitive advantages; they must be transformed into a product or service that those external to the firm will value enough to purchase.

Here are some of the many possible bases of competitive advantages: product-line width, size, price, quality, reliability, availability, performance, styling and image.

Just as beauty is in the eye of the beholder, so is it *the perception* of these competitive dimensions by current and potential customers that is important. One person may view his own big car as a high-performing, safe and luxurious

Strategic Planning Management, January, 1983; Commerce Communications, Inc.

automobile, while someone else considers the same vehicle a cumbersome, gas-guzzling, inefficient and unreliable monster.

Firms typically seek competitive advantages by combining several elements. The battle between personal computer manufacturers is currently being waged along the dimensions of number of uses, service, performance, software availability and compatibility, company image and product-line width (a means of enticing distribution support). In the following discussion, the focus is on consumer and industrial products, but the same essential questions can be asked in service industries.

WHAT IS THE PRODUCT-MARKET?

Any consideration of your potential advantages depends heavily on your perception of the relevant "product-market(s)"—that is, the set of product characteristics bought by a market segment, or set of customers. Indeed, if you specify your product-market incorrectly, your efforts to develop competitive advantages will probably be ineffectual. You must therefore ask two critical questions: (1) What is our product? and (2) What is our market?

In defining the product, begin with as broad a conception of your product as possible to avoid overlooking any potential basis for competitive advantage. What is the bundle of tangible and intangible benefits that the purchaser or user is likely to obtain? How can the product be used? Whether your firm produces soap, perfumes, automobiles or personal computers, be sure to define the product by listing *all* of its attributes—both those that are tangible (size, color, shape, texture, etc.) and those that are intangible (images, "style," etc.). Leaving out a feature that your customers value can be devastating to your analysis. It is the risk of inadequate definition that makes the apparently simple question of "What is the product?" a potentially hazardous and slippery mine field.

The next task is to define your market. Who can use the product? What are the users' socio-demographic characteristics? What is their geographical distribution? Critical questions related to developing your competitive advantage are: "What will the customer value?" and "Why?" If you don't ask and get defensible answers to these questions, you're likely to become just another legend about a product failure in the marketplace.

If you correctly identify the products but mis-specify your markets, important competitors could be omitted from the analysis. For example, if different firms are serving distinct market niches, a misconception of those niches may prevent you from anticipating the competitors moving across niches. Many banks have recently been surprised to find customers for many of their services abandoning them in favor of other types of financial institutions. In short, seeking competitive advantage without an accurate identification of current and future competitors is risky indeed.

WHAT ADVANTAGE IS DESIRED—AND WHY?

You must understand how *and* why you want to use a particular competitive advantage. For example, what would be the purpose of an aggressive price-reduction program? To secure a disproportionate share of market growth? To drive marginal competitors out of the product-market? To penetrate a competitor's distribution system? To signal to a competitor that you intend to "battle it out" and stay the course as growth rates slow?

Similarly, why might you want to develop an after-sales service capability? To broaden the concept of the product? To create a new image for the firm? To facilitate new product introduction?

These examples illustrate why you need to gain a detailed understanding of what your focal product-markets are and how your company wants to position itself within them.

HOW DOES IT COMPARE WITH COMPETITORS' OFFERINGS?

The notion of establishing a competitive advantage inherently presumes that you are seeking ways to surpass current and potential competitors. Here are some of the key questions in assessing current advantages: What (if anything) is the dimension upon which we have an advantage? Why is it an advantage? How large is it? How important is it?

You must assess each dimension to gauge how much the user will consider it a distinct advantage. These are some examples of specific inquiries you can make: What price differential is needed to constitute a significant price advantage? What kind of warranty would provoke customer interest? What degree of product-line width is important to distributors, the trade and customers? What mix of these would make the firm's offering superior?

IS IT FEASIBLE?

Once you've come up with a host of good ideas for creating and marketing an outstanding product, you must ask whether it is technically or physically feasible. For example, is it possible to extend the product life or modify the basic product in order to entice distribution support or broaden customer appeal? Or, how can the product be differentiated in the customer's mind in terms of image, styling, design, functionality, etc., to justify charging a premium price? (This is one of the challenges now confronting personal computer manufacturers; as they become more like commodities, price will be the dominant differentiating criterion.)

This question of feasibility forces the firm to look at itself. Does the firm have sufficient people and skills to offer after-sales service? Does the firm have the marketing expertise and sales force personnel to introduce a continual stream of product modifications to the market? Does the firm have the R&D, engineering and/or manufacturing capability to infuse the product with innovative features or superior performance?

WHAT WILL IT COST?

There is indeed no free lunch. A competitive advantage may be organizationally and technically feasible, but its cost may be prohibitive. Creating a strong brand image may be desirable, for example, but it obviously entails large marketing and advertising costs. Similarly, if you enlarge your manufacturing capability you may achieve production scale economies that allow you to lower your product price, but this expansion involves substantial investments.

If your firm is a multi-product business, remember that there are trade-offs in strengthening one product line. When you commit organizational resources and time to developing a competitive advantage in one product sector, your other products will receive less attention. Management must decide which product areas will receive emphasis.

HOW WILL YOUR COMPETITORS RESPOND?

A competitive advantage will endure only as long as competitors allow. If competitors recognize the advantage, they may choose to ignore it, copy it (in part or fully), or outdo it. Whatever response they adopt will shape the competitive dynamics among the firms in the market. You must therefore anticipate these responses and then assess your firm's own possible reactions to them.

These assessments will strongly influence whether you decide it is worth pursuing a given competitive advantage. If your competitors are likely to match a price reduction, then lowering your price may simply trigger a price war that ultimately results in reduced profits for all. Under these circumstances, it is certainly preferable to seek an advantage on other dimensions.

For example, an alternative to price wars in the airline industry is for the companies to compete on such other dimensions as availability (routes served), service (advance check-in), comfort (wider seats, more leg room) and promotions (free tickets upon completion of some minimum mileage).

CAN IT BE COPIED?

The speed, nature and intensity of competitors' responses are largely determined by whether other firms can duplicate or exceed the initial move. If you make only minor changes in price, product size, styling, promotion and packaging, your competitors can match them relatively easily. More substantial product improvements due to technological advances or innovative changes in the distribution system (such as moving from a two-step to one-step distribution chain) are less susceptible to quick-fix responses.

The intangible product attributes that are often the most painstaking to establish can also be the most difficult to match or overcome. In the soft drink industry, for example, Dr. Pepper and 7-Up have been fighting a long uphill battle against the potent image which Coke and Pepsi have established in the consumer's mind.

CAN YOU SUSTAIN YOUR ADVANTAGE?

You need to determine what further competitive moves *and* organization resources will be needed to sustain the advantages in the face of anticipated competitive responses and market changes. What new product introductions and line extensions will be required to sustain an image as the "market leader"? What incentives can the firm offer distributors and the trade to discourage them from supporting competitors' products? Does the firm have enough resources to engage in these competitive moves?

WHEN WILL THE ADVANTAGE NO LONGER BE WORTHWHILE?

In the battle for competitive advantage firms sometimes doggedly pursue their "advantage" long after some competitors have usurped it or after distributors or customers have ceased to value it. In either case, the company is simply throwing good money after bad.

Unless you periodically question the potency of your alleged advantage, you are likely to miss timely opportunities to establish new competitive superiority. The firm could then find itself trying to respond from a position of weakness in the product market.

CONCLUSION

Developing and sustaining competitive advantage(s) is a core task in formulating a competitive strategy. Yet many firms, by their own admission, frequently fail to ask fundamental and unavoidable questions, or, if they do so, fail to give them adequate attention. This case has briefly highlighted the most critical of these questions.

□

HOW LONG CAN YOU SUSTAIN
A COMPETITIVE ADVANTAGE?

IAN C. MacMILLAN

Your competitors are not likely to be either asleep or stupid. No matter what comparative advantage you may enjoy now, your competitors will almost certainly erode that advantage eventually. But how soon will they do it? To design effective strategies for the future, you must understand the dynamics of the competitive environment in which your business is embedded.

STRATEGY AND COMPETITIVE DYNAMICS

By launching an appropriate strategy, a firm achieves a "takeover"—that is, secures some kind of strategic advantage. It takes time—labelled period "A" in Figure 2-1—to build this advantage. Next there is a lull (period B), during which competitors notice and attempt to respond to this advantage largely by modifying *their* existing strategies.

When the competitors finally realize that these initial attempts at responding are not going to work, they start to seriously attack the strategic advantage directly. During period C the firm falls from its dominant position as its advantage is eroded by the competitive counter-actions. So, if the firm is to retain its superior position it must come up with a new strategy that creates a new advantage—which thus initiates a new strategic round.

In studying this three-phase process with two of my colleagues (Mary Lynn McCaffrey and Giles VanWijk), we recognized how important it is for a firm to estimate how long it can sustain its competitive advantage. It is during that "response lag" that the firm captures what the economists call "abnormal profits," and temporarily achieves profitability that is above average for the industry. The duration of these response lags is determined largely by "competitive dynamics" of the industry. The three key determinants of competitive dynamics are these: (1) how long it takes to create an advantage; (2) how large an advantage can be achieved; and (3) how long it takes competitors to respond.

First, the time it takes to create a competitive advantage is often a function of the competitive conditions. In some businesses, period A (the takeover) may be very short, particularly in service businesses where little in the way of new equipment or revised logistical systems is needed to implement a strategy. By contrast, in capital-intensive industries creating an advantage can take a long

Strategic Planning Management, January, 1984; Commerce Communications, Inc.

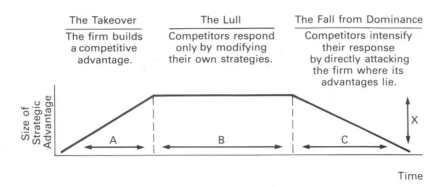

Figure 2-1 The rise and fall of a competitive advantage

time (building new chemical plant capacity based on a painfully developed new production process, or totally replacing old assembly line capacity with a new numerically controlled or robot controlled plant). It is important to identify the specific factors which delay or inhibit implementation of a proposed competitive advantage.

In some industries, it may take so long to create the advantage that the costs in expenses and effort are never really recouped. In fact, sometimes the benefits are actually lost to the competitors. This occurs particularly when a relatively innovative strategy must be "sold" to reluctant channels or end-users who shy away from the novelty of the strategy. When they eventually are convinced, the period of exploitation of the competitive advantage is short lived, because competitors swoop in and entice away the converts as soon as the viability of the strategy is proven.

Second, the *size of the advantage* that can be achieved also affects industry dynamics. In some environments, particularly where there are high entry barriers, it is possible to achieve much larger advantages than in others. Thus, the size of the advantage (indicated by "X" in Figure 2-1) may be either large (as in the pharmaceutical industry, where robust patents for new drugs permit substantial advantages) or small (as in financial service businesses, where new products tend to be easy to copy).

The third factor affecting competitive conditions is the *response lag—* the time it takes competitors to respond aggressively enough to erode the competitive advantage. The length of the lag is critical for three reasons. As we already discussed, it places an upper limit on the period in which abnormal profits occur. Also, during this time period two things must happen: (1) the next strategic advantage must be developed; and (2) the firm must profitably recoup the investment it made to create the first advantage. It is important to identify, for a specific strategy, what increases or decreases this advantage.

Estimating this response lag calls for a thorough understanding of the "inertia" of the competitive environment. Competitors in the investment banking industry, for example, respond to new product introductions in just a few weeks. On the other hand, competitors in capital-equipment businesses may take several years to respond, because of the time it takes to develop and field test new products whose long-run reliability must be assured. Our studies revealed that each industry and, in fact, each competitor had different response lags to specific competitive advantages. The effective strategist today cannot afford to ignore the factors which extend or shorten these competitive responses.

As you develop new strategies, you clearly need to understand whether you can expect large, long-lasting "waves" of dominance, as General Motors enjoyed from the 1930s until the mid '70s when they were unseated by Japanese automakers, or whether to expect short, choppy "saw teeth" periods of advantage, as in the commerical banking industry.

THE COMPETITIVE ENVIRONMENT: YOU DON'T CONTROL IT

To a large extent, the dynamics of the competitive environment also set limits on what *can* be accomplished: as research has consistently shown, there are some environments in which levels of profitability are inherently low or high, and in which a competitive advantage is either sustainable or hard to maintain. So, little of what you can accomplish is entirely under the control of your organization. Yet, managers frequently assume they have a great deal of room in which to maneuver. They do not sufficiently recognize how much competitive, market, and environmental conditions constrain their opportunities.

The fact is that you have little control over external conditions. So you need to identify which of the variables in your business you can control, and which are "environmental" and, therefore, largely beyond your control.

A major danger is that if you do not try to identify which factors influencing your business are uncontrollable, you may assume that you have much more room to maneuver than you actually do. This will likely result in very unrealistic strategies, or in a complete lack of concern with changing environmental conditions, and over-confidence in your organization's ability to respond to its environment and to handle competitors.

WHAT DO YOU CONTROL?

Evaluating controllable versus noncontrollable factors also helps you assess the reasonableness of proposed strategies. If a recommended strategy claims to be able to achieve and maintain a 20% ROI, in an industry where the average ROI is only 10%, then you should ask two questions. First, what competitive advantage will produce such sustained, abnormal profits? And, second, do we have control over the variables which seem to be critical for the success of that strategy?

To help identify which industry factors are likely to be relatively "uncontrollable," a colleague, Don Hambrick, and I conducted a study in 1980 in which we approached fifteen experts in strategic planning. We asked them to rate a set of factors affecting businesses according to how much "control" the managements in their industry have over each. We used variables selected from the PIMS database of SP1.

The experts were presented with a seven-point scale for rating each variable: low numbers classified a factor as being uncontrollable ("environmental"), whereas high numbers were assigned to completely controllable ("strategic choice") factors. The medium range was used for "position" factors that are somewhat controllable, though they do involve considerable time and expense.

Factors classified as uncontrollable ("environmental") included industry concentration, industry stability, relative importance to end-users, raw material cost growth, purchase frequency by end-users, real market growth, industry imports, typical purchase amount by end-users, relative importance to immediate customers, industry exports and industry wage-rate growth.

Moderately controllable ("position") factors included market share rank, percentage employees unionized, capital intensity, purchase frequency by immediate customers and percentage of sales from new products.

Factors classified as highly controllable ("strategic choice") included product R&D/revenue, process R&D/revenue, sales force expenses/revenue, relative product line quality, advertising and promotion/revenue, percentage of raw materials purchased from the three largest suppliers, value added/revenue, relative service, capacity/market size, capacity utilization, relation price, capacity/market size, capacity utilization, relation price, inventory/revenue, relation product quality and relative image. The environmental factors, therefore, form the *context within which strategy must be formulated:*

There are basically four types of uncontrollable, or environmental, factors:

1. Nature of the product (importance of product to end users and to immediate customers, purchase frequency, and typical purchase amount);
2. Industry growth rate;
3. Industry rivalry (industry instability, entry/exit of competition, industry concentration, and level of imports and exports); and
4. Inflationary conditions (raw material cost growth, industry wage growth).

The nature of these four major factors in an industry plays a decisive role in shaping what levels of profits can be achieved in an industry, and how responsive your competitors may be to your strategic moves. After all, it is within the context of these environmental constraints that you—and your competition—must make your strategic moves.

CONCLUSION

By evaluating the competitive dynamics of your industry you can gauge how long you can sustain a competitive advantage. You can also assess exactly where you (and your competitors) are the most constrained by uncontrollable environmental factors, which can help you evaluate alternative strategies. Any strategy that assumes it can alter these factors is unrealistic.

Finally, once you understand your competitive advantage, and what factors in your business are beyond your control—then you can develop a strategy that will take fullest advantage of those opportunities that are truly within your reach.

□

TO BUILD OR NOT TO BUILD: THE MARKET-SHARE QUESTION

V. K. NARAYANAN

Strategic planners generally share the belief that the most profitable businesses are those with the highest market shares. And for good reason! Look at IBM in mainframe computers, Proctor and Gamble in a variety of consumer products, McDonald's in fast food restaurants, and CocaCola in soft drinks. They all enjoy the highest shares in their product markets along with very attractive earnings.

It seems such an obvious choice: if you want to improve profitability, simply focus on increasing your market share. Yet many firms that embarked on programs to build market share have failed. In their enthusiasm for pursuing profitability, these firms never asked some basic questions about how realistic it was for them to be able to gain market share.

So before you undertake a program to increase market share, consider the following set of 10 basic questions. They may save you from squandering your effort and resources on an unrealistic target.

1. HOW LARGE IS YOUR MARKET SHARE?

Calculating your market share seems like such an easy task: simply divide your sales by total market sales. But it is really not so easy. Determining your share depends entirely on how you define your market. For example, if your product line is very limited, should you measure your portion of either the market that includes only the products that you sell, or the market that includes all the products of your full-line competitors? Similarly, if you compete in only one region of the United States, is your market only that region or the entire country?

Strategic Planning Management, June, 1983; Commerce Communications, Inc.

These may seem like trivial technical questions, but their answers can profoundly influence your analysis. For example, if Crown Cork and Seal Co. defines its market as the container market, then it has a low share. On the other hand, if its market is defined as metal containers for hard-to-hold applications (e.g., aerosols and beverages), then it has the dominant share.

It is tempting to gloss over the problems of market definition and "get on with it," but don't fall into that trap. If the market is defined inappropriately, then any subsequent analysis will be misguided. Market definition for any share-building program must be based on a clear understanding of the scale economies of operation (technology, manufacturing, or distribution) and of the geographic niches due to transportation costs, political or regulatory barriers, or genuinely unique customer needs or preferences. There are no ready recipes to the thorny question of market definition.

2. IS THERE REALLY AN OPPORTUNITY TO INCREASE SHARE?

Not all markets present good opportunities to increase market share. Here are the conditions that offer the greatest potential for a company to increase its share substantially:

Rapid market growth.   Where markets are growing rapidly, there is more opportunity to increase share, because some competitors may lack the resources or the capability to keep up with a fast-growing market. In the burgeoning microcomputer industry, for example, many larger companies have been able to steal share from smaller firms that simply don't have the resources to keep up with the competitive pace.

Changing technology, social values, or legislation.   Technological advances can offer great opportunities to build share; for example, the invention of the stationary-carriage typewriter enabled IBM to become the share leader in the office typewriter market with its Selectric models. The social trend toward more informal lifestyles in the '60s gave Levi Strauss its chance to expand its market share by developing a broad line of denim clothing, and legislative changes in banking and securities laws have allowed several firms to increase their share of the turbulent financial services market.

Complacent competition.   Market shares can also be increased when competitors have overlooked an opportunity either to differentiate the product or to reduce costs. Miller was able to increase its share in the mature beer industry, both because none of its competitors was using very sophisticated promotional techniques, and because no other company had recognized that a fitness-conscious public might appreciate a light beer.

If one or more of these conditions is present, you probably have an attractive invitation to build market share. Otherwise, a share-building program is less likely to succeed.

3. WHAT DOES IT TAKE TO SUCCEED IN THE MARKET?

Every strategy for building market share grows out of a set of presumptions about what it takes to be successful in the market. The fact that so many share-building attempts fail suggests two things: first, that managers frequently misestimate the success criteria in their business; and second, the determinants of success change over time.

The determinants of success in any business may include a combination of several factors such as research and technology capability, marketing expertise, knowledge of customers, ability to monitor and predict economic, social and legal trends, and brand awareness and loyalty. Each market or business may have its own unique set of success criteria.

A key point here is that while managers may have a strong gut feel for what will make them a winner in a particular market, these implicit criteria need to be explicitly identified, then monitored and critiqued. This approach will help you avoid the plight of a certain firm that maintained a large, extremely well-paid salesforce because it believed personal selling was the key to competitive success, only to find itself dramatically outperformed by smaller competitors with little or no salesforce!

4. DO YOU HAVE (OR CAN YOU GET) THE NEEDED RESOURCES?

Clearly, adequate resources are essential for building market share. Unless the managers can secure needed resources, the program cannot succeed. You need to assess how feasible it is that you will be able either to: (1) retain your existing resources for the program, (2) attract resources from other parts of the company by selling your superiors on the importance of the program, or (3) purchase resources outside the firm.

If you underestimate what is required to conduct a share building program, or if you can't line up all the necessary resources before launching the campaign, your offensive will soon be stalled.

5. DO YOU HAVE A COMPETITIVE ADVANTAGE?

Before you begin your market-share building efforts, you need to ask, "How can we distinguish ourselves from our competitors?" Only if you have a distinctive competence can you hope to take market share away from your competition.

For example, the reason that Timex succeeded in claiming the majority of the low-priced watch market in the '50s was that the company offered a product of exceptional durability (as illustrated in the famed "Torture Test" ads).

6. HOW WILL COMPETITORS RESPOND?

Don't make the mistake of using your competitors' current market-share positions as indicators of their future strategies or likely responses to your moves. Small-share competitors may fight even more fiercely than much larger-share firms to hold their ground, particularly if they have staked out a specific market niche (e.g., a geographic region, a particular distribution channel, a specific end-user type or market need). The owners of Ragu spaghetti sauces, for example, have tenaciously succeeded in fighting off encroachments of several large companies.

What a competitor *will* do is strongly influenced by what he *can* do. Developing a viable strategy that a competitor can't imitate is the best protection against harmful competitor response. But often that goal is not possible.

7. HOW SHOULD YOU SEGMENT THE MARKET?

It is easy, but dangerous, to assume that all segments of a market (customer types, geographic regions, age groups, etc.) have similar needs and preferences so that all segments can be reached and served in the same way. After all, the reasoning goes, a beer is a beer, everybody needs to use toothpaste, or people buy automobiles for pretty much the same reasons.

Yet beer-drinkers' preferences vary across geographic regions, consumers exhibit different degrees of brand loyalty for toothpaste, and autos are purchased for all sorts of reasons. Thus any share-gaining program will probably need to involve a *set* of strategies for penetrating individual market segments.

However, some caution is also in order. Although segmentation is useful, because it allows you to meet the distinctive needs of customer groups, sometimes it is wise not to splinter your market into different segments. If you can offer several segments of the same product (i.e., one that has higher quality, lower price, or both) you can take advantage of scale economics—as Japanese firms have successfully done in their mass-marketing of products such as consumer electronics.

8. DOES MARKET SHARE ACTUALLY REFLECT CONSUMERS' PREFERENCES?

Sometimes we tend to assume—erroneously—that high market share indicates consumer acceptance of a product. Such an assumption could lead to disaster, because tastes are always changing. Not only do the preferences of your current customers change, but the actual group of consumers changes as different types of consumers come into play at various times. Consider how much the auto industry has had to reassess consumers' needs in light of developments such as the emergence of the "singles" market, the increasing number of two-car families, and the rise in fuel costs.

Consequently, before you launch a share-building program, carefully assess the likelihood that you can sustain the loyalty of your existing customers.

9. WHAT ARE THE ASSOCIATED COSTS—AND BENEFITS?

Acquiring market share does not come cheaply even if the firm has a low-cost position. It often requires investment in technology development, additional capacity, inventory and marketing expenditures—all of which require financial resources.

Although many firms do calculate the direct costs of a share-building program, most firms neglect to assess the opportunity cost involved in not deploying the same financial resources elsewhere to support another strategic move. In other words, you must identify any opportunities that you are foregoing, and compare the costs of doing so (the potential benefits you will sacrifice) with the anticipated returns from the proposed share-enhancement program.

10. DOES MARKET SHARE REFLECT RELATIVE COST POSITIONS?

Conventional wisdom suggests that the larger the market share, the lower the per-unit costs due to experience-curve effects. Market shares, however, do not simply reflect relative cost positions. Share positions may indicate successful offensive strategies (product differentiation, past marketing campaigns, etc.) or current constraints (such as limited plant capacity).

The illusive connection between market share and costs often leads to erroneous inferences. Thus, it may be very misleading to infer that when firms in an industry have displayed relative share stability, their cost positions are reflected in their market shares. For example, a firm may have built its market share based on product differentiation, only to discover that other factors become far more important during industry maturity.

In a similar vein, even if your firm holds the low-cost position, share building may not be easy. Strategies for market-share acquisition have to address how to overcome entry barriers, such as consumer loyalty or access to distribution networks.

CONCLUSION

Market share is never the only issue confronting a firm. You must assess the tradeoffs involved in pursuing market-share growth, profitability, cash flow, etc. A myopic fixation on market share can lead you to stumble on obstacles that were beyond your immediate focus. Only if you carefully assess whether the conditions are ripe for you to launch a share-building initiative, can you ensure that your efforts will be successful.

☐

STRATEGIC SIGNALING: CONVINCING COMPETITORS YOU MEAN IT
COLIN CAMERER

The art of convincing your competitors that you're serious about pursuing certain strategic objectives is known as "signaling." Firms that thoroughly understand economic signaling can use that knowledge to their advantage in two ways: first, by devising clear signals that will deter competitors; and second, by interpreting the signals of competitors in order to anticipate their moves.

WHAT IS AN ECONOMIC SIGNAL?

An economic signal involves a costly action by the management of a company which is designed to communicate information about the firm's motives.

Although a company sends out many types of signals, a lot of ordinary signals have little impact because a competitor regards them as insignificant or merely bluffs. Because talk is cheap, many ordinary signals *are* merely bluffs. Economic signals, on the other hand, are convincing because they require investments that are too expensive for liars.

For example, any firm can inundate the media with press releases announcing tentative plans for an "exciting new product." But only the truly committed firm will put their money where their corporate mouth is, spending hard cash to advertise the new product, or making difficult-to-reverse investments in new plants or in high-priced managerial talent.

The range of information that a company must communicate to make its strategy work varies widely. Sometimes only a minor signal is needed: a modest increase in sales promotion activities may signal distributors that your firm is committed to specific products. But sometimes signals may be a company's only lifeline: if travel agents believe a struggling airline is sinking and they stop booking flights on it (thereby sinking it), the airline must convince agents of its ability to stay aloft or else it is doomed.

Strategic Planning Management, November/December, 1983; Commerce Communications, Inc.

THE THREE C'S OF POWERFUL SIGNALING

To transmit an effective economic signal, three factors are required. You can remember them as the "three C's": commitment, credibility, and communication.

To illustrate the importance of these factors, consider the dangerous game of "chicken," often used by "game theorists" as an example of how strategic jockeying can be very destructive if players err. In chicken, two drivers speed toward each other in cars and the first to swerve is "chicken," and loses face. If neither swerve, both can be badly hurt or killed.

Corporate and political analogies to this game are abundant: labor-management negotiations, local price or product wars, and international arms races are games of chicken. To win, you must convince your opponent of your irrevocable *commitment* not to swerve (or back down); if your opponent is convinced you will not veer, then he will swerve to avoid a collision, and you will win. But any such commitment must be *credible* and must be *communicated*, and you must be sure your opponent has received the communication.

To these ends, an imaginative chicken-player might pull the steering wheel from his car, thereby irreversibly (and credibly) committing himself to not swerve. But he must also display the detached steering wheel to his opponent, communicating his commitment. The hapless opponent has no choice but to swerve and lose—unless he has detached his steering wheel too! (In these games, the first to make and then communicate an irrevocable commitment is the winner.)

HOW TO SIGNAL COMPETITORS EFFECTIVELY

A primary purpose of signaling is to discourage competition. By conveying information about your firm—tenacity, plans for innovation, an undying pledge to customer service—you can scare off competitors and win territory without even having to fight battles for it. In the short run, however, you may have to be willing to pay a stiff price to avoid bigger warfare later on.

For example, consider the case of the Kroger chain of supermarkets in Nashville, Tennessee. Kroger was being hurt by competition from huge low-priced, no-frills warehouse markets, so they decided to communicate a strong signal that they were still a powerful force in the market. The Kroger store closest to a pesky competitor, Waremart, circulated special fliers announcing painfully low prices. Though the tactic probably cost Kroger dearly that year, and ran the risk of being labelled "predatory pricing" by the FTC, it convinced the battle-scarred warehouse owner never to open another store in Nashville—and many other potential competitors got the signal, too. (In addition, the FTC decided the tactic did not constitute predatory pricing.) As this case illustrates, costly investment in strengthening your reputation can yield large payoffs in lessened competition in the future.

The power of a signal is measured not simply by its costliness but by how that expense reflects long-term commitment. An *irreversible investment* in projects such as building a new plant designed exclusively for one product is a useful signal of intention, because competitors recognize that the company must be confident about their plans or else they would not spend money on assets that cannot be recovered or resold. Deliberately holding excess capacity may be a signal to potential entrants that a firm can easily create a market glut by lowering prices if entrants dare to invade.

If what you want to communicate is your firm's aggressiveness, you can get your signal across by using *cross-market retaliation.* That is the technique Bic used when they plunged into the disposable razor market after Gillette had begun competing with Bic throw-away pens.

Similarly, Maxwell House launched cross-market retaliation against Folger; when Folger invaded their Eastern markets, Maxwell House moved to increase their penetration in Folger's Western markets.

Although a retaliating firm may be at a comparative disadvantage when it crosses over into a competitor's market (as Bic's early losses in razor-making attest), the act of retaliation communicates that the firm has important qualities, such as tenacity and ferocity. After all, weak firms will not make costly retaliatory strikes. Cross-market attacks reflect something of an eye-for-an-eye approach—in the sense of "If you eye my market, I'll eye yours."

Keep in mind that although retaliation can be both costly and even brutal in the short run, the signal it communicates can help build long-term competitive strength. Another example of corporate toughness, well-signaled, is the way Proctor and Gamble reacted when Union Carbide test-marketed disposable diapers designed to compete with P&G's successful Pampers. As soon as Union Carbide introduced their brand in Maine, P&G muscled in, using local promotional gimmicks and price-cutting tactics that were designed not only to foul Union Carbide's test results, but also to convince the potential competitor (and others) that P&G would fight tooth-and-nail in *every* market Carbide might enter. (Union Carbide eventually gave up.)

CHOOSING THE RIGHT SIGNALS

The following steps will help guide you toward choosing the right signals by providing a framework within which you can conduct rudimentary signaling analysis. This evaluation process will probably resemble a lively, subjective brainstorming session far more than a methodical financial analysis.

1. *Decide what information must be conveyed, to whom, and for what purpose.*
   Begin by asking which competitors should be targeted, and what information you want to communicate in order to achieve the intended effects.

Identifying which competitors to signal, and what you want to signal to them, is a critical first step and is not as easy as it may appear. Different managers may consider different competitors as more likely to initiate threatening moves or to respond more viciously to your strategic moves. Your organization may also be undecided on whether to attack existing competitors or to ward off likely new entrants. You can only answer these questions by examining your strategy vis-a-vis different competitors. Unless you know what strategy you wish to pursue, you may end up sending confusing or misleading signals and, thus, provoking unintended competitive behavior.

Also, you must consider the risks involved. Is it possible that signaling this information might tip off the competitor(s) to your impending actions and cause long-term damage? For example, lowering prices too much to deter one entrant may alert tougher entrants to how much profit you have to protect, thus sparking further attacks on your turf.

2. *Make a rough guess about how much economic value will be created if you can signal credibly.* How much will a reputation for toughness benefit you in the long run? What will be gained by attacking a competitor in another market?

To determine how much economic value will be created, you will probably want to consider the following:

- What will the competitor be inhibited from doing or provoked into doing?
- Why will the competitor adopt these responses?
- What will be the impact on your sales, market share, and profitability, and over what time period?

In making such guesses, you will need to blend the insights of functional specialists (accountants, marketers, planners), line managers, and others with relevant expertise.

3. *Generate a set of potential signals, and evaluate their likely impact.* Once you've decided what you want to communicate, you can begin to generate a large range of possible signals. For example, you can consider using signals involving the following:

- long-term contracts with suppliers and customers;
- investments in plant;
- dramatic price or marketing changes;
- implicit guaranties or explicit warranties;
- instigation (or perhaps cessation) of costly lawsuits;
- public announcements in a costly medium or through a reputable source; or
- announcing or initiating an attack on a competitor in another geographic market or in another product market

For each possible signal, you must assess to what extent it is likely to deter the competitor from undesired behavior or provoke the competitor into the preferred response. For example, if you announce or even initiate a plant capacity extension as a means of conveying your commitment to a particular product market, will it inhibit new competitors from entering the market or will it dissuade current competitors from enlarging their own production facilities? Unless you make this assessment, you will likely choose signals that will not achieve the intended effects and, thus, waste your resources.

4. *Evaluate whether you could afford each signal if you were not telling the truth about your plans or intentions.* This is a most important step. If you could easily afford a signal, then it will not be credible. You should only consider signals that would be too costly for you if you were bluffing.

It is useful to put yourself in the position of the signal receivers to determine what might influence their perceptions of credibility. Then, once you've determined how expensive it will be to communicate your message convincingly, you can begin to compare this cost to the benefit you estimated in Step 2.

5. *Once you have chosen credible signals that will reflect substantial commitment, decide how you can best communicate them to the desired signal-receivers.* Remember, the power of your message will be lost if your target never tunes in to your signal.

MEASURING THE IMPACT OF SIGNALING

Paradoxically, signals are often more cost-effective when they are more costly. An advertising blitz, for example, tells consumers, "We expect to be so successful with this product that we'll earn back all these ad expenses plus ample profit." Extravagance—in building new capacity, designing opulent headquarters, hosting parties for suppliers, and printing glossy annual reports—can, of course, get some firms in trouble. But this "first class" approach can also yield some hidden benefits that you may not be able to see on balance sheets: namely, extravagance signals confidence and optimism. A prosperous company with strategic confidence must spend a little extra to distinguish itself from tight-fisted marginal companies whose future is dim (assuming, of course, that the prosperous company wants competitors or stakeholders to know of its prosperity).

It won't be easy to perform any cost-benefit analysis of an economic signaling effort because it yields "assets" that are intangible: pride, prestige, or reputations for quality (among customers), reliability (among suppliers), honesty and truth-telling (among stockholders), or aggressiveness (among competitors). A widespread reputation for these qualities can result in higher profits, but these benefits will only be seen in the long-run, and in ways that are hard to quantify. However, despite the difficulty of pinning numbers on intangibles, their financial impact can be huge, even if unmeasurable. As any corporate culture maven can tell you, intangibles and perceptions invariably reach the bottom line—sometimes invisibly, but often with an explosion.

CONCLUSION

Incorporating signaling into strategy analysis requires both imagination and careful analysis. The best signals are often out-of-the-ordinary actions: unorthodox legal arrangements, major new investments, or eye-catching tactics. The signals must be costly enough to demonstrate true commitment so they can earn credibility from competitors and consumers. It takes real guts to transmit a bold signal, but as long as competitors know the message is not merely a bluff, your firm can substantially increase its competitive power.

In short, signaling forces you to think through your competitive strategy, and to identify and assess the strategy of your competitors. Signaling considerations will likely help you avoid wasting your resources in competitive battles you cannot win; you will not take for granted either your own firm's strengths and position or those of your competitors.

CHAPTER

3

MACROENVIRONMENTAL ANALYSIS

■

□

UNDERSTANDING THE MACROENVIRONMENT: A FRAMEWORK FOR ANALYSIS

LIAM FAHEY

Environmental analysis is receiving increasing attention in many firms. This is well exemplified in the words of one senior executive, "my firm is only now clearly recognizing that industry analysis is not enough. We must understand the broader environmental forces that influence so much of what happens within our industry." However, many firms are struggling in their efforts to do environmental analysis. The purpose of this article is to suggest a framework for environmental analysis that is a composite of pieces of analysis conducted by a number of firms. Rather than taking the environment as a whole, the framework is illustrated in the context of lifestyles; that is, changes in family structure, work, education, consumption, and leisure patterns.

The suggested approach to environmental analysis consists of five steps:

1. Understanding the environmental segment
2. Understanding interrelationships among trends
3. Moving from trends to issues
4. Forecasting the future direction of issues
5. Deriving implications

Strategic Planning Management, September, 1984; Commerce Communications, Inc.

UNDERSTANDING THE ENVIRONMENTAL SEGMENT

For the purposes of analysis, the macroenvironment surrounding an industry is frequently divided into segments such as demography, lifestyles, social values and attitudes, the economy, technology, and the political and regulatory arenas. Of course, the segments strongly influence each other. The analysis of any segment can be organized around the following questions.

1. What Are the Current Key Trends?

An effective starting point in any effort to understand how a specific environmental segment may impact your organization is to begin by identifying the key current trends within the segment. This tells you in broad terms what is happening in that segment.

In the case of lifestyles you need to capture household, work, consumption, education and leisure related trends. Various external sources such as the Census Bureau, governmental agencies, consulting firms, assorted experts (e.g., demographers), and specialist publications (e.g., *American Demographics*) can be used to augment your internal resources in identifying trends.

2. What Are the Indicators of These Trends?

It is not enough to know that a trend exists. You need to know what data or evidence supports the existence of the trend. These indicators are also needed to facilitate monitoring the trend and forecasting its future direction and evolution.

3. What Is the Historic Evolution of the Trends?

Trends often have distinct lifecycles; they emerge, develop, mature (peak) and decline. They may not necessarily disappear. Thus, it is important to identify where a trend is in its evolution. Unfortunately, it is not always easy to do so.

What you can do is trace the evolution of the trend. For example, you can trace the pattern in the trends toward dual-career families, single parent families, participation in adult education programs, involvement in various leisure pursuits, and work-related activities. Understanding the history of trends is a prerequisite to identifying their future course.

4. What Is the Degree of Change Within Trends?

More insightful than simply outlining the evolution of the trend is to identify the degree of change currently evident within the trend. Is the trend gaining momentum, slowing down, or remaining stationary?

UNDERSTANDING INTERRELATIONSHIPS AMONG TRENDS

In any segment of the environment (and, of course, across segments of the environment) trends may conflict, reinforce and support each other or, possibly, have relatively little bearing on each other. Thus, you must investigate how individual trends are related. A major result of looking at trends collectively is that you see more than from any single trend individually. Broader patterns begin to reveal themselves.

1. Identify Interrelationships Among Trends

There is no simple methodology to search for and develop linkages among trends. It requires that you be inventive and creative. One company has found the following approach extremely beneficial. First, the firm looks for interrelationships at the sub-segment level. For example, in the case of lifestyles, how are "family life" trends related? How are trends in the area of cohabitation (unmarried individuals of the opposite sex living together), singles (individuals living alone), geographic mobility, single parent families, divorce rates, etc. related? Do they evidence a (continuing) breakdown in "traditional" family life? Do they reflect new definitions of "family"? Are there different lifestyles among different types of families?

A similar approach could be adopted with regard to trends pertaining to work, education, consumption, and leisure.

Second, the firm looks for relationships across sub-segments. That is, how are trends in the areas of households, work, education, consumption, and leisure related? For example, how do work, consumption, and leisure patterns differ across different types of households (single breadwinner, single parent, dual career, single individuals, etc.)? The firm then searches for conflicts among the identified trends.

2. Identify Conflicts Among Trends

The search for relationships among trends inevitably points up conflicts. Trends may push in opposite directions. If these conflicts are not noted, you may be too quickly lulled into drawing false inferences and making bad forecasts.

In the area of lifestyles, there is much data to suggest that many people are becoming less involved in and committed to their work, while others are becoming more involved and committed. A number of public and private studies have documented these counter trends. Real and apparent conflicts can be explained if we carefully look at the data. For example, with regard to the above counter trends different individuals relate to their work differently. Some working mothers view their jobs as careers; others see employment as economically necessary.

MOVING FROM TRENDS TO ISSUES

Not all trends are of equal importance to your organization. Some may have direct impact, others may have only tangential impact, if at all. Moreover your organization is not likely to have the resources or the energy to track and forecast all trends. In fact, you probably shouldn't even try to do so; the benefits would not exceed the costs.

You therefore need to determine those trends or combinations of trends that are likely to have most impact on your organization. Of course, the impact may be either negative or positive. These trends then become "issues" within the organization. That is, they are now declared to be worthy of analysis as to their likely future direction (forecasting) and impact on the organization.

The following is a list of "issues" in the area of lifestyles that different firms are currently addressing:

- dual-career families
- changes in consumption patterns
- the physical fitness boom
- changes in leisure patterns
- adult (continuing) education
- changes in the distribution of jobs

FORECASTING THE FUTURE DIRECTION OF ISSUES

To assess the potential implications of an issue for your organization, you have no choice but to make some forecast of the future evolution of the trend or set of trends within the issue. To do so you need to examine the forces underlying or driving the issue, and then lay out alternative forecasts (more precisely, projections) of the issue's evolution.

1. Assessing the Underlying Forces

Trends don't just happen. Something is driving them. The failure to try to understand the underlying forces driving trend(s) or issues is probably the most important reason why so many environmental projections miss the mark.

The challenge is to identify the most pertinent forces. For example, demographics, values and attitudes, technology, the economy, and political and regulatory change, individually and in combination, can drive lifestyle changes.

The aging of the population is changing leisure patterns. Value and attitude shifts directly influence many lifestyle trends. Changes in social values with regard to the role of women in society have helped propel and sustain changes in many facets of work and employment.

Rarely will all forces push trends or an issue in the same direction. In environmental analysis, countervailing forces almost always seem to exist. For example, demographic trends, such as the increase in the elderly population and married couples without children, underlie some of the rapid increase in the movement toward "condominium living." On the other hand, deeply entrenched social values around the preference for detached single family dwellings and, in some areas, legal restrictions, work toward inhibiting "condominium living."

2. Alternative Projections of the Issue

Multiple projections or scenarios are necessary in order to avoid the limitations inherent in making only a single "best guess" or forecast. All too often, in making only one projection of the evolution of an issue, organizations gloss over the difficulties involved in projecting the future (e.g., the conflicts among trends). Moreover, it becomes all too easy to accept as "fact" your single projection.

One consumer goods firm lays out at least three scenarios for each lifestyle issue. Each scenario represents a different picture of the future that is carefully developed around clearly identified trends (some of which may be only emerging). The initial intent is to create different scenarios.

Each scenario is then evaluated by different individuals as to its reasonableness: What is the evidence that its component trends are valid? Do the interrelationships among the trends make sense? What underlying forces are propelling the trends? Will they continue? Questions like these allow the management team to evaluate each scenario.

In this particular firm, a most likely scenario is created. This often involves picking and choosing pieces of the original scenarios to constitute the new, most likely scenario. It is this scenario that then forms the basis of the firm's planning.

DERIVING IMPLICATIONS

It is sometimes easy to forget that the purpose of doing environmental analysis is to enable your organization to do better strategic planning. You therefore need to derive the implications of your analysis for your organization. Implications should be noted at two different though directly related levels.

First, what does the analysis mean for your industry? That is, how will current and future developments in and around lifestyle issues affect the so-called structural forces within the industry: suppliers, distributors and customers, new entrants, substitute products, and rivalry or competition among the existing competitors? Each of these should be examined separately, and then these implications should be pulled together to identify key industry efforts.

Second, implications for the firm's current strategies should then be noted.

One firm, for example, is currently assessing the implications of a number of lifestyles issues for the current strategy of each of its major product lines.

An assessment of implications at these two levels will provide key inputs into determining what the firm's future strategies should be.

CONCLUSION

This article lays out a sequence of analytical steps which a number of firms have found useful in doing environmental analysis. The suggested framework for analysis is intended to guide you through the tortuous path of building bridges between environmental analysis and strategy formulation. It is only when you cycle through the steps in the analysis a number of times that real insight is gained into environmental segments or specific issues.

□

INTEGRATING MACROENVIRONMENTAL ANALYSIS INTO STRATEGY ANALYSIS: SOME PROBLEMS
LIAM FAHEY

Although the importance of understanding the macroenvironment, that is, the environment outside the industry or industries within which the firm is competing, is often recognized within firms, macroenvironmental analysis all too often contributes little to strategy analysis and formulation. Some firms have become so frustrated by the absence of apparent benefits from their efforts to understand and anticipate change in the macroenvironment that they have discontinued formal programs to do so.

Some of the major problems or issues that seem to account for the inability of firms to successfully conduct and utilize macroenvironmental analysis were identified in the course of a study of how macroenvironmental analysis is conducted in large corporations.

MISCONCEIVING THE MACROENVIRONMENT

The conceptions of the macroenvironment in the minds of key decision makers and ways of relating to it often act as a strong hindrance to effective environmental analysis.

Strategic Planning Management, June, 1985; Commerce Communications, Inc.

The environment poses uncertainties for the organization; thinking about the macroenvironment is a messy process. The scope of the analytical tasks in environmental analysis can be challenging as revealed by the complexity and interconnectedness of the segments that may need attention: demographics, lifestyles, social values, the economy, technology, and the political and regulatory milieus.

Consequently, it is convenient at one level to put these challenges aside because the environment appears too formidable to do anything about. The catch-cry becomes, "We can not impact the macroenvironment, therefore, we should not pay attention to it."

At another level, it is easy to discount potential environmental impacts based on the presumed capabilities of the organization. Here the catch-cry becomes, "We can react to events in the macroenvironment as they happen."

Either of these attitudes acts as a strong inhibition to environmental analysis. Such beliefs on the part of management often manifest themselves in the treatment of environmental analysis as an afterthought and as a symbol of progressiveness in management style without any real impact on decision making or by not engaging in it at all.

There are a number of potential reasons why this problem often exists in organizations. Culturally, the organization may be dominated by an operating as opposed to a strategic orientation; thus, the problems of today displace the possible concerns of tomorrow.

Alternatively, environmental analysis may have very low credibility at the top levels of management. This can easily happen. For example, in one large multidivisional firm, macroenvironmental analysis was deemed "a failure" and not likely to significantly contribute to enhancing managerial knowledge because the environmental analysis team had not foreseen the level of the economic recession.

Politically, environmental analysis has the potential to redistribute resources within the organization; politically motivated vested interests may prevent consideration of environmental issues lest it endanger their power position or resource base.

For example, in one single business corporation, the business development/strategic planning and public affairs departments fought each other over who should have responsibility for macroenvironmental analysis. The result is that each group persists in challenging each other's macroenvironmental analysis outputs.

Structurally, the individuals, units or groups may be located well away from the organizational centers of strategy formulation and implementation and thus have little real influence on the process. On the process side, individuals performing environmental analysis may be perceived as having low competence or not providing inputs into strategy formulation perceived as relevant by key decision makers.

INAPPROPRIATE REFERENCE FRAME

Closely related to inadequate conception of the macroenvironment are the frames of reference brought to bear when doing macroenvironmental analysis.

Too often the dominant frame of reference is "inside out" rather than "outside-in."

By inside out, we mean that macroenvironmental analysis is dominated by a current conception of the organization—its products, markets, technologies, etc. This leads to a narrow view of macroenvironmental analysis. An outside-in approach tackles macroenvironmental analysis in the absence of a current conception of the organization: it seeks to identify the dominant trends and patterns in the macroenvironment and then derive implications for the firm.

It is of course essential to integrate outside-in and inside-out approaches to macroenvironmental analysis; unfortunately this is much easier said than done in organizations. Much of the organization's attention is focused on the interface between the organization and its immediate task environment; that is, the industry within which it operates. The macroenvironment is viewed as far from the immediate concerns of management; moreover, its impact is often indirect and delayed. Thus, the pull toward inside-out analysis is great; outside-in analysis may be invoked when the organization finds itself in the midst of a crisis.

At first glance, this may appear to be a failure of analysis; however, the basis for this failure may lie in the nature of the organization's functioning. Cultural forces such as an operating orientation at the top levels of management, absence of structures for "doing" outside-in analysis, and political factors which inhibit search for new avenues for business development often engender a predominantly, if not exclusively, inside-out orientation.

MISUNDERSTANDING UNCERTAINTIES

A third problem that emanates from a lack of understanding of the macroenvironment is a low level of appreciation of the kinds of uncertainties involved in environmental analysis. Environmental segments differ in terms of their uncertainties: for example, demographic trends are relatively predictable in the short term, whereas technology change and political change can produce surprises even in the very short term. Thus, the kinds of analytical issues are different across segments. In a similar vein, the time frames of impacts are also different. Despite this, amid the push and pull of organizational life, the tendency to treat uncertainties as if they are similar is indeed great.

Furthermore, the greater involvement in the competitive environment which is relatively certain in the short-run predisposes managers to look for certainties which do not exist in the macroenvironment. For example, projections and forecasts are tentative statements about alternative futures; yet the tendency is often to treat them as "real" statements about the future. This not only misses the point of forecasting, but often results in disappointment and loss of faith in environmental analysis, as the forecasts turn out to be very much off the mark.

Structural, process, and political factors may underlie this problem. Structurally, where linkage mechanisms between environmental analysis and strategic analysis are weak, understanding of these uncertainties and its implications is less likely to be widespread in the organization.

On the process side, exclusive focus on the outputs of environmental analysis without attendant appreciation of the importance of involvement in the process often leads to misunderstanding the role of different uncertainties.

Finally, entrenched political interests can always play up the differences as a means of ridiculing environmental analysis itself.

INADEQUATE REFLECTION TIME

Beyond early convergence during scanning, a related but broader issue is common in environmental analysis: analysts may find themselves with inadequate time for reflection in the process of drawing inferences that are a central component of environmental analysis.

Here again, we need to note that environmental data do not yield inferences; analysts must exercise their creative and intuitive capacities to weave inferences from the data. This requires that time be devoted to reflection.

All too often, those conducting and using environmental analysis, by not giving themselves enough time for reflection, draw premature conclusions: conclusions that are later changed with more time for reflection. For example, in one consumer goods firm, a quick assessment of demographic trends yielded the conclusion that the firm's products were not affected by demographic changes. Further analysis, however, revealed that many of the firm's target markets were severely impacted by demographic change.

Reflection requires a certain organizational milieu; many of the structural, process and political impediments to effective environmental analysis already noted may inhibit the emergence and maintenance of this milieu.

INADEQUATE LINKAGE

Perhaps the most significant problem in many organizations is inadequate linkage between environmental analysis and strategy analysis: the outputs of environmental analysis are weakly or not at all linked to further stages in strategy formulation.

This problem manifests itself in several ways: uncertainties postulated by environmental analysis are neglected; weak signals are not further pursued;

operating assumptions from the past continue to shape strategy formulation; and no specific action plans emanate from environmental analysis. The effects of such inadequate linkage are often not immediately clear. However, over the long run, organizations typically face "foreseen" crises and continue to be driven by short-term issues.

While several factors may inhibit adequate linkage, structural factors are perhaps the most important in effecting adequate linkage. Isolated environmental analysis units, staffed by individuals with high technical expertise, often develop into "fortune tellers," with their own language and their own agenda and objectives, and, as a consequence, lose touch with the needs of the organization. It is not surprising then that the outputs of environmental analysis are not seen as action relevant, and the value of the process to those engaged in strategy analysis is lost.

On the process side, the absence of linkage could emanate from not tailoring the outputs of environmental analysis to planning cycles and lack of continual exchange of information between environmental analysis units and those engaged in strategy analysis. Communication becomes important not only to educate individuals to the differing kinds of environmental uncertainties, but to underscore the fact that environmental analysis addresses different timeframes. Political factors such as the top management's view of environmental analysis as merely window dressing can also inhibit these linkages.

□

HOW THE BROADER ENVIRONMENT CAN SHAPE INDUSTRY ELEMENTS

V.K. NARAYANAN

It is almost an accepted axiom that the starting point of any strategic analysis is some form of environmental analysis. In practice, however, environmental analysis is often not much more than industry structural analysis.

It is the thesis of this article that the environment beyond the boundaries of an industry almost always significantly influences, and sometimes largely determines, what actually takes place within the industry. Thus, the intent of this article is to show how various segments of the broader environment such as demographics, social lifestyles and values, technology, politics, and governmental regulations impact some key elements of an industry: industry boundaries, customers, suppliers, product substitution, strategic groups, and key success factors.

Strategic Planning Management, June, 1984; Commerce Communications, Inc.

IMPACT ON INDUSTRY BOUNDARIES

Of perhaps the greatest importance is the impact of environmental change on the survival of an industry or specific industry segments. Environmental change can sometimes have more sudden and significant impact on industry (segment) boundaries, and thus survivability, than the structural and competitive forces within the industry.

For example, in recent years regulatory changes have transformed the boundaries of such industries as financial services, telecommunications and airlines. New competitors have been allowed to enter each of these industries. They now offer more products or services than previously. Indeed, it is difficult to define what precisely is meant by the financial services or telecommunications industries—the scope of the products and services offered is changing so quickly.

Social values manifested in political and regulatory change and technology difficulties have transformed the nuclear power industry in the United States in the past decade from one which was considered an attractive investment into one riddled with inefficiencies, cost overruns, and shut-downs.

Economic progress can be viewed as one long history of technology change contributing to shifting industry boundaries. For example, technology advances underlying frozen foods and personal computers have irrevocably altered our conceptions of food and computer industries.

IMPACT ON CUSTOMERS

The size, characteristics, and behavior of a firm's customers can also be severely influenced by environmental change. In the longer term, demographics affect the size and potential of almost all markets. For example, reflecting the aging of the population, we now see a number of different types of firms marketing directly to senior citizens.

Changes in social values and lifestyle can exert a significant impact on customers' behavior and sometimes do so rather swiftly. The rise and subsequent decline of jeans in general, and designer jeans in particular, aptly illustrates the sensitivity of many markets to the tastes preferences and propensities of major segments of customers. The rapid rise and subsequent decline of the bowling industry is another example of where "customers" succumbed to other leisure activities and the "product" did not fit with the lifestyles of the younger generation.

In industrial markets, changes in technology can radically alter the products and/or processes of customer firms. These technology advances, of course, often take place outside of the user or customer firms.

IMPACT ON SUPPLIERS

Changes in environmental conditions can directly affect the number, type and location of suppliers as well as the products they produce and their supply cost.

Changes in the political and regulatory climate can affect the structure and competitive dynamics within the supplier industry. Taxation policy, direct subsidies, and import quotas may facilitate or constrain increases or decreases in the number of suppliers and the degree of competition among them.

More directly, regulatory actions may impact a supplier industry. The Federal Drug Administration, for example, may approve or ban products (e.g., saccharine).

Technology developments often change the competitive dynamics of suppliers; they may leapfrog and obsolete each other's products. Microprocessors and semiconductors are highly visible examples. Sometimes technology advances lead to the emergence of a new type of supplier. Computer-aided manufacturing improvement techniques have been initiated by a small number of firms over the last two to three years as a means to effect efficiencies in firms manufacturing operations and enhance product quality.

IMPACT ON PRODUCT SUBSTITUTION

Environmental change can result in product substitution. For example, changes in lifestyles such as an increasing tendency for people to move from suburbs to "the city," changes in work patterns, dual-career families, and later marriages, have contributed to condominiums replacing single-family homes for many individuals and couples. This movement also received impetus from, and was reinforced by, regulatory factors: rent controls in many cities and prohibitions on building more apartment complexes.

Changes in social values also often contribute to product substitution. Concern with health maintenance and improvement has led to the emergence of new products and much product substitution; diet foods and drinks are frequently purchased in preference to "regular" foods and drinks.

Technology developments sometimes lead to dramatic product substitutions. Developments in glass, plastics, and aluminum technology have led to these products replacing steel as a supply source to many other industries.

IMPACT ON STRATEGIC GROUPS

In addition to tracing the influences of environmental changes on an industry as a whole, it is important to note the differential impact of the changes on various strategic groups within the industry. Environmental changes, to the extent they affect customers' preferences, suppliers' capabilities, substitute products, etc., could potentially enlarge or decimate the product-market arenas in which different strategic groups operate.

Perhaps, more importantly, environmental changes may afford opportunities for firms in a specific strategic group to overcome mobility barriers, that is, the barriers inhibiting a firm from moving from one strategic group to another. Deregulation of the airline industry in the late 1970s had adverse impacts on longer-haul firms relative to shorter ones, thus facilitating restructuring of the routes of larger airlines and the capturing of these by smaller airlines.

IMPACT ON KEY SUCCESS FACTORS

Environmental change can potentially affect the key success factors in almost any industry or industry segment. This impact often differentially affects firms in an industry; some firms adapt to the environment by existing and exploiting new success factors, others may only partially do so, others may not be able to do so and exit from the industry, while other firms may be enticed into the industry.

Technology is frequently exploited to create new success factors. For example, when electronics firms entered the watch industry, that had traditionally been the province of Swiss and other manufacturers relying on mechanical watches, their technology capability enhanced the quality of watches along many dimensions, such as precision in keeping time and ease of repair.

At a minimum, environmental changes need to be assessed in terms of their impact on firms' relative cost positions, product quality and functionality, image, reputation and resource requirements for major product-market segments. Technology change can reduce product cost and/or improve product quality. Increasing low rates can erode firms' competitive cost position, as many manufacturers have discovered in the United States. Changes in social values and lifestyles often require variation in desired image and reputation.

A major success factor in the motel/restaurant industry—location—has recently been impacted by environmental change. A number of motel chains traditionally located near highways due to the continually increasing volume of highway traffic. However, with gasoline becoming increasingly expensive, some motel chains have decided upon employing non-highway sites based on their assessment that the potential of highway locations is likely to decline considerably due to decreased automobile travel.

IMPACT ON GENERAL EXPECTATIONS

Perhaps the above discussion can be summarized by noting that environmental changes potentially affect general expectations about an industry and of the firms within it. These general expectations are important, as they may have an impact on the level of investment funds into the industry and on the stock price behavior of the firms within it.

Similarly, firms which have not had to contend with major competitive battles may be completely misled if they do not carefully assess environmental change. Their prior general expectations may be no longer valid. For instance, after the deregulation of the telecommunications industry, many telephone companies are discovering that their assessments of competitors' responses shaped by past behavior are no longer valid.

CONCLUSION

The purpose of this case has been to demonstrate that environmental changes help to shape and drive so-called "industry forces." This case has briefly illustrated how various types of environmental change, taken together or in isolation, affect key structural elements or forces within an industry. Stated differently, industry forces alone do not fully explain what happens within an "industry."

However, in thinking through how environmental change affects an industry, you should not fall into the common trap of glossing over these impacts. This often takes place in the form of unquestioned commentaries ("it's too vague"), or a pretense of invulnerability ("it will not happen here") or wishful thinking ("we can lick it").

Assuming that your environmental analysis efforts have identified the relevent current and potential environmental changes in order to avoid the inertia underlying these traps, you should ask and explicitly answer the following questions:

1. How will these major environmental changes individually and in combination affect each of the industry elements discussed above? (Of course, some environmental changes may be only minimally relevant to some industry elements, if at all.)
2. How are these impacts, in turn, reflected in
   a. product-market opportunities within the industry?
   b. threats to your firm's current position and strategies or possible strategic moves?
3. What strategies can you develop to exploit these opportunities and/or fend off these threats?
4. What strategies can your competitors develop to exploit these opportunities and/or fend off these threats?

One result of persistently asking these questions is that you will more likely find yourself anticipating rather than merely responding to the forces shaping your industry.

CHAPTER

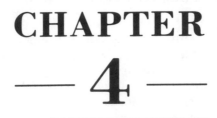

INDUSTRY AND COMPETITIVE ANALYSIS

COMPETITIVE ANALYSIS: UNDERSTANDING WINNERS AND LOSERS

WILLIAM E. ROTHSCHILD

In any given industry, all firms do not perform equally well. Some are winners and others losers. To identify who the winners and losers are, and to assess whether they will continue to win and lose, you need to address the following questions:

1. What are the criteria of winning (success) and losing (failure)?
2. What differentiates the winners from the losers?
3. What could happen to cause a change in winners and losers?

IDENTIFYING THE WINNERS AND LOSERS

To determine winners and losers and what differentiates them, you need some criteria or bases of assessment. It turns out that who the winners and losers are is often a deceptively difficult question to answer. This is because, in many industries, different criteria will give you different winners and losers.

Possible criteria which you can use are the following:

■ Profitability (e.g., ROI, ROE, ROA, ROS)

Strategic Planning Management, May 1984; Commerce Communications, Inc.

- Market share
- Sales and profit growth
- Cash flow
- New product development
- Creation of new markets

Since different criteria may give you different winners and losers, it is almost imperative that you use a variety of criteria. By using different criteria you are likely to acquire different perceptions and insights.

For example, in many businesses, a ranking of winners and losers will be quite different depending upon whether profitability, cash flow or market share are used. Cash flow winners may have more liquid resources to invest in the business. Market share winners may be somewhat vulnerable if they are deficient in cash flow.

USE MATRICES TO VISUALIZE

The differences in winners and losers are likely to be more evident if you represent them in the form of matrices where the axes reflect different criteria. By varying the intersection of the two axes or criteria (e.g., you may want to use your own firm's performance as the key average, or you may use the industry average), you will obtain a different depiction of winners and losers (e.g., those above and below your performance, or the industry average).

DETERMINING THE DIFFERENCES BETWEEN
WINNERS AND LOSERS

Depicting the positions of all the firms in an industry on a matrix does not explain why some are winners and other are losers. You need to investigate what makes the difference between them, i.e., why have some won and others lost.

Isolating what makes the difference between winners and losers may provide you with a listing of success factors which can be used later when you assess how you compare to the competition, and whether industry and environmental changes are likely to affect these factors.

There are four fundamental aspects to analyze in determining why some firms win and some do not:

1. Is there a unique vision, direction or strategy?
2. Were there different explicit assumptions about the market, technology and/or supply?
3. Were there unique combinations of resources?
4. Were there other unusual factors?

1. Vision, direction and strategy.   Winners are frequently driven by the "vision" and strategy of either their founder(s) and/or a strong leader. Alfred Sloane's restructuring of General Motors is a classic example. He put in place a strategy which was the basis for many years' success. Clearly, you need to know what strategies winners and losers have followed.

2. Different assumptions.   A major reason why we see different firms pursuing different strategies in the same industry is that they make different assumptions about the future. It is, therefore, important to try to deduce the assumptions that winners and losers have made and to assess whether or not they will change in the future. The four major areas to look for key assumptions are markets, technology, suppliers and the macroenvironment.

Market assumptions: assumptions about how and at what rate the market will develop undergird most firms' strategy. For example, in the energy industry, some firms are assuming that conservation is only a fad, and that it will disappear once oil and gas become plentiful and their cost stabilizes. Others are assuming that conservation is here to stay, and are busy developing products and services to meet conservation and efficiency needs.

Industry assumptions: assumptions about the industry are also obviously important. Will the industry continue to grow or will it decline? What will be the rate of growth or decline? These are particularly important questions in maturing commodity industries such as steel, aluminum, autos, and transportation.

Technology assumptions: assumptions about technology development are often a critical determinant of winners and losers. Some firms rush to displace old technologies with new advances, while others strive to make existing technology more competitive, and some firms may even ignore the entire question. These differences are evident in many industries.

Supply assumptions: assumptions about capital, people, raw materials, and natural resources can also make the difference between success and mediocrity. Assumptions about capital availability and its price, workforce productivity, wage rates, raw material availability and its quality, and cost influence the strategies adopted by firms. For example, assumptions about labor productivity have led many firms to more production facilities off-shore. However, this has helped some firms to become winners, but it has hindered others because they have not been able to adopt quickly enough to technology change.

Macroenvironmental assumptions: assumptions about the broader societal environment may also determine the winners from the losers. Consumer products firms may be vitally concerned with whether the trend toward working wives and feminism will continue. Assumptions pertaining to political trends influence the strategies of firms in many industries.

3. Resource differences.   Resource differences in many cases separate the winners from the losers. A careful assessment of the firms identified as winners and losers often quickly leads to significant sources of success and failure.

Resources should be broadly interpreted. Marketing skills, design and product differences, production capabilities, financial wherewithal, and managerial and workforce talents are frequent bases by which truly successful firms differentiate themselves.

What is important is to identify how these resources contribute to success (or, the lack of them contributes to failure). IBM had excellent cash flow from its old keypunch business, and used the money to enable its customers to rent or lease computers rather than buy them. McDonald's has been a winner because it has been able to deliver a fast, consistent-quality product on an economical scale.

4. Luck.   It is easy to underestimate the importance of luck. It may play an important role in explaining the differences between winners and losers.

Luck is often a matter of a firm being in the right place at the right time. Companies with energy-efficient cars, motors, appliances, and generators have prospered because of the energy crisis and concern about availability and cost. Companies with the ability to respond rapidly to a given fad, or unique once-in-a-lifetime need, are the winners for the short term, although not necessarily the long term.

Consideration of luck forces you to ask whether the successful firm can sustain its winning streak. If its success is largely due to luck, and conditions change, the winner may be very vulnerable. Consideration of luck may also help you to avoid overly attributing the success of the winners to vision and strategy, appropriate assumptions, and/or well-exploited resources.

WHAT WILL CHANGE WINNERS AND LOSERS?

Although it is important to know why *current* winners and losers are winning and losing, from a strategy formulation perspective it is even more important to know whether these firms will continue to win and lose, and why they will do so. A number of questions can be raised to guide this phase of assessing winners and losers.

1. *Will complacency and fear affect the winners?* A dominant reason why many winners lose their position is that they become complacent and fear that they will be affected negatively if they change. They do not adapt their strategy to competitive and environmental changes.

    A&P (the supermarket chain) stopped innovating and leading. They refused to follow their customers to the suburbs, and did not offer a combination of brandname and store-label products. Their stores became outmoded, and their prices became uncompetitive. This was caused by complacency and/or fear of losing what they had.

2. *Substitution.* Winners are often displaced by the introduction of a superior product or service. Competitors—not necessarily existing competitors— find a better way of providing the same function or an improved version of it.

   Addressograph Multigraph and AB Dick were the leaders in office products. Xerography substituted for the wet copiers and thus changed their standing. Technological improvements often result in the displacement of winners. It is also important to note that substitution can happen in specific market niches, rather than in total industries.

3. *Innovative followers.* It is not just substitution of new products that can cause displacement. Quite often the threat to position comes from those who are smarter in adapting or even following the leaders. You need to identify who the competitors are who can add or innovate on what already exists, and how they may do so.

   For example, in autos, computers, hotels, and financial services firms which were once followers have outpaced the initial leaders. Quality and reliability were added to autos; systems services and leasing were added to computers; clean, attractive, limited menus were added to fast food; elegance at moderate prices to hotels; and full services at moderate fees were added to the financial service markets.

4. *Environment.* Many factors in the environment can cause changes in the positions of winners and losers. Changes in social values, demographic shifts, governmental regulations, and labor militancy have dramatically affected the success factors in many industries. Our major purpose here is to emphasize the need to go beyond the borders of your industry in searching for reasons why the current rise of winners and losers might change.

CONCLUSION

The process outlined above provides a framework for identifying and assessing the winners and losers in an industry. It particularly emphasizes the need to determine the differences between winners and losers; that is, those factors which have led to success or failure. You then need to assess whether these factors will lead to future success, or, more generally, what is happening inside and outside of the winners and losers which will lead to a change in their position.

☐

APPLICATION IN STRATEGIC MANAGEMENT:
Identifying Potential New
Industry Entrants
LIAM FAHEY

Few events surprise firms as much as the unexpected emergence of a new competitor. All too often the cry, "We should have known," is heard after the entry of the new competitor(s).

New entrants usually are the harbinger of major change in at least one industry segment. Sometimes, their impact is felt in a number of segments of an industry. They frequently result in new product developments, new ways of marketing the product, and technology advances.

One firm in a service industry found itself the victim of new entrants in three of its most important market segments over the course of one year. One result was that the firm had to dramatically reshape its strategy in each market segment to counteract the new entrants.

The CEO of the firm asked the head of corporate planning to pull together a management team "to see if it was possible to identify potential new entrants into the industry."

After much deliberation, the management team evolved the following four-step approach to identifying likely new industry entrants.

MAPPING THE INDUSTRY

The first step in the analysis was to develop a map of the industry. The intent of this step was to answer the following questions.

■ What products are included in the industry?
■ What markets or customers are served by the industry?
■ Who are the current firms in the industry?
■ Who are the competitors in each major product-market segment?

To answer these questions, a large "product-market matrix" was developed. All the products were listed on the vertical axis and all the markets were listed on the horizontal axis. The matrix provided a picture of all the current product-markets in the industry.

Next, all the major competitors in each product-market were entered. Most competitors were in many product-markets. Only a few were in a single product-market.

Strategic Planning Management, July/August, 1984; Commerce Communications, Inc.

This map of the industry was a prerequisite to the following three steps. One unexpected side benefit of constructing the map was that it allowed the management team to trace the evolution of the industry, that is, product and market evolution. As part of this evolution, the team was able to identify the sequence of new industry entrants over the previous decade.

NEW PRODUCTS AS INDICATORS OF NEW ENTRANTS

Each of the three new entrants that inspired this analysis had introduced "products" that were new to the industry. In effect, two were, in large measure, combinations of existing products and one represented an extension and development of a product which was a relatively small item in the portfolio of many firms.

As a consequence, the management team decided to try to identify potential new products (i.e., products new to the industry) and what *types* of new entrants (i.e., firms new to the industry) might be likely to offer these products. Rather than get bogged down in trying to identify specific new entrants, the management team sought to identify the *types* of firms that would have the capacity—the skills, technologies, and resources—to develop and market these products.

To identify possible new products, the management team analyzed existing products and various "market needs" which had been surfaced by the firm's market research department. Various other managers were also asked to identify new products which might emerge in the industry, or market needs which were now unserved. Outside experts were also asked for their inputs.

The team created a short list of possible new products. For each product, a brief rationale was developed, as to why it might emerge. Is it an extension of existing products? What market need will it serve? How is it superior to existing products?

It proved surprisingly easy to identify types of firms that might market these products, some of whom would represent new entrants into the industry. This was largely because of the diversity of firms already in the industry.

The team identified the types of firms for whom each potential product would be a good "fit." This involved asking very specific questions:

- Does it represent an extension of existing products?
- Do these firms have the "technology" base to create and continue to develop the product?
- Do these firms have the requisite market skills?
- Do these firms have access to and knowledge of the targeted customer base?

In summary, identifying potential new products was relatively easy; most of them were products that had already received some public discussion within the industry. While all these products could be introduced by firms already in the industry, some of them were assessed as very likely to lead to new entrants into the industry.

COMBINATIONS OF EXISTING FIRMS AS NEW ENTRANTS

The recent history of the industry suggested that new entrants, both to the industry and to specific product-markets within it, might arise through some form of combination of existing firms. Mergers, joint ventures and distribution agreements were noted as possible combinations.

The management team focused upon two types of combinations. Combinations between firms within the industry and combinations between firms within and outside the industry. For the purpose of the analysis, any new combination was defined as a new entrant.

To identify potential combinations, the management team tried to match current and potential products with the skills, capabilities, and competences of firms currently within and outside the industry. The intent was to identify synergies across firms.

One particularly fruitful avenue of identifying combinations was to ask what liaisons could be formed among "suppliers" and "buyers" as a means of cutting out "middlemen." Another fruitful question was what liaisons might evolve between competitors in different product-market segments. Another question posed was what types of firms outside the industry might best help competitors within each major product-market.

Again, the purpose of this phase of the analysis was to identify types of combinations rather than the specific firms that might constitute any one combination.

BARRIERS TO ENTRY

Identifying potential new products and types of firms that might be new entrants does not mean that they will actually enter. Barriers to entry may either prevent them from entering or make it difficult to do so.

The management team tried to identify entry barriers for firms coming into the industry with a new product and for firms coming into existing product-markets. Some entry barriers were relevant to both types of entry, others were not.

Legal factors emerged as a major entry barrier for some of the new types of firms that had been identified as possible entrants. Some combinations of firms were not allowed legally, and there were some prohibitions on how some types of firms could operate (e.g., restrictions on doing business in more than one state).

Where legal barriers did not exist, resources and knowledge of the industry were identified as the most common entry barriers.

What proved illuminating for the management team was that financial resources, per se, might not be the dominant resource related entry barrier for many types of firms. A major resource was identified as "access to customers." If a potential entrant did not already have access to customers, the difficulties and time involved in building access to customers would be prohibitive almost irrespective of the firm's financial wherewithal.

An interesting sidelight of this insight was that the management team prophesied that the problems involved in gaining access to customers would lead to new forms of combinations among firms within the industry, and new combinations between firms within and outside the industry—something which is increasingly happening in the financial services industry and in the health-care industry.

Knowledge of the industry was also seen as a potential entry barrier. The management team argued that some previous entrants had not performed nearly as well as anticipated because of their lack of understanding of "how to do business" in the industry. However, it was also noted that some other recent entrants were successfully changing the "rules of the game" in some segments of the industry.

Considerations of entry barriers served to further refine the types of firms that might enter the industry and, more specifically, which product market segments they might enter.

MAKING USE OF THE ANALYSIS

The purpose of this analysis was not simply to identify potential new industry entrants. It was to determine how these potential entrants might possibly affect the industry and, more specifically, what implications they might have for the firm's current and future strategies.

The following questions guided this part of the analysis:

- Will each new entrant give rise to a new product-market?
- How will each entrant affect current product-markets?
- How might current competitors respond to each new entrant?
- How will targeted customers respond to each new entrant?
- What competitive advantages (if any) will each new entrant possess?
- What might be the major vulnerabilities of each new entrant?
- What can our firm do to preempt and respond to these entrants?

Although the answers to these questions were regarded as "informed guesses," they provided valuable inputs to the firm's strategy analysis. This occurred in three ways.

First, they indicated sources of opportunity as well as threats. A number of new product opportunities emerged, some of which are now under serious consideration.

Second, the firm began to see its industry in a much broader perspective. The winds of change that were sweeping it began to be much more visible. For example, it became much clearer to some managers why so many new combinations of firms had already taken place.

Third, senior managers began to see the need to take preemptive and "anticipatory" actions rather than their typical reactionary actions. For the first time, managers were heard to talk about the need to be the "first mover" under some circumstances.

CONCLUSION

The firm's management team now has a much better understanding of what some of its future competition may look like. It is using its profile of likely new entrants as a key ingredient in the development of its short-run and long-run strategies.

Competitor Analysis

☐

EVALUATING A COMPETITOR'S PRODUCT STRATEGY
WILLIAM E. ROTHSCHILD

Evaluating a competitor's product strategy is important to determining whether there is consistency among the elements of that strategy. Inconsistencies among a competitor's product positioning, development, funding, breadth, and depth reveal an inconsistency with the firm's strategic driver(s)—the force(s) behind its overall strategy. Once you have identified the inconsistencies in a competitor's product strategy, you can begin to look for the causes and to formulate plans for taking advantage of them.

Strategic Planning Management, June, 1986; Commerce Communications, Inc.

PRODUCT POSITION

A first step in assessing a competitor's product strategy is determining the company's product position. Is the company a leader or follower? Does it strive to differentiate or to standardize its products?

A competitor may wish to be the leader—real or perceived—in product innovation. Obviously, if the strategy is product-driven, it must have a consistent supporting implementation strategy and resource commitment. Has the competitor allocated enough financial, human, and physical resources? Where is this strategy being implemented? Does the competitor have centralized or decentralized laboratories? How successful has it been in innovating? What has contributed to its success? Can it continue to be successful in the future?

Some companies, with the reputation and thrust of being leaders, have a tremendous track record. AT&T, via its Bell Labs, is clearly an innovative organization and has received a high return on its commitment. DuPont, Kodak, Xerox, and Polaroid all have had varying degrees of success in leadership strategies.

A company may lead in some businesses and not in others, an indication that the R&D is done on a local or business-by-business basis, not on a centralized, corporate basis. Consistent with the portfolio concept, some companies excel in some lines, but not in others. It is useful to understand the reasons for such variations in leadership. Selecting priorities may be a corporate or local business decision.

It could be a funding decision. National priorities may emphasize some businesses or segments over others. Understanding how the funding is made is also useful. Is it done directly through contracting or through subsidiaries?

A company with a product-driven strategy does not need to be a leader; it can also be a follower. Why would a company elect a follower, product-driven strategy? It might decide it has a lot to lose by being the leader. A company that is already number one will be interested in protecting its position and will not want to make its product obsolete.

But a strategy of following is tough to implement. It will take extraordinary competitive/market intelligence and research and development. The competitor must know what the next generation of the product will be and also what the likely substitute products will be. It must be willing to invest in programs and projects that will prepare it to introduce the product when the timing is right.

Timing is critical. Following too early may mean reducing the company's own sales by substitution. Following too late can also mean lost sales.

Following can be rapid or slow. Rapid following is difficult and can be very expensive, possibly more expensive and complex than leading. The company that can move rapidly is unique.

At times, the company may be strong enough to get the customer to wait until it has an equal or better product to compete with somebody else. For example, when companies like Remington, Honeywell, Burroughs, and Amdahl introduced bigger and better mainframe computers, IBM announced that it was going to introduce the next generation soon. Since prospective users already had their software and systems geared to IBM, they were willing to wait and to convert.

At times, the problem is not rapidity but quality. The challenger must be capable of providing quality and reliability, or its challenge will not be successful.

Example: General Motors followed Volkswagen and Mercedes-Benz in providing diesel engines at the peak of the oil crisis, but the GM diesels did not measure up. They needed more battery power than ordinary internal-combustion engines, they ran rough, and they had trouble with water seeping into their tanks. Many of these problems were also true of the original entries, but GM may have been wiser not to have followed in this case. If the quick follower does not respond with quality, it may accelerate its decline.

An alternative is for a company to follow at its own pace, when it is ready. This is the option traditionally employed, and it is especially suited for a leader. This approach can be especially successful if the innovator's product fails. But it also can represent significant risk, since the innovation may take hold, develop rapidly, and require costly catch-up

Many American companies have adopted the slow-follow position. Kodak took over a decade to follow Polaroid in the instant-photography market. Kodak spent a great deal of money trying to catch up before relinquishing the field to Polaroid. The same thing happened with the 35-millimeter camera when Kodak permitted the Japanese to gain a superior position. American auto companies have followed the European and Japanese companies slowly in the small-car field. American consumer electronics firms have reluctantly followed the Japanese in videotape players. RCA, which already had its own videodisc, waited until Philips had units on the market before introducing its own.

Some companies decide not to follow at all. Such a strategy may be smart if the competitor's innovation does not work out. Mazda introduced a rotary automobile engine; no one followed and Mazda discontinued. Gulf General offered a gas-cooled nuclear reactor, and no one followed. Polaroid developed an instant movie camera, and no one followed; it did not succeed.

Not following, however, is not smart if it means missing significant opportunities and never being able to catch up. We've seen that with many losers—in steam engines, vacuum tube radios, electromechanical controls, and propeller-driven aircraft.

The final question about product positioning relates to how a company may wish to position itself in terms of product differentiation. The company may elect not to be different at all, but rather to be like all other companies. Others may want to create the standard and have others replicate them. This helps to increase the organization's ability to learn and to reduce costs.

If everyone follows, then savings are produced and even licensing fees

are generated. Philips of Holland created the audio cassette and licensed
the industry. Unfortunately, the industry followers were more successful than
Philips, and it did not gain the desired results. RCA standardized color television
in the United States and was the leader in creating an industry. Kodak has
standardized film in the United States and has been the winner in a number of
ways.

Despite such successes, standardization may not be as preferred as differentiation. A company can be different by providing unique features, quality,
or styling. The video cassette provides unique features such as the ability to
record at chosen times or the ability to record for a longer time.

Some companies distinguish themselves by reliability and quality.
Uptime—that is, operating for long periods without interruption—guarantees
are major selling points in many capital-intensive industries, including electrical
generators, farm equipment, aircraft, and computers—the less maintenance, the
better. In automobiles, time between tune-ups and oil changes is a key. Providing longer warranties or guarantees can also be vital and may provide a means
of making a product standard. Styling and appearance can also be important
(for example, the automobile model-change game—making cars look more
sporty, more affluent, or more sexy). There is no one winning combination,
and in any given industry, different companies select variations. In cameras,
Kodak emphasizes standardization; Canon, innovative features. Both are winners in their niches. Followers have tended to be losers—Bell & Howell is an
example.

PRODUCT DEVELOPMENT

Another way of determining a competitor's product strategy is to assess its
ability to develop and commercialize products.

If the competitor is in a leadership role, it may rely on its own developments and use its own proprietary and dedicated laboratory. This is typical
of companies clearly perceived as innovators and technology leaders: AT&T,
IBM, Siemens, Philips, Xerox, Wang, DuPont, Union Carbide. Many of these
companies have combinations of centralized and decentralized labs. The centralized labs concentrate on basic, forward-thinking research and development,
while the decentralized labs concentrate on the application and implementation
of basic research.

If a company is both multi-industry and multinational, it might have
product-development activities in many locations and permit competition to
stimulate innovation and provide it with alternative R&D approaches. Encouraging multiple solutions can make it difficult for a project to be killed.

Idea reviews are also important. If reviews are made by lower-level
managers who are concerned mostly about profits, ideas that take too long
to turn a profit will be ignored. If ideas can reach upper management and the

company considers innovation vital to success, then they have a greater chance of review.

At times it does not make any sense for a company to develop a product on its own. Licensing another's design and using it can be extremely powerful if you have a clear strategy and the willingness to admit someone else may have the better idea.

You may license not only from other companies, but also from laboratories and universities. Many companies consciously seek out other sources by financing research at universities, hospitals, private labs, or even individually run enterprises. AMF finances universities to develop products even if it does not have complete control of the results. Hoescht has financed work at Massachusetts General Hospital. Battelle Memorial Institute will contract to do exclusive company-funded projects as well as joint development ones. Another approach is to establish a venture-capital organization to support innovation and later acquire the innovating company.

There isn't anything magic about which approach to use. It depends upon product positioning, strategy, resources, and ability to capitalize on others' ideas. Wishing to protect its lead, a leader may wish to closely monitor and tie up an innovator's right to sell to others or even disclose any knowledge. Thus, approaches such as the direct funding of universities and private labs or the establishment of venture-capital companies make the most sense. These approaches are geared to getting innovation at the lowest cost and the least risk.

But a company must be willing to fund for the long term. If you are ranked second or third, then sharing costs and results may be more advantageous.

The issue of financing is critical. If R&D must be funded by the individual business unit, then the results will be directly related to that unit's prosperity. The rich units will get funding and the poor units will not.

This is fine if the rich units are the long-term winners and have better opportunities than the poor. If, however, the poor units are in growth industries, but cannot afford to capitalize on their opportunities, such a strategy will be detrimental to total corporate health.

Some companies have development funds that can be used "ex budget." In this case it is possible for poorer business units to get funding from other sources. Funding sources do not have to be restricted to inside the company. Outside funding might be obtained from the government or venture capitalists, or even by pooling resources with competitors, customers, or suppliers. Many companies seek out government contracts in fields of interest in order to gain a technological lead and use public funds.

Some would argue that if it were not for the space program, microcomputers and minicomputers would not have been developed.

Government funding, however, can be a tough way to fund because it is restrictive and the patents often become public and available to the competition. But smartly administered programs need not face this problem. It is possible to get a proprietary position or at least to have the running start on knowing how to make the product or mastering key timing and scheduling problems.

Some companies separate new ventures from the parent company and seek outside funding. This approach is typical for the emerging company, but it can also be used by the diversified or multinational company. Some Japanese companies separate their new ventures from the parent and then sell equity in the new companies. Most of this equity is owned by banks, which permits some financing off the balance sheet and gives access to new sources of funds. This approach also permits losses that will not reduce the return on investment or equity—a plus to financially oriented companies. However, the disadvantages include a reduced ability on the part of the parent company to use innovation and be synergistic.

Another way of financing is through joint venturing. This may be critical if funding requirements are high or if the company is so weak that it cannot afford to develop on its own. In the race for developing the videodisc and its related software, many companies joined together. By joint venturing, companies can bring complementary strengths to the development of a new industry. In this type of venture, it is important that the companies be compatible and that one of them be in a clear leadership position. Too many chiefs or incompatible objectives and talents will make a poor joint venture and probably result in a loss for all.

DEGREE OF SELECTIVITY

Having specified the desired product position and the means of funding and managing the outcome, you should now aim at determining whether the competitor is interested in being a specialist or a generalist in the marketplace. Some questions to answer:

- How selective is the competitor? Does it carry a full, partial, or minimum line?
- Does the competitor offer a wide variety for every style or model?
- Is this changing and why?

A broad competitor will offer a complete line, though possibly only a single item or a few items of each style or model.

For example, a women's clothing competitor would sell all styles and fashions—contemporary, high-fashion, traditional—in a wide variety of sizes. If the competitor were selling automobiles, it might sell a full array varying in size, price points, and so on to fit the multiplicity of needs and wants.

The true generalist in a particular market is very broad and not very selective. This is the philosophy of the mass merchant or discounter in the retail trade. If someone has a need, the company will fill it. An innovator is likely to be more selective and unwilling to be very extensive.

A company may be fairly broad and deep—not quite a specialist but certainly not a generalist. This can be done by concentrating on a moderate number of styles and models. However, companies in this category are typically in trouble. They cannot provide the necessary variety of generalists and do not have the reputation or power of true specialists.

The true specialist is narrow and deep. This is the entry strategy of many companies. They select niches that will permit specialization and, normally, innovation. Because a new company's product is untested and is resource limited, it keeps its initial offering limited. Once the product or service is accepted and its reputation has been made, the company gradually increases in depth—providing more and more variations and then extending to other sizes and configurations.

CONSISTENCY OF PRODUCT STRATEGY

It is important to determine whether a competitor's product positioning, development, funding, breadth, and depth fit together. If they do not, the firm's product strategy is not consistent with its strategic driver(s).

The strategic driver concept is built on the premise that there must be one thrust, more important than any other, behind each successful strategy. A firm can choose one of several strategic drivers—produce drivers (unique products, differentiation, standardization); marketing drivers (creating demand, distribution and sales, geographic expansion, pricing, service, applications); production drivers (capacity, process innovation, productivity, supply); and finance drivers (acquisitions, equity ownership, joint ventures, etc.). Any of these drivers can be followed successfully, as long as the implementation programs are uniformly consistent with that driver.

A product strategy that includes leadership, licensing, external funding, and a broad and deep line, on the other hand, does not hang together. If this is your assessment of the competitor's strategy, you would be wise to probe why it is being followed. Does the competitor have a "fatal flaw" that will knock it out? Does the situation indicate an inexperienced management team, poor organization, confusion, or financial problems?

Once you have explored the causes of any inconsistencies, you can act to use the inconsistencies to your advantage. For example, a competitor may be following a strategy similar to the one described above because financial difficulties are preventing it from committing sufficient resources to product development. Against such a competitor, you could gain a competitive advantage by funding the R&D necessary to leapfrog to the next generation of product development.

Probing the causes of any inconsistencies you identify before acting is critical. Occasionally, a strategy can succeed despite apparent inconsistencies.

The strategies a firm uses to implement its strategic driver(s) include not only product strategy but also investment, marketing, production, and management strategies. Evaluating all of these strategies is important to a thorough analysis of your competitors.

Obviously, this type of analysis can and should be done for your own firm as well. It is critical to avoiding self-deception and understanding whether you are really pursuing the strategic driver you think you are pursuing. Saying one thing and doing something else, or not having the resources to follow the game plan, results in failure.

☐

UNDERSTANDING YOUR COMPETITOR'S FUNCTIONAL STRATEGIES
ROBERT M. FIFER

Ultimately, the competitor analyst must address strategy at the business level. Just as most business organizations include individuals responsible for the various functions—marketing, manufacturing, sales, etc.—the competitor's business strategy is in fact the sum of its various *functional* strategies.

From a strategic standpoint, there are nine key functions: product R&D, process R&D, purchasing, manufacturing, marketing, wholesale distribution and sales, retail distribution, service, and finance/administration. A solid understanding of the competitor's strategy in each of these nine areas provides the analyst with the key ingredients necessary to portray the competitor's business-level strategy.

PRODUCT R&D

The role of the product R&D within a business strategy is very much a function of the stage of the product life cycle at which the industry is currently operated. It is important to understand whether the competitor's product R&D efforts are well-tailored for that life-cycle stage, in an absolute sense, and relative to the product R&D strategy of one's own company.

Early in the life cycle, product R&D is a highly speculative venture. Competitors have not yet figured out what features customers want, and experimentation, creativity, and the ability to "guess right" are key.

As the industry leaves the embryonic stage and growth begins to slow, scale in R&D becomes most important. IBM and Apple may spend similar

Strategic Planning Management, February, 1985; Commerce Communications, Inc.

sums of money to develop a new personal computer, but the impact on IBM's bottom line is minimal while Apple's margins will be very much affected.

Finally, late in the life cycle, the impact of product R&D is more subtle. Successful competitors do one of three things: re-design the product to reduce costs, extend the technology to serve new market applications, or "tinker" with the product features to stay marginally ahead of the competition.

PROCESS R&D

Manufacturing processes can be measured in terms of four variables: cost, quality, flexibility, and dependability (the ability to meet promised delivery dates). The competitive analysis should include an assessment of the competitor's ability to design manufacturing processes that meet these criteria.

Again, however, the stage of the life cycle is critical. Early on, flexibility and quality are most important. In the mature stage, competitor's offerings become more similar and more stable, and the customer's choice of vendor is based primarily on cost and dependability.

The *fit* between the competitor's product R&D and process R&D strategies is also critical. In the '70s, Federal Express decided that there was a need for reliable overnight package delivery among major cities. However, it was the company's *process* design—specifically, the creation of a Memphis hub and an entirely owned, dedicated fleet of aircraft—which made its product breakthrough possible.

Other key questions include:

- Where does the competitor acquire its process technology? Is it internally developed, or acquired from outside sources?
- How critical is process R&D to the competitor's competitive strategy?

PURCHASING

Analysis of the competitor's purchasing strategy is most important in industries where purchased goods represent a large percentage of costs, and/or suppliers are very powerful. The questions to ask depend upon the nature of the purchased items.

For raw materials, key issues are the competitor's use of long-term contracts, volume discounts, or superior access or proximity in order to reduce costs.

For labor, which is also a "purchased" input, key questions are:

- To what extent is the competitor unionized?
- How does it make use of international labor to reduce costs?
- Does it have different strategies for securing skilled vs. unskilled labor?

Finally, for purchased components, it is usually informative to compare the competitor's make-vs.-buy decisions to those of one's own company. Key questions include:

- What components, supplies or products does the competitor purchase, and from whom?
- What are the conditions (example: contracts, prices) under which they are purchased?

MANUFACTURING

Manufacturing processes, like products, evolve over time. Industries typically start with job shops, and proceed through batch, assembly, and continuous flow stages. Where does the competitor lie along this continuum? How does that compare to where one's own company is located? Does the competitor segment its plant by manufacturing stage, producing its low-volume specialties in job shops while commodities are produced in more automated facilities?

A great deal of emphasis has been placed on understanding the competitor's manufacturing cost, and we will not be able to do justice to this topic here. However, it is important to recognize that even if the analyst does not have detailed cost data, the competitor's general cost position can usually be accurately predicted based on an analysis of more qualitative factors such as process, scale, and purchasing strategy.

MARKETING

Marketing consists of three basic functions: selecting the target customer segment, specifying the product to meet the customer's needs, and choosing the communications program to get the message across. The competitive analysis should address each of these issues. Data should include: sales by customer segment, product mix, advertising expenditures and media, and promotional programs.

The consistency of these various ingredients should also be evaluated: Is the competitor merely scrambling to get business wherever it can, or does it have a premeditated, well-integrated marketing plan?

Two key questions are:

- What are the elements in the competitor's marketing plan, and how do they fit together?
- What does the competitor do that gives it a competitive advantage with its current or potential customers?

WHOLESALE DISTRIBUTION AND SALES

In more and more mature industries where technology is readily available, distribution has become a key battleground separating the winners from the losers. In these industries, the competitor's cost of distribution must be carefully assessed. Scale in distribution and "lock-up" of scarce distribution channels are the ways in which competitors typically attempt to lower distribution cost.

In specialty industries, measuring the *quality* of the competitor's distribution is more important, as measured by the knowledge level and professionalism of dealers and/or salespeople, as well as the level of responsiveness to customer requests.

RETAIL DISTRIBUTION

Retail distribution is an issue only in some industries. For firms which sell through retailers, the extent of representation regionally or nationally is critical. Smaller personal computer companies sink or swim on the basis of whether Computerland or other large retailers carry their product.

In addition, the development of shelf-space control through reputation or scale is of prime importance. Procter & Gamble's immensely successful introduction of Pampers disposable diapers was made possible by its ability to persuade retailers to allocate shelf space to the bulky product.

SERVICE

Service has many forms: repair capability, design help for the customer, training, parts availability and logistics, and "intangibles" such as reputation and the customer's sense of security.

The analysis should include an assessment of the competitor's ability and inclination to provide quality service in each of these areas. Specific information gathered may include the number and background of service personnel, the relationship between the service force and the sales force, the number of service options offered, the role of service within the competitor's overall strategy (e.g., profit center vs. support for sales), and the competitor's view of third-party service.

Other key questions include:

- How does the competitor use service to differentiate itself from other competitors?
- Can the competitor sustain the service levels it currently offers to customers?

FINANCE AND ADMINISTRATION

For some competitors, superior administrative or financial systems are crucial ingredients in their strategy. Radio Shack's information systems, McDonald's training programs, and General Electric's strategic planning process all have constituted important competitive advantages.

In terms of finance, Computerland (working capital), the Bell Operating Companies (accounts receivable), and Japanese competitors (debt) all derive important advantages from superior financial management. The analyst should compare the competitor's management of current assets, current liabilities, debt, and dividends to that of one's own company.

CONCLUSION

The analyst typically has at his or her disposal a wealth of information on the competitor's business strategy. The framework outlined above helps bring structure to that information by dividing the competitor's strategy into its nine component functional strategies. By recognizing the existence of these different functional approaches, the competitor's strategies can be investigated and portrayed in a more clear, orderly fashion.

□

UNDERSTANDING COMPETITORS THROUGH FINANCIAL ANALYSIS

ROBERT M. FIFER

Of all the types of techniques suitable to analyze competitors, financial tools are perhaps the easiest to use. The data are readily available, the techniques (after some practice) are relatively simple, and implications are often easy to discern.

The intent of this article is to provide an overview of analysis techniques to examine three basic aspects of any competitor's performance:

1. Stock market performance;
2. Financial ratios; and
3. Cash flow position.

Strategic Planning Management, October, 1984; Commerce Communications, Inc.

THE COMPETITOR'S STOCK MARKET PEFORMANCE

The stock market valuation is an important piece of competitor data. First, the competitor's stock price represents a consensus evaluation of the firm's prospects by people who are comparing the firm to other investment opportunities and who have every incentive to remain objective. Second, stock market valuation is central to every corporation's goal to create value for its shareholders. Third, the share price is an indicator of the firm's ability to raise capital for new investment through the issue of equity.

Analysis of stock market performance helps answer several key questions about any competitor:

1. *What is its primary goal, growth or profitability?* A competitor with low profits and poor stock valuation, which is investing heavily and retaining most of its earnings, is undoubtedly more concerned with growth than with profits. It may also be reinvesting the shareholder's cash in unproductive new assets.

2. *Is the competitor likely to significantly change its strategy in the near future?* Successful firms that have satisfied shareholder requirements will be less likely to change management or strategic direction than poorly valued, less successful competitors. In addition, the stock market's reaction to a competitor's new strategy will often determine whether the strategy is adhered to over time.

3. *How can the competitor acquire new capital?* Competitors with high market-to-book valuations can more easily exploit investor confidence to issue new equity. Competitors with low market-to-book values will be more likely to issue debt.

4. *Is the competitor vulnerable to takeover?* Competitors that are poorly valued may be likely acquisition targets of larger firms that can improve financial management or exploit their assets.

FINANCIAL RATIO ANALYSIS

Balance sheet and income statement data can be used to generate the basic financial ratios needed for competitor analysis. Ratio analysis yields considerable insight into a competitor's capabilities, constraints and strategies.

Return on Sales measures the profit earned on every dollar of sales. It is useful in comparing the cost management and pricing capabilities of firms in similar industries. However, average return on sales varies between industries with different cost structures.

Return on Assets measures the profits earned on every dollar of total net assets. Since it is not directly affected by cost structure or debt levels, it is the best cross-industry, cross-company profitability measure.

Turnover measures sales relative to total net assets. As a measure of asset productivity, it links operating profitability to investment profitability; return on sales times the turnover rate equals return on assets.

Return on Equity measures the profits earned on the average dollar of common equity over the previous two years. Companies with declining or below-the-cost-of-equity returns have fewer degrees of freedom in designing their strategies than more profitable companies. Analysis of the various components of return on equity (return on sales, asset turnover, debt, and free money) indicate the source of the financial pressure.

Net-to-Gross Fixed Asset Ratio measures net fixed assets as a percentage of gross fixed assets. It indicates whether the competitor is replenishing its depreciated property, plant, and equipment. A decreasing net-to-gross ratio indicates a lack of re-investment in fixed assets.

Debt/Equity Ratio is the ratio of total debt to total equity and indicates the competitor's balance sheet leverage. The history of the debt/equity ratio can be particularly illuminating, especially when compared against the industry average debt/equity or debt capacity (.5:1 is a benchmark in many American industries today). For example, Gulf and Western reduced its debt-equity ratio from a high of 1.97 in 1979 to 0.62 in 1983, as part of an intentional and much publicized corporate strategy. Given management's commitment to that strategy, it is unlikely that the company would pursue an aggressive business-level strategy if a significant increase in debt-equity were required.

Retention Rate is the percent of profits retained by the corporation and reinvested in new assets. Plotting "retention rate" and actual total dividend dollars paid on the same chart is the most efficient way to highlight the implications of dividend policy. For example, in order to keep its dividend at eighty cents in 1981 and 1982 despite declining profitability, Champion Spark Plug reduced its earning retention rate to zero—it paid out all of its earnings (and more) in dividends. Competitors of Champion could assume that there would be tremendous pressure on Champion's operating managers to avoid major investments during those years. Alternatively, Digital Equipment Corporation and Hewlett-Packard have always maintained retention rates above 90%; this has enabled them to keep up with their rapidly growing markets without ceding market share.

CASH FLOW POSITION AND ANALYSIS

The competitor's future cash flow is a major indicator of its ability to fund its strategies. While a wide variety of simple and sophisticated cash flow models are available, we recommend a relatively simple one (See Table 4-1).

This model can be used to estimate expected net cash flow—the difference between cash outflow and cash inflow. The model measures three sources of cash: additions to retained earnings, additions to debt, and additions to free

TABLE 4-1　Five Year Cash Flow

Net Cash Outflow

Base Year Sales $\times$ 5-Year Compound Growth = Target Year Sales
　4271　　$\times$　　$(1 + .20)^5$　　=　　10,628

Target Year Sales $\div$ Target Year Turnover = Target Year Assets
　10,268　　$\div$　　.98　　=　　10,844

Target Year Assets $-$ Base Year Assets = Net Cash Outflow
　10,844　　$-$　　4,541　　=　　6,303

Additions to Retained Earnings

Target Year Sales $\times$ Target Year Margin = Target Year Income
　10,628　　$\times$　　.10　　=　　1,063

Target Year Income + Base Year Income $\times$ 5/2 = Cumulative Income
　(1,063　　+　　284)　　$\times$ 5/2 =　　3,367

Cumulative Income $\times$ Retention Rate = Additions To Retained Earnings
　3,367　　$\times$　　1.00　　=　　3,367

Additions to Debt

Additions To Retained Earnings $\times$ Debt/Equity Ratio = Additional Debt
　3,367　　　　$\times$　　.04　　=　　135

Additions to Free Money

Target Year Sales $\times$ Free Money/Sales $-$ Base Year Free Money = Additional Free Money
　10,628　　$\times$　　.21　　$-$　　891　　=　　1,341

Additions To
Retained Earnings + Additional Debt + Additional Free Money = Net Cash Inflow
　3,367　　+　　135　　$|$　　1,341　　$-$　　4,843

Net Cash Inflow $-$ Net Cash Outflow = Net Cash Flow
　4,843　　　6,303　　=　　(1,460)

money. (The model ignores exogenous cash sources such as new equity issues or divestitures, which can be added separately.)

The major outlay of cash is for new asset investment. The model compares the cash sources to the cash outlays to calculate net cash flow over a five-year period.

Assumptions must be made for six financial ratios: Sales Growth, Turnover Rate, Return of Sales, Retention Rate, Debt/Equity Ratio, and Free Money-to-Sales ratio. Recent trends in these ratios, as well as expected changes in the competitor's performance, should underlie these assumptions.

The results of this model are highly dependent on the assumptions; therefore, sensitivity analysis is imperative. The cash flow analysis shown in Table 4-1 represents a "best guess" scenario. In pessimistic and optimistic scenarios, assumptions for the competitor's growth rate, turnover, and margin should be reduced/increased.

Implicit in this discussion is the relationship between growth, profitability, financial policies, and cash flow. Not only is cash flow extremely important, because of its impact on the competitor's stock valuation, but it also has a major impact on its operating strategies. A competitor projected to generate a positive cash flow has the ability to raise its dividend or to invest in existing or new businesses. This investment could take the form of fixed assets, reduced prices, or increased expenditures on technology, manufacturing, or marketing. For this reason, a firm with excess cash can be a dangerous competitor.

Conversely, a negative cash flow forecast reveals a weakness in the competitor. Firms can not remain in deficit forever. They must find ways to fund negative cash flow through additional equity, additional debt, reduced dividends or reduced investment in their businesses.

CONCLUSION

These financial analyses, at the least, provide a context within which one can view the results of the other competitive analysis techniques. Indeed, any *operating* analysis of a competitor should be placed side-by-side with the financial analysis, so that the impact and implications of changes in a competitor's strategy can be considered. Moreover, in a large number of cases these tools provide insights and surprises which are significant enough to drive the entire competitive analysis and help shape the strategic response to the competitor.

$$\Box$$

UNDERSTANDING YOUR COMPETITOR'S "PERSONALITY"

ROBERT M. FIFER

Much of the emphasis within the competitive analysis field focuses on gathering and analyzing quantitative data concerning the competitor's financials, manufacturing operations, or marketing strategy. This information reveals much about the competitor's capabilities, but often does not tell enough about how the competitor is likely to *use* those capabilities over time.

A relatively "ignored" area of competitive analysis—the competitor's *personality* or culture—provides the key which places the other data in perspective.

Strategic Planning Management, December, 1984; Commerce Communications, Inc.

Analysis of the competitor's personality allows one to "get inside the head" of one's competitor, and learn how the competitor thinks. Armed with this knowledge, one is much better able to anticipate the competitor's future moves, and predict how the competitor will react to different strategies that one's own company could pursue.

The following nine different pieces of analysis can be used to develop a picture or profile of the competitor's personality.

1. THE COMPETITOR'S GOALS

Every company has a set of objectives, and these are often explicitly stated in the President's Letter in the Annual Report, or in top management interviews with the press. These objectives usually fall into six basic areas:

- Profit targets;
- Growth targets;
- Cash flow or financial policy targets;
- Portfolio objectives (e.g., diversification or "pursue high-tech businesses");
- Operating objectives (e.g., 90% capacity utilization or add 100 new accounts);
- Employee satisfaction goals.

Understanding a competitor's goals reveals much about its personality and the strategies which it is likely to pursue. A company that is committed to not laying off employees will have difficulty pursuing a low-cost strategy in a declining market. Similarly, a company with high growth targets is more likely to price aggressively than one which emphasizes profit over growth.

2. THE COMPANY'S "INVESTMENT HISTORY"

The Investment History is perhaps the single most useful tool within all of competitive analysis. The Investment History Chart plots each of the competitor's businesses on a two-dimensional map, with the market growth for each business on the y axis and the business' actual sales growth on the x-axis. A 45-degree line is drawn to indicate the region where market growth is equal to sales growth. Businesses to the right of the 45-degree line are growing faster than the market, and therefore are gaining market share. Conversely, businesses to the left of the 45-degree line are losing market share.

Important insights about the competitor's personality can be developed based on the *pattern* of businesses on the Investment History Chart.

- Are all high-tech businesses gaining share, while mature businesses are losing share?

Figure 4-1   Investment history chart

- Are "manufacturing"-oriented businesses gaining share, while businesses where marketing is key are losing share?
- Are all businesses growing at the same rate (indicating a uniform growth target, rather than strategic portfolio management), or are all businesses gaining share (indicating a very aggressive company focusing on growth over profit)?

The answers to these questions provide the analyst with a view of the basic philosophy of the competitor.

3. BUSINESS STRATEGIES

Although one may compete against the competitor only in one business area, a quick review of the competitor's strategies for other business units can be very helpful. Most companies have consistent *strategic themes* which run across many of their businesses; by studying the competitor's strategy in a seemingly related business, one improves the ability to predict the competitor's strategy in the business of interest.

Themes to look for include:

- Does the competitor tend to price high or low?
- How aggressive is the competitor?
- Does the competitor focus on the commodity or specialty portion of the market?
- Is the competitor an R&D leader or follower?

4. ACQUISITION/DIVESTITURE HISTORY

Even something as "factual" as a listing of the competitor acquisitions and divestitures over the last 10 or 15 years reveals a lot about how the company thinks.

Questions to ask include:

- Are unprofitable businesses quickly disposed of, or does the company tend to throw good money after bad?
- Does the competitor acquire outside companies to bring necessary skills in-house, or does it develop those skills internally?
- Are the majority of the company's financial resources being devoted to existing businesses, or to new acquisitions?

5. COMPANY OWNERSHIP

Basic data on the ownership of the competitor can be gathered from the Form 10-K filed with the SEC, and from a literature search. The major shareholders and their percent ownership should be recorded and analyzed.

Key questions include:

- Is the company publicly or privately held? Privately held companies often have lower profit objectives, making them difficult competitors;
- Does an individual, institution, or group of individuals or institutions control a major portion of the stock? If so, what are the objectives of the major shareholders: dividends, growth, diversifications, etc.?
- What does the competitor's ownership structure say about the likelihood that it might be acquired?

6. BOARD OF DIRECTORS

Much can be learned about a competitor's personality from the make-up of its board. Board members, although usually not involved in the day-to-day operations of the company, have considerable say over the competitor's long-term direction.

A key question is whether the board is dominated by "inside directors," i.e., directors who also hold management positions at the company, or "outside directors." As a generalization, inside directors tend to focus more on operations, while outside directors, depending on their backgrounds, give emphasis to financial performance.

The backgrounds of outside directors are important. Are they financial managers, lawyers, businessmen with manufacturing backgrounds, or university professors? What skills, biases, and perspectives are they likely to bring to the board?

For example, one company in a financially troubled industry recently removed three "operating managers" from the board, and added two financial managers and one finance professor.

One can expect that the competitor will look to tighten financial controls and "clean up" its businesses, potentially at the expense of growth.

7. KEY MANAGERS

Understanding the backgrounds of the key managers of the corporation and those in the business unit against which one competes is also helpful. Managers, even more than corporations, tend to rely on strategies that have been successful for them in the past, at other companies or at other business units within their current company.

Knowing whether the division manager came up through the manufacturing, marketing, or technical organizations tells a lot about the types of strategies with which he or she will be most comfortable.

8. EMPLOYEE POLICIES AND NORMS

Many companies have very strong internal cultures which are reflected by their employee policies and norms.

- Are individualism and entrepreneurialism rewarded, or does one get ahead by "not rocking the boat?"
- Do employees work long or short hours?
- Are politically-motivated decisions the norm, or is there a strong attempt to minimize the impact of politics?
- Are salesmen paid commissions, or are they paid on a straight salary basis?

These and many other "employee" questions can be invaluable in understanding the past and future behavior of competitors.

9. MARKET COMMUNICATIONS

Finally, even the competitor's advertisements can be an input into an analysis of its personality.

- Does the company position itself as the "Cadillac" or the "Chevrolet" of its industry?
- Does its corporate advertising emphasize growth, dividends, superior product, etc.?

- Does it portray itself as an aggressive company or a "solid," mature one, an innovator or a cost-reducer?

The answers to these questions will usually be consistent with insights derived from the other eight analyses described above.

CONCLUSION

There are two important lessons to be learned about the competitor's personality. The way that it behaves and thinks—*is* "knowable"; there is a tremendous amount of relevant information available. Second, understanding the competitor's personality is the most crucial portion of competitive analysis. Facts and figures tell you how the competitor is *able* to compete; analysis of personality or culture tells you how the competitor is *likely* to compete. It is the latter which is the final objective of any effort to analyze competitors.

Customer Analysis

□

UNDERSTANDING YOUR CUSTOMERS THROUGH MARKET AUDITS
MICHAEL FREEHILL

Audits have long been a routine process in finance and accounting, and recently—especially since competition from overseas has heightened—audits have been used in the areas of human resources and manufacturing to determine worker productivity. Now a newer kind of audit is attracting attention: the market audit, which provides valuable information for planning how to compete in the '80s and beyond.

WHAT IS A MARKET AUDIT?

A market audit is a formal evaluation of a company's customers. It typically covers such questions as these:

- Who are the firm's current and potential customers?

Strategic Planning Management, March, 1984; Commerce Communications, Inc.

- What are the customers' demographic characteristics, buying behavior and perceptions of the firm's products?
- How do current and prospective customers view the firm's performance and capabilities relative to competitors?

Thus, the goals of a market audit are threefold: (1) to identify and assess the firm's position in the market; (2) to pinpoint current and likely problems and opportunities; and (3) to suggest ways to manage these threats and opportunities.

MARKET AUDITS IN ACTION: SOME EXAMPLES

Many corporations have developed their reputations for excellence largely from their sensitivity to customer perceptions and needs, as assessed in regular market audits. Since its inception, for example, IBM has positioned itself as the master of service. Iowa Beef Processors was addressing their customers' needs when they developed boxed beef, a superior method of preparing and shipping. Caterpillar gained its leadership position in the construction equipment industry by virtue of its superior sales and technical support skills. These are classic examples of how companies audited their market position in order to seize opportunities in their markets.

Manufacturing or technical firms whose products are essentially commodity items can also benefit from market audits. Consider the example of a company that manufactured a chemical item. The company agreed to grant its customers their request for a price break on the item. But when their sales didn't increase as much as they had forecasted they wanted to know why.

A market audit revealed the following problem. The discounted orders were very slow to be processed, because the company had a credit-clearance policy requiring each salesperson to report back to the district manager, who in turn must get final approval for the discount from corporate headquarters. The process took several weeks, so often prospective customers moved on to another supplier rather than wait for the approval. The market audit helped alert top management that it was this clearance policy that had hindered sales.

In another case, an audit revealed that a problem in one area actually extended across several other functional areas. A company was losing accounts because of late delivery of dated commodity items, but an audit revealed that the problem was not just on the loading dock. In commodities, where the product is readily available from many sources, timely delivery is an important point of differentiation. In assessing the situation, an in-depth review of the manufacturing and marketing policies revealed that they were not coordinated, which contributed to poor communication and cooperation between these areas, and ultimately caused the late deliveries.

HOW TO IMPLEMENT AN AUDIT IN YOUR FIRM

Once you've recognized the need for an audit, there are four key steps in implementing it.

Step 1: *Identify the different markets (i.e., customer groups) your firm serves.* Categorize the markets by product, industry, geographic region, demographics, etc. Then develop an analysis and profile of each segment you serve. Some sample profiles: "six manufacturing clients in the southwest who buy our chemicals to make industrial cleansers;" or "all companies nationwide who purchase our chemicals for use in printing processes."

Step 2: *After you have categorized your customers, break them into tiers.* First, list the customers within each grouping who are most important to your firm. Then list those customers who, regardless of grouping, are most important to your firm's overall success. This second list is your core group of customers. If you are failing to meet their needs, you may be facing severe problems in the near future.

Step 3: *List each function or service your company provides its customers.* Include such items as product line width, pricing, product quality, sales and technical support, service responsiveness, delivery systems, returns policy, and other relevant elements which can be used by customers to differentiate your firm from its competitors. Then ask selected line managers and staff to rate the firm on its performance in each area. This exercise will reveal your company's internal perceptions of what it does well and badly.

Step 4: *Test your internal perceptions against those of the marketplace.* Otherwise, you will mistake your own views for those of your customers. There are four key steps involved in this process.

First, ask a small sample of your customers what they think about your firm. In particular, ask them what constitutes the basis of their purchasing decisions, what qualities of your firm they find appealing or unappealing, and on what dimensions your firm compares favorably and unfavorably to competitors. Typically, 10 to 15 open-ended in-depth interviews are sufficient to complete this phase.

Second, with those results in hand, select the research staff and/or consultant to devise a questionnaire to survey a sample of your customers in each of your customer groupings and tiers. The questionnaire should be designed to get a measured response from clients and would-be clients about your company's perceived performance along the dimensions noted above.

Third, execute the research. Use the questionnaire you have developed to conduct in-depth interviews with your sample of clients and prospective clients.

In a market segment that is important to your firm, 50 to 100 interviews may be necesary to generate a reliable picture of how the segment views your firm. For most audits, telephone interviews of 20 to 30 minutes can provide the requisite data.

Fourth, evaluate the results. Often a comparison of the internal perceptions and the customer responses surprises the firms who undertake a market audit. The surveys frequently indicate that firms are perceived quite differently by customers than by those who are inside the companies.

Sensitive analysis of the research will reveal not only what the clients' perceptions are, but also those areas where the company excels but has not been exploiting its capabilities. It is this kind of information that helps reallocate resources and repositions a firm for maximum effectiveness relative to its most important customers.

This last phrase bears repeating: you should strive for effectiveness with your *most important customers.* A market audit is not designed to reveal what the "ideal" company should do in the marketplace. This is neither an affordable nor desirable idea. Rather, the audit seeks to match the priorities of key customers with the performance capabilities of the firm—and it is this which spells differentiation, competitive advantage, stability and profitability.

The analysis and result should present this in the form of a final written report. It should be short and succinct and should emphasize findings and implications.

One of the merits of a final report is that the audit's findings can be widely disseminated within the organization. If the audit is comprehensive in scope, top management, line managers, strategic planners, marketing personnel and other functional areas will probably find its conclusion and implication of relevance to their own organizational roles and responsibilities.

ORGANIZING INTERNALLY TO PERFORM MARKET AUDITS

The impetus for performing an audit must come from senior management, if possible the CEO or general manager. The executives must convey both their seriousness in undertaking an audit and their commitment to making the changes that it may suggest. They must impress upon their turf protecting managers that the audit is designed to help them, not hurt them, and that it is a tool for developing strategy that will better integrate the company's functions and activities.

Firms have adopted quite different approaches to conducting market audits. The self-audit is the cheapest method, but it is also the least reliable. Its main shortcoming is that it possibly will not be as objective because the auditors may be too close to the situation to perceive problems. Another approach is the "top-down" method, where a group of top managers conduct the audit. These audits often run into trouble because the process seems arbitrary to lower-level managers, who are not involved in the process.

A better approach is to establish a standing auditing office or task force. These semi-autonomous units have more objectivity, independence and authority from top management. The task force or auditors should design the process and, then, either implement it themselves or delegate that task to outside consultants. Another effective approach is to have consultants work closely with strategic planning staff in determining the strategic goals of audits, devising the research instruments, executing the questionnaires, and, finally, evaluating the results together.

Again, the keys to a successful market audit are support from top management, a striving for objectivity and independence and, of course, keeping the expense of the whole procedure within reason.

AVOIDING PITFALLS IN MARKET AUDITS

Auditing your firm's customers is not easy, but it is likely to be much more instructive if some common pitfalls are avoided. You should involve those who will be responsible for implementing the findings of the audit as early as possible in the auditing process. If the managers who must make use of the market audit are not involved in its design and implementation, they will not have ownership in it, they may not understand its objectives, and they are thus likely to dispute its findings.

Flexibility and adaptability in the course of the audit are important. You may find that fruitful sources of information emerge that you had discounted or had not taken into account. These would need to be incorporated into the audit. Also, you may be surprised by your preliminary or early findings, and you should be ready to incorporate any changes they suggest in the scope and direction of the audit. For example, if you discover that your image is very much poorer than you expected (by comparison with competitors), you may need to add a segment to the audit questionnaire to help explain why this is so.

To the extent possible, you should use multiple sources of data. Data from different customer groups or tiers may paint quite distinct pictures. Also, various elements in your distribution channel and your end-user customers may have quite different assessments of your product, service, image, etc.

Finally, audits and the auditing process must be oriented to action. An audit is not intended to generate "nice-to-know" information. The emphasis must be on how to make use of the findings. The persistent theme should be "what actions do the findings suggest?"

CONCLUSION

Market audits may represent your only formal and systematic means of truly capturing and understanding how your customers view your firm, its products, and its services. Periodic audits can provide you critical data to help strategically position your products in the eyes of your customers.

☐

APPLICATION IN STRATEGIC MANAGEMENT:
Understanding Your Customers
LIAM FAHEY

Exactly why do your customers choose your products or services?

Low prices, high quality, quick delivery, reliable servicing, catchy advertising, or a personable sales force? Unless you know precisely what attracts them now and how their preferences are likely to change in the future, you may eventually find yourself without a clientele. The following case study offers you one effective approach to gathering intelligence about your customers.

Few events can unsettle your company as much as the unanticipated actions of your customers. How do you respond if many of your customers suddenly start purchasing competitors' products or demand better service, lower prices, or guaranteed delivery? If you're caught off guard and don't move quickly, you'll risk losing your best customers. But if you understand your customers well, chances are that you'll be able to execute a plan to win back your lost customers or to meet their demands.

It's dangerous to rely solely on "gut feel" for your understanding of your customers. You need to implement a systematic, ongoing analysis of customers. The following case study will show you how a small firm (annual sales of $35 million) put such a system into practice successfully.

This small firm couldn't understand why sales in its major industrial market had begun to taper off. The company had continually improved the quality of its product line, while competitors had hardly made any recent innovations. So why had its sales begun to stagnate or even decline in some geographic regions?

The management of this company, realized that they didn't understand the change in their customers' buying habits, so they decided to conduct a thorough investigation.

DEFINING THE PURPOSE OF CUSTOMER ANALYSIS

The firm decided for two reasons to begin by clearly laying out the goals of its customer analysis efforts. First, managers were afraid that the information they collected would never be seriously scrutinized; after all, they already had plenty of data on their customers (from internal salesforce reports and outside market research) that had never been systematically analyzed. Second, senior managers wanted to ensure that the customer analysis would not simply become another

Strategic Planning Management, March, 1984; Commerce Communications, Inc.

short-term preoccupation, producing reports that would soon be confined to the dustheap on somebody's shelf.

As a result, they articulated these three clear goals:

1. To systematically identify and test the firm's current knowledge base about customers;
2. To identify the major gaps in that knowledge base and fill them; and
3. To ensure that the outputs of the customer analysis were actually integrated into the firm's decision making.

IDENTIFYING WHO YOUR CUSTOMERS ARE

Although there was initially resistance to pursuing the deceptively simple question, "Who are our customers?," it proved illuminating as a point of departure. The firm's customer base was divided into segments using a number of different criteria:

- end-use application (e.g., technical requirements, fit with customers' own production processes);
- buying methods;
- demographic characteristics (size, industry type);
- geographic location; and
- needs (services, quality, function, financing, etc.).

Different segmentation matrices were developed using these criteria. For example, for each sales region, customers were segmented in groups based on end-use application, demographic characteristics and buying methods.

Two major conclusions were drawn from this analysis. First, the firm was able to identify some market niches that the firm had previously not considered targeting. One such market segment was small current or potential user firms who might be induced to buy more of the product if the financing terms were more favorable. Second, the firm was ready to begin identifying gaps in its customer knowledge base—that is, to determine exactly where it lacked knowledge about certain customer groups.

DETERMINING WHAT YOU NEED TO KNOW

Once they had completed a preliminary segmentation of customers, the next step was to note carefully the critical gaps in the firm's knowledge base about its customers. These questions would then become the focus of later data collection and analysis efforts.

First, they drew up a laundry list of questions they needed to ask about each customer group. Here are some sample questions:

- What customer needs do our products satisfy?
- What are the unmet needs of our customers?
- How technologically sophisticated are the customers?
- Who are the purchase decision-makers and decision-influencers within our customer firms?

Next, the questions were grouped into categories based upon similarity in focus. The questions fell into clusters around topics such as these:

- customers' needs;
- buying behavior;
- buying criteria;
- size and growth of customer segments; and
- customers' perceptions of the firm, its products and services.

Each group of questions was then condensed into no more than two or three key issues or questions around each topic. This step forced the management team to focus on the important elements of each group of questions.

Finally, to prevent the firm from collecting useless data (i.e., information that would not be of direct use in decision making), the managers addressed a more basic question: how would answers to these questions about our customers help us position our products more effectively to compete successfully in the marketplace?

This question was not as easy to answer as had been expected. For example, if the analysis showed that their customers considered the company's products inferior to those of competitors, what type of action would the firm be willing to take? Would that finding imply that the firm should emphasize research and development, a new promotional program, or a redirecting of the salesforce's efforts? Raising this question forced the management team to think through fully why customer analysis was necessary, what analysis should be done, and the magnitude of the implications it might produce.

COLLECTING THE CUSTOMER DATA

The managers used a variety of approaches for conducting their analysis. Before they began collecting information, they needed to decide these two issues. (1) Who should collect the requisite data? (2) Who should analyze it, and what form should the findings take?

They decided that the data would be gathered via several specific projects conducted by the salesforce, the market research department and outside consultants.

The salesforce was chosen as the best source of information on buying behavior, buying criteria and customer demographics. The market research department interviewed a sample of salespersons as to how and why customers purchased the firm's products. The market researchers then developed a brief questionnaire which was completed by the entire salesforce. Next, the questionnaire was administered to a stratified sample of customers.

Another brief data form was provided to the salesforce so that they could continually report to the marketing personnel changes in customers' buying behavior and buying criteria, as well as any other changes which they considered important.

The market research department was charged with pulling together information from the firm's own records on broad customer trends such as product usage by customer type, growth in new customers by product type, and customer's preferences for financial arrangements.

The market research department also went out and conducted a small number of primary research projects. These projects focused upon identifying new customer segments for the firm's existing or potential products. Market research staff would conduct in-person interviews with a small sample (maximum of 10) of potential customers. This was the first time the firm had engaged in this type of focused customer research.

WHO ANALYZES THE INFORMATION, AND HOW?

A consulting firm was retained to perform two types of analysis. First, the consultants were asked to develop a report outlining current and emerging technological developments in customer firms that might affect the firm's current and potential products. The consultants were asked specifically to identify market opportunities—that is, unmet customer needs or applications.

Next, the consulting firm was asked to perform a "market audit." (For a description of a market audit, see Michael Freehill's article.)

TAKING ADVANTAGE OF THE ANALYSIS

Reports resulting from each project team were widely circulated within the company. Several efforts were made to ensure that these reports were used for some actual decision making, rather than merely being skimmed and then tossed aside.

First, the findings of each project were formally presented not only to the marketing and sales departments but also to representatives from other functions, especially R&D and engineering. This explanation of the findings allowed those who had to interpret and use the data to understand how it was collected and analyzed, and how particular conclusions were drawn.

Second, marketing, sales and R&D managers were asked to pinpoint specific implications of this customer analysis. How would they do things differently, what new actions should they undertake, what further analysis was required?

The managers who participated in the study subsequently undertook a number of commitments to build and sustain an effective intelligence-gathering effort about the customers. Marketing instituted some new promotional activities and literature. The salesforce required special training to better equip them to "sell" to different types of customers. And R&D launched or intensified its efforts to design new products or product improvements.

Finally, in presenting their marketing plans to senior executives, the marketing managers now were required to mention explicitly how they had built customer analysis into their planning efforts. By testing each plan against the findings of the customer analysis, the executives could judge whether the plan was compatible with these findings and whether the marketing tactics made sense. Once they truly understood their customers' needs, they could begin to anticipate how these preferences would change in the future.

CONCLUSION

The firm discovered that its sales fall-off was due to poor marketing and sales programs—a problem that the company is rectifying. Some lost customers have been won back, largely through the efforts of the salesforce. Specific new customer segments have been identified and programs put in place to sell to these niches. Finally, some new products are being introduced to satisfy specific customer needs.

Supplier Analysis

☐

MANAGING SUPPLIERS: THE
STRATEGIC IMPLICATIONS
ALBERT W. ISENMAN

A Canadian manufacturer of electronic devices entered into a supply contract with a Japanese maker of subassemblies, specifying a 5 percent defect rate, according to the company's usual purchasing practices. Sure enough exactly 5 percent of the subassemblies that began arriving were defective;

Strategic Planning Management, December, 1986; Commerce Communications, Inc.

conveniently, the defective devices were packaged separately from the good ones, and were labelled as such.

Astonished, the Canadian purchasing manager inquired about this anomaly, and was informed by the Japanese agent that his company was happy to supply the defectives but had been wondering why the Canadians *wanted* them in the first place.

A domestic auto-parts supplier, closely held by an American car manufacturer, provided a standard automobile component to a Japanese car maker as part of a well-known joint venture. Extra care was taken to assure that the shipments abroad contained zero defects; even so, a portion of shipped goods were identified by the Japanese as substandard and were returned.

What happened to the defective parts? The American plant manager, whose bonus was tied to production volume, "salted" the defectives into shipments to the domestic parent, where they ultimately were installed in American cars.

Why do such perverse results so frequently occur? How can managers undertake and sustain symbiotic rather than parasitic relationships with suppliers? To answer these questions, let's examine the assumptions that underlie our understanding of the supply relationship.

SUPPLIERS AS ADVERSARIES

In conventional textbook treatments, managing the supplier is couched in terms of "minimizing your input costs," and assumes that you principally are concerned with prices and quantities while maintaining an arm's length bargaining position with your supplier.

For example, the classic "make-or-buy" decision (whether to acquire supplies on the open market or to integrate backward into production) requires you to consider the gain from recapturing the supplier's margin versus the investment costs of self-manufacture. Similarly, determining the optimal "economic order quantity" for inventories is a model for minimizing supply and inventory costs (subject to constraints of stockouts).

Hence, the adversarial view of suppliers suggests finding ways to minimize their bargaining power in order to obtain better terms. The following prescriptions are part of the adversarial recipe and often are suggested as ways to keep suppliers in line and supply agreements favorable:

1. Locate and exploit alternative sources of supply. This will reduce your dependency on any one supplier, and mitigate against the likelihood of a single source becoming a significant portion of your unit cost.
2. If only one or two suppliers exist, reduce their bargaining leverage over you by actively seeking or promoting the emergence of substitute suppliers (e.g., plastic containers instead of glass).

3. Demonstrate that you are capable of integrating backward (by making some of your supplies yourself). Thus you have the potential of becoming a competitor to your supplier instead of simply a customer. In addition, your experience with self-manufacture gives you precise information about your suppliers' manufacturing and raw materials costs: hence you will be an informed bargainer at contract time.

4. Whenever possible, exclude from your product's design any critical component not available from multiple sources.

5. Select suppliers that are small relative to you. Your purchases will be an important part of their revenues, making you very important to them; but they will lack the capacity to lean on you.

SUPPLIERS AS PARTNERS

The cooperative model of supplier relationships—often labelled a Japanese invention but common in Western Europe, too—assumes that you principally are interested in stability of supplies, consistency of quality, and maintaining a long-term but flexible relationship. This may require trading off absolutely low input costs when it gives you a competitive advantage in design, delivery, or features; or even if it is done to enable your supplier to survive and prosper. It recognizes, for instance, that your inventory decisions and delivery terms become part of the supplier's cost structure and affect the relationship itself in the long run. Managing suppliers as partners is a *negotiating* rather than a *bargaining* arrangement.

Advocates of cooperative relationships with suppliers emphasize practices that are rather different from the adversarial ones. While the price/quantity mix is important, it takes a back seat to policies that encourage a mutually beneficial relationship:

1. Consider longer-term contracts with suppliers rather than episodic discrete purchases. This has the advantage for both parties of building some certainty into the future of the supply relationship. In many instances, suppliers may be willing to enter into *exclusive* longer-term contracts, which has the added advantage of denying their supply to your competitors.

   Contracts need not build out strategic flexibility as some would complain: a well-prepared longer-term contract requires thinking through the contingencies and "what-ifs" that the future may bring (such as demand changes, product line extensions, service, and customization requirements of customers), and working out a mutual understanding of what both sides expect of one another in such eventualities.

   This will have implications for how you specify inventory and delivery terms, supply specifications, even the number, mix, and location of suppliers. Since this is precisely what strategic thinking is about, why not extend that intellectual habit to supplier management?

2. Invite your supplier to join you in "getting close to your customers." You are downstream, after all, from the supplier, and hence you are closer to the end user. Your customer intelligence can be useful to the supplier in helping him serve your needs (and ultimately the customer's) more effectively.

    Additionally, a demonstrated strong supplier relationship itself can be a competitive advantage. For example, I know a large printing concern that specializes in consumer product packaging, both paper and plastic. When working with their customers (all large food, beverage, and tobacco companies), the firm takes care to involve their suppliers of paper, plastic, ink, and film color separations to produce the industry's best quality to customer specifications.

3. Share your supplier's risk. This is the "upstream" version of servicing and customizing for your customer's needs. For example, work closely with your suppliers to promote the introduction of quality improvements or manufacturing practices that may lower his (and your) costs. Sometimes this may even include investing in the supplying firm to assist in the acquisition of new technology or capacity expansion. Sears, for example, has long been an equity partner in firms that supply Kenmore appliances.

    This works in reverse, too: aluminum companies actively helped can manufacturers acquire the process equipment that accelerated the shift from three-piece steel cans to two-piece extruded aluminum containers. Many companies have undertaken joint ventures with their suppliers in research and development or to penetrate new markets.

MANAGING YOUR SUPPLIERS

What can we learn from the two models that can help you manage supplier relationships? It's unlikely that your situation exactly fits either model: if you are purchasing strictly commodity-like supplies and serving extraordinarily price-sensitive customers, your relationship may look very much like the classic adversarial bargaining situation. If, on the other hand, you face changing customer expectations, evolving technologies, or have a need for balancing stability with flexibility at the supply end, you may draw on elements of both models or begin to look very much like the cooperative model.

In any case, managers and planners should consider some of the following practices in order to help avoid pitfalls like the ones in our opening examples:

1. Develop a supplier intelligence capability. Firms have become quite sophisticated in customer and market research; more recently, analysis of

competitors and competitive dynamics has come into vogue. Supplier analysis by comparison is in its infancy.

Basic information about a supplying industry would certainly include:

- The number, mix, and availability of alternative sources of supply or the possibility of locating suppliers of acceptable substitutes.
- The amount that your purchases contribute as a percentage of the supplier's revenues. This is a proxy measure of how important you are to the supplier.
- The supplier's interest in and capability of integrating forward into your industry; becoming your competitor.
- The terms and conditions of suppliers' arrangements with your competitors.

Other components of supplier intelligence suggest the kind of attention sophisticated firms give market and competitor analysis and would include:

- What is the supplier's strategy? For example, if the supplier desires high growth or increased share while you are in a mature industry, you'll be less attractive to the supplier than a growing competitor unless you can demonstrate some unique potential that exploits the supplier's strategic capabilities.
- What is the supplier's cost and manufacturing structure? Is the supplier equipped to customize, to meet your needs in terms of cost, delivery, etc.? The information is essential if one is an adversarial bargainer, but may also reveal potential competitive advantages.
- Can the supplier give you a technical or design advantage? For example, are there ideas in the supplier's research pipeline that you could translate into a market opportunity as a new product or as an improvement on a current product?
- What is the supplier's financial capacity? Is the supplier able to help you buffer your working capital and inventory requirements; or are there opportunities to solidify and stabilize your supplier relationship by offering such help to the supplier?

2. Link your supply strategy to your overall strategy. In one of our opening examples, the American car maker's practice of rewarding its vendor on price/volume considerations clearly was at odds with its intentions to boost product quality.

Coordinating purchasing with your strategy is no different from linking other functional areas (sales, finance, etc.) with strategy, and bears similar pitfalls. Purchasing is a function, and in large complex organizations, purchasing agents may have particular parochial views or beliefs. And because purchasing is principally a *staff* function, purchasing managers (like human resource managers) frequently are excluded from strategy making and line of business decisions. And as we have seen, the reward system often motivates purchasing managers to treat vendors as adversaries, rather than managing them as partners.

3. Similarly, consider your supply strategy when other strategic decisions are made. For example, a decision to advance your process technology may have important implications for your supply relationship, such as changing delivery or packaging specifications, product form, inventory quantities and timing, or financial needs.

4. Finally, think about your suppliers as a *resource* with the potential to help you develop or sustain a competitive advantage:

   ■ By improving your cost position if your strategy is to be an industry price leader

   ■ By helping with features or design if product attributes are important to you

   ■ By managing inventory and delivery arrangements if service and availability are part of your strategic thrust.

   The price/quantity mix is the classic economic treatment of the supplier/buyer relationship, the basis of all the "tools of the trade." But minding p's and q's is only part of thinking *strategically* about managing your suppliers.

☐

SUPPLIER ANALYSIS:
THE SUPPLIER PERSPECTIVE
LIAM FAHEY

Increasingly, firms are finding themselves at the mercy of their suppliers or, at a minimum, finding their negotiations with suppliers more protracted and onerous.

On the other hand, suppliers are also attempting to gain a better understanding of their manufacturing customers. To this end, one supplier, a provider of components used in the manufacturing process by industrial firms, conducted a detailed analysis of its customer organizations.

The analysis was conducted by a team or task force composed of indi-

Strategic Planning Management, December, 1986; Commerce Communications, Inc.

viduals from a variety of functional areas. As the analysis progressed, the team identified serveral key questions:

1. What do we provide our customers?
2. What do our customers buy from us?
3. What is our product?
4. How do we learn about our customers?
5. What do we know about our customers?
6. What do we need to know about our customers?
7. What is the nature of our relationship with customers?

WHAT DO WE PROVIDE?

The team quickly decided that this was the appropriate point of departure for their analysis.

As the team began to explore this question, however, it became evident that the question was better asked in the following way: What is it that the customer buys from us? The way the question was originally posed, the team noted that the viewpoint or perspective they were adopting was that of their own organization and not that of their customers—which was the rationale for embarking upon the analysis.

WHAT DOES THE CUSTOMER BUY?

As with many of the questions that were addressed in this analysis, the answer largely turned on the specific product considered. However, a number of broad generalizations did emerge.

First, customers bought the products to satisfy some functional need: "to facilitate manufacturing operations" in the lexicon of the team.

Second, customers bought a bunch of "services" that were required either to install the product, to make it more functional, or to adapt and improve the product (or, more specifically, the product's performance) over time.

Third, in the case of some products, what the customer was buying was knowledge—a knowledge base that it did not have itself (and would probably find too difficult and expensive to develop) and which it could obtain only from a few suppliers—at best two or three. This knowledge base resided in the firm's technical and engineering staff. Its existence and value was conveyed to the customers' personnel through discussions, on-site visits, product specification details, project proposals, etc.

Fourth, some members of the team, as they spent more time contemplating what it was that the customer really purchased, began to suggest that it was something beyond simply a product or bunch of related services.

They argued that what customers ultimately were acquiring was something on the order of peace of mind: a long-term relationship without which it would be difficult to produce their own products as efficiently or with the quality they desired.

WHAT IS OUR PRODUCT?

Some team members, echoing sentiments widely held within the firm, thought that this question was not worth asking—the answers were obvious. Everyone knew what products the firm produced and sold.

However, as they probed along the lines noted above in trying to determine what it was that customers bought, it became readily apparent that many misconceptions abounded in the firm as to what "products" they provided their customers.

Principal among these misconceptions was that many individuals in the firm defined each product as simply the sum of its tangible attributes. In the vernacular of the firm, a hardware conception of the product was emphasized.

Stated differently, the services component of the product received relatively little attention; the knowledge element received almost no attention; and, the nature of the ongoing relationship between provider and customer was accorded no attention at all.

HOW DO WE LEARN ABOUT OUR CUSTOMERS?

One other question persistently raised its ugly head in the team's deliberations—how does the firm acquire its knowledge about customers?

The team intentionally decided to raise this question before it asked "what do we know about our customers?" The thinking behind this sequencing of questioning was that a familiarity with the way in which the firm learned about its customers (and how that information was disseminated within the firm) would temper what otherwise might be extravagant claims about what they actually knew about customers.

Team members created a long enumeration of items, each of which represented a means by which someone in the firm was able to gain a better understanding of customers. The list was then pared down to what the team considered the most significant items.

Personal contacts with customers was rated as the most important and most reliable source of information about all aspects of the customer's business. While this did not come as a great shock to team members, they were surprised to discover the variety of interpersonal contacts they had with many of their customers, particularly their larger customers. The following contacts were deemed to be the most valuable access points:

- Design/engineering staff working in conjunction with the customers' counterparts
- Salespeople (most of whom are engineers) calling on customers (generating among other things a profile of different customers' needs, current operations characteristics, etc.)
- Line management and finance/accounting staff negotiating contract terms
- Various personnel speaking with customers at product or trade shows

Although they were not deemed nearly as important as personal sources of information, the team did develop a long laundry list of secondary (i.e., non-personal) sources of data about customers.

The team did note, however, that different individuals or functions tended to utilize different secondary sources. For example, the engineering staff culled data from very different types of publications than did the marketing/sales function.

As the team began to examine the nature of the data that could be extracted from secondary sources, two conclusions emerged.

1. Such data could be used to reveal much more about customers than most team members had realized. For example, it quickly became evident that trade literature pertaining to customers often revealed significant details about customers' competitive strategy—what the strategy was, why it was being pursued, what results it had generated or were expected, etc.
2. Such information could prove useful to the firm's personnel in preparing to meet with customers. For example, salespeople could be provided with a greater understanding of each major customer's competitive strategy and how they could help the customer to execute the strategy.

WHAT DO WE KNOW ABOUT OUR CUSTOMERS?

To grapple with this question, the team identified different types of customers, and then developed another list of those things which they were reasonably confident they knew about each type of customer. In order to give the analysis a specific anchor, the team zeroed in on the one or two largest customers in each customer class.

To focus the analysis, the team asked a series of questions about each of the following customer aspects:

- Manufacturing processes
- Technology capability
- Engineering capability
- Product strategy
- Key personnel
- Organizational policies

- Financial condition
- Purchasing criteria

A number of conclusions emerged from this analysis.

First, it became apparent to the team that a lot of information about customers already existed within the firm, but it was highly disjointed and distributed across various functions. In other words, it had never previously been pulled together and analyzed.

Second, in the words of one member of the team, "the vast preponderance of the data about customers was of a very specific nature—it was largely about individual aspects of the customer: its manufacturing, technology, engineering, etc. There was very little data about the customer's overall competitive or business strategy."

Third, the team realized that in order to negotiate effectively with its customers, the firm needed a much broader base of knowledge about its customers than had previously been appreciated. Indeed, this question became a large and very significant part of their analysis.

WHAT DO WE NEED TO KNOW?

In the view of most members of the team, answering this question proved most enlightening.

A large portion of the enlightenment stemmed from the recognition that this question could only be answered by placing it in a broader context. That broader context was identifying and assessing the firm's strategic options. Asking what they needed to know about their customers compelled the team to assess the firm's own strategic options, and then to ask what customer knowledge was required not just to assess strategic options but to identify the options.

To provide a framework for assessing customers within the broader context, the team identified the following questions as the most important inputs to effectively linking customer knowledge and strategy analysis:

1. What is the customer's business or competitive strategy? (i.e., what is its strategy in the marketplace?)
   - What are its market share goals?
   - How does it price its products?
   - What non-price elements are important?
   - What role does product development play?
2. What contribution does each functional area make to the business or competitive strategy?
   - What is expected of manufacturing? Is it product quality, production flexibility, or cost efficiencies?

- How important is cost control in its strategy? Where is cost control accorded most attention—product development, engineering, manufacturing, marketing, general administration, etc.?
- What is the role of the engineering function in product development, prototype testing, manufacturing, etc.?
- What role does the finance/accounting function play? When are the finance/accounting personnel brought into the decision-making process? Are finance/accounting criteria strictly adhered to?

3. What is the decision-making process within customers with regard to the firm's products?
- Who is typically involved in the decision process?
- What role does each play?
- What is the duration of each phase in the decision process?
- Where does authority to make the decision reside?
- Who are the most significant influencers in the decision process?
- When the decision process becomes protracted, who or what tends to be the cause?

WHAT IS OUR RELATIONSHIP WITH CUSTOMERS?

As the team considered each of the questions noted so far, it became increasingly clear that customers could only be fully understood in the context of their relationship with the team's own firm.

Not surprisingly, the team determined that the firm had a wide range of relationships with its customers, spanning a spectrum from what various team members described as "friendly, close, cordial, and close-working" to "hostile, distant, arms-length, and disfunctional."

The team concluded that two factors seemed largely to determine the nature of the firm's relationship with customers: the degree of dependency between the firm and the customers and the character of the relationship that had evolved over time between their respective personnel.

In assessing the extent of dependency between the firm and specific customers, the team raised the following questions:

1. What percentage of the customer's product requirements are accounted for by our firm's sales?
2. What percentage of our sales (by product type) is accounted for by each customer (and customer type)?
3. How critical are our firm's products to the operations of each customer? Are they critical to the customer's efforts to produce a (superior) quality product? What contribution do they make to the customer becoming more cost-efficient?

4. What options do customers currently or potentially possess with regard to other suppliers? Is the firm a single source supplier, one of a few, or one of many?

In assessing the nature of the interpersonal relationships the firm has with different customers, the team asked the following questions:

1. Who are the key contact persons within our own firm? The importance of this question became manifest when it transpired that some key individuals within their own firm (engineers, salespersons, line managers) seemed to do a much better job at "cultivating" appropriate individuals within customer organizations.

2. What key events seem to have influenced the relationship? A wide range of events were identified as having positively or negatively influenced how the firm and customers viewed each other. Negative events included protracted bargaining between the parties, problems about credit terms and payment, personality clashes between personnel, and post-installation product problems.

A greater awareness of the importance of these concerns led the team to conclude that the firm needed to develop an explicit strategy or approach to managing its multiple relationships with customers.

MAKING USE OF CUSTOMER KNOWLEDGE

The team continually emphasized that gaining knowledge about customers was not an end in itself. The ultimate intent was to use that knowledge to formulate better strategies to strengthen customer relationships.

Although the team identified innumerable ways in which such knowledge could be used, three uses were accorded most significance:

1. Identifying strategic (product) options
2. Assessing strategy options
3. Managing customer relationships

In large part because of the nature of the firm's products, knowledge of the operations of customers' organizations was a key input to developing new products and modifying existing products. In many instances, the products had to be developed or modified around a customer's specific needs. Such custom products could not be first developed and then adapted to fit customers' unique requirements.

This was not news to the team. What did come as a surprise was how little effort was expended by the firm in studying customers (or more precisely working with customer personnel) with the specific intent of identifying new product options.

The firm has now developed project teams to work closely with customers in product development, particularly in the development of products new to the firm.

Also, stemming from its broader understanding of what the customer buys (or what product the firm provides), the firm is now developing different "product packages" for each customer type (and, in some cases, for specific customers). Different service mixes are now being made available.

The firm now specifically "tests" product options by asking how and why customers may respond to them. For example, they now ask how will the product help the customer? How does it meet the interests of individual functional areas within the customer organization?

Members of the analysis team also claim that their better understanding of customers is also helping them to anticipate how customers may respond to the offerings of competitors, and how the firm itself should respond to competitive threats.

The firm is also now establishing some programs to manage all aspects of its relationships with customers. At the broadest level, the firm is developing a strategy to exert maximum leverage upon some large customers. This includes proposals to develop products jointly, perform assessments of the customers' needs, provide alternative service options. The intent is to make customers as dependent as possible upon the firm.

At a more specific level, it involves the provision of training and development programs for all personnel that interact with customers. For example, salespeople and engineers are being trained in negotiating and bargaining tactics.

The firm is now extensively refocusing its approach to doing business with customers. In line with that effort, the team has decided to continue to work together as a means of formalizing ongoing learning about customers.

Analysis of Strategic Alliances

☐

STRATEGIC ALLIANCES: A NEW COMPETITIVE FORCE

JAN HERRING

More and more American companies are finding it advantageous to form strategic alliances with firms in other countries—or even, in some cases, at home—as a way of doing business in an increasingly complex and competitive environment.

Strategic Planning Management, May, 1986; Commerce Communications, Inc.

According to a report recently published by *Dataquest,* in 1980 there were three strategic alliances between Japanese and U.S. and other Western semiconductor makers. By 1985, that number had grown to 54. While there was no evidence of affiliation activity among Japanese semiconductor equipment manufacturers in 1980, by 1985 there were 17 such alliances.

The benefits of doing business through strategic alliances have not escaped the notice of other industries. Consider the following examples:

- Caterpillar Tractor Co.'s lift trucks are built by South Korea's Daewoo Heavy Industries Ltd.
- Hewlett-Packard Co. has its printed circuit boards manufactured in Taiwan.
- U.S. firms such as Microelectronics and Computer Corp. have formed R&D consortia.
- Honeywell, Inc. gets the central processing "brain" for its biggest mainframe computer from a Japanese manufacturer, and two other mainframes that Honeywell sells in the U.S. are imported as finished products from Europe.

By analyzing the number and nature of such alliances, a company can learn a great deal about the strengths and weaknesses, as well as the strategic intent, of its competitors. Such information can then be used in a company's own strategic planning, both in drafting its own alliances, and in anticipating a competitor's next moves.

DEFINITIONS AND GOALS

Strategic alliances are generally defined as contractual agreements that firms enter into with each other. These may take the form of mergers, joint ventures, licensing arrangements, acquisitions, or shared research and development projects, among others.

Many companies enter into such affiliations as a way of achieving a specific strategic objective. This may be an expansion of technology, access to certain markets, or the acquisition of manufacturing skills and capabilities that the firm does not possess on its own. In arranging a strategic alliance, a firm generally seeks a business partner that can help it compete better internationally. Such alliances, however, are not exclusively the domain of international business. A company may also seek a domestic alliance that would give it the ability to compete more effectively on a global basis.

FORCES BEHIND AFFILIATION ACTIVITY

There are many forces driving firms to engage in a high level of affiliation activity, particularly in high-technology fields, such as the electronics industry.

To maintain historical revenue growth, firms are using affiliations to gain market access, to develop technology, to broaden product lines, to strengthen parts sourcing, to manufacture products, and to enter new businesses.

The forces of change having the greatest impact on company affiliation activities today are: the high rate of technological change, globalization of the industry, and increased worldwide competition. In addition, foreign governments have increasingly developed policies that encourage the formation of affiliations, either directly or indirectly, as a way of strengthening their electronics industries and facilitating exports. It is worthwhile to examine each of these forces a bit more closely.

HIGH RATE OF TECHNOLOGICAL CHANGE

The high rate of technological change is increasing the demand on research and development resources of electronic firms. Shorter product life cycles are reducing technological lead times, demanding rapid and repeated development of new products, and increasing R&D costs. The convergence of computers and communications requires broadened capabilities from system suppliers. Users demand systems and services that are increasingly complex and difficult to provide.

Companies are turning to affiliations as a way of leveraging or supplementing their own R&D resources, in order to cope with the fast pace of technological change.

GLOBALIZATION OF INDUSTRY

While globalization does offer many advantages, it also tends to make running a business more complex, more costly, and more risky. Companies are entering foreign markets to maintain historical growth rates, which are no longer possible in many domestic markets. Entering new foreign markets requires development of new sales and distribution channels; but successful entry offers a solution to potential protectionist and cultural barriers.

To reduce costs and improve market access, firms are increasing the manufacturing and sourcing of parts on a global basis. Worldwide manufacturing networks put demands on coordination of operations, and increase risks associated with currency fluctuations and governmental regulations. Affiliations are being used to reduce the costs and risks of foreign market access, and to speed product penetration.

INCREASED COMPETITION

Increasing international competition in a maturing industry, such as electronics, puts pressure on company growth and profitability. In many industry segments, there are already too many participants to support traditional growth rates, and yet new entries continue to proliferate.

Even traditionally non-electronic firms are entering electronics, often through acquisitions or joint ventures. General Motors is now involved in data processing and defense electronics; British Petroleum is developing software; and Kawasaki Steel produces semicustom ICs. Additionally, large electronics companies are horizontally integrating into new businesses: for example, Mc-Donnell Douglas has expanded into data networks, and AT&T into computers.

Governments of the Newly Industrializing Countries (NICs), such as Singapore, Korea, and Taiwan, are targeting electronics as a growth area for domestic industries. As a result of these factors, electronics firms worldwide are spending more on R&D and capital investment relative to revenues in an effort to remain competitive. Affiliations are being used more often to enter new businesses, or to maintain or develop a broad product line as competition intensifies.

GOVERNMENT POLICIES

Governments in Europe, Japan, and the NICs are pursuing policies that are increasing affiliation activity. European governments are encouraging inter-country programs to advance European technology. Japan is encouraging its companies to affiliate internationally to avoid trade barriers and to reduce trade friction. Some NIC governments are requiring foreign firms to enter into affiliations with local companies before allowing access to local electronics markets.

PLANNING FOR A STRATEGIC ALLIANCE

Before embarking on an affiliation strategy, a company must be prepared to undertake a great deal of research. Motorola, for example, has looked at hundreds of companies' track records seeking ones that offered an appropriate fit. Companies that seemed to show potential were examined for how well they matched Motorola's own culture and values.

For each prospective ally, a company must conduct a strategic analysis and ask: What is this other firm's strategy? What is it trying to accomplish? What are its strategic objectives?

All aspects of that company's business—its distribution methods, financial picture, R&D capabilities, marketing expertise, product line, etc.—should be scrutinized carefully. That information can then be used to infer what the firm's strategy might be with regard to product development, manufacturing, marketing, etc.

It is also important to analyze the other affiliations the company has made over the last 5-10 years. By examining the company's past record of affiliation activity, including its acquisitions, joint ventures, second sourcing, etc., it is possible to determine whether there are emerging patterns in the company's affiliation activities. It may help to make a graphic representation of past events as a way of understanding the relationship between the past and the current situation.

UNDERSTANDING THE ALLY'S GOALS

In examining a company's past affiliation activity, it is helpful to recognize that firms enter into such arrangements for a variety of reasons, not all of them apparent.

Some companies will enter into strategic alliances as a way of staking out claims for the future, hence precluding competitors from coming in ahead of them. AT&T, for example, identified the leading companies in countries where they wanted to be doing business in 5 to 10 years. They entered into alliances with those companies now, intending to follow up on them at an appropriate time in the future.

A variation on this type of strategic alliance is a preemptive alliance. Some companies form alliances with other companies chiefly as a way of keeping major competitors from entering the arena, even if they have no real intention of making use of the alliance. This practice is used chiefly as a time-buying strategy.

SOME EXAMPLES

We have already outlined some of the major forces that have led to increased affiliation activity in recent years. It may be helpful to consider some specific examples of recent alliances to illustrate the variety of reasons why a company might consider this particular strategy.

1. **Worldwide marketing.**   At the time of divestiture, AT&T had little international experience. The company knew that the only way it could gain access to multinational markets quickly was to enter into an alliance with another company—in this case, Olivetti—with global experience.

2. **New products.**   AT&T's alliance with Convergent Technologies provided it with the capability to produce a PBX product it could not have developed on its own, or at least not quickly enough to be competitive.

3. **Vertical or horizontal integration.**   IBM sought access to advanced microprocessor equipment. By vertically integrating with Intel, it was able to accomplish that goal. IBM's alliance with Rolm enabled it to complete its advanced office communication capability.

4. Access to markets. In order to gain access to a country, a company must often affiliate with a local partner. In China, Korea, and Taiwan, for example, the government may require that a company enter into a joint venture in order to have access to local markets and to establish manufacturing facilities there.

5. Gaining time. Strategic alliances may also be a time-enhancing element. It could, for example, take 2–3 years to train Americans in a particular field and send them around the world to open markets. The alliance route allows a company access to capabilities it couldn't gain on its own in the same amount of time. Even IBM, traditionally a company which preferred to go it alone, has found that in many areas affiliation has been the only route available for achieving its objectives.

6. Guarding valuable customers. In a world where acquisitions and takeovers have become common, a company may find its relationship with a former good customer undermined if that customer forms an alliance with a competitor.

UNDERSTANDING COMPETITORS

The same information a company uses to locate a possible strategic partner of its own may also be used to analyze the kind of affiliations a competitor is engaging in, or is likely to undertake.

A competitor's affiliation activity will often reveal what that firm is doing to achieve a new objective or ameliorate a weakness. For example, the Japanese are weak in software development. To remedy that deficiency, they have formed many software alliances, often with American firms, and have established facilities jointly with companies in Singapore and China to exploit the programming support that those countries might offer.

However, strategic alliances may also give misleading signals. For example, in the GE-RCA alliance, it was easy for competing companies to get so caught up in the possible governmental aspects of the alliance that they missed what this alliance might mean for them. Companies must analyze all the parts of an alliance that have potential for a direct impact on them. A focus on the larger issues may divert attention from the more mundane, but ultimately more important, aspects.

FUTURE PROSPECTS

The four major forces currently affecting affiliation activities—the high rate of technological change, globalization of industry, increasing worldwide competition, and government actions—will continue into the 1990s. Thus, affiliations probably will continue to be important strategy tools for electronics firms, as well as for others, for the rest of this decade.

Large firms such as AT&T, General Motors, IBM, and Japan's NTT will use acquisitions and joint ventures to move into new electronics businesses, especially where the time and costs of internal development are prohibitive, such as large computers or factory automation. They will also use affiliations to penetrate new markets rapidly worldwide. Smaller firms will compete to establish strong supplier relationships through partnerships with large firms to survive industry shake-outs. Finally, most firms will try to use affiliations to leverage financial, technological, marketing, and human resources to gain competitive advantages on a global basis.

Affiliation attempts, however, will probably continue to fail as often as they succeed. The entry cost will be high in funding, technology, and particularly in the commitment of key personnel. But those firms that are able to manage affiliation complexities are likely to gain important strategic advantages over those that cannot or are not willing to try.

☐

SECURING COMPETITIVE EDGE THROUGH STRATEGIC INFORMATION SYSTEM ALLIANCES
CHARLES WISEMAN

The strategic use of computer-based information systems is accelerating as intra- and inter-industry competition intensifies in the 1980s. Increasingly, such systems are emerging as potent weapons in the battle to gain competitive edge.

Some examples can quickly illustrate the potency of information systems as a source of competitive advantage. Despite the complaints of travel agents and rival airlines, American and United still enjoy the fruits of their online reservation systems: priority flight listings on agents' screens, ticket-payment float, and market analysis. By providing electronic order-entry and inventory control services to hospitals, American Hospital Supply supports its business strategy by raising entry barriers for competitors and switching costs for customers.

In the financial sector, Merrill Lynch's Cash Management Account, a product based on database and laser printing technology, illustrates the preemptive power of information systems. It enabled Merrill to sustain a monopoly position, to win more than 500,000 new customers, and to collect over $60 million annually in fees.

Strategic Planning Management, April, 1984; Commerce Communications, Inc.

STRATEGIC INFORMATION SYSTEMS

The above examples are instances of *strategic information systems* (SIS). Unlike traditional information system product lines such as *management information systems* (MIS), intended primarily to automate an organization's basic business processes, or the more recent *decision support systems* (DSS), aimed at satisfying its managerial information needs, SIS are used principally to support an organization's business strategy and, particularly, its efforts to gain competitive advantage.

The emergence of SIS marks the start of a new era in information system application opportunities. To realize these, you need to think systematically about the strategic *uses* of information systems. You can begin by asking the following two questions:

1. What Is the Strategic Target of Your Information System?

Among the strategic targets you should consider are your *suppliers* (providers of raw materials, capital, labor, or services), *customers* (those who retail, wholesale, warehouse, distribute, or use your products), and *competitors* (those currently in the industry, possibly new entrants, firms in other industries offering substitute products, or other organizations competing for scarce resources).

2. What Strategic Thrust Can Be Used Against the Target?

There are three basic categories of a strategic thrust that may be aimed at your suppliers, customers, or competitors: differentiation, cost and innovation.

The aim of a *differentiation* thrust is to either (1) reduce the differentiation advantages that strategic targets enjoy vis à vis your organization, or (2) increase the differentiation advantages you enjoy vis à vis your strategic targets.

The aim of a *cost* thrust is to (1) reduce or avoid your costs vis à vis your strategic targets, or (2) help your customers or suppliers reduce or avoid their costs so that you gain preferred treatment from these stakeholders, or (3) increase your competitor's costs.

The aim of the *innovation* thrust is to find new ways of doing business through the use of information systems. These new ways include, but certainly are not limited to, the use of information systems to transform steps on an existing industry (value-added) chain, diversify into new industries or markets, redefine the existing business or create new businesses. Innovative SIS applications, like the airline, financial, and health care examples previously noted, are preemptive strikes. They are major moves made ahead of the competition allowing the firm to secure an advantageous position.

INNOVATIVE SIS THRUSTS: SIS ALLIANCES

A special class of innovative SIS thrusts may be called "SIS alliances." Your organization may attempt to forge a SIS alliance if the following conditions hold:

1. Your organization identifies an opportunity to support its competitive strategy through the use of information systems.
2. The opportunity requires a negotiated relationship with one or more other organizations.
3. Either your firm or some of its partners have already developed the information systems to be used, or have the expertise to develop them.

You need to distinguish three generic forms of SIS alliance opportunities. These are opportunities for your firm (1) to leverage the information systems it has already developed by arranging a deal with another party, (2) to exploit the information systems developed by another organization through some kind of negotiated agreement, or (3) to form a joint venture with another organization to develop a new information system.

1. Leveraging Information Systems You Have Already Developed

American Express's recent agreement to buy Investors Diversified Service (IDS) from the Allegheny Corporation illustrates one firm's efforts to leverage existing information systems-based products and services. Founded in 1894, IDS has about 1.1 million customers located primarily in small and medium-sized cities. The 4,500 IDS salespersons sell mutual funds, life insurance, tax shelters, and other investments to their clients.

American Express saw in IDS a vehicle for distributing its information systems-based products and services and those developed by its various units: Shearson in the brokerage area and Fireman's Fund in the insurance realm. The acquisition of IDS will permit American Express to tap into a massive market that, up to now, it has only been able to penetrate via the direct marketing route.

Joint marketing ventures represent another form of SIS alliance where you can leverage information systems assets you already have developed. I call this form the "IBM Connection" because so many deals have been cut between organizations that have developed software products and IBM. But certainly this form of SIS alliance is not limited to IBM: "AT&T," "WANG," "PACTEL," and the like could be substituted for "IBM." Here are some recent instances of this SIS alliance form.

Computervision Corp., the leader in CAD/CAM software, has decided to become a value-added remarketer for IBM's various hardware products. While IBM is Computervision's closest competitor in this market segment, it realizes that it cannot satisfy the needs of customers in every niche. Most analysts believe that the agreement will increase the sales of both vendors. It is interesting to note that IBM did not purchase a minority equity interest in Computervision, as it did when it signed major OEM deals with Rolm (for PBX's) and with Intel (for microprocessors). In the latter two cases, it was IBM that became the value-added remarketer.

Geisco, General Electric's information services company, has signed an agreement with IBM to be a value-added remarketer of the IBM PC. Geisco can parlay some of the information systems it offers via timesharing by repackaging them on the PC.

2. Exploiting Information Systems Already Developed By Others

SIS alliances can be arranged with your rivals as well as with your suppliers or customers. In the increasingly deregulated financial services sector, competitors often find it profitable to trade with each other. This is particularly true when your potential partner is a player in an industry encroaching on your territory. Dreyfus Corp., the large mutual fund organization, recently cut a deal with Chase Manhattan Bank to manage funds for its clients. Bank of America has arranged with a large insurance company to provide facilities for the sale of the firm's insurance products to Bank of America's customers.

Paine Webber, the large brokerage house, has just seized an SIS alliance opportunity that no other broker has been able to capture. It seems that Paine Webber, because of its close ties with the State Street Bank and Trust Company of Boston, has been able to penetrate the nationwide automated teller network run by MasterCard International. Paine Webber is the first and only non-bank in this network. Banks had been very careful, up to this time, to use this service to differentiate themselves from their rivals.

Now Paine Webber customers can use credit cards issued by State Street to get the same 24-hour access to cash that bank customers enjoy. Because of this SIS alliance, they can withdraw money from their Paine Webber accounts at ATMs of local banks, nationwide.

The story of how Paine Webber will use this new alliance in packaging its products and services has yet to unfold. In any case, to exploit the information systems assets of another, you may want to consider partial or complete acquisition. This is the route followed by Fireman's Fund and Merrill Lynch.

Fireman's Fund is a large insurer locked in an intense battle to save its network of salespeople through an agency automation program. In 1982, for example, the firm spent $100 million for minicomputers for its agents. To further support this strategic initiative, it has acquired the ARC Automation Group, a software house serving the insurance industry. This initiative should bring Fireman's up to par with its competitors, Travelers and Hartford, who already own software vendors.

Merrill Lynch, on the other hand, opted (like IBM with Rolm and Intel) to shape an SIS alliance by purchasing an equity interest in Institutional Network Corp. (Instinet), a firm that offers customers an information systems-based service that automatically executes stock trades, without having to be matched with other trades in the traditional auction market. Merrill will use the system as the over-the-counter market maker for about 100 stocks. Currently, Merrill makes the market for about 1000 OTC stocks. Whether Merrill will try to trade N.Y. Stock issues on Instinet is still an open question.

The newly emerging field of software distribution presents another SIS alliance opportunity. The book publisher, Addison-Wesley has seized it by inking a pact with Infocom, Inc. to distribute Infocom's packages to book stores.

JOINT VENTURING NEW INFORMATION SYSTEMS

The last area of SIS alliance opportunity covers joint ventures by two or more firms to produce new information systems-based products or services. This area differs from the two previously discussed, in that SIS alliances formed in those areas are based on already developed information systems.

In 1982, Kroger Company, a supermarket chain with 1200 food stores, 500 pharmacies, and 32 food processing plants in 21 states, announced that it had begun selling insurance, money market funds, mutual funds and IRAs in one of its stores. Behind the announcement, believed to be the first example of a financial services operation set up in a supermarket, lay an SIS alliance with Capital Holding Company, an insurance company with assets of $3.8 billion.

The joint venture entailed costs of approximately $2 million, a substantial chunk of which was used to develop an information system that immediately compares a customer's current automobile and home insurance with the offering at the supermarket. For Capital, the alliance represents an opportunity to move into another distribution channel, different from the agency route. For Kroger, the aim is the same as it is for any new specialty service offered by the chain. "It is a service customers want, and we are in the business of serving customers," the president of Kroger said.

CONCLUSION

Strategic information systems represent a major new source of competitive advantage. Frequently, this type of competitive advantage is difficult to dislodge. With innovative strategic thinking, you may be able to exploit your own information system capability or that of others, to forge such a sustainable competitive edge.

CHAPTER

— 5 —

ORGANIZATIONAL ANALYSIS

■

BUILDING DISTINCTIVE COMPETENCES INTO COMPETITIVE ADVANTAGES
LIAM FAHEY AND H. KURT CHRISTENSEN

Every successful company has found at least one way to out-perform its competitors. This capability, whatever it may be, is called a *distinctive competence;* that is, the ability of a firm to do something better than competitors. Here are some common distinctive competences that firms develop:

- the ability to carry out innovative ideas (the capacity to introduce new products or product modifications);
- superior production skill (the ability to produce high quality products and/or to produce products at lowest cost);
- exceptional marketing (an effective sales force or the creation of a strong brand image);
- effective management of R&D; or
- superior financial management skills or the development of superior management expertise.

Other less-discussed distinctive competences include such areas as these:

- an organizational culture that is particularly conducive to handling strategic change;
- incentive systems which motivate more effectively; or
- superior planning and control systems.

Strategic Planning Management, February, 1984; Commerce Communications, Inc.

DISTINCTIVE COMPETENCES VS. COMPETITIVE ADVANTAGES

A cardinal strategic error is to assume that your firm's distinctive competences (i.e., what your firm does better than its competitors) are also your firm's competitive advantages (i.e., what favorably distinguishes your firm or its products *in the eyes of your customers*). Although some distinctive competences may translate easily into competitive advantages, others will not.

Many firms have developed products that out-perform their competitors in some way—only to find that customers did not value that factor in making their purchase decisions. Some personal computer manufacturers are trying to achieve distinctive competence along speed or capacity dimensions, when many customers are primarily interested in IBM-compatibility.

Perhaps the reason that managers so often mistakenly assume that whatever the firm does well will be valued by the customer is that they become overly preoccupied with the internal affairs of their firms. In short, managers fall into the trap of making decisions based on their own view of the world rather than from the perspective of the customer, distributor or competitor.

BEGIN BY IDENTIFYING DISTINCTIVE COMPETENCES

Exactly what *does* your firm do particularly well? If you ask four or more executives to list what they consider the firm's distinctive competences, you're likely to get a range of quite different responses.

A more effective way to grapple with this broad question is to break it down into these three more focused areas: what does this firm do well. . .

- in each of the functional areas?
- in developing linkages across the functional areas?
- in managing relationships with external entities (suppliers, customers, distributors, research establishments, governmental agencies, etc.)?

One way to ensure that the firm actually possesses the distinctive competences that some managers assume it does is to answer this question: what evidence is there to prove that the alleged distinctive competences actually exist? For example, many companies allege that customers buy their products because of their "quality," which is not defined more explicitly. While market studies could be made to provide such data, this is often not the case.

You may be surprised at how little support there may be to verify that a firm is indeed as relatively strong in one area as many managers may assume it is. In examining evidence about whether a distinctive competence actually exists, you may find it useful to address the following set of specific questions:

1. What type of evidence exists (cost data, market research data, numbers of personnel, financial measures, numbers of patents, comments of secu-

rity analysts, consultants or other knowledgeable outsiders, comments of suppliers or customers)?

2. How credible is the source? Did the information come from an employee within the firm who is merely aggrandizing the strength of his department?

3. How strong is the firm's capability *relative to its competitors?* You may have identified competences of your firm, but you do not know whether or not they are *distinctive* competences. For example, a company may be more competent at marketing than at manufacturing its products, but the firm is not necessarily distinctly stronger than its competitors at marketing.

LINKING DISTINCTIVE COMPETENCES TO COMPETITIVE ADVANTAGES

Gaining an understanding of what it takes to turn your distinctive competences into competitive advantages requires you to adopt an external perspective—that is, to consider whether or not your distinctive competences are important to your current or potential customers.

It can be either very easy or very difficult to identify how distinctive competences can become competitive advantages. It's simple enough to understand that superior production efficiencies (a competence) could readily translate into lower prices (a competitive advantage), or that the capacity to develop branded products (a competence) could generate consumer awareness and loyalty (an advantage).

However, it's not nearly as straightforward to comprehend exactly how competences such as an exceptional strategic planning system, a superior organizational culture, or greater managerial expertise contribute to specific competitive advantages.

To understand the relationships between distinctive competences and competitive advantages, approach the task in two complementary ways.

1. *The "inside-out" approach*—For each distinctive competence you identify, show how it can be built into a competitive advantage. For example, if your firm is exceptionally competent at raising capital, how can you or how should you use these funds to generate and sustain competitive advantages—by producing higher quality products, greater product differentiation, better service, lower costs, or more sales force attention?

2. *The "outside-in" approach*—Determine what competitive advantages you desire, then identify what distinctive competences are required to create and maintain each one. For example, what distinctive competences are required to create and sustain superior customer service?

The outside-in approach requires you to begin by determining your strategic goals, and then work backwards to identify what distinctive competences will permit you to attain those goals. For example, if a company decides it wants to compete in a low-value-added field, like discount retailing, it will need to develop competence in cost control. Similarly, if a retailer wants to concentrate on upper-income customers, it must develop special competence in merchandising to this customer segment.

HOW DID YOU DEVELOP CURRENT DISTINCTIVE COMPETENCES?

You need to understand not only what your firm's current strengths are, but you must know exactly what factors are contributing to those competences. Begin by identifying which functional area(s) has seemed most important—marketing, finance, production? But don't stop here. You then need to identify what specific activities or skills within the functional area have built that distinctive competence, and toward product-markets with which specific characteristics are they aimed.

Failure to take the second step by Heublein in the mid-1960s had adverse consequences. Assessing its distinctive competence as marketing alcoholic beverages, it purchased Hamm's Breweries, only to find that its ability to market liquors did not translate effectively into ability to market beer. Heublein mis-identified its distinctive competence by defining it too broadly. While both products were alcoholic beverages, they required different types of marketing competence. Further, the meaning of the product, the customer, and the motivation to consume were sufficiently different that Heublein was not successful and eventually divested the unit.

A superb information system can be a distinctive competence, especially for a company in a paper-processing industry like banking, brokerage or insurance. Is the system speedy or slow, expensive or inexpensive to operate, oriented toward gathering funds (deposits) or disbursing them (loans), and oriented toward mass or select markets?

DISTINCTIVE COMPETENCES FOR THE FUTURE

What distinctive competences will you need in the future? After all, markets, products, technology, competitors, and customer needs all change over time. As you modify your strategy to anticipate and respond to those changes, you'll probably need somewhat different distinctive competences.

In particular, if your company depends highly on a particular product-market, you're likely to need new competences to fend off competitors. Similarly, carrying out a new niche strategy will probably demand a new distinctive competence.

In any industry, the marketplace may eventually cease to value the distinctive competence(s) held by one firm. This situation is sometimes triggered when new competitors enter the market.

For example, when low-priced foreign steel producers entered the U.S. market, the most desirable competence suddenly sought by domestic manufacturers was low-cost production. In the long run, U.S. steel producers will either have to develop competence in production efficiency or develop new competences for some type of niche strategy.

THE CHALLENGE OF CHANGING YOUR DISTINCTIVE COMPETENCES

It's not necessarily easy to alter what it is that your firm does particularly well. After all, your firm's strengths are so much a product of the resources, systems, and people of your organization that changing those capabilities requires altering many aspects of the company simultaneously—but you *can* develop new distinctive competences, provided you follow a few guidelines.

1. Specify precisely the distinctive competences you want to develop and identify the competitive advantages to which they should lead, in light of the capabilities of present and potential competitors.
2. Comprehensively outline the nature and timing of changes that will be required throughout the organization, such as new systems and trained personnel.
3. Solicit the participation of people at all levels in planning and implementing the change.
4. Remember that this process of change is a slow one.

Consider the case of a large consumer goods firm that recently committed itself to developing a distinctive competence in marketing—that is, to be a better marketer than its competitors. Here are some of the steps the company has taken within the past year to enhance its marketing capability.

1. It rewrote its statement of mission to reflect a marketing emphasis.
2. It has restructured its divisions into more focused groups.
3. It has hired several new managers with marketing expertise.
4. It has launched a series of marketing-oriented seminars for both marketing and non-marketing personnel.
5. It has changed its reporting and control systems to incorporate more marketing-specific data.

Finally, keep in mind that instead of trying to change your competences, it may be easier to find new opportunities to apply your existing distinctive competences in a new product-market.

CONCLUSION

To develop the competitive advantages necessary for achieving your strategic goals, you must first build distinctive competences that are valued by present and potential customers. This requires first dispassionately identifying your current distinctive competences. Then, you can gain competitive advantage in one of two ways: (1) by developing new distinctive competences for your present product-markets, or (2) by seeking new product-markets in which you can exploit your current strengths more effectively. Neither process is speedy, but when it is thoughtfully done and implemented with care, the results can be impressive.

□

EVALUATING YOUR COSTS STRATEGICALLY

FRANK T. PAINE AND LEONARD J. TISCHLER

Few firms take advantage of one of their richest—and most readily available—sources of strategic information: the company's own data on its costs. Strategic planners typically leave cost analysis to the domain of accountants and financial analysts responsible for budgeting and control.

But, an evaluation of your firm's costs can yield information that is critical for developing effective strategies. This article will illustrate how you can use some extensions of standard cost accounting and budgeting procedures to reveal some of the most serious constraints and greatest opportunities facing your firm.

First, we'll discuss some ways to assess costs related to two areas: product lines and customer groups. We propose one type of analysis to use in evaluating these costs, the "what if" approach, and then we discuss issues involved in integrating strategic and operating data.

STRATEGIC ANALYSIS OF PRODUCT-LINE COSTS

The first step is to prepare a strategic analysis of product-line costs that will enable you to identify two things: (1) what the major controllable elements of your strategy-related costs are, and (2) whether or not those elements are actually being controlled. This analysis will help us to begin to answer some critical strategy-related questions such as:

- Are managers actually influencing discretionary items to support the current strategy?

Strategic Planning Management, September, 1985; Commerce Communications, Inc.

- Are managers laying the groundwork for future strategies or are they tipping the scales toward achieving primarily short-term profits?

The framework for your analysis will be a modified version of a standard income statement showing contribution margins. In this statement you will list separate costs for each product line, and you will also distinguish between operating and strategic costs.

"Strategic costs" include discretionary expenditures related to executing a strategic move, such as campaigns designed to increase market penetration, expand into a new market, shift production into a different mix of products, or improve quality. The condensed modified statement, shown in Table 5-1, includes only one general category for strategic costs, but in a more detailed statement you can report several accounts separately, either within or as an addendum to the statement.

Here are some examples to help you determine which expenses to classify as strategic costs rather than as discretionary operating costs. Costs related to strengthening your strategic position would include such items as new programs for attracting customers, strengthening distribution coverage, or developing a new technology. Discretionary operating costs (that is, costs related to maintaining current operations), on the other hand, would include expenses such as sponsoring weekly specials, handling customer complaints, and solving warranty problems.

Your company will need to establish clear guidelines for distinguishing between these categories to ensure that data is properly categorized and consistently used. Electronic spreadsheets can speed the process of working with the data and setting up this modified version of the contribution-margin income statement. These spreadsheets are also useful for changing from book income to cash flows.

The type of statement set up in Table 5-1 helps you see that Product 3 is the most profitable line due to its lower operating costs (manufacturing, SG&A, and other allocable fixed costs). The least profitable line is Product 2, both because it entailed some higher operating costs and because it received the least support from discretionary strategic expenditures.

You should realize, of course, that a high level of spending for strategic purposes does not necessarily guarantee profitability. Although more "strategic funds" were spent on Product 1 than on both the other products combined, its high SG&A costs seriously eroded the profitability of this product line.

Cash-flow information should be included, if possible, for two reasons. First, it reveals the various times when each product line either requires or generates cash, which identifies both constraints and internal investment opportunities. Second, in making projections you need to use cash flows, rather than book income, to discount for future risk and inflation.

It should be noted that, in certain data generation systems, it could be very costly to generate cash-flow information from accrual-basis accounting

TABLE 5-1 Product-line Contribution to Income (Operating vs. Strategic Costs—Condensed Version)

	Company		Product 1		Product 2		Product 3	
	$000s	% of sales	$000s	% of sales	$000s	% of sales	$000s	% of sales
Net sales	900		300		200		400	
Mfg. cost of sales	535	(59%)	120	(40%)	155	(78%)	260	(65%)
Mfg. contribution margin	365		180		45		140	
SG&A expenses	95	(11%)	60	(20%)	15	(7.5%)	20	(5%)
Contribution margin	270		120		30		120	
Discretionary fixed operating costs	31	(3.4%)	10	(3.3%)	6	(3%)	15	(3.8%)
Operating performance margin	239		110		24		105	
Discretionary strategic costs	55	(6%)	35	(12%)	4	(2%)	16	(4%)
Strategic performance margin	184		75		20		89	
Other allocable fixed costs	43	(5%)	20	(7%)	15	(8%)	8	(2%)
Product-line margin	141	(16%)	55	(18.3%)	5	(3%)	81	(20%)
Nonallocable costs	88							
Net income before taxes*	53							

*Net cash flow is another approach.

data. Adding an additional level of data categorization and coding, at the data input stage, can be the most expensive change of all. Before making extensive changes, you will want to weigh the benefits of improved planning, implementation, and control against the costs. When the costs of adding coding for cash-flow conversions are too high, many firms use one of their staff accountants or planners to estimate the figures or manually make the accrual-to-cash-flow adjustments. These firms find that the added information on cash flow and strategic costs is valuable enough to be well worth the extra effort required to generate it.

IDENTIFYING YOUR BEST CUSTOMER GROUPS

The next step of your strategic cost analysis is to examine the costs related to each customer group for each product line. Although we commonly break down sales figures by customer group, we less frequently consider *costs* in the same manner. Such a cost analysis may be helpful in selecting which customer groups to emphasize or deemphasize.

Economic and marketing analysis of customer groups includes evaluating customers' needs, each group's growth potential, their bargaining power, and price sensitivity. In addition, we can analyze net cash flow and switching costs.

In certain product lines it may be possible to categorize all costs, or nearly all costs, of the product line to the various customer groups. For example, you may sell different versions of your product to different customer groups and have a separate sales staff for each group.

To the extent that you can separate costs without arbitrary allocations, you can analyze the profitability of each customer group in the same way that you typically analyze the whole product line or company.

Next, you can acquire more valuable information about your customers by trying to identify how high or low the "switching costs" are for each customer group. If you can assess how easily or costly it would be for each customer group to switch to one of your competitors (e.g., specifications may have to be tied to the new supplier, or high investments may have to be made in retraining personnel), then you will have a better idea of how much you may need to spend to keep a good customer group.

Similarly, the level of new cash flow generated by each customer group suggests how desirable the customer is to your firm. Once you have identified your best customers, you may wish to consider ways to add additional switching costs to keep those customers.

This breakdown of your costs by customer group offers insights into both internal control and competitive position. Internally, the analysis tells you how much income, cash flow, or marginal contribution each customer group is making. You can use this information to evaluate the relative value of customer groups, which helps in planning where the firm should focus its resources on retaining customers. The analysis also reveals if the firm has sufficient resources, in case it needs to fight to keep this group.

To use this analysis for evaluating competitive position, you do not need precise numbers. A competitor intelligence system needs only enough precision to yield comparative graphs or charts. Even rough comparative figures, or "guesstimates," can help show you how much fighting you may have to do with your competitors to hold onto, or to increase your share of, the customer group. They will also tell you what chances you have of winning the fight.

THE "WHAT IF" APPROACH TO COST PLANNING

After you've evaluated your firm's past costs by product line and customer group, you can consider alternative ways of strategically altering future costs. This approach involves asking some "what if" questions such as these:

- What if we increase advertising?
- What if we make certain improvements in the quality of the product?
- What if a certain competitor uses its excess capacity to flood the market and lower the price?
- What are the cost implications of new legislation?

You can consider a full range of alternatives for changing both operating and strategic expenses: adding discretionary costs, controlling certain existing costs, or undertaking various strategic options such as increased market penetration, adding capacity, expanding or contracting a product line, or responses to competitive or regulatory changes.

Again, the electronic spreadsheet is the easiest way to perform this type of analysis. It allows you to manipulate a set of figures quickly, in many ways, and it readjusts all the figures almost instantly, based on a change in just one "what if" figure.

The "what if" procedure allows us to test many changes before we make them. You must be aware of the risk of becoming overly dependent on spreadsheet results. Keep in mind that results of any analysis are only as good as the data and assumptions that went into it. Watch for assumptions about relevant ranges for models. For example, although your model may assume that certain costs remain "fixed," as production volume increases beyond a certain range, some "fixed" costs may increase to cover the expenses of a new factory or bigger equipment.

Assumptions about factors that are not under the firm's own control, such as inflation or labor and material costs, can also cause problems. A model may have certain costs or inflation adjustments built into it. As these change, the model becomes less useful. For example, if your forecasting model is based on a 15% inflation rate, the model would give us faulty predictions if the inflation rate drops to 5%.

You'll want to be alert for environmental changes or competitors' moves that also can render a model ineffectual. For example, a merger or acquisition can change the entire posture of a competitor, so our model of its past behavior will no longer be as useful as it had been.

Even supposedly straightforward matters, such as methods for calculating net present value, internal rate of return, or net cash flow are laced with assumptions that could invalidate your results.

These problems can be warded off by building into the software various automatic warnings about assumptions and limitations when different techniques are applied, or specific models are being used. Also, a knowledgeable staff person should be assigned to check models and assumptions periodically for internal and external consistency.

INTEGRATE STRATEGIC AND OPERATING DATA

As long as the basic information system of all firms continues to center on standardized financial accounting guidelines, firms must maintain an accounting-oriented information system. At the same time, planners are overcoming the limitations of traditional accounting data by establishing an additional set of information referred to as a "strategic database." Unfortunately, the two databases usually aren't very closely linked.

One problem is that accounting financial data is reported for traditional divisions, while strategic plans are based on product lines or SBUs. Thus, managers usually receive reports on operating performance only, without any information about their progress toward strategic targets. Consequently, they only work toward improving operating (rather than strategic) results, because those results are their only benchmarks.

Higher-level executives, on the other hand, may focus at least as much on the strategic information that they get in special reports, as they do on the standard financial information. Moreover, their strategic decisions on matters, such as expansion or contraction of a product line, are based primarily on how well the product line is progressing toward its strategic goal.

Here we have a classic case of lack of integration. Because their decisions are based on different information, the various levels of management inadvertently end up working against each other. To avoid this, you need to begin to integrate the operating and strategic information. Although no established procedure exists yet for combining these two types of data, the product-line and customer-group analyses can be used to achieve at least partial integration of these databases.

CONCLUSION

Making use of cost analysis in strategy appraisal and development is difficult, but the insights gained make it worth the effort. A prerequisite to realizing these benefits is to get those involved in strategy analysis and cost analysis to work together.

CHAPTER

— 6 —

MANAGING MACROENVIRONMENTAL, INDUSTRY, AND ORGANIZATIONAL ANALYSIS

■

☐

MANAGING MACROENVIRONMENTAL ANALYSIS: ORGANIZATIONAL PREREQUISITES

V. K. NARAYANAN

Organizational factors strongly influence how well macroenvironmental analysis is conducted and to what extent it is integrated into strategy analysis. Stated differently, the analytical side of macroenvironmental analysis takes place within an organizational context.

Thus, the organizational factors that affect macroenvironmental analysis need to be managed. Some of the managerial issues involved can be divided into three sets of organizational factors: cultural-political, structural, and managerial process.

CULTURAL-POLITICAL PREREQUISITES

There are some key cultural-political prerequisites to getting macroenvironmental analysis initiated, sustained, and integrated into the strategic manage-

Strategic Planning Management, June, 1985; Commerce Communications, Inc.

ment process in organizations. These are necessary for maintaining the legitimacy, visibility, and credibility of macroenvironmental analysis.

1. **A macroenvironmental analysis champion.** Beyond top management commitment, macroenvironmental analysis, especially in its early stages, requires a credible champion to make it visible within the organization. The champion should ideally be from the line management—someone who can wield sufficient influence in the organization.

   The role of the champion is important because not all members of top management can pay continual attention to environmental analysis issues, given the demands on their time. Secondly, the champion's role is to nurture environmental analysis efforts; this includes political "amnesty" to those engaged in environmental analysis who are likely to be viewed with suspicion in the organization.

2. **The sustenance of ambiguity.** A key role for top management and the environmental analysis champion is to create and sustain a sufficient level of ambiguity in the process of doing macroenvironmental analysis. This implies an ability to live with uncertain information, uncertain interpretations, and to downplay expectations of certainty, often demanded by the operating sectors of the organization.

3. **Interfaces into strategic management.** Commitment to macroenvironmental analysis at the operating levels in the organization needs to be generated primarily by highlighting the role of environmental analysis in strategy analysis and particularly the need to weave macroenvironmental assumptions into strategy analysis. This could be accomplished by having senior line management ask macroenvironmental-related questions in strategy presentations and making macroenvironmental analysis a formal part of analysis in strategy decisions, strategy development, and implementation.

STRUCTURAL PREREQUISITES

Structural prerequisites are important because they delineate allocation of tasks and responsibilities for doing macroenvironmental analysis, impact on the quality of outputs, and usefulness for strategic analysis. Four key issues:

1. **Multiple structural mechanisms.** A wide number of choices are available to an organization in terms of structural mechanisms that facilitate a macroenvironmental analysis. At the simplest level, an organization could rely on outside agencies to provide it with the

requisite analysis; at the other end of the spectrum, an organization may have a unit devoted entirely to macroenvironmental analysis.

Most organizations use multiple structural mechanisms for environmental analysis. What structure is used depends on the purpose of the analysis and the amount of resources available. Outside agencies very often provide routine data (e.g., economic data) or quite sophisticated data analysis and forecasts (technological and political issues); ad hoc teams are frequently assembled to identify and assess strategic issues; task forces involved in such strategic activities as new product development or diversification may include environmental analysis representatives; more generally, environmental analysis units can serve multiple functions in ongoing strategic planning processes.

2. **Linkage mechanisms.** Without linkage mechanisms, macroenvironmental analysis is not likely to be integrated into strategic analysis.

Linkage problems are likely to be acute in the case of reports from outside agencies. Thus, sufficient time must be devoted to understanding the implications of outside agency reports. This may involve getting such reports on the "agenda" of ad hoc committees, task forces, or regular management meetings.

3. **Location of environmental analysis center.** We use the term "analysis center" to emphasize that macroenvironmental analysis may be conducted within many different structural mechanisms— irrespective of the structural mechanism employed, in attempting to assure linkage, it is important to place macroenvironmental analysis as closely as possible to strategy analysis so that its outputs are useful for and utilized in strategy analysis.

Unless there is close interaction between the two streams of analysis, the value of both the process and the products of environmental analysis will not be fully realized. Such proximity in location enables those engaged in macroenvironmental analysis to (1) portray the outputs in terms meaningful to strategy analysts, (2) fine-tune the process and outputs of macroenvironmental analysis so that they correspond to the strategy analysis requirements, thus enhancing the chances that action implications are relevant and meaningful, and (3) help strategy analysts to think through the implications in specific action terms.

4. **Design of environmental analysis units or task forces.** Heterogeneous viewpoints need to be represented throughout environmental analysis and especially in the early stages to avoid premature convergence.

This necessitates that design should focus on creating groups with a heterogeneity of perspectives. Diversity should be maintained on specific projects over time. This is particularly important for long-standing environmental analysis units so that "group-think" (that is, individuals with similar assumptions or causal beliefs) does not ensue. New blood with fresh viewpoints brought in over time can resuscitate what may be an ossified analysis unit.

MANAGERIAL PROCESS CONSIDERATIONS

Process considerations involve the dynamics of managing environmental analysis. They influence how environmental analysis gets done and also how it is linked to strategy analysis.

1. **Managing the design process.**   It is critical to manage the process of setting the overarching premises of environmental analysis and how it gets done. The premises involve two key issues: that environmental analysis outputs should be included in strategy analysis and that environmental analysis is not a quick fix or panacea for organizational problems.

   Setting these premises is not an exercise in rational analysis but should be viewed as an educational effort: the key individuals who play a role in strategic analysis need to be educated about the role of macroenvironmental analysis. Managing these expectations about the role, scope, and nature of macroenvironmental analysis is a key to the success of macroenvironmental analysis.

2. **Managing the internal process.**   Managing the internal dynamics of environmental analysis units or task groups is another important consideration. Two issues related to macroenvironmental analysis activities deserve mention.

   First, the macroenvironmental analyst is expected to exercise judgment, intuition, and sometimes speculation. This necessitates internal norms different from those in many firms. Norms of decisiveness, specifity, and consensus are not always functional; in contrast, norms of reflection, ambiguity, and legitimacy of differences in viewpoints need to be nurtured.

   Second, it is critical to manage the time frame of those engaged in macroenvironmental analysis. It is always easy to focus on the current environment because data is plentiful and analysis is relatively straightforward; but as the time horizon lengthens, data becomes murky and interpretations are much more difficult. Where individuals are rewarded on short-term considerations, the focus will be predominantly short term. It is therefore necessary to manage the motivational and reward schemes so that individuals are focused not merely on the short term but also on the long term.

3. **Managing linkages.**   Just like the structural factors, managing the process of linkage is important if macroenvironmental analysis is to be useful for strategy analysis. Four key issues need to be considered.

First, and perhaps most important, the macroenvironmental analysis outputs should have direct utility to the strategy problems at hand. Thus, the kind of outputs useful for corporate strategy are likely to be different from those at the business unit or functional levels. Loss of linkage results when the outputs are mismatched.

Second, and related to the above, environmental analysis outputs should be timed to fit into different planning cycles. The short, medium, and long-term characterization of environmental issues is useful for different planning horizons.

Third, the form of macroenvironmental analysis outputs should be intelligible to those engaged in strategy analysis. While environmental analysis is facilitated by the use of several methodologies and its own jargon, the outputs of these are not necessarily intelligible to those not familiar with them and thus may be ignored.

Finally, environmental issues should be given visibility at all stages of strategy analysis. The role of the linking person is often to make sure macroenvironmental issues are raised at the various stages of decision making.

4. **Evaluation of environmental analysis.**   Of particular importance to organizations where macroenvironmental analysis has been in existence as a formalized process, is the need to periodically evaluate its performance. The function of environmental analysis should be audited with a view to assessing its contribution to strategy analysis.

For example, at the analytical level, as the environment changes, previously held definitions of the environment will have to be discarded. At the organizational level, structures and processes will have to be changed, given the particular set of circumstances facing the organization. At the cultural-political level, leadership changes may necessitate that environmental analysis redefine itself and renew its legitimacy and utility.

□

BUILDING COMPETITIVE ANALYSIS INTO YOUR PLANNING PROCESS

CRAIG W. MOORE

Every manager knows how devastating competitors' moves can be, but few firms are armed with an adequate arsenal of knowledge about their competitors either to anticipate attacks or identify competitors' vulnerabilities. In our company we recognized that our "competitive analysis" consisted mostly of the uncollected casual impressions in managers' heads. So two years ago we decided to build a systematic analysis of our competitors into our planning process.

EXPLODING MYTHS ABOUT COMPETITORS

Competitive analysis demands that you not only identify and assess your competitors' strategies, but it also forces you to test the effect of your own current and potential strategies against theirs in the marketplace. In the process you're likely to discover that some of what you thought was competitive knowledge is actually mythology. In our case, for example, our strategic plans had indicated that we were following a price-leadership strategy in particular market segments, but we quickly found that our pricing policies did not comply with that strategy. Rather than being the price leader, we were actually trailing second- and third-position competitors in our pricing. These competitors were not following the pricing strategy we had attributed to them.

We also found that we were simultaneously labeling certain characteristics strengths in our organization, but weaknesses in our competitors. Similarly, the same factors we viewed as weaknesses in our company were initially considered strengths of our competitors. We saw a full product line as our strength and its absence as a weakness of our competitors. This perception prevented us from truly understanding—from the customers' perspective—where our competitive advantages lay and how to exploit them.

Overall, by systematically analyzing our competitors, we began to explode many of the organizational myths that had been obscuring a clear view of our strategic options. Then, we could start to replace the myths with factual data and tested assumptions.

Strategic Planning Management, November/December, 1983; Commerce Communications, Inc.

CREATING COMMITMENT TO COMPETITIVE ANALYSIS

Before you can strengthen your firm's competitive knowledge, the managers must, of course, recognize that their information is deficient. But this concession is not a guarantee that the organization will seek a better understanding of its competitors. Line and staff members at all levels of the organization must somehow be motivated to enhance what they know about current and potential competitors.

Many individuals in our company viewed competitive analysis as unnecessary, particularly in the near term. They continued to focus on their operational goals, although they agreed that it would be "nice," and their general attitude toward the idea of performing competitive analysis was "show me a real reason why we should to this."

To build sufficient commitment among the staff to the idea of improving competitive knowledge, we found that the following steps are essential:

1. The CEO and other senior managers must communicate their interest in—and willingness to help perform—competitive analysis.
2. One person must assume responsibility for instituting and overseeing all activities involved in competitive analysis. This person must have sufficient stature to lend organizational credibility to the whole effort.
3. Competitive analysis must be an explicitly assigned job responsibility for some line and staff members.
4. Most important, this process must focus on producing *useful* results whose value can be appreciated by those who help perform the analysis within the organization.

As the senior management team began to grapple with how we might set up a process for analyzing competitors, two central questions dominated our discussions:

1. Who should do the competitive analysis, and how should their effort be organized? and
2. What analysis should be done?

In this case, we will discuss the first of these questions.

WHO SHOULD BE INVOLVED

Because such a broad range of data must be collected and analyzed from various perspectives, it's wise to include line and staff members representing many different functions and levels in various stages of the process. We can cite three reasons for this recommendation:

1. The CEO, diverse functional managers, and various line and staff personnel can each bring useful and different perspectives and knowledge to the process.
2. If your firm has done as little competitive analysis as we had previously conducted, you'll realize that a comprehensive effort simply cannot be done by only a small team.
3. Broad-based participation yields not only better data but, ultimately, real organizational commitment to the process. This support is essential for sustaining a long-term effort.

DEVELOPING A BROAD ORGANIZATIONAL APPROACH

In designing and implementing a competitive analysis system, you can choose from a variety of approaches. In our case, the CEO called a series of senior management meetings specifically to identify and discuss these options. We outlined and debated three major options.

First, we considered appointing a task force or committee to design and coordinate the effort. But we felt that although a task force would involve many key individuals in the process, it would also entail unnecessary formality and it might not produce results as quickly as desired, because no single person would be spearheading the effort. Morever, staff members would probably resent the extra burden of being assigned to the task force, since the organization had not yet become committed to the concept.

Our second option was to assign one person the formal responsibility for the effort and then organize all participants into teams that would analyze a single competitor. As with the other approach, this option suffered from the problem that no one in the organization had experience that could help guide this kind of analysis. In addition, we recognized the likelihood of political conflicts when we would cross organizational boundaries to assemble the appropriate teams from the different functional areas.

So we settled on a third option: assigning the responsibility for guiding the process to an external consultant who had expertise in competitive analysis, and then organizing our own staff into teams to study separate competitors. The VP of Marketing and Business Development was designated as the internal "project leader."

The selection of the consultant proved to be critical to the process. In developing an approach to competitive analysis, the staff needs to be convinced that the consultant is someone capable of translating his knowledge and experience into practical products. Since any organization is generally limited in its ability to stretch and challenge its own behavior, we wanted an independent consultant to help us break out of these constraints and guide us in properly (re)structuring our thinking.

One example of how the consultant helped trigger fresh insights was in the way we assessed our sales force. We have an extremely effective sales organization that is generally credited as a strength in each market segment. Through analysis, though, we came to understand that customers did not peceive that strength in several very specific market niches. Because of our internal pride in our sales force, we had been unable to challenge and recognize that weakness. Without the consultant asking us to justify the value of a sales force in that segment, we would not have gained this insight.

DEFINING THE CONSULTANT'S ROLE

In a series of meetings, the CEO, senior management, and the consultant defined the role of the consultant as follows:

1. to lay out a range of broad alternative approaches to competitive analysis for management's consideration;
2. to work with management in developing a detailed blueprint of the chosen approach;
3. to oversee each step in the process and provide frank feedback to management; and
4. to be available to anyone engaged in the process for individual consultation and as a sounding board for ideas.

The consultant was essentially to serve as an "objective outsider" or catalyst to help participants gain insights they otherwise might not have reached. The consultant was urged to be candid and critical in the joint role as teacher and group leader.

CHOOSING THE TEAMS

As we mentioned, we decided to establish teams to conduct the analysis because of the amount of work involved. We also thought teams could speed the effort, so we could complete a first pass at competitive analysis in the five months before the beginning of the organization's next planning calendar.

Six teams were created, each comprising three to five members. We limited the number of teams, because we felt that in our first attempt to conduct formal competitive analysis, any larger might prove to be unmanageable. A marketing manager was designated as a leader for each of the teams, which included product and assistant product managers, market research staff, and other marketing and planning specialists. Manufacturing, financial, and other specialist personnel were made available to the teams on an as-needed basis. To the extent possible, team assignments were made on staff members' prior knowledge of particular competitors and business segments.

CHOOSING THE COMPETITORS

Senior management and team leaders were asked to designate competitors who might be the subjects of analysis. From their suggestions, the consultant and the project leader compiled a listing of more than twenty firms. They then met with the team leaders and some team members to choose the competitors.

Four criteria were used in making the selections. First, we wanted to study only "large players" in the industry or major segments of it. Second, any competitor should be a firm against whom we competed directly in at least one business segment, and preferably in more than one. Third, the competitors should represent a mix of product technologies prevalent or emerging in the industry. Fourth, we wanted to be sure to look at a variety of sizes and types of competitors: small emerging venture firms, divisions within large corporations, and corporations with different divisions in multiple markets that we serve.

Using these criteria, we narrowed the initial list down to about eight or ten firms that seemed especially worthy of analysis. Team leaders, as representatives of business segments, were then asked which of these firms they would most like to see analyzed and why. From their recommendations, six firms emerged as the most desired candidates for analysis.

SEMINARS ON COMPETITIVE ANALYSIS

Few of our staff members had previously been involved in any organized effort to study and predict the strategies of competitors. Moreover, preliminary discussions with various managers suggested that there was much confusion as to what competitive analysis entailed. So the consultant, in conjunction with senior management, developed three "seminars" on competitive analysis. They were designed to provide a common understanding of why competitive analysis was needed, how it should be performed, and what benefits could accrue.

The primary focus of the seminars was on what analysis should be done and how it might be done. The consultant described each broad segment of analysis, along with discussing why that analysis is considered important and how the segments of analysis fit together. (Table 6-1 identifies the analysis segment.)

Before the first seminar, the consultant met with the team leaders to give them an initial briefing, describing their roles as team leaders and what the seminars would cover, as well as answering any major questions or concerns they might have. At this meeting, it was decided that the participants should be exposed to some background reading material on competitive analysis. Michael Porter's *Competitive Analysis* (The Free Press, 1981) and three articles were immediately made available. These readings served as the basis for much discussion during the seminars.

TABLE 6-1   Competitive Analysis:
Major Analyses Segments

1. The competitor's *current* product-market strategy
2. Major recent and current strategic moves
3. Competitor's goals
4. Competitor's commitment to its strategies, markets, and the industry
5. Key assumptions of competitor
6. Key strengths/weaknesses of competitor
7. Key distinctive competencies of competitor
8. Special relationships with other entities
9. Strategic implications
10. Issues for further analysis

At this initial meeting, the group also decided that the first seminar should not take place for at least six weeks. This timing would allow the participants to familiarize themselves thoroughly with the readings, and it would also allow the teams to hold a preliminary meeting. The next two seminars would then take place a month apart.

The initial seminar was very important for several reasons. It was the first occasion when all participants came together, and it provided an opportunity for them to air all concerns about the process. (Why did we pick these competitors? What will we really learn from this process? How can we use the information gained? How does it fit into our broader strategic management activities?)

Finally, and probably most importantly, the first seminar was critical for achieving consensus on what the product would be and how that product in turn would provide dollars-and-cents value to the participants of this process.

THE SECOND SEMINAR

Six weeks after the initial seminar, a second seminar was held in which the teams provided a preliminary progress report on both the process and the emerging output. At this stage, the discussion focused on issues and problems the teams had encountered in data collection and analysis, and in drawing inferences or conclusions.

Each team made a brief presentation covering the following key points: types of data being acquired, data sources being exploited, internal and external resource persons who had been helpful in generating and interpreting data (e.g., individuals at other divisions of the corporation, sales force, distributors, customers, security analysts, etc), and the types of analyses underway.

A central data analysis problem received considerable attention. Teams had begun to experience the difficulties inherent in drawing inferences or conclusions from complex and incomplete data. It had become evident to the teams that conflicting inferences could readily be drawn from any given data set.

Three related methods of dealing with this problem were suggested by the consultant. The first approach is to carefully lay out the "logic" in the analysis (i.e., the steps involved in moving from the data to an inference or conclusion). The purpose here is to clearly indicate the rationale(s) that allows one to reach an inference from a given set of data. For example, what is the logic or rationale(s) which allows one to make connections between the competitor's financial position (e.g., cash flow, capital structure, etc.) and its capacity to launch a major marketing program?

The second method is to identify the key assumptions necessary for reaching a conclusion. Assumptions become a major component of the rationale(s) connecting data and inferences or conclusions. For example, what assumptions do we make about the competitor's ability to raise capital from external sources?

The third method is to use scenarios as a means of developing alternative interpretations of the data. Each scenario carefully lays out the logics and assumptions involved in it. This gives everyone the opportunity to critique and challenge the plausibility and likelihood of the elements within each scenario.

THE THIRD SEMINAR

The intent of the third seminar was to deal with any new problems or issues which had arisen for the teams as they did their analyses, and to flush out in some detail what their final product should look like. Most of this seminar was spent in refining many of the topics covered in the second seminar.

Particular emphasis was placed upon the need for team members to continually challenge each other—to search for data which might refute a conclusion and to develop alternate scenarios. In this way, teams could explicate and test their thinking.

In order to assist team members in the process of critically challenging each other, the consultant asked some teams to present some of their tentative conclusions and the analyses supporting them, and then "attacked" their mode of analysis and conclusions by searching for data which would not support their conclusions, developing rationales which might lead to different conclusions, and challenging their assumptions. Team members could then employ this thought process in their own group sessions.

FINAL PRESENTATIONS

The culmination of our competitive analysis efforts was a full-day meeting in which each team presented its findings to senior management, the other teams, and the consultant. The teams' final reports covered all of the items noted in Table 6-1.

In making these presentations, each team was asked to especially emphasize the strategic implications for our firm, and to support these implications with the strongest possible arguments which could be derived from their analysis.

CONCLUSION

Competitive analysis is too important to be left to chance. If you don't organize to do it, competitive analysis most likely will not be done as well as it should.

□

APPLICATION IN STRATEGIC MANAGEMENT:
Building a Competitor Analysis System
LIAM FAHEY

In recent years, competitor analysis has begun to receive significant attention in many corporations. However, firms have experienced varying degrees of success in creating systems or processes to do competitor analysis.

This report outlines an approach adopted by a division of a major corporation to build a competitor analysis system. The division had two major product lines that it sold to industrial customers. It confronted five major competitors. These firms were the focus of its initial competitor analysis efforts.

This report briefly outlines the nine major steps that were involved in getting competitor analysis off the ground.

STEP 1: ESTABLISH AUTHORITY

Senior management decided that one person would have division wide responsibility for designing and implementing the competitor analysis system. The management team felt strongly that somebody should clearly be seen to be in charge of this new activity.

To help choose the appropriate person, three criteria were established:

1. The individual should already have some familiarity with the division's principal competitors;

Strategic Planning Management, November/December, 1984; Commerce Communications, Inc.

2. The individual should have some experience in data collection and analysis;

3. The individual should have a proven capacity to work with others in different functional areas.

The person who best met these criteria was the Manager of Market Research, whom we shall refer to as the CA (competitor analysis) Manager.

He began the competitor analysis system on a part-time basis. If the benefits of the process are considered sufficient enough, a full-time position, possibly titled Manager of Competitor Analysis, may be established. (This is now under consideration by the division.)

STEP 2: ASSIGN RESPONSIBILITY

Because it was a new functional activity for the organization, management considered it imperative to lay out the specific responsibilities involved in the new part-time position.

Three primary tasks were identified:

1. To stimulate each functional area and other designated individuals to collect and forward competitor data;

2. To coordinate the collection and analysis of this data;

3. To disseminate the results of the data to senior management, the functional areas, or anybody who could use them.

STEP 3: MEET WITH FUNCTIONAL AREA HEADS

The CA Manager recognized that he alone could not do competitor analysis. He would have to work through many others to do the requisite data collection and analyses.

Through the Division President's office he arranged a meeting with all functional department heads or their representatives. The purposes of the meeting were three-fold:

1. To enhance awareness of the division's efforts to develop a competitor analysis system;

2. To solicit support for this effort; and

3. To identify specific action items which each department could initiate to better collect and analyze competitor data.

In this meeting, the CA Manager briefly outlined what he saw as the benefits for each department of being involved in competitor analysis. He also asked each department head to identify the benefits and problems they foresaw in collecting, analyzing, and using competitor data.

A major part of this meeting was devoted to describing and discussing what each department currently did in the area of competitor analysis. This discussion served a number of purposes. It showed that some competitor analysis was already being conducted—the organization would not have to start from ground zero. It also convinced those present that much more competitor analysis was required.

STEP 4: MEET WITH EACH FUNCTIONAL AREA

The general meeting with the department heads provided much of the basis for individual meetings with each department.

The key issues discussed in each meeting centered around the following questions:

1. What competitor data does each functional department require?
2. How is the data used and how might it be used in decision making?
3. Who uses it?
4. What current or potential data sources exist?
5. Who currently collects that data should collect that data?
6. What are the current or potential problems in collecting the required data?
7. How is the data currently analyzed and who should be involved in doing so?
8. What data does each department require from each of the other departments?
9. What individuals (if any) from other departments should be involved in data analysis and interpretation?

Particular emphasis was placed up with questions 1 and 2. A laundry list of key questions about competitors was developed within each functional area. Each question was then appraised as to whether the requisite data was available and how it might be used in decision making.

This appraisal process served two functions. First, it focused each department's data collection and analyzed efforts. Many questions initially on the list for each department were eliminated entirely or combined into more global questions. This occurred because many questions were largely of the nice-to-know variety.

Second, it served to emphasize the need to integrate the data into decision making. The purpose was not to collect competitor data for its own sake. Rather, the purpose was to better understand competitors and, thus, to make better decisions.

A major output of each meeting was a tentative work schedule to accomplish specific analysis tasks.

STEP 5: WORK WITH FUNCTIONAL DEPARTMENTS

In order to get the competitor analysis system off the ground, the CA Manager devoted some time to working with each functional department. He primarily concerned himself with the following issues:

1. Who should collect which data.
2. How it could be collected and analyzed; and
3. What reports could be developed.

A major focus of his early efforts with each department was to build up what competitor analysis was already taking place. The intent here was to benefit from what each department was already doing.

This required a careful documentation of what each department was doing to understand its competitors. The marketing and R&D areas paid considerable attention to competitors. However, it was not well coordinated and little of the information generated was disseminated outside of these departments.

Specific individuals were assigned data collection tasks. For example, within the R&D function, some individuals were asked to collect competitor data on different occasions or opportunities to do so: trade shows, conventions, technical meetings, etc.

Within the marketing functions, salesforce, product managers, promotions and communications managers, and the market research staff were asked to focus upon specific aspects of competitors. For example, the product managers were asked to detail the overall marketing appraisal of their top competitors for one or two product lines.

In part because of his own background, and in part because the salesforce had paid little attention to competitor intelligence, the CA Manager spent a considerable amount of time working with the regional sales managers to develop a process whereby individual members of the salesforce could collect and transmit competitor data. The salesforce was asked to pay particular attention to five items:

1. Product developments and modifications;
2. Pricing;
3. Credit terms;
4. Salesforce activity; and
5. New customer development.

Each salesperson was asked to make a brief bimonthly report to the Regional Sales Manager. They were also asked to immediately report "exceptional events" such as patented new products, major pricing changes, pursuit of new customer types, etc.

In the early stages of working with each department, the CA Manager also found himself confronted with data source problems. "What are or might be the sources of different types of data?" was a question he frequently heard. Thus, for each type of required data, the CA Manager in conjunction with department personnel identified one or more data sources. Then, to the extent possible, an individual was assigned to collect data from that source.

STEP 6: DEVELOP PARTIAL COMPETITOR PROFILE

Each department was asked to develop preliminary partial competitor profiles. These profiles were to be completed within four months of the initial meeting between the CA Manager and the department heads.

The content of these preliminary profiles varied considerably by department. This was in part because of the different focus of each department, but also in part because the CA Manager felt that each department could best answer specific types of questions about competitors.

In order to maximize the potential insight from the preliminary profiles, the CA Manager met with each department to develop an outline for the report. The outlines served to focus each department's efforts to analyze their competitors.

STEP 7: DEVELOP COMPETITOR PROFILE

Next, the CA Manager developed a complete competitor profile from the partial profiles submitted by each department.

These profiles emphasized two elements: a description of the competitor's current strategy, and likely future strategies. The future strategies were developed in scenario form. If certain things happened, the competitor's strategy would be. . .

In developing these profiles, the CA Manager worked with various members of different departments. This enabled him to get answers to questions which arose from the preliminary reports, and to test his own interpretations of all the data provided. Through these meetings, the CA Manager developed his own understanding of each competitor.

STEP 8: FEED BACK COMPETITOR PROFILES TO DEPARTMENTS

Once the CA Manager pulled together a profile of each competitor, he presented it to multiple representatives of each department in a single meeting.

The CA Manager specifically wanted to get all the functional areas together in one meeting for a number of reasons. First, he figured it would facilitate a cross-fertilization of ideas and perspectives. Second, he wanted to get each department's reaction to the competitor profiles at the same time.

Third, he hoped that the meeting would tend to better relationships among the functional areas.

As a result of this meeting, a number of changes were made in the competitor profiles. The changes were largely a result of the discussion in the general meeting.

STEP 9: FOLLOW-UP WITH THE DEPARTMENTS

These competitor profiles were regarded by everybody involved in their development as merely first pass attempts to understand competitors. Thus, the CA Manager and the department heads worked out a follow-up program to make competitor analysis an ongoing aspect of the division's activities.

The follow-up program was centered around the following:

1. Specific competitor analysis tasks;
2. Cross-departmental teams to execute these tasks; and
3. A timetable for their implementation.

APPLICATION IN STRATEGIC MANAGEMENT:
Don't Let Data Collection Bog Down Your Strategic Analysis
LIAM FAHEY

If your firm is launching its first strategic analysis effort, the task of collecting sufficient information can loom menacingly. But you do not need to begin with a gargantuan data-gathering program.

Even if your firm has much experience in conducting strategic analysis, troublesome questions about data collection and analysis are still likely to arise.

In either case, your firm probably already has more than enough data on its markets, industry, and environment to trigger creative strategic thinking. Your efforts to get real strategic analysis off the ground could get sidetracked, or even paralyzed, by an overzealous pursuit of all possible data.

Once a firm commits itself to building a more formal system for strategy analysis, it must begin helping its management team develop their strategic and operating plans based upon thorough analysis of the firm's environment, industry, market, competitors, resources, etc. Many issues quickly arise: how

Strategic Planning Management, January, 1984; Commerce Communications, Inc.

will that analysis be conducted, what kinds of insight will be gained, and how can you be sure that your line and staff will be committed to the process?

One of the biggest challenges is to decide where to compromise your "ideal" form of strategy analysis to settle for what you feel the firm can reasonably achieve, within constraints of time and resources. And one of the more critical tradeoffs involves setting standards for the quantity and quality of data to be collected and disseminated.

To offer you some guidance in establishing standards, here is an account of how one large multi-divisional firm handled these tradeoffs in its early formal strategy analysis efforts.

THE IDEAL VS. DATA AVAILABILITY

The first task was to determine what the ideal breadth and scope of the information for comprehensive strategy analysis was, and then assess how much of that data was already available or quickly obtainable.

Different executives had different opinions on how to proceed. Some thought that a major data-gathering exercise should first be conducted before formal strategy analysis could take place. Others argued that they should begin with the data available to them.

The company decided to rely largely on its existing information pool, despite some glaring gaps, for a number of reasons. It would be difficult to persuade managers to help gather more data because formal strategic planning had a poor reputation in the firm, and some managers were skeptical about the usefulness of formal strategy analysis.

Also, some senior managers were convinced that data insufficiency was not to blame for the absence of strategic thinking on the part of many managers. Rather, it was their inability or unwillingness to use the data already at their disposal.

Since the first phase of building a system for strategy analysis was designed primarily to identify key strategic issues facing each business unit, senior management believed that they could achieve this goal by depending on the judgment of managers at all levels, rather than by collecting extensive new data. So, although they acknowledged that this strategic information base was insufficient to support comprehensive and detailed strategy analysis, they could launch their analysis by identifying issues based on available information.

DATA QUALITY VS. EXPENSE

Another issue quickly presented itself. Executives in the firm generally agreed that the data quality (i.e., accuracy and reliability) left a lot to be desired. But, collecting more accurate data would involve a considerable expense.

For example, some managers contended that they did not have precise market share measurements. However, obtaining more accurate market share measurements would entail much time, effort, and expense.

Once again, senior management decided to trade off in favor of working with the existing data base, despite its defects. They would rely on managerial judgment, where in-house data was unavailable, rather than impose an immediate and large data-gathering burden on line management and staff.

By not saddling line and staff with tedious extra work, the senior managers knew they'd have a better chance of gaining their cooperation in the strategy development process. Senior management also reasoned that highly precise data wasn't essential for many of the initial tasks such as business definition, identification of current strategy, and competitors' strategies.

One manager reasoned as follows: "we seem to spend too much of our time worrying about whether we have the right data, or enough data, and too little of our time as to how we can better use the data we have." Another manager declared that if the firm was able to develop better ways of analyzing the data it had, it might not need a lot more.

Also, the executives made it clear in a number of announcements and memoranda that as the strategy analysis and development program progressed, the firm could improve its information. Indeed, one output of this first phase was to identify how best to tackle this challenge.

WIDE VS. NARROW DATA DISSEMINATION

Another tradeoff involved determining how widely or narrowly strategic information should be disseminated within the firm. Should truly "strategic" information be restricted to a few managers?

Previously, market, competitive, and environmental data had not been circulated beyond the marketing function and some senior management. Budgetary statements and financial projections had received even less circulation.

This company decided that since one of their goals was to open communication channels, so line management could help formulate strategy and develop a common understanding of the strategic thrust of the firm, they would favor wider information dissemination wherever possible.

As one manager put it, "unless we can get relevant and valid data diffused throughout the organization, we will never get multiple layers of management participating in strategy analysis."

Senior management recognized that the dangers in doing so were not trivial. Broad-based participation made information overload a real possibility, which might result in more protracted decision making.

Also, if lower levels of management had access to more information, senior management would have less decision-making leeway. Moreover, extensive sharing of information might make managers more aware of the personal risks involved in pursuing existing or potential strategies, which could make them balk at carrying out certain plans.

To ease some of these risks, a specific timetable was set for some key decisions. Managers were given deadlines for completing analyses and making their recommendations. Senior managers also agreed to provide feedback to lower-level managers within certain time periods.

MAKING USE OF DATA

Based upon the experience of this firm, a few points are worth emphasizing about collecting and using strategic information.

First, if you want your formal strategy analysis to promote insightful and creative strategic thinking, the way you manage the analysis effort is critical. If you begin by burdening managers with a huge data collection task, the analysis is likely to bog down under its own weight. The participants will focus more on completing their documentation and meeting deadlines than engaging in challenging and innovative thinking.

Second, you should not try to move too quickly. You should probably avoid setting high expectations—they will likely result in frustrated participants. If you encourage individuals to learn on the job, as they collect and analyze data, draw inferences from the data and think about their implications, they will better understand what data gaps exist, which data voids they should try to remedy, and how to go about doing so.

Third, you need to realize that merely collecting and disseminating information is not your goal. Exposing individuals to new information does not automatically mean that they will pounce on that data to do more and better analysis or engage in more insightful and creative thinking.

You'll need to set up mechanisms to facilitate and support creative strategic analysis. Consider using methods such as brainstorming, scenario development, playing devil's advocate, taking time out to develop your own strategic "think-tank," or taking managers away for off-site strategy development.

These processes may be as important—or even more so—than simply making data more generally available, especially in your early efforts to do more formal strategy analysis.

After all, producing useful results right from the start will help you to generate and sustain long-term commitment to and interest in strategic analysis.

CHAPTER

— 7 —

STRATEGY UNDER DIFFERENT ENVIRONMENTAL CONDITIONS: FITTING STRATEGY TO THE MARKET AND INDUSTRY CONTEXT

■

☐

STRATEGIES FOR STAGNANT BUSINESSES

JOEL A. DYSART

If your company's businesses are in embryonic, high-growth markets such as genetic engineering, you can skip this case. But if you have to worry about a business that is "stagnant," read on.

In the go-go days of the 1960s and 1970s, we were told that gaining long-range success was as easy as filling the corporate portfolio with businesses that have strong competitive positions in fast-growing markets. If only it were this easy!

Our disinflating economy has dampened the growth prospects of many industries. And many corporations are beginning to question how much competitive edge they have relative to overseas competition. But what happened to

Strategic Planning Management, January, 1983; Commerce Communications, Inc.

the businesses that were lackluster performers in the 60s and 70s? Were they all liquidated by aggressive corporate managers?

WHAT'S A STAGNANT BUSINESS?

A stagnant business will have many, if not all, of the following characteristics:

- *Slow growth and low returns* over a long period of time.
- *Undifferentiated,* commodity-like products nearly indistinguishable from those of competitors.
- *Equal market power among competitors* where business can be moved on price, but market share shifts are minuscule. Competitors quickly retaliate to price reductions because of:
  1. *Approximately equal manufacturing costs among competitors* because all producers have achieved production scale economies; consequently, transportation costs are often more crucial to the purchase decision.
  2. *Slowly-evolving product and process technologies* that are well understood by competitors and customers alike.
  3. *Low entry and exit activity in the businesses* where no one is getting into the business and those in it can't or won't get out.
  4. *Strong impact from economic cycles* where in booms, the business is just O.K. and in recessions, things become "awful" fast.
  5. *Uniform management policies and practices among competitors* which are usually heavily rooted in "tradition."

THE TROUBLE WITH STAGNANT BUSINESSES

In fact, stagnant businesses are still found in abundance in corporate portfolios. In many corporations, the portfolio is dominated by the original, or "core," business which is now stagnant. Top management is naturally reluctant to divest a business that accounts for a large proportion of revenue and profits.

Some corporations only operate in a single stagnant business and are then trapped in their circumstances. In other cases business may possess a strong sentimental attachment to the business, which they repeatedly give "one last chance" to return to prominence in the portfolio.

Some stagnant businesses are now so unattractive that the corporation cannot find a buyer. Outright liquidation might entail large write-offs which most CEOs are loathe to take; better, they say, that we just hold onto the business and let it limp along.

Finally, some stagnant businesses are passed along with other more valuable assets in corporate mergers. Only the most aggressive acquirers dispose of the declining businesses almost immediately.

If they haven't been divested, stagnant businesses are often shoved into the "backwaters" of the corporate portfolio where they drift until they dissolve. These corporate pariahs receive no investment of money, people, or management attention. Young ambitious managers quickly learn to avoid these businesses, lest they jeopardize their career aspirations.

Interestingly, all industry participants may be treating these businesses in the same fashion—particularly if the competitors are all large corporations with diverse portfolios.

This neglect, then, presents an opportunity. If all industry participants are virtually ignoring the stagnant businesses, your corporation may have an excellent chance to stimulate its neglected segment into becoming a better performer. You may have an excellent investment opportunity because no one else in the industry is willing to put anything into the business.

However, to gain ground in a stagnant business, *your management must be able to shift the competitive balance in the industry,* which is a difficult feat.

PRUNING FOR PROFITABILITY

Stringent expense controls are typically one of the first remedies employed to improve returns in a business that is beginning to stagnate. As profits begin to slip, managers focus on tightening expenses because they suspect that the build-up of organizational "fat" is the main culprit in reducing their profits.

Organizations do tend to gain weight over time. And cost-reduction measures can improve returns quickly. But these benefits are mainly temporary.

In their efforts to "cut out the frills," companies often eliminate staff analysts first. But the loss of these analytical capabilities and the possible dilution in overall management talent merely accelerates the decline rather than removing the causes of the downslide.

A more effective approach entails pruning the business's product portfolio. In this case, management cuts out any products or ancillary services that aren't pulling their own weight financially.

Narrowing the product line can dramatically improve your returns since it increases profitability while reducing investment. This disinvestment approach actually represents a shift of business strategy that is often referred to as a "niche" or "focus" strategy.

The most common shortcoming in the way managers prune the product portfolio is just that they rarely go far enough. Top management is too often easily swayed by the argument that a broad product line is necessary to compete in the market.

Consider the case of a catalog retailer whose sales had stagnated even while the direct mail retail industry was growing at a fairly good rate. The company was a "full-line" catalog house carrying everything from fashion apparel to office furniture. Sales were generated by three channels: mail, phone, and catalog order stores. The catalog stores contributed 40% of total volume.

Managers had consistently worked on keeping costs down, and the organization was considered relatively lean. While the managers recognized that certain merchandise lines were only marginally profitable, all lines did contribute something to overhead.

Management was convinced that the catalog store channel produced most of the firm's profits and that catalog stores gave them a local presence that was necessary to compete with their department store and discount chain counterparts. But nothing could have been further from the truth.

The fact that a major attraction of any mail-order business is that it offers customers the convenience of shopping without going to a store contradicted these managers' belief that their walk-in catalog stores were their primary profit producer. Closer analysis revealed that maintaining the catalog stores had resulted in duplicate operating systems, personnel, and merchandise-handling activities. In fact, the stores were actually *un*profitable.

After much debate, a new management team was put in place to restructure the business. Many merchandise lines were eliminated and others were scaled back significantly. The catalog-order stores were closed over a period of 18 months.

After nearly five years of massive restructuring, this business has regained its growth momentum and is much more profitable. As an aside, many of the catalog store customers were converted to mail and phone-order shoppers by the company's carefully planned promotions. In some areas where catalog stores were closed, sales even increased!

So pruning the business is often a strategic approach that allows for higher growth and profits by focusing the firm's resources on a few areas where the chances for success are highest.

But what about businesses that offer only a single product? How can competitive balance be shifted in an industry where all competitors focus on the same product?

DIS-INTEGRATING THE BUSINESS

A much more ticklish strategy is to "dis-integrate" the business—that is, to divest certain portions of the business that do not produce a competitive advantage in the marketplace.

This strategic approach will always be met by high levels of resistance by management. After all, tampering with vertical integration attacks the basic "way the industry works."

After all, vertical integration did not develop accidentally. During an industry's growth phase, there are a lot of good reasons for companies to integrate vertically backward (to raw materials procurement) and/or forward (to the end-user customer). Here are some of the good reasons for integration:

- If raw materials are in short supply, obtaining an assured source offers a competitive advantage in meeting a growing market demand.
- If competent suppliers of components cannot be found, a firm may be forced to manufacture nearly all of the product's components.
- If the product's application is highly technical, the company may need to maintain its own highly-trained sales representatives to market the product.

While these factors might have been critical at one time, they may no longer be valid in a mature industry.

For example, many forest products companies have been divesting themselves of timberlands and sawmills. Owning the source of raw materials was once a strong competitive advantage in this industry where prime hardwoods and softwoods were required for making building products. But today the industry technology has evolved to the point where scrap lumber and sticks can be used to manufacture the product.

Divesting timberlands and sawmills, therefore, has allowed these companies to redirect funds into more profitable endeavors, and shareholder returns will likely improve over time. However, it remains to be seen if these companies can improve their competitive position as well.

One often overlooked area of opportunity for dis-integration is the marketing function—that is, to use independent distributors or manufacturers' representatives instead of the company's own sales force. A direct sales force somehow seems to give managers greater comfort in dealing with the marketplace, perhaps because they're reluctant to relinquish total control of distribution of the product from the manufacturer's dock to the customer's door.

It seems odd that managers pay attention to economies of scale in manufacturing but only infrequently investigate this phenomenon in their selling operations. Clearly there are marketing scale economies, both in personnel and sales promotion.

However, these economies can be eroded as a business matures. What was once a technical product may now be well understood by customers. In some industries, customers might even have a better grasp of the technology than producers.

One thing is for certain: the impact of inflation on selling costs never abates. If a business cannot pass these rising costs on to the customers via price increases, the direct selling organization will be slowly rendered uneconomic.

Shifting to independent distribution may result in both cost savings and increased market power. It is important to understand that this is a high-risk strategy that should be carefully analyzed and planned. The critical factors for success are to choose the most powerful distributors available and then build a strong relationship between the manufacturer and the sales representative.

This strategic move can result in several benefits:

- Selling costs can be lowered dramatically, giving the manufacturer a clear cost advantage over competitors even though their production costs tend to be nearly equal.
- You can enhance your competitive power and ability to respond quickly to market changes by using local distributors who can more effectively service customers in this area. Also, distributors are frequently hungrier for new business than their salaried counterparts in direct selling organizations.
- The manufacturer may be better insulated from the sharp economic cycles that tend to go hand-in-hand with stagnant businesses. Entrepreneurs simply respond more swiftly and effectively when their personal income is threatened.

Vertical dis-integration is one of the more daring strategic moves. In fact, it may be more daring than total divestiture. But if you've reached the end of your rope with a stagnant business, it may be worthwhile to ask yourself the following set of questions about whether you should consider restructuring the business.

1. Are all of our assets in this business contributing to a competitive advantage? Would we really be at a competitive *dis*advantage without them?
2. Could we find competent suppliers of our component parts? Do we really achieve a cost advantage from manufacturing rather than buying outside?
3. Is our power in the marketplace enhanced by the full range of products we sell? Is it hard (and costly) for our customers to switch suppliers?
4. What is the advantage we gain from having our own direct sales force? If we eliminated some portion of our product line, could we still afford direct sales?

These general questions may give you a better insight into why your business is stagnant and what leverage you can use to change its fortunes.

CONCLUSION

Today many top executives seem enamored with major acquisitions and divestitures. No doubt these are exciting to execute and in some cases produce powerful new enterprises. In contrast, stagnant businesses seem dull and appear vastly inferior to their faster-growing counterparts in the corporate portfolio.

But in general, corporate management may be giving up too easily on stagnant businesses. Some of the success stories of the '80's may well be about firms that have successfully come to grips with their stagnant businesses, finding ways to make them more productive and profitable.

STRATEGIES FOR SMALL-SHARE FIRMS IN MATURE MARKETS

STANLEY F. STASCH AND JOHN L. WARD

The vast majority of all firms or product lines ultimately face the difficult question of how to cope with no better than second position in a mature or soon-to-be mature market. For many firms, this situation arrives much more quickly than they would like. While small-share firms in mature markets are often quite profitable, many of them feel boxed-in by their larger-share competitors.

Conventional wisdom, however, suggests that two basic strategies can lead to share increases for small-share firms in mature markets.

- Invest selectively in fast growth market segments; and/or
- Seek and develop specialized niches with a highly differentiated offering.

These two broad strategies offer some hope for small-share firms in mature markets through the marketing strategies of *segmentation* and/or *differentiation*. The purpose of this case is to develop in greater detail the *marketing tactics* and *competitive circumstances* of firms which have successfully implemented one or both of these broad strategies.

REFINING THE GROWTH DIFFERENTIATION STRATEGIES

Among the small-share companies in mature markets that we have studied, the following three strategy elements or factors have substantially contributed to market share gains.

1. Their strategies included some effort to maximize the *competitive differentiation* between themselves and their competitors.
2. Their strategies were ones which tended either to *minimize or avoid competitive response.*
3. They developed a *significant distribution* "advantage" to help secure their accomplishment.

Strategic Planning Management, July/August, 1984; Commerce Communications, Inc.

Each successful firm we have studied exploited at least two (and occasionally all three) of these factors. This suggests that, to be successful, small share firms in mature markets probably must do more than just pursue either one or both of the two basic strategies of seeking growth segments or developing differentiated products.

It is our contention that the above three factors are "refinements" to the two basic strategies, and that these refinements are as important as the two basic strategies themselves. In fact, it seems that success is more likely to be assured as more of these "refinements" are incorporated into the "growth segment-differentiated niche" strategies.

STRATEGIES TO MAXIMIZE COMPETITIVE DIFFERENTIATION

Rarely will much be gained if a small-share firm only duplicates, or copies, the success formula used by the dominant competitor. The small-share firm is much more likely to attract the attention of consumers and distributors by creating points of difference between itself and its major competitors. It can do so in at least three ways.

1. Create Strong Brand Identity

In virtually every case we studied, the small competitor went to considerable expense and determined effort to develop a brand name which became identified with the product form and/or with the highest quality. Successful examples of building a brand name to be synonymous with newer product forms include Miller's Lite (for a type of beer known as "light"), Mr. Coffee (for a new type of coffee brewing device), Perrier (for naturally carbonated mineral water), and BIC (for inexpensive, disposable ball point pens).

2. Develop a New Product Form

A number of the successful cases we studied involved the introduction of a new product form—disposable pens, light beer, etc. A new product form can make existing products look obsolete to consumers. Also, at the very least, new product forms can undermine existing brand loyalties. New product forms may out-date the existing production systems of the dominant competitors, thus requiring considerable product and manufacturing research which is both expensive and time consuming.

Examples of new product forms include Johnson and Johnson's *non-aspirin* Tylenol, Quaker Oats' Tender Chunks *soft-dry, complete meal* dog food, and Polaroid's *instant* photography. Lorillard offered Kent Golden Lights as a cigarette with only *8 milligrams* of tar at a time when no other cigarette brands were being offered in the range of 5–10 milligrams of tar.

3. Change the "Rules of the Game"

The rules of the game can be changed by introducing new and different competitive variables into the industry's traditional marketing mix. If a firm can make a significant and effective change in its marketing relative to the industry's traditional marketing practices, it may create a difference which competitors will not immediately duplicate because (a) they don't think it will succeed, (b) it's not easy to change "traditional thinking" in a short time, and/or (c) they are unable to do so except at great expense.

One of the most successful examples of this strategy is Hanes' marketing of hosiery (L'eggs) as a consumer package good on consignment with direct distribution through food and drug stores. It was the first time a major competitor made a serious attempt to employ this strategy. Once it became established in these channels, competitors found it difficult to duplicate L'eggs' strategy.

Heublein led the way in changing the nature of whiskey marketing from a "price and distribution" orientation to a "promotion" orientation. They were the first to use heavy advertising to create brand awareness and a favorable brand image for their Smirnoff vodka that would permit the company to charge premium—rather than equivalent—prices. This strategy's success is evident from the fact that Smirnoff became the #1 brand among all alcoholic brands.

STRATEGIES TO MINIMIZE LIKELIHOOD OF COMPETITIVE RESPONSE

If a small-share firm can successfully employ one or more of the three foregoing strategies to create a noticeable and effective difference between itself and its competitors, it will have made a good start toward increasing its market share. However, the firm can further improve its position if it also takes steps to minimize the likelihood of a competitive response. There seem to be at least three ways this can be done.

1. Be First to Vigorously Enter a New Growth Segment

A firm has a better chance of capturing a sizeable share of a growth segment if it establishes itself in the segment while it is either unnoticed or too small to attract the attention of important competitors.

Heublein was one of the first to recognize the trend toward increased consumption of light and "white" liquors, due in part to changing demographics—more young drinkers in the late 1960s and the 1970s. Heublein devoted considerable resources to its Smirnoff vodka, and exploited this light trend by promoting a number of drinks such as Bloody Marys and Screwdrivers.

Other successful examples of firms capitalizing early on the trend to "lightness" in beverages include Miller's Lite and Perrier. Lorillard's Kent

Golden Lights was the first to exploit the trend toward low-tar cigarettes by aggressively going after that segment, and L'eggs success was due in part to their recognition that there was a small but growing trend of sales of women's hosiery through supermarkets.

2. Compete Against Many Products to Avoid Direct Competition Counterattack

Probably one of the fortunes for Lorillard's Kents, Miller's Lite and Heublein's Smirnoff was that their gains came at the expense of many competitors—each losing only a scarcely noticeable amount. The small-share firm that competes in this manner may be graced with a period of "competitive peace" which will allow its brand to become established. One way a small share firm can avoid a direct counterattack is to seek situations in which it can take sales away from a number of competitors who each market a number of different brands.

Successful examples of firms competing against many products include Hanes' L'eggs (who competed against many small unadvertised private brands of hosiery being sold in food and drug stores), Mr. Coffee's coffeemaker (who competed against many producers of various coffeemakers), Vlasic's pickles (who expanded from regional supplier to national supplier by frequently displacing a small, local brand of pickle from the retailers' shelves), and Perrier (who essentially competed against many small, little-known brands of mineral water). Even Miller's Lite probably took sales away from the various brands of all breweries, rather than from only one or two brands.

3. Compete Where Competitors Fear Their Response Might Hurt Them More Than You

The strong, established competitors to Bic's stick pen, to Hanes' L'eggs, and to Quaker Oat's Tender Chunks had to be hoping that those new product forms would not attain market acceptance. Each was taking share, and profits, from a mature product form and from a different production and or distribution system. If the established competitors aided in the market development of the new segment and form, they would cannibalize their own well-established products and be forced into costly new production and distribution efforts.

Such inactivity on the part of big competitors can give the small-share firm time to consolidate its new production and distribution systems and to establish its brand in the market place. For the market leaders, it's a heads-you-win, tails-I-lose situation—at least until they ultimately forge a significant powerful response. Two particular types of product concepts can create this dilemma for the established leader: *disposable* products and *"straddle"* products. The market leaders would prefer not to switch over to a disposable product, because it is likely to require an entirely different production system while yielding a smaller per unit profit margin. Bic's disposable pen caused such a dilemma for Scripto, Paper Mate, and others. Quaker Oats' soft-dry, complete meal dog food competed with canned dog food because of its lower price and with dry dog food because of its additional benefits.

A new product form which successfully "straddles" two established product categories by offering the best of both in one product form (such as Tender Chunks) also creates the same dilemma for the established competitors. They must broaden their product line and develop a brand preference that will take more sales from their existing products than from the smaller competitor. "Straddling" also has the advantage of competing against several products or brands, as discussed earlier.

STRATEGIES USING DISTRIBUTION TO SECURE AN EARLY ADVANTAGE

In a number of the cases studied, distribution became important to the long-term defense and exploitation of a growing market segment or differentiated product niche. Such distribution strength was developed in two ways.

1. Provide Distributors With a Full, Relatively Broad Product Line

Independent distributors tend to want a full product line in order to maximize the returns from their efforts. From the firm's viewpoint, a full line helps a firm maintain distributors' loyalty due to the larger sales volume accruing from the line. Certainly a full line makes it more difficult for competitors to tag onto your distributors or to capture retailer shelf space left vacant due to an incomplete line.

Heublein provided its distributors with a line of vodka brands in addition to Smirnoff. Other examples where a small-share firm offered its distributors a more full line relative to competitors were Vlasic, BIC, and Miller Brewing.

2. Control Your Own Distribution

Both Hanes and Entenmann's developed their own direct distribution and in-store display management. Once established, competitors found it extremely difficult to overcome these distribution methods. As a result, these methods provided the small share firms with a solid basis for defending their market gains.

CONCLUSION

Successful strategies for small-share competitors in established markets are not simple or accidental. It is not enough merely to seek high growth or specialized market segments. You need to systematically investigate how you can attain and defend your position in these market niches. The strategies discussed in this article may be a useful starting point in this analysis.

☐

ENTRY STRATEGIES IN EMERGING MARKETS
TERI LOUDEN

Emerging markets are the frontier regions of business, where the rules of the competitive game are not yet established. Projecting growth and the direction of an emerging market is a demanding task requiring a systematic evaluation of many facets of the emerging market. Particular attention must be paid to the peculiarities of these markets in comparison to established markets.

Before you commit your organization to entering an emerging market, you should carefully analyze the following:

1. broad environmental forces that are shaping the emerging market;
2. the key characteristics of the market segments;
3. market segment potential;
4. the strategies of current and likely competitors;
5. distribution channels; and
6. the organization's resource base.

Only when you have conducted this analysis are you in a position to determine your entry strategy. Of course, if you are already in a segment of the emerging market, this analysis will be helpful as you assess your organization's performance. The first four elements above are discussed in this case. The home health care industry is a current example of an emerging market and provides the focus for much of our discussion. We begin by addressing some of the peculiarities of emerging markets.

PECULIARITIES OF EMERGING MARKETS

Like other frontiers, emerging markets can be defined as terrains of high risk yet high potential reward. In general, emerging markets are characterized by a lack of hard data in comparison to more established markets. This greatly limits the use of traditional market analysis techniques and market share and growth estimates. There is typically much uncertainty about the future direction of the market, what firms are likely to enter the market, and what strategies they may pursue. Further, there is great variance among products and services as the entering firms struggle to establish product and technology standards and market leadership. Emerging markets also often lack established channels of supply and distribution.

Strategic Planning Management, May and June, 1984; Commerce Communications, Inc.

The adventuresome firm entering an emerging market faces an array of risks that further complicate planning efforts: risk of investing in obsolete technology; risk of confusing consumers with new products; and risk of confronting regulators. In the emerging home health care industry, a major source of risk is the government and third-party insurance reimbursement structure. Changes in the kinds of products and services that can be reimbursed can drastically affect a company's position in this emerging industry.

ENVIRONMENTAL FORCES INFLUENCING THE MARKET

The first questions to address are what environmental forces are helping to shape the emerging industry, and how are they influencing the emergence of the industry? In the case of home health care, demographic, technological, political/economic, and social/psychological forces have each contributed to the rapid growth of this industry segment.

Demography: as the number of people aged 65 and older increases in the population, there is a greater need for long-term care and support services for home based elderly and their families. Also, the greater proportion of the aging population is women, which further impacts the kinds of products and services needed.

Technology: computer science, miniaturization, and other electronics advances make home health care feasible by creating easy-to-use, inexpensive products which may be used outside of a hospital setting (e.g., inexpensive and easy-to-use home feeding pumps). Future technological devices such as home telemetry will also impact the home health care market.

Political/Economic: the demand for cost control in health care creates opportunities for low-cost alternatives. The deficit in the Medicare trust fund has compelled the government to institute a new rate structure for reimbursing hospitals and physicians. These new, flat rates create incentives to move people out of their high-cost facilities as soon as they are able—or risk carrying them at a loss. Home care provides an attractive alternative to costly in-patient care.

Social/Psychological: a combination of fitness and health awareness, plus the strong preference to avoid institutionalization has generated a market need for home health care goods and services. The combination of these environmental influences has in effect created the home health care market segment. An analysis of broad environmental forces such as these will indicate whether the market is likely to be longlasting or merely a fad. You now need to turn to what is actually happening in the market.

UNDERSTANDING THE MARKET SEGMENT

The choice of market entry mode is strongly dependent upon an understanding of the evolution of the market segment to date, and an assessment of the path of its future evolution. One useful point of departure here is to identify and assess how various players in the industry have responded to the environmental forces shaping the emergence of the industry segment.

In home health care, for example, hospitals are now integrating forward with home care and with offsite facilities for physical therapy and geriatric care. The large hospital supply companies are attempting to serve the new markets through a variety of high tech home care therapies such as antibiotic therapies. Retail franchise drug stores are already expanding their services to include sales and rental of home health care equipment and supplies.

A systematic approach to segment analysis is required to help focus your firm's efforts to the precise market niche(s) it hopes to serve. An analysis of the home health care industry segment could include the following elements: type of disease treated, type of treatment, types of products or services, and who the decision maker is. Here is a delineation of this breakdown:

Addressing the market by type of disease:

- specialization in cancer treatment products and services (e.g., chemotherapy)
- specialization in diabetes care (e.g., home insulin pumps)
- specialization in kidney disease care (e.g., home dialysis)
- other disease-specific products and services

Addressing the market by type of treatment:

- diagnostic products such as home testing kits (e.g., pregnancy, blood pressure, diabetes)
- preventive medicine products (e.g., exercise equipment products)
- acute care products (e.g., traditional home care, post hospital care)
- maintenance (treatment) products (e.g., hospice pain unit, daily living support devices)
- delivery of health care services (e.g., nursing, therapy, housekeeping)
- delivery of health care supplies and equipment (e.g., manufacture of items and/or delivery through appropriate distribution systems)

Addressing the market by who the decision maker is:

- medical focus: health care referred by the physician
- wellness focus: consumers are the decision maker

The primary output of this analysis is the identification of possible market segment opportunities. You must now assess the potential of these opportunities.

ASSESSING MARKET SEGMENT POTENTIAL

Because of the previously noted characteristics of emerging industries, assessing the potential of individual market niches is difficult at best. Forecasts of market growth, product acceptance, and competitors' responses must be treated with caution. You must carefully monitor evolution of the emerging industry to verify the reliability and accuracy of such forecasts. For example, while the home health care market is predicted to accelerate in growth due to the previously discussed forces, the lack of physicians' acceptance could greatly reduce projected growth.

COMPETITIVE ANALYSIS IN EMERGING MARKETS

In the absence of attention to competitors, the market potential in emerging industries often looks enticing. However, when competition's actions and responses are taken into account, the industry segment often looks considerably less attractive. You need to address the following questions on competition:

- Who are the firms you are most likely to take on in head-to-head competition? Who will the other competitors be in specific segments?
- If they are already in the emerging market segments you wish to enter, what are their strategies?
- If they have not already entered, what are their strategies likely to be?

Competitive information is difficult to obtain in emerging markets. As such, you have to be prepared to make decisions based on educated guesses about your competitors. Other questions on competitors include:

1. What is the structure of the emerging industry segment (e.g., fragmented or concentrated)?
2. Can one or a few firms dominate the industry segment?
3. Are new entrants coming in horizontally in diversification moves? or,
4. Are they entering vertically, in a move to integrate forward or backward into the emerging industry?

In home health care, hospitals and product companies are entering the new market from different angles. Hospitals are integrating vertically into home care, extending their existing patient care services outside of the institution. Meanwhile companies like Servicemaster are integrating horizontally into home care—applying their experience in hospital housekeeping services to the delivery of home health care services.

Because competitive information is especially difficult to obtain in the early stages of an emerging market, it is imperative that you identify the competitors *as soon as they enter the market.* To do so, you may have to develop relationships with customers, distributors, suppliers, and/or industry experts or observers; these sources of information can alert you to new market entrants. Once you have identified these entrants, you can then begin to track their behavior.

Once the above analysis has been conducted, you need to match these conclusions with your firm's own evaluation criteria, e.g., how much risk are you willing to take, how much are you willing to invest, and what can you afford to lose.

DISTRIBUTION CHANNEL ANALYSIS

Once you have identified a promising emerging market, a major area to be addressed is which channels you will use to serve the markets you have selected. This includes selecting the distribution channels and the appropriate advertising, promotion, and service activities.

One of the significant trends in home health care is the emergence of mail order as a means of distributing products. Even an established firm in the health care industry seeking to directly market its products through mail order may have difficulty in adjusting to this channel if it has not had direct experience with this form of distribution. Another major way to reach most emerging markets is of course through retailing. It provides the most effective, though not necessarily the most efficient, means of reaching the mass market. Manufacturers seeking to integrate forward into retailing may be surprised to learn some of the problems involved. The cost of recruiting and maintaining a retail sales force has surprised many firms. Also, firms entering retailing through forward integration often find themselves competing with their former suppliers and customers. Thus, they often face retaliation in the marketplace. A firm launching such an integration must carefully identify how it will be able to withstand such stiff competition: how well it will be able to respond to likely competitive moves. This is where the previously discussed competitive analysis is highly relevant. Often, emerging industries or industry segments manifest distribution channel peculiarities. For example, in the personal computer industry quite different distribution channels have evolved compared to those employed in the more established mainframe industry segment.

In home health care, understanding the referral network which underlies the distribution channels is essential. Today, as in the past, the physician is the primary source of patient referral to outside sources of home health care products and services. But in the increasingly decentralized home health market, anyone at any level of care may be an important referral source—discharge planners, nurses, social workers, hospital staff, and especially friends and family members. These multiple sources make the task of marketing a product or service quite complex. Solving the problem is based on developing a marketing strategy that responds to the structure of the segments you wish to serve, as well as a strategy that reflects an understanding of the information flows within the segments.

RESOURCE ANALYSIS

Even though you have identified an emerging market with substantial potential, and you have carefully assessed the current and likely competition and the distribution channels to reach the market, a most critical question still remains: does your organization possess the resource base to successfully establish competitive advantages and sustain its position in the marketplace as the emerging market grows and matures?

Perhaps the single most important issue is whether your firm has or can develop the necessary competencies to succeed in the emerging market. Again, this is a difficult question because of the uncertainties and peculiarities inherent in emerging markets. However, as in other markets, shirking from this question could be suicidal.

Market, competitive, and distribution analysis provide indicators as to required competencies. Market analysis indicates what customers want: product characteristics, service levels, price levels, etc. Competitive analysis indicates what competitors are doing and how they may resond to your moves. Distribution analysis indicates what you have to do to establish and sustain means of getting your products or services to your customers. You must then assess whether you have or can attain the resources to create and maintain these competencies.

Another central element in performing resource analysis is determining what level of risk your firm is willing to accept to enter an emerging market. Given the uncertainties in entering an emerging market, the risks involved may be substantially greater than entering more established markets.

Thus, your organization must identify and assess these risks. If it does not, it may lose more than its financial investment. You would hurt the image of your firm in its industry, and thereby make it difficult to raise capital and/or undertake other ventures. There is also an opportunity cost: investing in risky ventures consumes valuable resources that could be invested elsewhere.

A most important factor in assessing the degree of risk you are willing to accept is knowing what your firm's capabilities or competencies are, both in terms of technical skill and managerial ability. Frequently, firms discover they have particular competencies that will not help them succeed in an emerging market. Having the right people is crucial to entering an emerging market. A firm can take much greater risks if it knows its people have the abilities, the entrepreneurial spirit, and the flexibility it takes to succeed in a new market.

CHOOSING THE ENTRY STRATEGY

The purpose of the above analysis is to help choose the most appropriate mode of entry into the emerging market. We shall discuss five different entry strategies.

1. Ownership/Internal Development

This is the most direct way to enter an emerging market. Here the firm assumes all the risk, but reaps all the reward. In home health care, a hospital integrating forward to open its own durable medical equipment (DME) retail sales and rental store is an example of entry through internal development.

The key concerns in pursuing an ownership strategy are the extent and cost of capital for start-up, the costs of carrying inventory, and the experience of the firm or institution in the new market. In this case, a major problem for a hospital entering the DME business would be generating and maintaining a sales volume high enough to justify continued presence in the market.

In this mode of entry, firms often assume they have the appropriate competencies or can easily attain them. This sometimes proves not to be the case. Therefore, you need to carefully identify the requisite competencies and challenge those who assert the organization already has them or can easily acquire them.

2. Acquisition

This is another method of forward integration where some of the risk is relieved by acquiring an existing company with experience and expertise in the new field. An example from home health care might be where a diversified health care firm acquires a DME company to add to its portfolio of products and services.

Major issues of concern with this option are management capability and valuation of the acquired firm. A firm seeking to enter an emerging market may need all the help it can get from the existing management of an acquired firm. On the other hand, the firm may see itself as better off installing its own management team. Putting an economic value on firms is particularly difficult in emerging markets. You must apply both your financial and accounting skills to determine the firm's current and potential value. The value of the firm will be highly influenced by your estimate of market size and growth, the competencies of the firm, and its capacity to reach the market. You may pay a premium to acquire a firm that will not show bottom line benefits in the short-term, but will pay off in the long-term.

3. Joint Ventures

In cases where the firm seeks to share the risk with another party, a joint venture provides a method of entry into an emerging market. There are many different ways to execute a joint venture, from complete "partnership" (sharing of risk and reward), to mere informal affiliation agreements.

A joint venture is sometimes the only way many firms can enter an emerging market. They simply do not have the resources to go it alone. Thus, suppliers or manufacturers and distributors frequently enter into joint ventures to gain an early foothold in an emerging market.

The key advantage of a joint venture is that it can marry complementary firms in such a way that efficiencies are gained for both firms. Joint ventures can also serve to bring competing firms together for mutually beneficial, cooperative efforts.

An example would be a home health care DME company seeking to establish a joint venture with a hospital. The former could be a supplier of products to the hospital's home health care system, with access to a steady pool of patient clients. The latter would maintain its integration into home health care with the benefit of controlled supply of products and services for the market, and quality check on the operation.

4. Contract Management

This method involves hiring an outside firm to come in and run an aspect of your business which relates to an emerging market. Contract management allows a firm to diversify into a new area without the problems entailed in operating the entire program itself. This means it can have a presence in the market, yet enjoy the experience and scale economies that an outside firm brings, with very quick entry into an emerging market.

Contract management allows market entry with minimal demand upon the firm's resources. This mode of entry often allows a firm to quickly learn about an emerging market at the same time that it is participating in the market.

The disadvantages are the lack of direct control over the program and the sharing of rewards with the contracted firm. However, since early entry is often so crucial for establishing competitive advantage in emerging markets, contract management can pay off in the long run as an entry strategy.

Again, an example is a hospital contracting out to another firm to come in and operate its home health care program.

5. Franchise

This is a method for a firm that has attained success in one region to create a broader presence in the marketplace. When the firm finds that its products or services can be standardized, it can license qualified franchisees to take on the "local" risk.

In this mode of entry, you may need to move very quickly if you have already attained success in one region; it is quite likely that word of your success will spread. If your product or service can be replicated, an entrepreneur or an organization seeking to expand its products or services may beat you to the market place.

Franchising allows a firm to establish precise criteria of quality and investment while permitting penetration of new geographic areas. In home health care, establishment of franchised retail outlets that rent and sell home health care equipment and supplies, and provide nursing services, are already well underway.

An important final note. You need to remember that the standard measures of success for investment, such as ROI, profitability, and stock value may not apply to emerging markets in the short term. An entry method that seems undesirable in the short term could have significant payoffs in the longer term. This trade-off becomes critical where significant strategic leverage can be gained by entering the market as early as possible.

CONCLUSION

The task of evaluating emerging markets is a complex one, requiring a keen sense of the changes and opportunities in the marketplace. Skillful analysis demands staying in close touch with the market and establishing good sources to give you the information you need to determine your initial strategy and modify it as circumstances change.

□

STRATEGIES FOR BUSINESS TURNAROUNDS
CHARLES W. HOFER

For one reason or another, entire firms or major parts of their product portfolio sometimes go into a tailspin: sales decline precipitously, profits may disappear altogether, and cash flows may become negative. That part of your business which has experienced this kind of performance decline faces three options: continued marginal performance, liquidation, or turnaround.

This case addresses the last of these options, turnaround strategies. It suggests that there are distinct stages in the turnaround process, and that one must distinguish between the strategic and operating health of the business.

Strategic Planning Management, July/August, 1983; Commerce Communications, Inc.

THE MAJOR STAGES OF THE TURNAROUND PROCESS

Although the terms used may differ, almost all those who have studied turnarounds identify four or five stages in the process. These are:

Stage 1: Management Change
Stage 2: Situation Diagnosis and Strategy Selection
Stage 3: Emergency Action
Stage 4: Stabilization
Stage 5: Return-to-Normal

During each of these stages, sharply different actions must be taken—each of which is critical to survival. So some understanding of each is necessary for effective turnaround management.

Stage 1: Management Change

Before any turnaround can occur, there must be a moment of truth when the board or president recognizes the seriousness of the situation. Then it will be necessary to decide who will be responsible for getting the business back on the right track. In the vast majority of circumstances, the existing top management team should *not* be assigned this job—usually for the simple reason that if they didn't know enough to keep the firm out of trouble in the first place, they won't know how to rescue it now.

I recommend definitely replacing top management if the short-range predictors indicate bankruptcy within a year, and possibly switching the management if the longer-term picture indicates trouble. In other words, allow the existing top management team to stay on only if they have identified the problems in the very early stages and brought them to the board's attention themselves.

Stage 2: Situation Diagnosis and Strategy Selection

The next stage involves diagnosing the situation and deciding what turnaround strategy should be followed. In general, this stage is the most important one and will be examined in detail in the second half of this case.

In choosing a turnaround strategy, the key is to keep it simple. There are usually insufficient time and resources to pursue an elaborate strategy, so a simple, powerful strategy will help avoid mistakes and subsequent backtracking.

Stage 3: Emergency Action

As soon as a turnaround strategy is chosen, the action must begin. Most turnaround situations are so critical that if action is not taken quickly, disaster is a certainty. The first action must focus on stopping the bleeding—that is, taking direct control of all major cash inflows and outflows while you put your strategy into action.

The second action is to unload all the budgetary fat and least-effective managers by following three rules:

1. Try to make all the necessary cuts at once (to avoid having the remaining staff waste time worrying about when the next axe will fall);

2. Cut too much rather than not enough (so you won't have to go back and make further cuts later); and

3. In borderline situations, compare the risk of your current situation against potential long-term gain. Thus, if a particular product still has the potential for high returns, you may want to keep it. But, if you're in real trouble, follow the "when in doubt, cut it out" guideline.

Stage 4: Stabilization

Once you've stopped the bleeding and trimmed the fat, the time has come to put the longer-term aspects of your turnaround strategy into effect. Basically, your attention must turn from plugging cash flow leaks to generating sufficient long-term profits to justify the continued existence of the business. Typically, this involves protecting its key assets, improving its existing operations, and repositioning it in the industry in order to maximize its future potential. The specific emphasis and direction of these tasks are decided on during the diagnosis stage. The two principal tasks during this stage are (1) to insure that the chosen turnaround strategy is actually being implemented by the organization, and (2) to monitor the company's continuing progress to make sure that the desired results are being obtained (if they're not, it may be necessary to liquidate the firm to get the desired returns).

Stage 5: Return-to-Normal

At some point, the turnaround ends and normal growth resumes. Although this stage is "normal," you should still consider it part of your turnaround process because it may involve choosing a different type of manager to guide, develop, and perhaps even create success, than was needed to turn the company around. In short, just as a turnaround almost always starts with new management, so it often should end with new management.

Fortunately, most managers who are turnaround specialists get their "kicks" out of the turnaround process itself and know when to move on. But what of those who don't? It all depends. If they are essentially generalists, they can probably adapt to the new situation. But, if they're really turnaround specialists, they may need to be replaced.

How can the board tell when the management must be replaced? Two guidelines may help. The first relates to having a preponderance of "good news" over "bad news." When this ratio swings to roughly two-to-one or better, it usually indicates that the business has stabilized and normal growth can begin. The second indication that management may need to be changed is if there has not been a "take-off" after the good news begins to strongly dominate the bad. Immediately after a turnaround has been completed, a firm should experience a positive take-off for a year or two: if this jump doesn't happen, change in management may be in order.

DESIGNING TURNAROUND STRATEGIES

Now that you have a framework for understanding the overall turnaround process, let's examine one aspect of the process in more depth: how to select the most appropriate turnaround strategy for your situation. (Our focus here is on business level strategy only: we do not address corporate level turnarounds.)

At the business-unit level, there are two broad types of turnarounds: strategic and operating. Each of these types is indicated below:

Strategic turnarounds

1. Move to larger strategic group
2. Change competitive weapons in existing strategic group
3. Move to smaller strategic group

Operating turnarounds

1. Revenue increasing
2. Cost saving
3. Asset reduction
4. Combination

To determine what type of strategy is most appropriate for your situation, you should first assess the current strategic and operating health of the business. For each of the following four key resource areas, you should evaluate factors such as those suggested in Tables 7-1 and 7-2.

TABLE 7-1   Operating Health Assessment

Key Resource Area	Sample Factors to Examine
1. Finance	Pro-forma cash flow; cash flow break-even chart
2. Market position	Sales of existing product vs. cash flow break-even point
3. Technology	New modified products available in one year
4. Production	Facilities replacement required/available for sale; variable costs vs. competitors' variable costs

TABLE 7-2   Strategic Health Assessment

Key Resource Area	Sample Factors to Examine
1. Market position	Unique competitive advantages: distribution strengths
2. Technology	Relative product, process, and basic R&D capabilities
3. Production	Experience-curve effects available; timing of required capacity additions
4. Finance	Long-term growth requirements vs. internal resource availability

When such assessments are completed, you can come up with overall evaluations of both your strategic and operating health as being strong, average, or weak. The business's current strategic and operating health can then be plotted on a nine-cell matrix, such as Figure 7-1, to determine which broad type of turnaround should be pursued in the emergency action and stabilization stages.

As this chart indicates, if your operating position is weak while your strategic position is average or strong, the situation calls for an operating turnaround (if possible), or if your analysis suggests that an operating turnaround won't be successful or that its costs outweigh the benefits, then liquidation is preferable. (Note: liquidation is usually preferable to divestment in such situations, since it is seldom possible to obtain a reasonable price for a company in such a weak position.)

The chart similarly indicates that if your strategic position is weak while your operating health is average or strong, the situation calls for a strategic turnaround (if possible) or sale/divestiture; under these circumstances, divesti-

Chart A

Current Strategy Health

		Strong	Average	Weak
	Strong	None Needed	None or Strategic	Strategic
Current Operating Health	Average	None or Operating	Strategic or / Operating	Strategic or Sale/ Divestiture
	Weak	Operating	Operating or Liquidation	Operating or Liquidation

Figure 7-1 Current strategic health

ture will normally bring a better return than liquidation if the turnaround effort is not likely to succeed.

When both operating and strategic health are weak, the situation requires either a combination operating/strategic turnaround effort, or liquidation if the situation is already too far gone.

OPERATING TURNAROUNDS

In general, a business can follow basically four different types of operating turnaround strategies: (1) *revenue-increasing strategies:* (2) *cost-cutting strategies:* (3) *asset-reduction strategies;* and (4) *combination strategies.* Before you implement any of these strategies, you should identify those resources and skills which will be essential in the stabilization and return-to-normal growth stages and which, therefore, must be protected during the emergency action stage.

Your choice of an operating turnaround strategy should be based primarily on how close the firm is to its current breakeven point, as illustrated in Figure 7-2.

Cost-cutting strategies are normally most appropriate if the business is relatively close to its current breakeven point, or is within 75% to 90% of breakeven and has high direct labor costs or high fixed expenses. The reason for their advantages in such circumstances is that they almost always will produce results more quickly than revenue-increasing or asset-reduction actions.

At the opposite extreme, if sales are less than a third of breakeven, the only viable option is usually an asset-reduction strategy, especially if the business is close to bankruptcy. Typically, the only assets which should be retained in such situations are those that the firm will definitely need over the next year or

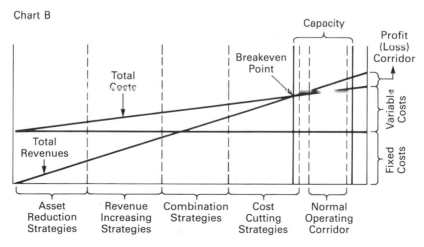

Figure 7-2

two. The rest should be sold—deliberately, if possible, rather than in a rushed or forced sale which will usually reduce the price attainable by 50% or more.

If sales are between 35% to 60% of breakeven, the most appropriate option is usually a revenue-increasing turnaround, unless finances are super-critical in which case some assets will normally have to be sold before the revenue-increasing effort can be made. The key point here, though, is that when a business is operating within this range, there is usually no way to reduce costs sufficiently to reach a new breakeven point, and the time and resources are usually not available for a combination effort.

Between about 60% and 80% of breakeven, combination strategies are normally the most effective, because the cost/benefit ratios for the best cost-reducing and asset-reduction actions are usually substantially higher than those of the third, fourth, or fifth-best resource-generating actions and vice versa. Such ratios should be calculated explicitly, however, without a substantial cost/benefit advantage, "single-focus" turnaround strategies are usually preferable because they are far easier to implement and control than combination efforts.

STRATEGIC TURNAROUNDS

Most strategic turnarounds involve circumstances in which the business either has begun or is beginning to experience major sales and share declines. Theoretically, there are three broad types of strategic turnarounds a business might follow: (1) *movement to a larger strategic group in the industry;* (2) *movement to a smaller strategic group in the industry;* or (3) *more effective competition within its existing strategic group.*

Not all these options are equally feasible, however. Movement to a larger strategic group is usually not feasible because of the weakened condition of the business, unless it has a corporate parent willing to fund its efforts.

Furthermore, even when such moves are possible, they are usually limited to one-level increases in strategic position, (e.g., if AMC were in a position to move up, the best it could normally do would be to displace Chrysler; that is, displacing Ford or GM would usually be totally out of the question).

Typically, then, most strategic turnarounds involve either movement to a smaller strategic group in the industry, through the use of segmentation or niche strategies, or regaining position in one's existing strategic group through the use of a more effective set of strategic weapons. Even the latter can be difficult, unless one gets an early start, for the simple reasons that (1) the market seldom rewards "copy cats" as much as "innovators," and (2) for strategic decline to have occurred in the first place, someone else in the industry must have already chosen and implemented a superior set of weapons. One guide for determining the specific type of strategic turnaround to follow is illustrated in Figure 7-3.

Chart C

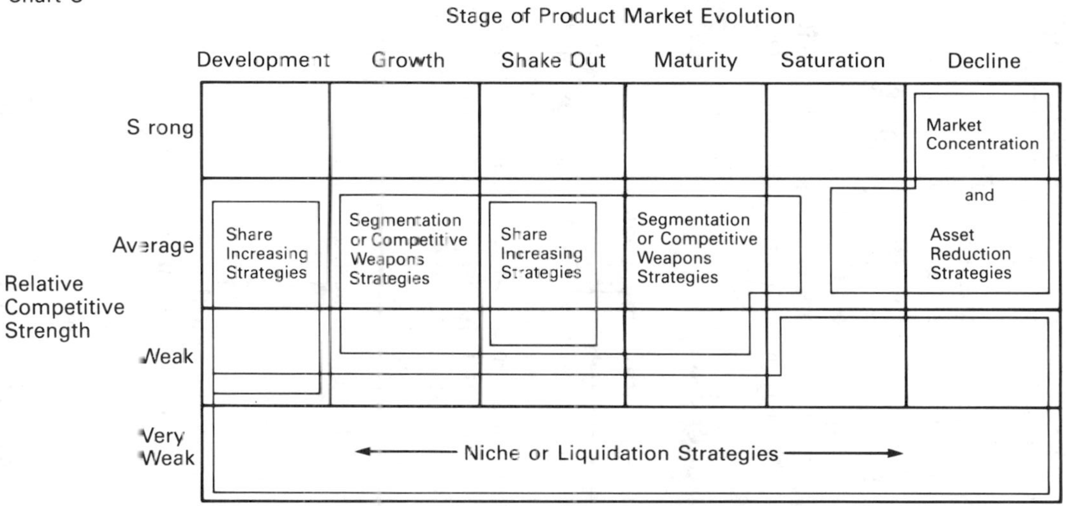

Stage of Product Market Evolution

	Development	Growth	Shake Out	Maturity	Saturation	Decline
Strong	Share Increasing Strategies	Segmentation or Competitive Weapons Strategies		Segmentation or Competitive Weapons Strategies		Market Concentration and Asset Reduction Strategies
Average			Share Increasing Strategies			
Weak						
Very Weak						

Relative Competitive Strength

←——— Niche or Liquidation Strategies ———→

Figure 7-3 Stage of product/market evolution

Usually, however, it would be much better to retrench to a solid position in the existing business, and then to seek future growth through diversification into new industries, than to buck the odds in one's own industry. Unfortunately, such common sense is all too often lacking in turnaround situations. What those who seek to emulate the heroics of the charge of the Light Brigade always seem to forget is that the Brigade itself was, for all practical purposes, totally destroyed in the effort.

The other key difference between strategic and operating turnarounds is that in strategic ones most current actions are taken in the expectation of long-term benefits. Thus, strategic turnarounds focus on the *future,* with the consequence that near-term performance improvements are expected to be positive but not dramatic. In operating turnarounds, by contrast, the focus is on *today* and on sharply-improved performance now. Given our cultural bias for action, this distinction again explains the preference for operating turnarounds.

SOME RESEARCH RESULTS

Our cultural bias for action may, unfortunately, have some negative results in turnaround situations. My research has shown that the vast majority of failed turnarounds involved situations in which the managers undertook operating turnarounds when strategic turnarounds were clearly required. Operating problems can be cured either through operating solutions or strategic solutions (the latter take longer, of course, and are less dramatic). Strategic problems can be cured *only* through strategic solutions, however. In short, what works appears to conflict with our natural cultural proclivity for action—which may help explain why Japanese and European managers have been successful in turning around businesses such as Motorola, that American managers felt were hopeless.

CONCLUSION

Since most turnarounds occur in situations where resources and time will permit only one turnaround attempt, it is crucial that the most appropriate strategies be chosen. An incorrect choice may result in bankruptcy—a situation usually far worse than even immediate liquidation.

In designing your strategies, keep two points in mind. First, before starting you must *explicitly* calculate whether it is worth attempting a turnaround at all. Too often, firms embark on turnaround efforts based solely on the "myth" that nothing can be worse than failure (i.e., liquidation). Such is not the case, however, and in many instances stockholders, employees, and other stakeholders in the organization would be better served if management faced up to the true prospects and benefits of long-run survival and was willing to liquidate the business for its current value.

Second, remember that the preponderance of research so far suggests that in non-critical turnaround situations, the greater danger lies in trying to use operating tactics when a strategic turnaround is needed rather than the reverse.

□

AVOIDING SOME PITFALLS IN COST LEADERSHIP STRATEGIES

RAPHAEL AMIT AND CHAIM FERSHTMAN

One of the most common strategic concepts is the notion of establishing a firm's cost leadership position as a means of gaining market share. The idea that underlies such a strategy is that by riding down the well-known Experience Curve, the firm may realize unit cost declines.

When unit cost declines are followed by a corresponding price reduction, the firm may be able to penetrate the market rapidly. As the firm penetrates the market, it can further reduce its costs to gain additional market share, and thereby further increase its profitability.

Adopting this strategy may also deter potential new entrants into the market, as it makes it harder for them to be able to price competitively without sustained losses since their costs, in the presence of the experience effect, must be higher. Therefore, the cost-price leadership strategy may also strengthen the firm's market position.

While such strategy is very popular and common knowledge among corporate strategists, it doesn't always work. For example, if your firm is faced with low price elasticity in its market, then pricing aggressively will not result in a meaningful increase in sales, since customers will not respond to lower prices by substantially increasing their purchases. In such a case, a cost leadership strategy is likely to be fruitless.

Another case where cost leadership may not yield the desired results can be drawn from the experience of a well-known consumer electronics and home computer company. While it focused on upgrading its production technology and automating its manufacturing facilities to achieve lower unit costs and to be able to price competitively without hurting its profit margins, a new entrant introduced a higher priced, technologically superior product that essentially made the firm's product obsolete. The new entrant's product was an immediate hit and the company couldn't produce the product fast enough to meet demand. Needless to mention that the electronics firm was unable to

Strategic Planning Management, April, 1984; Commerce Communications, Inc.

increase its market share despite its improved relative cost position. The market had simply shifted to more advanced products so that consumers were just not interested in purchasing a cheaper, but technologically inferior, product.

IS COST LEADERSHIP SUSTAINABLE?

To ensure the sustainability of a cost leadership strategy, it is imperative to carefully consider alternate market responses and potential competitive reactions similar to the ones described above. However, prior to embarking on a comprehensive strategic analysis that is required to substantiate the long-term viability of a cost leadership strategy, a much simpler, often overlooked issue needs to be examined: will the ride down the Experience Curve result in a permanent reduction in cost, yielding cost leadership and enabling the firm to establish its competitive advantage?

The interrelationship between the factors that determine the firm's cost structure may be such that no long lasting advantage can be obtained by riding down the Experience Curve. This is the case when the firm does not realize any economies due to learning. A declining Experience Curve then merely reflects cost savings due to increasing returns to scale, and a firm that invests in new plant and equipment to reduce its costs will not obtain a sustainable improved relative cost position.

It is important to note that the data required to address this issue are available internally in most organizations. What are frequently misunderstood, however, are the assumptions underlying the Experience Curve and the distinction between scale offsets and learning offsets as sources of the Experience Curve. Unless these are properly understood, it is very likely that your firm will misallocate resources in its search for a cost leadership position.

ASSUMPTIONS UNDERLYING THE EXPERIENCE CURVE

The use of the Experience Curve phenomenon as an element in a firm's strategy is based on the following interrelated assumptions:

1. The reduction in real unit costs of value added as cumulative output increases. If this causes a shift downwards in the firm's average cost curve it will permanently reduce production cost, and thereby establish the firm's competitive advantage.
2. The positive correlation between cumulative output and market share. If the realized cost reductions are followed by a cut in prices, the firm may be able to rapidly penetrate the market and thus gain market share. Therefore, the higher the cumulative output, the larger is the firm's relative market share at any point in time.

3. The positive relationship between relative market share and profits of the firm. The share-profitability relationship provides the fundamental justification for gaining market share, and the Experience Curve phenomenon is the vehicle used to establish the firm's competitive advantage.

To the extent that these assumptions do not apply, a strategy based upon riding down the Experience Curve is not likely to generate the hoped-for results.

DISTINGUISHING SCALE AND LEARNING EFFECTS

As previously noted, the sustainability of a cost leadership strategy is dependent upon the source of the unit cost declines. There are two fundamental sources that underlie unit cost declines along an Experience Curve. These are:

1. Cost declines that may occur as a result of movements *along* a given long run average cost curve, where unit costs are measured as a function of the production rate. For example, if a firm operates along the downward sloping portion of its cost curve, cost declines will be realized through an increase in the production rate. These increasing returns to scale, which are often referred to as the *scale effect,* may be realized at *any point in time* through adjustments in production capacity and substitution in the factor input mix, so that the least cost combination of factors and plant size is chosen for each production rate.

2. Cost declines that may occur *over time* which are reflected by movement *of* the long run cost curve. For example, as a result of gains in labor efficiencies often realized when cumulative output rises, a movement downward of the average cost curve occurs, since less labor input is needed to produce a unit of the product. Clearly, the more labor intensive the production process, the greater will be the overall cost savings that result from this learning-by-doing process. Alternatively, the cost curve may also move downwards due to a technological breakthrough that allows for less imputs per unit of output, or due to standardization or product redesign, or due to other conservation measures that facilitate greater efficiencies in manufacturing. These changes in unit costs that occur over time may be referred to as the *learning effect.*

The experience curve is commonly presented as a single curve that displays the inverse relationship between cumulative production, which is a measure of learning and/or process related technological advances, and average costs. However, the preceding analysis suggests that there is an additional important factor that is hidden in this two-dimensional display of the experience curve, which affects the desirability of an investment in cost leadership. It is the impact on costs of changes in the production rate, which in turn is a measure of the scale effect.

As is highlighted in the following examples, it is simply incorrect to draw any strategic conclusions on the attractiveness of an investment in cost leadership without an in-depth, company-specific, structural analysis of costs that focuses on the interrelationships between the scale and learning effects.

Consider for example the case where you observe increasing returns to scale in the manufacturing process but learning does not take place. This may occur in a production environment in which average fixed costs are relatively high while average variable costs are only a very small fraction of the value added. Further, suppose that the production technology is well established and it is unlikely to materially change.

Under these circumstances, the company clearly needs to increase its market share to enable it to produce at a higher volume, which in turn will result in lower average costs due to the increasing returns to scale phenomenon. The question now is whether an investment in cost leadership is the most attractive and sustainable way to increase market share or whether other ways to reach the firm's objective should be explored.

You should note that the lack of learning in the manufacturing process that was assumed suggests that the mere increase in cumulative production will not yet yield any reduction in costs. The traditionally displayed downwards sloping experience curve will reflect only the so-called scale effect, namely the reduction in costs that results from producing at a higher rate. There are clearly no long-lasting cost reductions, as no downward shift in the average cost curve occurs when cumulative output increases.

The point here is that the experience curve phenomenon exists only on the surface, and it is very misleading under these circumstances. Cumulative production is unimportant strategically. New entrants can penetrate the market by producing at the same rate as experienced producers. In this environment, a strategy that is based on riding down the experience curve will not yield a sustainable relative improvement in costs and is, therefore, undesirable.

Another example that highlights the importance of considering the interrelationships between the learning and scale effects, when you are contemplating an experience-curve based strategy, can be drawn from a company whose production technology displays *decreasing returns to scale,* yet learning is present. This company may easily find itself in a trap: the purpose of investing in cost leadership is to increase market share. However, the presence of decreasing returns to scale implies that unit costs will increase as the production rate increases, which will occur if you are successful in increasing your market share. You then run the risk that the reduction in cost which is due to learning will be entirely offset by these cost increases and you will actually realize higher unit costs. Such a result is clearly an undesirable outcome of your strategy that was primarily aimed at giving you a relatively improved cost position. Here again, drawing any strategic conclusion by examining the traditional experience curve may indeed be very misleading.

FOCUS ON YOUR COST STRUCTURE

Identifying the structure of your firm's cost function and its behavior over time is clearly an important input into strategy determination. It is essential to verify the presence of a learning effect in the manufacturing process in order to be able to gain a sustainable improved cost position. This, however, is not sufficient as you should also analyze the impact of changes in the production rate on unit costs. A proper analysis should consider the marketing side as well: you will need to examine the implications of an investment in co-leadership, at the anticipated higher production rate that will have to be maintained if the company is successful in increasing its market share. The need to estimate scale and learning effects can be illustrated through the following example.

A bank embarked upon an advertising campaign to attract many new depositors. At first, the bank gained many efficiencies in handling the increased volume of business. The tellers and others learned about the intricacies of the new accounts.

However, the advertising campaign, over time, generated so many new customers that the bank decided to stay open longer, paying tellers overtime and incurring other increased overhead to keep the facility open. Although the tellers and others continued to learn, that is, to become more efficient in handling the high number of customers, the other costs (giving rise to decreasing returns to scale) associated with the process began to outweigh the learning effects.

CONCLUSION

The morals of this discussion can be summarized as follows:

1. Do not invest in cost leadership as a strategy if price is not a point of differentiation in the marketplace.
2. Do not invest in cost leadership if other firms can imitate easily. You will therefore not be able to sustain your competetive advantage.
3. Riding down the Experience Curve can be misleading. You need to estimate both scale and learning effects. If you do not, even though some learning may be taking place, your overall costs may actually be increasing.

CHAPTER

8

BUSINESS-LEVEL STRATEGY: ATTACKING COMPETITORS

◼

FRONTAL STRATEGIES: ATTACKING COMPETITORS
LIAM FAHEY

In a pure frontal strategy, the attacking firm goes "head-to-head" with its competitor: it matches the competitor product for product, price for price, promotion for promotion, and so on. Of course, the aggressor also goes after the same customer group(s), by trying to win away the competitor's current customers.

Thus, a pure frontal attack is largely a "me-too" or "look-alike" strategy. The attacker tries to do everything in the same way that the target competitor does.

LIMITATIONS OF A PURE FRONTAL ATTACK

In a pure frontal attack, customers have no reason to buy from one firm as opposed to another. In other words, customers are not provided with any means to differentiate between the offerings of rival firms. For example, if one car rental firm attacks another with a pure frontal strategy—that is, it provides the same types of cars, from very adjacent locations, at the same rates, with

Strategic Planning Management, August, 1985; Commerce Communications, Inc.

the same insurance coverage, and the same mileage allowance—customers are given no reason to buy from one firm over another.

Thus, the primary limitation of a pure frontal attack is that it does not provide the attacking firm with any form of competitive advantage—that is, a reason why the customer should buy from it rather than its competitors.

DANGEROUS ASSUMPTIONS UNDERLYING FRONTAL ATTACKS

A common assumption underlying frontal attacks is that superior resources are sufficient. All the attacker has to do is pump greater resources into the attack and the competitor will be eventually worn down. Yet, quite frequently, this is not the case. In a pure frontal attack, the resource advantage does not translate into a competitive advantage—customers do not see the benefits of the superior resources.

Another set of dangerous assumptions often pertains to competitor responses. It is assumed that the competitor will not or cannot respond to the attack. And, even if the competitor does respond, it can be beaten off. In all too many cases, these assumptions are simply the consequence of not thinking through whether competitors will respond and how they may and can do so. They may also be the consequence of presuming that resource superiority is sufficient.

Because resources alone are not sufficient and competitors most likely will be provoked to respond, some form of modified frontal attack is always preferable to a pure frontal onslaught. Modified frontal attacks seek to create and sustain some form of competitive advantage—they are not just a replication of the competitor's strategy. Three types of modified frontal attacks are often employed.

LIMITED FRONTAL ATTACK

One form of frontal strategy is to limit the scope of the attack: to focus on specific customers and commit substantial resources to winning them away from competitors. In narrowing the scope of the attack, the intent is to be able to create differentiation—to do something different than competitors that provides value to customers.

Japanese firms have frequently employed a limited frontal attack against their U.S. competitors. For example, in semiconductors, Japanese firms identified select U.S. customers and pursued them with vigor. They worked with them to develop product specifications, provided product demonstrations, offered very favorable price terms, and committed themselves to extensive after-sales service. In short, these Japanese firms tried to outcompete their U.S. competition along several dimensions simultaneously.

PRICE-BASED FRONTAL ATTACK

Perhaps the most common frontal strategy is a price-based frontal attack. The intent of this strategy is to match the competition on other dimensions but to beat it on price.

This is a frequently employed strategy in consumer goods industries. Many firms basically adopt this strategy in trying to enter and penetrate major retail outlets such as supermarket or department store chains. Firms in industries as diverse as autos, steel, tires, computers, and textiles often use this strategy.

Japanese firms have become notable purveyors of the strategy. For example, many Japanese producers of television sets, in their efforts to penetrate the U.S. marketplace, matched their U.S. competitors on many dimensions but charged lower prices, and in some cases, considerably lower prices.

Price-based frontal attacks are more likely to succeed if competitors do not retaliate by cutting price or if they do not retaliate by trying to convince the market that their products offer superior customer value. Thus, it is in the attacker's interest to devise a frontal strategy that buffers it from competitive retaliation. One such strategy is an R&D-based frontal attack.

R&D-BASED FRONTAL ATTACK

In an R&D-based frontal strategy, the attacker tries to imbue its product with features that may allow a number of different frontal attacks in the marketplace. Product and process R&D-based frontal strategies are possible.

Product R&D-based strategies strive to create value-based frontal attacks. Value is imbued into products by creating product improvements and establishing features not found in a competitor's product. The intent is to achieve product differentiation based on factors other than price. For example, many pharmaceutical firms pursue customers of competitors by introducing new products or radically improving existing products that treat the same disease, ailment, or health problem as competitors' products.

On the other hand, many process-based R&D strategies are intended to effect lower manufacturing costs and thus facilitate an attack on competitors based on price. The hope is that it will be much more difficult for a competitor to respond to an R&D-driven, price-based strategy by cutting price because of its higher-cost structure.

Process R&D investment may also lead to product improvement in the form of higher quality such as superior performance and greater reliability. Of course, it may also lead to these features plus lower cost.

CONDITIONS FACILITATING A FRONTAL STRATEGY

From the above discussion, it will be evident that a number of conditions are conducive to a successful frontal strategy. These conditions should be carefully assessed since an unsuccessful frontal attack is most likely to result in significant financial loss and fall-off in organizational morale.

First, sufficient resources are required to support a frontal strategy. When frontal attacks degenerate into head-to-head battles, a firm's endurance is facilitated by its available resources.

Second, since resources alone are not sufficient, a frontal attack must be built upon the creation and maintenance of competitive advantage. The frontal attack should result in distinguishing the firm's offerings from those of competitors.

Third, frontal attacks succeed or fail to the extent they attract customers away from competitors. Unless product and brand loyalties can be overcome, the likelihood of a frontal strategy succeeding is small.

SOME RISKS IN FRONTAL STRATEGY

Finally, it is worth noting that frontal strategies are not risk free. First, they absorb plenty of resources. Thus, substantial losses are possible.

Second, frontal strategies may only serve to awaken sleeping giants. Thus, competitors may retaliate with much more vigor and venom than they previously exhibited.

Third, frontal strategies may only intensify competition, resulting in a depression of profits for all participants in the marketplace.

CONCLUSION

Frontal strategies should only be adopted under certain conditions. They make the most sense when the attacker has greater resources and possesses some form of a sustainable competitive advantage. Otherwise, the result is likely to be a severe contest of wills and a show of brute force, where even the winner is likely not to emerge unscathed.

FLANKING STRATEGIES: COMPETITION BY AVOIDANCE
LIAM FAHEY

Rather than going directly head-to-head against each other, firms frequently find it much more appropriate, given the circumstances confronting them, to try to flank their competition. Thus, a "flanking strategy" serves quite different purposes than a "frontal strategy."

Strategic Planning Management, October, 1985; Commerce Communications, Inc.

But what is a flanking strategy, what are its goals, what are the conditions under which it is appropriate, and what are the risks attendent to it?

WHAT IS FLANKING?

Flanking is, in essence, a niche strategy. It involves identifying an unserved market niche—discovering market needs and serving them. Successful flanking strategies are often built around initiating shifts in market segments or market evolution and capitalizing on these shifts by developing them into strong market segments.

The driving thrust of a flanking strategy is not to engage the competition in hand-to-hand battle. Rather, it is to fight competitors in those segments of the market where they have little presence or are nonexistent. Thus, flanking is premised upon the hope that you can identify substantial market segments not presently inundated with competitors.

FLANKING GOALS

Firms pursuing a flanking strategy are typically seeking one or more of the following goals:

- to avoid taking on well-entrenched competitors
- to avoid awakening some "sleeping giants"
- to create and develop a market segment or niche
- to build a market position that will be sufficient to attack competitors at a later time

Typically, a flanking strategy involves a combination of these goals or possibly all of them.

THE CASE OF TIMEX

The strategy pursued by Timex Corp. during the 1950s introduction of its watches manifests an almost classic flanking strategy. Timex's strategy was designed to avoid direct competition with established watch manufacturers.

First, the watches were considerably different from those of competitors. They were simpler, styled differently, and had additional features such as being shockproof, waterproof, and antimagnetic.

Second, Timex priced its watches considerably lower than did competitors. Its initial watches were priced at less than $10.

Third, the product was not aimed at the conventional watch purchaser. It was aimed at customers who felt they could not afford the "conventional" watch, or the customer who wanted a second watch, or even watches for different occasions. In the late 1950s, Timex even introduced a line of watches aimed exclusively at the women's market. In short, Timex tried to flank its competitors not just in terms of its products but also with regard to its target customers.

Fourth, Timex also flanked its competitors in its choice of distribution channels. Timex initially tried to distribute its products through the conventional channels—jewelry stores. However, the jewelry trade rebuffed it, considering Timex watches not in keeping with their image of dealing in high price, high quality merchandise—and because margins would be much lower.

Thus, Timex had to seek other avenues of distribution. As a result, it began to distribute its watches directly through retail accounts, primarily drugstores. In the early years, drugstores accounted for over 70% of Timex's sales.

In summary, Timex flanked its competitors in terms of product, pricing, distribution, and target customers. It sought to develop a market niche and use it as a springboard for an attack on other segments of the watch industry—and it succeeded.

TYPES OF FLANKING STRATEGY

Firms can pursue several types of flanking strategy. Indeed, many firms have employed more than one type simultaneously.

Geographical flanking. In this type of strategy, the firm flanks the competition on a geographical basis: it focuses on particular areas of the country or the world where opponents are either nonexistent or quite weak. Thus, they are highly vulnerable—in military parlance, their flanks are exposed.

It is important to note that a geographical flanking strategy may be built around selling identical or largely similar products to those of the competition and thus satisfying an identical or broadly similar market need or niche. The intent is to do so in geographic markets where the competition is poorly positioned or before the competition has reached the market.

Segmented flanking. A segmented flanking strategy does not try to avoid competitors on a geographic basis. Rather, it aims to identify and serve market niches and needs that are being neglected by competitors within a given geographic area.

Segmented flanking strategies are potentially much more powerful than geographical flanking attacks because they are inherently built upon satisfying market needs and doing something different from the competition. They entail providing products that are different from competitors; they often involve the creation of new market niches, that is, new needs and/or new customers; in short, segmented flanking strategies allow firms to compete in new and different ways in the marketplace.

Segmented flanking strategies may take many forms:

1. Introducing products with significant differences to those of competitors—for example, smaller products, more or less features, "stripped-down" versions of competitors' products.
2. Pricing products much lower or higher than competitors.
3. Private labeling.
4. Developing new distribution channels or using channels neglected by competitors.
5. Pursuing customer groups neglected or not considered by competitors.

Companies typically combine a number of these elements in their flank attacks as noted in the Timex example discussed above.

Entry flanking.   Segmented flanking strategies are often used by firms in entering markets, as Japanese firms have done in entering the U.S. market. For example, Honda, when it first entered the U.S. market in the early 1960s, flanked its U.S. competitors by introducing smaller motorcycles at a lower price. Japanese television manufacturers also used this route.

FACILITATING A FLANKING STRATEGY

When should a firm choose a flanking strategy? There are a number of specific conditions that greatly contribute to the desirability of a flanking strategy.

- The existence of substantial market segments that are distinct from the prevailing dominant product markets and that are not being served, or served well, by the current producers.
- Substantial growth in the market or industry as a whole. This renders competition a positive-sum game (that is, gains are not at the expense of competitors' growth) rather than a zero-sum game (that is, one firm's gain is another firm's loss).
- Entrenched competitors are complacent and generally consider the new entrants as "non-runners" or "upstarts" who will not be able to stay the distance in a competitive battle.
- The firm does not have the resources or capabilities to confront competitors head-to-head, or to develop a major onslaught on the market.
- Even in situations where firms do not face severe resource constraints, the absence of market and competitive knowledge may strongly suggest a flanking strategy. By choosing a strategic posture that does not result in immediate direct competitive conflict, you can learn enough about the market and the requirements for success before finding yourself confronting combative competitors.

RISKS IN FLANKING STRATEGY

Even though flanking strategies do not consume resources on as large a scale or as quickly as frontal attacks on competitors, they are nevertheless not risk-free.

One risk is that the strategy may be directed at a very small or nongrowing market. The pay-off is thus not likely to be worth the cost.

Another risk is that even under growing market conditions, it may take too long to realize the fruits of the strategy.

A related risk is that the competitors being flanked may be provoked into retaliating—they may directly invade the niche. One consequence may be that the flanking firm succeeds only in creating a market opportunity for the larger firms in the relevant product markets.

CONCLUSION

Flanking strategies can provide a fruitful avenue to attack competitors indirectly. As with any type of strategy, however, there are certain conditions that are conducive to choosing a flanking attack, and there are also inherent risks. These conditions and risks should be carefully assessed before choosing a flanking strategy.

ENCIRCLEMENT STRATEGY: ATTACKING COMPETITORS BY SURROUNDING THEM

LIAM FAHEY

Frontal and flanking strategies, if successful over time, may evolve into an encirclement strategy. By continuing to modify and develop its products and to pursue all available market or customer niches, the attacking company may find that it has encircled a competitor or competitors. It may, however, take a number of years for this situation to evolve.

WHAT IS ENCIRCLEMENT STRATEGY?

An encirclement strategy simply means that the attacking firm encircles the competitor's position in terms of products or markets or both. It has greater product variety than the competitor and serves more market or customer

Strategic Planning Management, November, 1985; Commerce Communications, Inc.

segments. No matter which way the competitor turns, it confronts the encircling firm.

The goals of encirclement are straightforward:

1. To lessen the competitor's possible retaliatory responses. If the competitor is surrounded by the attacking firm on every side of a given product/market, the competitor's options are severely circumscribed.
2. To compel the competitor to defend its front, side, and rear all at once, thereby forcing the competitor to disperse its resources in defending itself. The hope is that the competitor will leave itself open to attack on at least some side—in short, the competitor becomes more vulnerable.
3. To make the front line or marketplace more fluid over time so that it can be more easily penetrated at a number of points and potentially developed into significant market niches for the attacking firm.

These goals of an encirclement strategy can be summed up in the following military principle:

> If he prepares to the front, his rear will be weak; and if to the rear, his front will be fragile. If he prepares to the left, his right will be vulnerable; and if to the right, there will be few on his left. And when he prepares everywhere, he will be weak everywhere.

TYPES OF ENCIRCLEMENT

As noted, there are basically two types of encirclement strategy: product encirclement and market encirclement. Although the two types are closely related and may be the same under some circumstances, they are conceptually distinct.

Product encirclement involves putting many more types, styles, and sizes of products on the market than competitors, including products that are more and less expensive. Ultimately, launching products in a multitude of qualities, styles, and features may swamp the competitor's product line.

Market encirclement involves making the attacking firm's offerings available to almost every possible market segment. The intent is to move into every adjacent market niche, thus leaving no market avenues open to the competitor.

Market encirclement may be focused at the end customer or at distribution channels or at the trade. Many firms have tried to encircle competitors at the level of end customers as Japanese semiconductor manufacturers are trying to do by now going after the "custom" end of the market.

Market encirclement at the level of distribution channels is also common. Seiko offers a good example. It has penetrated every possible type of distribution channel for watches and through its product line proliferation, it has sought to absorb as much shelf space as possible.

Product and market encirclement are closely related, though they do differ in focus. It is not sufficient to engage in product proliferation; there must also be distinct market or customer segments to absorb the product varieties.

CONDITIONS FACILITATING ENCIRCLEMENT

As with other strategy types, a number of conditions facilitate the employment and likely success of an encirclement strategy.

First, encirclement usually depends upon the attacking company having superior resources to its competitors. To develop and proliferate products and to go after many adjacent market niches requires not just a substantial resource base but one that is superior to competitors.

Second, the firm must be willing to commit its resources for an extended period of time, if it is to achieve strategic encirclement. Success in encircling a competitor is not likely to be accomplished quickly.

It is this latter condition that has clearly distinguished many Japanese competitors from their U.S. counterparts. They were willing to commit their resources to winning the competitive war. Many U.S. firms, even when the Japanese attack was at an advanced stage, did not make the necessary resource commitments to repel the attack.

Third, a diversified resource base is necessary. All too often, U.S. firms overemphasize the importance of financial resources. No doubt financial wherewithal is important, but it is often not sufficient. If the attacking firm has superior R&D capability, it will find it much easier to continually modify and develop products. Similarly, if the firm has superior access to distribution channels and the trade, it is much easier to go after multiple market segments.

Fourth, as is the case with frontal attacks, encirclement attacks are more likely to succeed if competitors are not willing to make the necessary long-term commitments to defend their market position. If existing competitors are not expected to compete on all fronts, then the encirclement strategy is more likely to succeed.

ENCIRCLEMENT STRATEGY: SOME EXAMPLES

Many Japanese firms have encircled their U.S. competitors or are well on the way to doing so.

Honda has clearly encircled Harley Davidson in motorcycles. Beginning in the early 1960s, when it first introduced its very small motorcycles into the U.S., Honda gradually upgraded the size and power of its machines until by the end of the 1970s, it had a much broader product range than Harley Davidson, and its products appealed to a much greater diversity of customer groups. Almost every year during the 1960s, Honda introduced new models, stretching its product line from under 100cc to almost 1000cc machines. During the 1970s, Honda introduced a number of machines to extend and solidify its hold in the heavyweight end of the product/market, the 500cc machines and above.

An almost classic example of encirclement strategy is Seiko in the watch industry. Seiko has encircled Swiss as well as American manufacturers. Over the last decade and a half, Seiko has dramatically extended its product line into both the upper and lower ends of the watch market. It introduced a series of lower priced watches under the brand name Pulsar. It also entered the upper priced end of the market with a series of specially designed watches aimed at the "luxury" segment of the market. In short, Seiko now encompasses the watch market from top to bottom in terms of price, quality, design, and features.

Other Japanese examples of encirclement abound: audio and stereo equipment, televisions, radios, and hand-held calculators. The Japanese are also on their way to encircling U.S. manufacturers in a number of other product/markets, for example, in autos and semiconductors. In autos, the Japanese dominate the lower end of the market and are moving rapidly into the higher end. In semiconductors, the Japanese not only are moving ahead of many U.S. manufacturers in terms of product offerings, but they are also beginning to go after such market segments as the custom chip market, long held by U.S. firms.

THE CONSEQUENCES FOR COMPETITORS

In view of the goals of strategic encirclement, it is also important to consider the position of competitors who become the victims of an encirclement strategy.

In this vein, it is instructive to examine the predicament that many U.S. firms find themselves in—the position of being followers rather than leaders. Partly as a consequence, it has taken some time for some of them to fashion successful strategic responses. Many U.S. firms have not yet done so. And, of course, some U.S. firms have withdrawn entirely from the battle with the Japanese.

The predicament that confronts a victim of strategic encirclement is that it requires a major expenditure of resources to outmaneuver the encircler and it also takes a significant amount of time to do so.

RISKS IN STRATEGIC ENCIRCLEMENT

Every strategy has its attendant risks. And the risks with regard to encirclement are considerable.

Encirclement of a competitor's position in the marketplace can consume substantial resources, managerial time, and organizational commitment. Thus, the primary risk is that the organization is betting a significant portion of its resource base that the competitive battle is worth winning.

However, the competitive gains may not be worth it. The battleground may have changed. The winner may be left with a stagnant or declining product/market. Technology developments, government regulations, changes in customers' tastes, etc., may result in making the old product/market obsolete.

A common risk with any type of strategy but one that may be particularly painful in the case of either a frontal or encirclement strategy (due to the level of organizational resources involved) is that the attacking firm may become absorbed with defeating a particular competitor. Such an orientation makes the strategy more risky because it is likely to result in the attacking firm aiming at the wrong target—the competitor rather than the customer or the broader marketplace.

CONCLUSION

Strategic encirclement, because of the extensive risks involved, must not only be executed with skill but must also be the product of thorough strategic analysis. Of particular importance is an assessment of competitors' likely responses and the evolution of products, markets, and technology. In other words, care must be taken to ensure that the battle is worth winning.

□

BYPASS STRATEGY: ATTACKING BY SURPASSING COMPETITORS

LIAM FAHEY

A common conception of the competitive marketplace is that of competitors competing directly against each other in well-defined product/market arenas. Competitors confront each other and fight for position in some specific product/market such as the high-priced or luxury end of the car market.

The implicit imagery is of combatants engaging in hand-to-hand combat. This imagery is dominant in each of the strategy types discussed previously in this chapter. Frontal attacks manifest direct confrontation in its purest form. Encirclement attacks also reflect an effort to directly confront (that is, surround) a competitor. Even in the case of flanking strategies, the driving thrust is against specific competitors even though the immediate battle may take place in markets where the competition is either weakly present or not present at all.

However, if we focus only on these direct forms of competitive confrontation, we miss a potentially powerful form of competitive strategy, which

Strategic Planning Management, December, 1985; Commerce Communications, Inc.

is frequently referred to as the bypass attack. This strategy type derives its name from the initiating firm's desire not to directly confront a competitor in a particular product/market. The bypass attack is the most indirect of assault strategies and avoids moving against the enemy in the current period.

GOALS OF A BYPASS STRATEGY

Although we shall see there are quite different types of bypass strategy, two overriding goals tend to characterize most of them:

1. The desire to avoid further competition against competitors in some specific product/market
2. The desire to move the competitive battle among firms to a new arena— one where competitors will have to play catch-up

A bypass strategy, therefore, unlike flanking, frontal, and encirclement strategies, takes the initiating firm into product/market terrain that is likely to be quite different than its current product/market domain.

TYPES OF BYPASS STRATEGY

A firm has three options in pursuing product/markets where competitors are now present:

1. Develop new products and thus satisfy customer needs that are unserved by any competitor
2. Diversify into unrelated products
3. Diversify into new geographical markets

The development of new products is perhaps the single most common form of bypass strategy. It is also the most aggressive form of a bypass attack.

New products are a clear signal to competitors: the firm is no longer content to fight in the marketplace with the current products but wants to change "the rules of the competitive game." The attacking firm seeks to gain a major competitive edge or advantage through its leapfrogging bypass moves.

Although the bypass element in new product development may take a number of forms, it is usually the consequences of R&D or technology advances. For example, programmable controls bypassed numerical controls as a means of automating machinery and equipment in many industrial markets. In ethical drugs, the discovery of new compounds often leads to new forms of the "product" to treat specific human ills.

DIVERSIFICATION INTO UNRELATED PRODUCTS

A quite different form of bypass strategy is diversification into unrelated products. Rather than trying to bypass the competitor in a product/market where they face each other, the attacking firm commits itself to product/markets where the competitor is not present.

This form of bypass strategy is often employed by a firm when it wishes to lessen its dependence on a single industry or a single segment of an industry. This is more likely to be the case where the firm presumes that by diversifying into unrelated products it can ultimately strengthen its position in its present or core business. Many consumer goods firms adopt this form of bypass attack; for example, cigarette firms have diversified into other consumer products in the hope of strengthening their marketing and distribution capabilities or creating other forms of synergy and thus being able to do better in the cigarette business.

NEW GEOGRAPHICAL MARKETS

The above two types of bypass attacks primarily revolve around products. However, another classic form of bypass attack is to diversify into new geographical markets by seeking new markets for existing products.

This form of bypass attack can be launched in conjunction with other forms of attack in existing product/markets. For example, it is not uncommon for firms to attack competitors with a frontal attack in one geographic market and simultaneously enter foreign markets where the competitor does not have a position.

Bypass via diversification into foreign markets can also be used to develop a position in the global market and then use that position to launch or intensify a frontal attack or a bypass attack via new product development at a later time. Many Japanese firms have used this strategy in their assaults on the U.S. marketplace. They bypassed their U.S. competitors by going after foreign markets, sometimes at the same time that they were beginning to enter the U.S. marketplace, other times before they did so.

CHANGING THE BATTLE ARENA

As noted above, each of the bypass strategies reflects an effort to evade the current or prevailing competitive battle. However, the different options manifest varying degrees of bypass.

Bypass via new product development involves moving the battle to a new product level within the same product/market area. For example, in the watch industry, a succession of new product-specific battlegrounds has evolved: mechanical watches were initially bypassed by electronic watches, and these, in turn, were bypassed by digital watches. As a result of each bypass, firms are still seeking position in the watch industry, often finding themselves up against both new and old competitors.

Bypass via development of new geographical markets, on the other hand, is intended to go around existing competitors completely or, at a minimum, to take the fight to a product/market segment where competitors are much less established.

Bypass via unrelated products is an attempt to avoid the prevailing competitive fight altogether, though firms may be able to derive benefits from this form of diversification in existing product/markets.

CONDITIONS FACILITATING BYPASS ATTACKS

The conditions required to successfuly execute a bypass attack depend to some extent upon the type of bypass strategy involved. Given the nature of bypass attacks, however, one condition is common: an existing market position that provides a springboard from which to bypass competitors.

Bypass strategy based on new product development is likely to require substantial R&D and technology resources and capability. At a minimum, if internally sourced, this strategy typically requires product development knowledge and skills that are different from those that gave rise to the bypassed products.

This is seen in some of the new product examples previously noted. Programmable controls necessitate a very different knowledge base than numerical controls; movement from mechanical to electronic to digital watches involves a progression through quite different R&D and technology bases.

Bypass strategy in the form of diversification into unrelated products may also require extensive R&D capability to the extent that it requires internally sourced R&D. Alternatively, it may require sufficient resources to acquire companies with the requisite R&D and technology capability.

Bypass strategy in the form of extending existing products into new geographical markets is most likely to require extensive marketing and distribution capability. This is particularly likely to be the case if the new geographical focus is foreign markets.

Another condition typically giving rise to bypass strategies is congestion in the competitive arena—many competitors fighting in the same product/market may spur some firms to try to bypass the fight.

Another condition that greatly facilitates a bypass strategy is not just the availability of resources but the intensity of the organization's commitment of resources to the strategy. It is evident from the above discussion that a bypass strategy involves moving the organization in new strategic directions. Moreover, it will often be the case that the payoff from the strategy may not be apparent for a number of years. Thus, success with a bypass strategy is likely to be a function of the organization's commitment to pursuing the strategy.

RISKS IN BYPASS STRATEGY

Bypass strategy is explicitly designed to create and exploit significant product/market opportunities. As a consequence, and because it almost always entails the firm doing something new and different, some major risks attach to bypass strategy.

First, the bypass strategy may exceed the knowledge, skills, and competency of the firm. Each type of bypass strategy typically requires the firm to develop new knowledge and competence. To the extent that the current firm's knowledge and skill base is lacking and it is not able to fill the void, the bypass strategy is at risk. The absence of an appropriate knowledge and skill base has especially haunted firms seeking to bypass via diversification into unrelated products.

Second, there is always the risk that a bypass strategy, especially one based on diversification into unrelated products or into new geographical markets, may entail conceding some existing product/market to competitors, at least in the short run. The avoidance or minimization of direct confrontation with competitors in existing markets leaves them free to penetrate those marketplaces even further. The danger is that the competitors may avail themselves of this opportunity to strengthen their position and use it as a base to attack the bypassing firm. If the strategy of the bypassing firm falters, it may be extremely vulnerable.

BALANCING RISKS AND BENEFITS

Bypass strategy, although it is an indirect form of competing against specific competitors, is perhaps the most aggressive and risky form of assault attack. It avoids attacking competitors in existing product/markets, but it inherently involves considerable risks since uncertainties are always attached to moving into new product/market domains.

For those firms intent on creating a major strategic initiative in their industries, or most likely, in some segment of an industry, executing a bypass strategy is the logical choice. If it results in a significant change in the rules of the game within an industry segment, it is a strong bet that the initiating firm will have left a number of competitors following its trail.

☐

GUERRILLA STRATEGY:
THE "HIT-AND-RUN" ATTACK

LIAM FAHEY

The strategies discussed so far in this chapter—flanking, frontal, encirclement, and bypass—are broad-based, continual, and extensive resource-consuming attacks on competitors. They represent large-scale combat that is fought out over a considerable period of time. Their aim is to defeat competitors.

These competitive strategies do not exhaust the gamut of possibilities. There is another form of attack strategy, one that is much less ambitious in scope and purpose but nonetheless is often highly successful in both military warfare and the business arena—guerrilla strategy.

Firms can pursue two types of guerrilla attacks: market-focused and non-market-focused attacks. Although the two forms of attack are quite different, they can also be highly related.

MARKET-FOCUSED ATTACKS

This form of attack is typically characterized by the use of small, intermittent assaults on different "territories" held by the competitor. It involves actions designed to harass a competitor as both seek to win the favor of some customer group. This type of guerrilla activity may take many forms.

1. *Price reductions.* A frequently employed form of guerrilla behavior is targeted price reductions. Rather than instituting a general price reduction, the attacking firm chooses to reduce prices in selected geographical markets, distribution channels, or even in some cases with specific customers or accounts.
2. *Special promotions.* These also are often targeted at specific geographical regions or types of customers.
3. *Distribution channel pressure.* A very effective form of guerrilla activity is to bring intense pressure to bear on specific types of distribution channels or individual members of a distribution chain. The pressure may be intended to acquire greater shelf space, greater promotional attention, or lower prices to the ultimate consumer.
4. *Advertising.* Another form of guerrilla tactics is to engage in brief but intense bursts of advertising activity in selected media.

Strategic Planning Management, January, 1986; Commerce Communications, Inc.

5. *Supply interference.* Some firms have successfully employed guerrilla actions to interfere with the flow of supplies to competitors. They may offer a higher price than the competitor to a supplier of raw materials or components for a specified volume of supply. The intent is to pressure the competitor to meet the higher price and/or to jeopardize the competitor's relationship with that supplier.

NON-MARKET-FOCUSED ATTACKS

Market-focused attacks are most guerrillalike in the military sense. To a large degree, they reflect the militarist's hit-and-run mentality, the aim of which is to keep the enemy guessing where the next attack will come from.

However, in the business or competitive arena, non-market-focused attacks manifesting guerrillalike behavior are also clearly evident and used by many firms to good effect. The following are some of the more typical forms.

1. *Legal actions.* Various forms of legal actions are becoming a common way to harass competitors. The intent is to cause sufficient delay or interruption to the plan of the competitor so that it will either give up the fight or be unable to realize its goals for a considerable period of time.
2. *Executive raids.* Another form of harassment is to raid competitors for executive talent. Although there are some legal stipulations as to how this can be done, firms can severely damage their competitors by hiring away key personnel.
3. *Acquisition of distributors.* Taking control of a distributor, either by buying it outright or entering into an exclusive arrangement, is a major way to inflict significant damage on a competitor. Many Japanese firms, for example, have used this tactic in their assaults on the U.S. marketplace.
4. *Information collection.* Much of the market and competitor intelligence gathering activities of many firms reflect guerrillalike traits. They tour competitors' plants, subject competitors' customers to intense questioning about their likes and dislikes of competing products, and they interview former employees of competitors. In the extreme, guerrillalike tactics in information acquisition become covert and illegal, as evidenced in the efforts of Hitachi to gain access to highly secret IBM data.

GOALS OF A GUERRILLA STRATEGY

The aims of a guerrilla strategy (particularly market-focused attacks) are typically clear and straightforward:

1. To harass the competitor so that it cannot concentrate on implementing its preferred strategy. The overriding intent is to keep the competitor

off balance. If the guerrilla strategy is successful, it will result in a disproportionate drain on the resources of the competitor.

2. To demoralize the competitor so that its commitment to doing what is necessary to win in the marketplace is weakened.
3. To use the attacks for short-run gains as a means of facilitating longer-run benefits such as greater market penetration.

The third goal needs particular emphasis. Harassing a competitor is hardly ever sufficient as a goal. The strategy must possess the potential to create some benefits for the aggressor. The damage inflicted upon the competitor must also benefit the aggressor in the long run.

CONDITIONS FACILITATING GUERRILLA STRATEGY

Guerrilla attacks could conceivably be used by firms of any size against any type of competitor under diverse market situations. However, there are several situations that make a guerrilla assault particularly appropriate.

First, guerrilla attacks are more likely to be appropriate if the attacking firm is working from a considerably smaller resource base than its competitors. Smaller firms simply may not have the resource base required to launch a frontal or even a flanking attack on competitors. Thus, a guerrilla strategy may provide the means for the undercapitalized firm to cause trouble for its bigger competitors, in particular by causing them to disperse their resources.

Second, comparative resources often say little about firms' relative market positions. Being a small(er) player in a particular market may also contribute to the appropriateness of a guerrilla strategy. The firm with the smaller market position may be able to harass the larger firm through price discounts, special promotions, focused advertising, etc.

Third, flexibility in taking action and dealing with competitors' responses is also needed by firms seeking to execute guerrilla actions. They need to be able to "hit and run." This requires them to be able to take quick and decisive action, withdraw, and move on to the next action or series of actions.

Fourth, a guerrilla strategy is more likely to be successful if the aggressor can muster a series of minor attacks rather than depending on a few major assaults. The experience in the military theatre shows that a well-planned sequence of minor attacks is more likely to keep the enemy off balance and confused than a few major ones.

Fifth, as we noted above, guerrilla strategy is more appropriate if it carries with it the threat that the aggressor can and will use it as a preamble to a larger fight. It requires a sufficient resource base to back this implicit threat. In short, a guerrilla strategy is not necessarily a cheap operation.

RISKS IN GUERRILLA STRATEGY

If a firm wishes to embark upon a guerrilla strategy, it must be aware of the risks involved. There are three major risks.

First, as in the case with a flanking attack, a guerrilla strategy may serve to awaken competitors, provoking them into taking severe retaliatory action. Price, promotion, advertising, distribution, and product actions may all stir intense competitive response. Without a sufficient resource base, the guerrilla strategy may crumble before the onslaught of competitors' retaliatory actions. This risk reinforces the need for any firm thinking about adopting a guerrilla strategy to carefully assess competitors' potential responses and their likelihood.

Second, a guerrilla strategy may provide very low returns compared to the volume of resources required to effect it. This may be especially true of major market-focused actions. The nature of this risk highlights the need to carefully assess the goals of the guerrilla activity.

Third, a firm may become so preoccupied in making successful hits on the competitor, that it may lose sight of its broader strategic thrusts. When we consider that the aim of this type of strategy is rarely—if ever—to attain significant short-run returns, either in the form of profitability or market position, the nature of the "returns" and linkages between short-run and long-run goals must be thoroughly assessed.

It may be that the returns are in the form of "damage" to the competitor rather than immediate profits to the initiating firm. Indeed, it is possible for the aggressor to actually incur a financial loss with regard to its guerrilla actions. Thus, again, the purposes of the guerrilla activity and where it fits in the firm's broader strategic game plan must be carefully evaluated.

APPLICATION IN STRATEGIC MANAGEMENT:
Choosing a Flanking Strategy:
Some Questions
LIAM FAHEY

Flanking strategies, just like any other type of marketing strategy, are appropriate under certain types of market, competitive, and environmental conditions. But they are not always the best choice.

What are some of the questions that a firm should pose as it seeks to determine whether the conditions it is confronting are amenable to the choice

Strategic Planning Management, October, 1985; Commerce Communications, Inc.

of a flanking strategy? Here is what one firm (which asked not to be identified) asked as it developed a strategy to flank well-established and much better known competitors.

The company was considering entering a segment of the consumer electronics industry that had been largely neglected by the dominant firms in the industry. It was looking at introducing a product that had some distinctive new features compared to existing products and that would sell at a lower price than competing products.

WHO IS THE CUSTOMER?

This question reflected the firm's concern that it not find itself going after only its competitors' customers. If it were, it would immediately invite a retaliatory response from competitors, and thus its efforts to follow a flanking strategy would quickly degenerate into frontal attacks on each other.

Thus, the firm tried to assess carefully whether its strategy would create new first-time customers for the product or simply take customers away from existing competitors. While the firm's strategy was intended to create new customers, the company also recognized that existing product users might also be enticed to use the product. Of course, the firm decided that it would not turn away these customers.

IS THIS A GROWTH MARKET?

Related to the first question was not just the issue of market growth but what part of the market was growing and at what rate? The company believed (and probably rightly so), that the lower the total market growth rate, the more likely that competitors would respond aggressively.

The firm felt it was especially important to estimate the likely size and growth rate of its target niche. Unless this niche could warrant a major marketing effort, the company would likely find itself having to aim at more established segments of the market—and, therefore, having to meet head-to-head entrenched competition.

This led the company to recognize an important facet of any strategy: it is not possible to forecast what results would accrue. The results must be carefully monitored as the strategy is rolled out.

WHAT IS OUR COMPETITIVE ADVANTAGE?

Why would customers buy from us rather than from competitors? What reasons are we giving customers to differentiate in our favor over the offerings of competitors?

The company tackled this question at two levels. Potential new customers, once they had become aware of their need for the product, could still buy the products of other firms. Existing customers for competing products needed to be persuaded to switch from their present choice of product.

For both classes of customer, the firm believed that superior product features, better product performance, and lower prices would constitute its competitive advantages.

HOW WILL COMPETITORS RESPOND?

The company quickly realized that the nature of the competition's responses would determine a number of things: how much time the firm would have to develop a position in its chosen niche; how quickly it might have to alter its strategy; and whether it would have sufficient time to learn about its customers and their responses to the firm's product before major strategy changes would become necessary.

The firm found that it had to look at different competitors in different ways. Some competitors seemed to be especially knowledgeable about technology in the product area. Other firms had greater resources and greater coverage of distribution channels, which would make it easier for them to respond quickly.

WILL THE TECHNOLOGY CHANGE?

A key underlying factor in the firm's efforts to flank its competitors was a technology advance that allowed it to develop and market a superior product— one that had features that competing products did not have—and made it possible to offer the product at a lower price. This technology advance greatly helped in introducing a product that avoided a direct confrontation with existing competitors and also facilitated the company's efforts to create new customers and thus not aggravate competitors by taking away existing customers.

Because of regular technology changes in the industry, a primary condition of success for the flanking strategy was that no major technology change would occur that would either obsolete the firm's product or considerably lessen its competitive advantages. Recognition of the importance of this condition led the firm to extend its efforts to monitor both the product and process technology programs of its competitors as well as those of a few firms not presently regarded as participants in the industry but which were deemed to have potentially relevant technologies.

ARE OUR RESOURCES SUFFICIENT?

Although the firm's choice of a flanking strategy was largely predicated upon its belief that a substantial market niche existed and that it could exploit the niche before competitors could mount an aggressive response, the company was also aware that it did not have comparable resources to many of its potential competitors. Management decided that company resources could best be used by trying to isolate and capture market segments that were not populated by larger, aggressive, and well-entrenched competitors.

What concerned the firm was not so much whether it had sufficient resources to develop and exploit the chosen market niche, but whether it would have sufficient resources if one or more of its competitors were to launch an attack on its niche. Were they to do so, the firm would likely find that its cash flow would be significantly affected, possibly resulting in the need for more debt to allow the firm to remain competitive. The management team had committed itself to keeping its debt burden to a minimum.

DO WE HAVE THE RIGHT KNOWLEDGE?

Related to the question of sufficient resources in the mind of some members of the management team was whether the firm had sufficient knowledge to compete successfully in this market. In particular, they were concerned whether the company knew its potential customers well enough to be able to establish a viable position in the marketplace before competitors might respond.

The following issues were raised:

- Does our sales force have the right knowledge to deal with the distribution system and knowledgeable customers?
- Does our marketing organization know enough about our customers to be able to mount an effective marketing program?
- Do we know enough about our competitors to be able to anticipate their responses and to be able to "read" their intentions once they respond?
- Does our manufacturing organization know enough about technology to be able to continue to manufacture a quality product at reasonable cost in the face of continuing technology change?

Each of these points was seen as important to the firm's strategy—each dealt with an important ingredient of the efforts to flank its competitors.

WHAT ARE THE KEY CONTINGENCIES?

Going through the above procedure allowed the company to identify "key contingencies"—events or actions of others that must be anticipated in developing plans. They revolved around five elements:

- Slower or greater than expected market growth or penetration
- Smaller or greater than expected product switching by customers now buying from competitors

- Rapid and aggressive response by competitors
- Major technology change
- Insufficient organizational resources

In essence, consideration of each of these contingencies led the company to review the validity of the choice of a flanking strategy. The biggest question was whether the firm could avoid a head-to-head confrontation with dominant competitors until it had built up the strength to take them on. The company found a positive response to each question and is now embarking upon the flanking strategy.

STRATEGY IN ACTION

How do you enter a mature, competitive product category? And, then, what do you follow with? Topol, "the smoker's tooth polish," produced by Jeffrey Martin, Inc., provides a good example. Now they have come out with a mouthwash, also targeted for smokers.

The negative side-effects of smoking—the cosmetic ones as well as the health-related ones—have become a matter of increased concern. Topol and several other early products have successfully responded to that concern with a product that offers a distinct benefit and isn't easily replicable by established brands—a perfect illustration of a flanking strategy.

Then what? Instead of going into the intensely competitive toothpaste business, Topol introduced another product—also a flanker—that built on the original product's reputation within a segment of the market. While the results aren't in, prospects for the line extension are good. The company has developed a sound strategy based on the psychographics of a segment of the market.

□

APPLICATION IN STRATEGIC MANAGEMENT:
Developing a Bypass Strategy:
Some Considerations
LIAM FAHEY

A potential bypass strategy must always be strenuously evaluated: the potential rewards may be substantial, but the risks are also great. For many smaller firms, bypass may be close to "abet the company strategy."

But it can work, here's how a small firm (small by comparison to many of its competitors) in an industrial market effected a successful bypass strategy,

Strategic Planning Management, December, 1985; Commerce Communications, Inc.

ensuring that the inherent risks were worth the gamble, especially in regard to the responses of customers and competitors.

THE STRATEGY

The company's intended strategy was an almost classic bypass attack on its competitors. It was composed of a number of elements.

1. Developing a new product that would be significantly technologically superior to the offerings of either competitors or the company's own current products
2. Imbuing the product with some attributes that would allow the company not only to take current customers away from competitors but also create new customers
3. Changing the competitive focus away from price and toward performance capability and service

Each of these elements could be viewed as part of the firm's effort to change the rules of the competitive game and move the battle to a new competitive arena.

MOTIVATING FORCES

As seen by the company, a number of forces added merit to the desirability of a bypass strategy.

First, the marketplace was crowded. A number of competitors produced products that were largely similar in terms of performance and price.

Second, many customers were becoming much more technologically sophisticated and were beginning to pressure suppliers to improve product quality, that is, supply products that would better meet their needs.

Third, no major advances had occurred in the core technology for almost four years. Competitors thus found themselves competing on price rather than on performance, quality, and service with a consequent decline in margins and profits for all the combatants.

NEW PRODUCT DEVELOPMENT

The wellspring of the bypass strategy was internally sourced new product development. The firm worked closely with a select number of customers in developing a line of products completely new to the market. The working relationship with these customers was highlighted by the following characteristics:

1. A group of the firm's engineers spent a number of weeks working with the technical personnel in each of the customers' plants. During this

time period, they established a detailed understanding of the customers' needs through intensive discussion with a wide variety of personnel and observation of their operations.

2. The engineering team made a particular point of not confining its discussions to their engineering counterparts. They felt that they needed to gain the perspective of others, especially those who were involved in using their products and those who were involved in the decision to purchase their products.

3. The engineering team also invited specific individuals in these client firms to make a presentation describing what they would like to see in the new product. This proved to be a valuable source of ideas.

CHANGING THE RULES

The explicit intent of the strategy was to bypass competitors in such a way that the rules of the competitive game would be irrevocably changed from the point of view of competitors. The firm sought to do this in a number of ways.

To start with, the product development program was oriented toward getting a product into customers' plants that would outperform anything offered by competitors. Superior performance was measured along a number of dimensions.

- Greater performance predictability
- Greater variety of uses
- Easier to service and replace
- Longer period of use

The firm planned to extensively "sell" each one of these dimensions to existing and potential customers.

Superior product performance was directly attributable to a new technology that the firm had largely developed internally. The technology was developed with the help of one outside organization—a small consulting firm that had considerable expertise in related technologies.

The technology was distinct from existing technologies in a variety of ways. Thus, it would not be easy for competitors to learn and replicate—a consideration that was key to allowing the firm some lead time in order to establish its position in the marketplace.

The company, however, was adamant that it would not fall into a trap it perceived had befallen many others in a similar position: a technologically superior product, that offered considerable advantages to the customer compared to existing products but which did not do as well as was expected because of a paucity of marketing clout behind its introduction and early market penetration efforts.

Consequently, the firm put together a marketing team to oversee the first installations of the product and to develop and execute a marketing plan to get the product into as many customers' plants as possible in the first two years.

It is also worthy of note that the marketing team was put together in the later stages of the product's development and spent a large amount of its time with the engineering team that developed the product. Thus, the marketing team, which consisted predominantly of engineers, was able to learn not just about the product and its attributes, but also about its application or trial in customers' plants.

The latter point was especially significant because the marketing team was charged with developing new product applications and new customers. Senior management insisted that the company could not sit on its laurels were the product to be a success.

WINNING THE CUSTOMER

In a bypass strategy, as in any other type of strategy, it is not enough merely to beat the competition. You must also win the customer.

The central thrust of the product development effort for this particular company was to provide a product that would satisfy the cusomer needs. Thus the question continually asked by the head of the product development team was: what does this do for the customer? This led to extensive interaction with the customer in all phases of product development.

Just as important, in the view of many company people, were the efforts to monitor customer response to the product once it was launched.

- Some members of the product development team visited several of the first major customers to gauge initial reaction to the product
- Each member of the marketing team visited different types of customers to learn as much about different applications of the product as quickly as they could
- In a few cases, members of the product development and marketing teams made customer calls together

Most customer calls also involved some degree of what one marketing team member called "on-the-spot fire-fighting." They had to deal with questions about the product: how it differed from existing products, what its limitations were, how it might be improved, what the next technology development might be, etc.

WILL COMPETITORS CATCH UP?

A critical assumption underlying the firm's strategy (as is always the case with a bypass attack) was that competitors would not be able to catch up to its product development achievement for some time, if at all.

The evidence used by the company to support this assumption was threefold:

1. Competitors had shown little capacity or inclination to engage in product innovation
2. Competitors had little, if any, knowledge of the technology underlying the firm's new product
3. Because it had taken the company over three years to develop the product, many company executives felt that it would take any firm that did not have their knowledge base considerably longer, even though the product was on the market.

There was, however, concern that the company would be facing new competitors. A bypass strategy inevitably brings the initiating firm into a new product/market domain. In this case, the technology in the new domain meant that the firm was now much closer to a large number of well-established firms that were heavily involved in related technologies.

Some senior managers in the firm suspected that some of these potential competitors could be enticed into the market if they determined that an opportunity existed. The irony for the firm was that the success of its product would signal the existence of an opportunity to competitors.

CHAPTER

— 9 —

CORPORATE-LEVEL STRATEGY: SOME DECISION CONTEXTS

■

□

THE STRATEGIC MANAGEMENT OF FIRST DIVERSIFICATION: A NEW PERSPECTIVE

CHARLES W. HOFER AND JAMES J. CHRISMAN

The first acquisitive diversifier faces the problems of:

1. Continuing major competition in its original business
2. Competing successfully in a new industry
3. Effectively integrating the newly acquired business(es) with its existing organization
4. Coping with the transition to a new, and more complex, set of strategic concerns.

The situation boils down to one of learning several quite different and quite difficult top management skills simultaneously.

Such a task would be challenging under any circumstances. It is, however, aggravated substantially when the first diversifier's acquisition(s) face major strategic opportunities and threats in its own industries. And this is normally the case, since both existing diversification theory and current management practice suggest that the preferred acquisitions should have high market attractiveness and at least average business strengths (see Figure 9-1). The major question,

Strategic Planning Management, October, 1986; Commerce Communications, Inc.

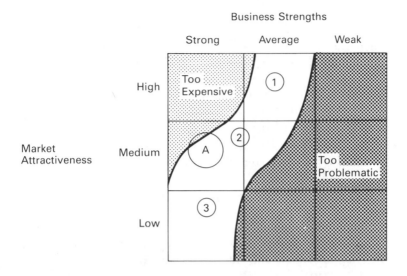

A Denotes the normal position of firms facing first
diversification acquisition decisions for the first time.

1, 2, 3 Denote the traditional priorities placed on potential
acquisition candidates in first diversification decisions.

Figure 9-1 First acquisitive diversification priorities: guidelines from existing diversification theory and management practice

then, turns to a consideration of what this all means for first diversification strategy.

SOME NEW GUIDELINES

It is clear that an organization's strategy for its first acquisitive diversification efforts should be formulated in such a way as to minimize the difficulties of integration and transition. Naturally, planning is important. Yet the question still remains: "How can an organization effectively plan the integration of new business(es) *and* the transition to a new level of strategic sophistication if it has never faced either challenge before?"

Perhaps the first thing that is clear when addressing the first acquisitive diversification problem is that past solutions will not do. Recent acquisition history is littered with the wreckage of firms that have followed these guidelines and failed.

Only two approaches suggest themselves. First, firms can try to develop different ways of coping with such first diversifying acquisition challenges. Alternatively, firms can try to reduce the complexity of the challenges such situations pose.

LEARNING TO COPE

The first acquisitive diversification problem has its genesis in the simultaneous influence of four major strategic challenges:

1. The continuing series of major opportunities and threats still confronting the firm in its own industry
2. The new opportunities and threats the firm will have to face in a totally new industry
3. The difficulties encountered in integrating the newly acquired business(es) with its existing organization
4. The difficulties encountered in learning how to manage a multi-industry firm.

The attempt to increase the firm's coping capacity seeks to "solve" this dilemma by minimizing the difficulties associated with learning how to manage a multi-industry firm.

In general, there are three approaches that a firm can use to try to improve its coping capabilities in first acquisitive diversification situations:

1. It can hire outsiders who have experience in running multi-industry firms to replace some or all of the existing members of its top management team.
2. It can hire one or more consultants experienced in the management of multi-industry firms to act as advisors for the initial years of the transition.
3. It can send some or all of its existing top management to executive training programs whose focus is the management of multi-industry firms.

Few, if any, top level executives are willing to consider the first option for understandable reasons. Almost every firm considering acquisitive diversification for the first time has normally experienced periods of high growth during which it has successfully met all the challenges encountered. As a result, it has usually become one of the leading competitors in its industry. It is also relatively young as firms go. Consequently, its top executives are usually still relatively young, and are considered by both their peers and their communities to be exemplars of success—modern Horatio Algers, as it were. To suggest that such individuals are incapable of successfully implementing a diversification program goes against the grain.

To suggest further that they need to step down so that someone with no experience in their industry or firm can take over just because that individual has experience in running a multi-industry firm would be the height of folly! Not only would this suggestion fall on deaf ears, the proposer would lose all credibility and influence over the firm's future direction! As well he or she should! Unless, of course, no other options are available. And the latter possibility will never occur as long as the management consulting community is alive and well.

Unfortunately, consultants are not normally the answer either. The problem is their work routine and fee structure. Consultants are accustomed to working on specific projects for which they use junior associates to do most of the detail work, while one or more senior members of the firm supervise the effort.

In making the transition to effective multi-industry strategic management, though, there are only a small number of specific projects to be done. What is needed, instead, is a change in the day-to-day activities of top management. Consequently, there are few contributions that junior consulting associates could make that would assist the transition process. Senior consultants could help, but most first acquisitive diversifiers would find it difficult to afford such assistance to the extent it would be needed because of the length of time necessary to complete the transition process and the typical billing rates of senior consultants.

Which leaves executive training programs. Unfortunately, little help is available here either, primarily because of the nature of such programs. Typically, they are of two general types: short (up to one week) programs on specific topics, or longer (three- to fifteen-week) programs aimed at improving overall management skills. The later programs are not of much use in the first diversification situation, though, because the three- to four-week programs do not spend enough time on issues of multi-industry strategic management to be of much help, while the ten- to fifteen-week programs take more time than the executives of the normal first acquisitive diversifier can afford to spend off the job—and even then the issues of multi-industry strategic management are usually not covered comprehensively.

Short programs on the latter topic would clearly be far more helpful. Regrettably, none of the major institutions offering such programs, including the American Management Association, the Conference Board, *Business Week's* Executive Education Subsidiary, and the executive programs of Harvard, Stanford, Wharton, Columbia, Northwestern, MIT, NYU, Michigan, Penn State, and UCLA, offer any programs on this topic. Nor is there a listing for any such programs in *Bricker's International Directory of University Executive Programs.* Thus, even if such programs existed, it is doubtful that most of the firms that would have need of them could find them.

This does not mean that first acquisitive diversifiers should not try to improve their coping capabilities. Clearly, they should, through efforts such as seeking new board members who have multi-industry strategic management experience, sending selected members of their top management team to some of the shorter general management training programs to improve their overall management skills, and possibly even by hiring a few executives with multi-industry strategic management skills for newly created top management positions such as that of corporate planner or internal corporate consultant.

What the above comments do imply, though, is that even if all such efforts were undertaken, they would generally prove to be insufficient to guarantee successful passage through the difficult transition associated with moving from the management of a single-industry firm to that of a multi-industry firm.

REDUCING COMPLEXITY

The only alternative left is that of reducing the complexity of the strategic challenges which first acquisitive diversifiers face. This means that transition and integration problems must take precedence over decisions with regard to the type of business(es) to acquire and/or the type of industry(ies) to enter. Recalling the basic causes of the first diversification dilemma indicates that there are two ways in which this might be done.

One is to delay all diversification efforts until the major challenges inherent in the firm's existing industry have been met. Unfortunately, this solution confronts the firm with three problems most managements are unwilling to face.

The first is that the failure to diversify will leave the firm vulnerable to the vagaries of a single industry. Of course, almost every firm faces this problem from the day it is founded. During the early years, however, when the challenges are ones of survival and growth, nothing else can be done. As both the firm and its industry mature, however, this is no longer the case. Therefore, whether seeking growth or the decreased risk that accompanies diversification, few managements are willing to wait until they have extracted the last ounce of growth out of their original industry before diversifying.

The second problem with delaying diversification is that the slowing of the firm's growth rate will normally substantially decrease its price earnings multiple, and, as a result, the resources it has available for its diversification efforts. Put differently, if diversification is delayed, a firm can no longer use its high P/E multiples to help pay for its acquisitions, but must, instead, either pay cash or issue enough new stock that earnings dilutions become possible. And, in both cases, the magnitude of the firm's diversification potentials will be reduced.

The final problem with delaying diversification is that it often restricts the number of industries which a firm might profitably enter, simply because the firm's increased size (as a result of its growth during the delay period) rules out entry into industries that once might have been attractive, but are now too small to make entry desirable. As a consequence, few firms that have the capability to diversify effectively are willing to substantially delay their efforts to do so.

The second option for reducing the complexity of the strategic challenges faced by the acquisitive first diversifier is to choose acquisition candidate(s) that will minimize the amount of integration time and effort required and that will also be able to stand on their own feet until the transition of the firm's top management to a multi-industry perspective is relatively complete.

NEW CRITERIA

This requirement of minimizing both the acquisition's integration time and the number and magnitude of new industry challenges it poses for the first diversifier's management dictates some changes in the traditional set of criteria used for such acquisitions. Specifically, it suggests that the initial diversification acquisition target(s) should:

1. Be in an industry not currently facing any major strategic challenges
2. Be either the dominant firm in that industry or the dominant firm in some unique segment of that industry
3. Be less than a third of the size of the first diversifier

The rationale for the requirement that the industry entered not currently face any major strategic challenges seems clear enough. Its implications need to be examined a bit more thoroughly, however. Most importantly, it eliminates from consideration all industries in which the bases of competition and/or relative competitive positions are changing. Thus, industries in the development, growth, shakeout, early maturity, and decline stages of the life cycle are out. Industries without some moderate barriers to entry are also out. Moreover, even industries in the late maturity or saturation stages of the life cycle that have moderate barriers to entry are eliminated if they are currently undergoing changes in their bases of competition.

It is interesting to note what the application of these criteria would do in Heublein's case (see **STR,** August 1986, p. 57). First, the acquisition of Kentucky Fried Chicken would have been eliminated since KFC's segment of the fast food industry was in the late shakeout or early maturity stage of the life cycle when Heublein acquired it. The acquisition of Hamm's would also have been eliminated because the beer industry was in the midst of a major shakeout as evidenced by both the increasing shares of the dominant firms in the industry and the fact that over 200 of the 350 competitors in the industry in 1945 had dropped out by the time Heublein acquired Hamm's in 1965.

The requirement that the firm acquired be dominant either in the entire industry entered or some unique segment of it stems from the fact that such dominance usually increases the stability of both the firm's sales and profits. Applying this criterion to Heublein indicates that the acquisition of Kentucky Fried Chicken would pass muster, but that the acquisition of Hamm's would again be rejected—unless Hamm's were to shrink its scope and become a regional brewer by concentrating its efforts in the North Central United States. Interestingly, the latter option is the only high-profit scenario generated by Howard Stevenson's financial model of the Hamm's acquisition.

The requirement that first diversifying acquisition(s) be less than a third the size of the first diversifier stems from our finding that firms should not undertake major new projects of any sort that require more than about 30% of the firm's normal cash flow, and from the common sense observation that the smaller the first diversification effort(s), the smaller the challenges they will pose for the diversifier. Applying this criterion to Heublein indicates that the Kentucky Fried Chicken acquisition was just slightly larger than would have been desirable. The Hamm's acquisition, however, was clearly far too big, as Hamm's was 75% of Heublein's size at the time of purchase. In fact, if federal excise taxes were deducted from both Heublein's and Hamm's sales figures, Hamm's was actually about a third larger than Heublein.

In summary, the revised acquisition criteria that we have proposed for first acquisitive diversifiers indicate that Heublein's acquisition of Hamm's would have been rejected by all three considerations, while its acquisition of Kentucky Fried Chicken passed one criterion, was marginal on another, and failed the third.

Our new criteria for first acquisitive diversifications also seem to work well in other situations. Thus, Phillip Morris' acquisition of Miller would have been approved because Miller was less than a third the size of Phillip Morris and Miller was the dominant competitor in the premium quality, light drinker segment of the brewing industry. Moreover, although the beer industry was still in the throes of a shakeout when Phillip Morris made the acquisition, even here there was a difference. Not only did Phillip Morris know about the shakeout, its strategy envisioned a restructing of the brewing industry that would be abetted by the shakeout already in motion.

From a portfolio perspective, our new criteria mean that a firm planning its first diversifying acquisitions should focus more on "cash cow" type businesses, than on the "budding star" type businesses that have been traditionally sought in such situations (see Figure 9-2).

This also illustrates a rather subtle benefit of our new criteria. It is the fact that "cash cow" businesses are not only more *stable* than "budding star" businesses, they also generate more resources than they consume. This means that these excess resources can be used to help a first acquisitive diversifier to meet the continuing challenges that it faces in its original business. Thus, rather than *doubly* compounding the strategic challenges confronting the acquisitive first diversifier, they *doubly* reduce them.

CONCLUSIONS

The central thrust of this article is that top management, when facing the unique situation posed by first diversifying acquisition decisions, should forego the deceptively attractive lure of high-growth markets and companies in favor of more stable ones. Implicit in this recommendation is the contention that

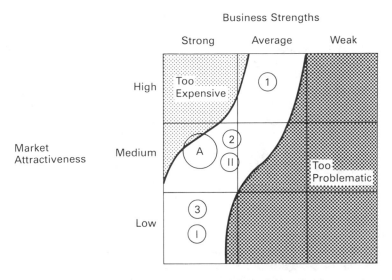

A Denotes the normal position of firms facing first
  diversification acquisition decisions for the first time.

1, 2, 3 Denote the traditional priorities placed on potential
  acquisition candidates in first diversification decisions.

I, II Denote the revised focus suggested for potential first
  acquisition candidates by strategic management
  considerations.

Figure 9-2   First acquisitive diversification priorities: new guidelines suggested by strategic management theory

the key task facing top management in these situations is that of learning
how to manage a multi-industry firm—a job that is sufficiently demanding
and that requires so much of top management's attention that it is unwise to
simultaneously undertake large risks in other areas.

At the same time, it should be emphasized that the revised first diversification acquisition guidelines presented in this article will not *ensure* the success
of any single diversification move, nor will divergence from them result in sure
failure. What they will do, however, is increase the *probabilities* of success,
other things being equal.

There is still much work left to be done. First, these new guidelines need
to be tested against a larger sample of first diversification results to ensure
that they are as generalizable as they appear to be. In addition, they prompt
several other questions about first diversification strategy and organizational
learning, such as: In first diversification moves, are there advantages in choosing
acquisitions over internal development? If so, what are they? And, will two
or more first diversification acquisitions shorten the time needed for a firm's

management to make the transition to an effective multi-industry strategic management?

The challenges are many, but the rewards should be correspondingly great.

□

THE STRATEGIC MANAGEMENT OF FIRST DIVERSIFICATION: A NEW PERSPECTIVE
CHARLES W. HOFER AND JAMES J. CHRISMAN

In 1965, Heublein, Inc., the manufacturer and marketer of Smirnoff vodka and other liquor and food products, made its first major diversifying acquisition—that of the Theodore Hamm's Brewing Co. Heublein's management felt that its distinctive skills in advertising and promotion, which had enabled it to increase sales 89% and profits 259% during the previous six years, would be transferrable to the brewing industry, enabling it to reverse Hamm's deteriorating financial and market position. However, Heublein, which was barely larger than Hamm's, was unable to direct sufficient resources or skills to Hamm's for it to gain ground on the market leaders in the brewing industry such as Anheuser Busch and Schlitz. In fact, Hamm's financial and market position continued to worsen to the extent that Heublein was forced to divest Hamm's in the early 1970s.

In 1971, just six years after its ill-fated venture with Hamm's, Heublein made another major diversifying acquisition when it acquired Kentucky Fried Chicken, the famous fast-food restaurant chain. Ten years later, the results of this acquisition could best be described as poor, and Heublein stockholders would have been better off had the acquisition not been made.

The Heublein story is particularly interesting because of the implications and insights it offers for management practice with regard to diversification, and especially first diversification, strategy. It is somewhat unsettling to note that Heublein, a company with proven management that was skilled in retail advertising and promotion, has been so unsuccessful in its major diversifying acquisitions. What is even more unsettling is the fact that *both* acquisitions were consistent with existing theory and practice regarding diversification strategy.

However, despite the convergence between Heublein's acquisitive diversification behavior and extant diversification theory, both acquisitions must be considered as failures, which raises the interesting questions: "Are the existing theories wrong?" "Or, are they correct, but incomplete?" "Or, was Heublein just plain unlucky?"

Strategic Planning Management, August, 1986; Commerce Communications, Inc.

REASONS FOR DIVERSIFICATION

It seems hard to deny the importance of relatedness and synergy in diversification, especially when strong evidence exists to support their relationship to performance. Yet, it is also evident that the benefits available are not easily obtainable, implying that diversification theory and its practical application is not as well developed as it should be. And this is especially true with respect to the approaches a firm should take in its initial diversification moves.

Several reasons have been proposed explaining a firm's decision to diversify. One basic contention is that diversification is motivated by the inability of a firm's existing line(s) of business to meet its growth objectives. A further elaboration cited additional reasons why firms diversify:

1. Their objectives can no longer be met within their current product-market scope.
2. Their retained earnings exceed their total expansion cash needs.
3. Diversification opportunities promise greater profitability than expansion opportunities.
4. Available information is not reliable enough to permit a conclusive comparison between expansion and diversification.

A firm's decision to diversify need not always be reactive (e.g., in response to problems such as declining demand); it can also be proactive (e.g., searching for new opportunities). Additional insights into the reasons firms diversify include:

1. To complete product lines.
2. To increase market share.
3. To fully utilize existing marketing capabilities, contacts, or channels.
4. To offset unsatisfactory sales growth in current product/markets.
5. To capitalize on distinctive technological expertise.
6. To obtain patents, licenses, or technical know-how.
7 To meet demand of diversified customers.
8. To fully utilize existing production capacity.

Other research on why firms diversify find the following:

1. Portfolio risk theories (firms diversify to reduce risk).
2. Escape paradigm (firms diversify to escape declining prospects in their existing business).
3. Organizational scale theories (firms diversify to obtain economies from overall size).
4. Systems effect theories (firms diversify to benefit from increased sophistication in reward systems, resource allocations, etc.).

5. Conglomerate growth theories (firms diversify to take advantage of book-keeping gains).

Different reasons for diversification usually lead to different strategic approaches to diversification, and may, therefore, affect performance differently.

CHOOSING ACQUISITION CANDIDATES

Research on the characteristics and performance of 69 acquisitions made by 20 companies between 1960–1965 demonstrates that firms utilizing explicit acquisition evaluation criteria were more likely to be successful than those that did not have any explicit criteria for evaluating acquisitions. Table 9-1 identifies various sets of such acquisition critieria.

Perhaps the most widely espoused criteria for a firm to consider in its diversification strategy, however, is that of synergy. This concept basically proposes that groups of functions and/or businesses can be combined in such a way that the resulting whole is greater than the sum of its parts. Sales, operations, asset structure, management systems and personnel, and start-up are the most likely areas in which potential synergies might occur for most normal diversification moves.

Other criteria have also been proposed. One suggestion is that a diversification move should be large enough to compete effectively in the entered business. Others argue that, at least in the case of unrelated acquisitions, the diversification should not be too large.

In the case of diversification by acquisition or merger, the most promising candidates are probably those that compete in a well-defined market niche, produce essential products with high value added, and are located in close proximity to the acquirer. However, other research studies specify that high market

TABLE 9-1   Acquisition Criteria

A	B	C
1. Sales stability	1. Financial position	1. Investment liquidity
2. General economic environment	2. Company structure	2. Societal responsibilities
3. Breadth of combined product market base	3. Growth patterns	3. Political risk
4. Operational compatibility	4. Market potential	4. Financial fit/risk pooling
5. Potential for increasing acquired company's strength	5. Standing with suppliers	
6. Potential for joint product development	6. Growth potential	
	7. Candidate's reason for selling	
	8. Seller's long-range objectives	
	9. Candidate's business philosophy	
	10. People who work in the candidate's business	

share is a more desirable characteristic. This would imply the acquisition of "stars" or "cash cows" rather than the acquisition of "question marks." Most researchers agree that "dogs" and businesses facing major turnaround situations should be avoided.

Research studies concerning the "best" industries to enter via diversifying acquisitions basically presume that high growth rates are essential to maximize the potential for success of the diversification move. However, at least one researcher asserts that entry into markets in the introductory *or* maturity life-cycle stages can be successful in less concentrated industries.

From a slightly different perspective, the most unsuccessful types of acquisitions have been those involving concentric marketing and concentric technology synergies, which accounted for 26% and 21% of all failures respectively. The reason for this somewhat surprising finding was the fact that such synergistic benefits were hard to achieve because the organizational structures and systems of the acquiring and acquired firms restricted the effective consolidation and integration of the two. This implies that unless such administrative problems can be avoided, or at least minimized, the probabilities of failure are increased, regardless of the potential benefits that might be achieved through such mergers.

Finally, a study of corporate strategy found that dominant constrained and related constrained corporate strategies produced the best overall performance, while dominant vertical and unrelated passive corporate strategies produced the worst performance. The most important implication of this research for potential acquisitive diversifiers is that performance differences among corporate strategy categories seem to be more closely linked to the ways in which the firm has related its new businesses to its existing ones, than to its overall diversity (see Figure 9-3 and Table 9-2).

INITIAL DIVERSIFICATION DECISION

Despite all the theory and research, little attention has been given to the special characteristics of the first diversification efforts of a firm. Especially ignored has been the fact that such moves represent, for the firm involved, a transition of somewhat unusual dimensions: namely, moving from a single business operation to a multi-industry one. Little research has been done on the management issues and actions appropriate for the transitions from one organizational configuration to another. Yet it is just these unique managerial and organizational aspects of an organization's first diversification moves which are responsible (in our opinion) for much of the gap between existing diversification theory and the poor performance of most of the organizations that have followed such theory.

Furthermore, while some of the diversification literature recognizes the problems inherent in integrating a new business unit into existing operations, none of it fully recognizes that such integration is merely the first part of the

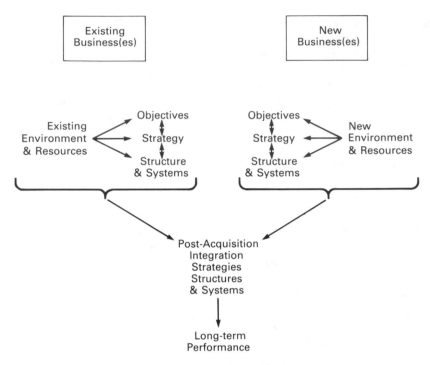

Figure 9-3   Determinants of diversification success

TABLE 9-2   Diversification in Proposition Form

---

1. The principal objectives of a firm's diversification efforts influence both the type of diversification strategy chosen and the approaches used to implement that strategy.
2. Explicitly planning both pre- and post-diversification corporate and business strategies
increases the probability of successful diversification performance, all else being held
equal.
3. Diversifications into related product-markets, especially those in which common core skills
can be built upon and exploited, will offer a greater probability of success than unrelated
diversifications, all else being equal.
4. The greater the market share of the acquired firm and the greater its size relative to that
of the acquiring firm, the greater the probability of successful diversification performance,
all else being held equal.
5. The greater the resistance to the integration of the acquired and acquiring businesses, the
lower will be the probability of successful post-acquisition performance of the diverisifica-
tion move, all else being held equal.
6. The post-diversification performance of the acquiring firm is contingent upon the diversification strategy chosen, its pre-diversification situation, the situation faced by the acquired
firm, and by how the intregation task is carried out.

---

task: once such integration is accomplished, the newly diversified company is faced with the ongoing, and somewhat novel, task of managing a multi-industry corporation—a task that usually requires major changes in most or all of its major management systems and processes (see Table 9-3).

In addition, the nature of the strategic management task is substantially different in multi-industry corporations than it is in single-business firms. In particular, top management in the multi-industry corporation must ensure both that the overall organizational corporate strategy and individual business unit strategies are compatible with the organization's objectives, and that the organization's macrostructure and major management systems and culture permit the successful implementation of these strategies.

These problems are also usually magnified because the first acquisitive diversifier still faces major strategic challenges in its original business and also the process of integrating the new business(es) usually requires the coordination of two (or more) different strategic thrusts and distinctive competences.

In short, the first acquisitive diversifier faces the problems of:

1. Continuing major competition in its original business
2. Competing successfully in a new industry
3. Effectively integrating the newly acquired business(es) with its existing organization
4. Coping with the transition to a new, and more complex set of strategic concerns.

The situation boils down to one of learning several quite different and quite difficult top management skills simultaneously.

Such a task would be challenging under any circumstances. It is, however, aggravated substantially when the first diversifier's acquisition(s) face major strategic opportunities and threats in their own industries. And this is normally the case, since both existing diversification theory and current management practice suggest that the preferred acquisitions should have high market attractiveness and at least average business strengths. The major question, then, turns to a consideration of what this all means for first diversification strategy.

□

MANAGING DIVESTITURE EFFECTIVELY
MARILYN TAYLOR

Today, in many U.S. firms, divestiture activity takes a significant portion of executive energy. Many firms are divesting their unrelated businesses in order to concentrate their resources and attention on their core business.

Strategic Planning Management, February, 1985; Commerce Communications, Inc.

TABLE 9-3 Strategy, Structure, and Systems

	Single Product Line	Multiple Product Lines
Product/service transactions	Integrated pattern of transactions	Non-integrated pattern of transactions
Distribution	One set of channels	Multiple channels
R&D	Increasingly institutionalized search for product & process improvements	Institutionalized search for new products and improvements
Strategic choices	Market share objectives Breadth of product line Degree of integration	Rate of growth Entry/exit from industries Resource allocation
Organizational structure	Functionally specialized	Specialized by products & markets
Performance measures	Impersonal Technical and/or cost criteria	Impersonal Market criteria
Rewards	Systematic Stability & service values	Systematic Performance value
Control systems	Strategic: Personal CEO control Operating: Policies & delegation	Corporate: Organizational results Business unit: Delegation

Source: Adapted from Bruce R. Scott, "Stages of Corporate Development—Part I," Harvard Case Services, No. 9-371-294, 1971.

Conversations with over twenty senior managers who managed divestitures for their companies, suggest that there are a number of issues which must be addressed if the firm's divestitures are to be carried out effectively. Seven of these issues are discussed below.

WHY DIVEST?

Perhaps it would be better to ask *when* should the firm divest? Firms divest for numerous reasons. Some are returning to an original focused strategy or moving to a new one. Others regularly buy and sell units in their portfolio.

A frequently heard comment is, "We should have sold that unit long ago." Recently, one executive went on to say, "You see, we consider ourselves a family (of businesses). The emotional attachment often gets in the way of good business sense." Such an orientation has multiple costs as division managers pursue the elusive and often unattainable goal of "turnaround." If the turnaround is *both* operational and strategic, the task may be insurmountable. It is not unusual for such division executives to come to corporate *after* the decision to divest is made and say, "Why didn't you sell our unit long ago?"

The current evidence suggests that many firms hold on to divisions past the parent company's ability to effectively manage the division strategically and, perhaps, even operationally. This observation leads to the recommendation that:

Firms should regularly screen divisions for potential divestment.

Such screening should include the following question: Which (other) companies might be better able to strategically position this business unit?

When suitable new potential "homes" for a division are forthcoming in a review, the time may be ripe for a divestiture that may be better for the current parent company, the subsidiary, and the new parent. Currently, the review for potential divestiture frequently consists of the CEO calling a halt by saying, "We can't afford to lose this much money."

Few company cultures have gone so far as to encourage initiation of divestiture from among the division managers themselves. In most instances, division managers are expected to present plans as though they will remain in the portfolio on an ongoing basis.

At least one company, however, has moved to make it "okay" for division managers to initiate consideration of divestiture. In this firm, multi-stream financial reward systems have been set up. Some unit managers are rewarded on the basis of contributing to the company's long-term growth, while others are rewarded for providing the financial resources for fueling that growth. Managers *are* rewarded even if their strategic plan may include divestiture of their unit. This situation is in stark contrast to most firms where initiation of divestiture comes strictly from corporate management.

The above leads to the following conclusion:

Firms should legitimize multi-level consideration of divestiture, because it may lead to earlier identification of divestiture opportunities that yield higher payoffs.

TO TELL OR NOT TO TELL?

Corporate executives agree that among the most difficult issues inherent in divestment are "personnel" problems.

First among these is *when* to tell division executives. As noted above, one firm legitimized initiation of divestiture consideration at the divisional level. At the other extreme is a CEO who called the division executive and said, "You're sold."

Part of the dilemma emanates from concern as to whether the key people will flee the division once the decision to divest is made. Most executives agree, however, that the longer the time period from the decision to divest to actual divestiture, the more likely the Rumor Mill will carry the news—however inaccurately!

The problem of rumors is exacerbated in instances where the parent company decides not to tell division executives, and then the first one or even two overtures to potential buyers are turned down. If the industry in which the unit operates is tight knit, there are few entrants, or the division executive has close relationships with many of the competitor firms, word is likely to get back to the division—fast. The recommendation from executives, therefore, appears to be:

If the time from decision to divestiture is to be short, division executives may be kept in the dark.

However, a number of other factors also enter in. In some instances, the unit to be sold is very specialized in terms of its products, market emphasis, or manufacturing processes. Corporate executives have little idea who would be a likely buyer. In these instances, division executives are often informed of the divestiture early. These observations suggest that:

Where the unit to be divested is highly specialized, or the time to actual divestment is expected to be long, division executives should be informed early.

SHOULD WE RENOVATE THE UNIT?

Unless the buyer has made the initial contact with the seller, there is often a considerable time lag between the decision to divest and closure of sale.

For example, in one firm which has undertaken a wave of divestitures, the time lag has varied from 90 days to three years. Another firm is still looking for a buyer for a "discontinued operation" three years after the decision to divest it.

The expected time to complete a sale impacts tremendously on strategic and operational choices in the interim. Other factors which are also critical are the current performance of the unit and the expected risks attendant with new investments in the unit. Some examples illustrate the importance of these factors. In one company, the business unit had a new product line ready to launch. All of the firm's analysis indicated that the product line should do very well. The corporation opted to make the investment and hold the unit for 18 months to three years. In another company, in which corporate management estimated that a buyer would not be forthcoming for at least a year, the decision was made to "trim" the unit's assets.

In those instances in our study where the decision was made to conduct "business as usual," the performance of the unit was typically good enough that the corporation would not suffer any cash drain.

One other factor must also be taken into account. Where the parent company has opted to tell divisional executives late, it is usually advisable to stick to the unit's strategic plan.

Significant deviations from the plan, especially if made midyear, raise the possibility of suspicion. Where division executives are informed early in the process, they can often be helpful in realigning the objectives and operations of the unit. The above leads to the following conclusion:

> Consideration must be given to realigning the objectives and operations of the unit, in order to enhance its value to potential buyers.

WHO'S THE "RIGHT BUYER"?

Just as motivations for selling differ, so, too, does choice of buyer differ. The processes the corporation uses in finding the buyer and selling the unit differ. At least three are frequently used.

1. Management leveraged buyouts. Management leveraged buyouts have received significant recent attention in the business press. Not so long ago, management buyouts were considered the "last resort" option. However, some firms now consider a management buyout *first*. At least two aspects are weighed in considering an early approch to division management:

- Is current management financially capable of effecting a buyout or of effecting a consortium of investors?
- Are we willing to carry paper on current management's ability to successfully manage this subsidiary as an autonomous company?

Observation of the firms involved in the study indicates that corporate executives could more frequently consider a management buyout than is currently done. Of course, the development of expertise on leveraged buyouts within various merchant and investment banking concerns is further encouragement to corporate executive consideration of management buyouts.

The above suggests the following recommendation:

Consider division executives as potential buyers early in the game.

2. Open solicitation.   Public "auction" can potentially derive an equitable price for the division. However, if corporate executives decide to publicly announce that one or more units are for sale, several advance preparations must be made.

First, someone must be designated as the initial contact point for all entities indicating interest in the unit. Among the firms participating in this study, the initial contact persons at corporate included the CEO, Corporate Counsel, Vice President of Strategic Planning, and the Director of Business Development.

Who should be the initial contact person depends upon the relative significance of the divestment, the legal issues expected to be involved, the amount of experience the firm has had with divestiture in the past, and who in the firm has greater knowledge concerning potential buyers.

Depending upon the saleability of the firm, the contact person at corporate should be prepared for an initial onslaught of calls from interested parties.

If the announcement concerning divestiture is made public, corporate must also decide what initial criteria will be used to screen interested parties. The most usual initial criterion is whether the party has sufficient financial backing to consummate the sale.

The integrity of the buyer is another criterion which is often utilized. Whether the caller is interested in the whole unit or some portion of the assets is also considered. How the buyer will treat personnel is another criterion. Whether the business makes strategic sense for the buyer is also considered.

Corporate executives must make an early decision whether the unit will be sold as an ongoing business or whether offers for portions will be considered. Of course, callers interested in portions of the unit can be told that they will be considered if buyers for the total unit cannot be found. Returning to such potential buyers after futile search or negotiations further depresses the sale value of the unit, however, and some firms prefer to put off potential buyers interested only in portions of the unit rather than make an explicit statement of their status in the consideration queue.

Is the caller someone we are willing to do business with? Corporate executives sometimes demur on considering certain potential buyers because of their negotiation style or their reputation in business circles for unreliability in their dealings.

How will this interested party treat the division personnel? Executives in companies that have a "family" culture often give heavy weight to this criterion. Especially where division executives are well-thought of, corporate executives may wish to give preference to a potential buyer who will "treat our people right." Such preference can take the form of opening negotiations earlier with that entity and helping to arrange financing.

Does this unit make sense strategically for this potential buyer? Where synergies can be effected, the selling company can negotiate for a higher price. However, emotional attachments may also play a role—for example, one firm sold an entire division to a competitor. The division came into the new company under the responsibility of an executive who had previously been with the selling company. The potential synergies made sense. The executive in the buying company knew the division well. The executives in the selling company had high respect for their past employee and were confident personnel in the divested unit would be treated fairly.

The above leads to the following recommendation:

> With open solicitation, corporate must be ready with an individual designated to receive inquiries and a set of criteria for screening would-be buyers.

3. Sequential vs. simultaneous negotiations. Most divestitures among the firms studied were sequential in nature. Sequential negotiations allow the selling company to have somewhat more control over the pace of negotiations. In some instances, of course, there is recycling since negotiations with Company A may be temporarily shelved and then resumed when negotiations with Company B are stalemated.

Only a few firms preferred simultaneous negotiations. These may be in the form of negotiations or bidding. The well-publicized case of the Vickers Petroleum divestiture by Esmark is one instance where a bidding procedure was used. In this instance, Esmark, the parent company, made clear that they would accept sealed bids for all or part of the division. The resulting sale price exceeded the parent company's original estimates. Of course, the parent company can always retain the right to reject all bids. Simultaneous or near simultaneous negotiations raise the complexity of the selling process, but also allow the possibility of increasing the price.

Thus we conclude that:

> The selling firm must consider whether sequential, simultaneous, or bidding negotiations may be most appropriate.

MAKING INFORMATION AVAILABLE

Several different sets of information must be prepared, and decisions made as to who will receive them. An *initial package of information* must be drawn up for parties who indicate initial interest.

If a public announcement is made, a brief summary of the company's operations and abbreviated financial statements should be all that is necessary.

The selling company must decide whether this material goes to all callers, or whether the material should be sent to interested parties after screening.

A second and more extensive package must be prepared for potential buyers that corporate wants to consider seriously. Usually on-site visits occur later in negotiations. Most often, private conversations with executives in the division to be sold occur very late in negotiations.

In the case of a bidding procedure, the same information must be given to all interested parties. In the case of the Vickers divestment, for example, Esmark set up centers where interested companies could go for information. Corporate and division executives were then very careful when they personally responded to informal inquiries from industry associates.

We therefore recommened that:

> The information relevant to potential buyers must be drawn up in advance of the public announcement or private solicitation, consideration must be given to what information will be made available, in what form, to whom, when, and by whom.

WHITHER THE DIVISION EXECUTIVES?

Earlier, we considered *when* to announce the divestiture to division personnel. Many firms, as indicated, wait until late to inform division personnel. However, informing division management early opens up an array of potential roles, especially for the most senior division executive.

What should be the role of the division executive? Whether the division executive is to be considered a potential buyer, is encouraged to seek potential buyers, or is to participate in negotiations should be made clear.

At the opposite extreme, the division executive may only be expected to operate the unit so as to minimize losses and to host would-be buyers when they make an on-site visit. The clarity of the role affects the basis upon which monetary rewards are effected.

Again, as indicated earlier, division management may become the initiator of the divestment. Depending upon the culture and reward systems in the firm, it may be "okay" for division executives to suggest that the division is no longer appropriate in the firm's portfolio. Under other circumstances, division management may initiate the idea by suggesting they would like to buy the unit.

In addition to being potential buyers, division executives may identify appropriate potential buyers. They, after all, know their industry and who among suppliers, competitors, and customers may be potential buyers.

Foremost among the roles of the division executive is to maintain the integrity of the unit. One of the greatest dangers in most divestments is that the key people will flee—leaving a shell of assets and a much deflated division. Judiciously designed reward systems and post-divestment assurances can do much to retain key people *and,* thus, the value of the subsidiary.

At least three variations of monetary rewards are used by firms which involve division executives in the divestiture:

1. A flat sum, negotiated at the time the divestiture was announced to the division executive. Usually this sum approximated the expected year-end bonus.
2. A designated but open-ended sum, to be paid depending on the subjective evaluation of the division executive's contribution to bringing the divestment to timely and effective closure.
3. A multi-criteria bonus, which depends upon (a) the performance of the unit during the divestiture negotiations and (b) upon the value obtained for the unit.

In many instances, the first-mentioned bonuses were made to key personnel at several levels. The second and, especially, the third bonus plans were reserved for the most senior of division executives. In some instances the bonuses are payable only three to six months after divestiture and only *if* the key personnel have stayed with the subsidiary, if so requested by the purchasing firm.

This leads us to conclude that:

Corporate executives must delineate the expected role of the division executives, the rewards, and post-divestment assurances

NEGOTIATING TERMS WITH THE BUYER

Although price is the critical factor, a number of other issues must be considered by the buyer and seller. Among these issues are

a. continuity of employment for personnel
b. pension liabilities
c. warranty considerations

The selling firm may have considerable emotional investment in obtaining assurances that employees will be treated "right." One firm has a firm policy that their key corporate executives will visit each site in the divested division to talk about the divestiture in an open forum. Each employee may request a private meeting with a representative from personnel, to go over their pension benefits and other issues. This company insists that the purchasing firm follow with open forum meetings several weeks later, and that each employee be entitled to a second private meeting with a personnel representative from the purchasing firms. Division employees are kept notified of current events, beginning shortly after the divestiture decision.

Why such an elaborate process? One senior executive explained, "All our divisions are in related industries. As you know, we acquire frequently and we also have carried out a number of divestitures. We want to be known as a firm of high integrity. We only want to buy under those circumstances and, when we sell, the buyer and the personnel in the divested unit know the sale has taken place under those circumstances."

Pension liabilities often have significant legal entanglements, giving rise to a number of innovative approaches. In one firm, corporate carries all vested employees in its plan until their retirement. The employee then receives two pensions—one from the selling firm and one from the acquiring firm. Employees not yet vested are vested for partial benefits if they remain with the acquiring firm beyond the original date when vesting would have been initiated. Such employees would also receive pension benefits from the selling and acquired firms at the time of retirement.

Warranty considerations are also complex. The selling firm prefers not to be liable after the sale because, as one executive put it, "The insurance is expensive. Imagine trying to resurrect records long since transferred to the new owner in order to settle a liability suit!"

On the other hand, the buying firm does not want to be held liable for products it did not manufacture. A compromise is usually necessary. Some firms have set up a reserve account based on past history. If the reserve is not utilized for liability action by a certain date, the balance reverts to the selling firm.

Warranty issues are difficult to resolve, however. As one executive noted, "As we approached the limitation date, they (the buying firm) just settled complaints. If they had pressed a little harder . . . but it wasn't their money." Our recommendation is that:

> Divesting executives can maximize their negotiations at the bargaining table if they consider alternative positions on problem issues such as pensions and warranties BEFORE negotiations begin.

DO WE NEED AN INVESTMENT BANKER'S HELP?

Should the divesting company call in their investment banker? It all depends. Where the divestment is large, relative to the rest of the company, firms generally find it advantageous to invite investment banking participation. In the case of small units, where the company has had experience with divestitures, the presence of investment banking personnel may be dysfunctional.

One senior executive described a recent experience: We had several smaller units for sale. We asked help from our investment banker. Suddenly, we had swarms of MBA types asking questions, gathering data. We finally withdrew the units from sale.

Even where the presence of an investment banker is appropriate, the role must be worked out. In some instances, investment bankers may solicit buyers, perhaps anonymously. It is not unusual for a firm to note, however, that the potential buyers presented by the investment bankers could easily have been identified by corporate or division executives.

In other instances, the investment banker will be present in negotiations, perhaps aiding where the negotiating executives feel weakest. As one senior executive put it, "I want the financial expert right at my elbow."

We conclude that:

> Whether the firm needs an investment banker, and what role the investment banker should play, must be considered carefully.

CONCLUSION

Divestment is a significant strategic activity which can do much to enhance the value of the firm. The process of divestiture, however, needs to be managed carefully. The issues presented here are key elements in this process.

□

APPLICATION IN STRATEGIC MANAGEMENT:
Problems in Managing a Divestment Decision
LIAM FAHEY

The decision to divest a business unit, or even a sector of a business unit, is usually a traumatic time for the managers involved. It may be particularly difficult for those who spent many years in establishing and maintaining the business.

However, the level of trauma and apprehension is often heightened by the way in which firms initiate, arrive at, and implement the decision to divest. This was the case in a recent divestiture of a small business (less than $20 million in sales) by a multi-business conglomerate.

INITIATING THE DIVESTMENT DECISION

The possibility of divesting the division was first raised by the corporate strategic planning department (CSPD). The CSPD argued that even though the division was showing some profits, it was in an industry where future growth prospects were dim. The CSPD also contended that the division did not "fit" with the recently chosen strategic direction of its group.

Strategic Planning Management, June, 1984; Commerce Communications, Inc.

The CSPD, following the instructions of the firm's president, organized a special task force to comprehensively investigate where the division should be divested, and if it should be retained what strategic focus it should have. No member of the division's management team was invited to participate in the task force.

REACTION OF THE DIVISION MANAGEMENT

The division's management was first informed of the impending task force review during its annual strategy review meeting with senior group and corporate management. It was a complete surprise. They resented not being informed of the establishment of the task force. They further resented the arrival of the corporate "whiz kids," the task force members who were assigned the responsibility of "appraising the division."

A consequence of this resentment was little interaction between the two teams, the task force members and the division's management. In the words of a senior member of the division's management, "we eyed each other with mistrust and with little confidence in each other's capabilities." This standoff lasted for the full month that the task force members spent on the division's premises.

THE TASK FORCE'S RECOMMENDATION

The task force unanimously and strongly recommended divestment. It laid out its arguments in a 20-page report. The report was made available to division management.

The division's management then prepared a document challenging the task force's analysis and findings. They identified the key points in the report and criticized each one. Their recommendation was that the division be retained, since it could be "turned into a winner." It would require much more integration with specific divisions in the group, and a modest influx of resources from the corporation—support which the division had never previously received.

The division's president requested, but did not receive, an opportunity to present the analysis to corporate management. The head of the CSPD informed the president, shortly after his request had been received, that corporate management had approved the task force's recommendation. Division management then publicly resigned themselves to their fate.

SELLING THE DIVISION

An explicit assumption in the CSPD analysis was that the division could easily be sold without sustaining much of a loss, if at all. They even identified a listing of potential buyers.

However, none of these "buyers" were interested in the division. The initial asking price was much too high. Even when the asking price was lowered, only one firm entered into serious negotiations. These negotiations collapsed when some key members of the division's management team informed the potential purchaser that if it took control of the business, they would immediately tender their resignations.

The corporation had set itself a target of six months to dispose of the division. When they were not able to do so, it quickly became obvious to all involved that little time had been devoted by the CSPD, or anyone else in the corporation, to developing a contingency program should they fail to sell the division.

The division management seized this opportunity to resurrect their own analysis, and sent it by mail to the head of the CSPD and to select other executives at corporate headquarters. Their intent was to spark some interest in "the possibility of retaining the division, pumping some resources into it, and developing it into a truly profitable unit." The response of corporate management was that the division would be given one year "to prove its case," but that the corporation would provide only minimal resources during this time period. The division's management team is now embarking upon this challenge.

CREATING THE TRAUMA

In most respects, the trauma surrounding this divestment decision was inflicted upon itself by the organization. Much of it also could have been avoided. It was in large measure a result of noncommunication and ill will.

1. Much of the noncommunication and associated ill will had its origins in the distribution of functions and roles within the corporation.

   The CSPD had the authority to examine the strategic condition and context of any division, with or without the consent and support of the division's management. As described above, it could also do so without the knowledge of division management: CSPD members did not interact with the division until after they had been instrumental in establishing a special task force.

   It is little wonder then that the division management was incensed to discover that a special task force had been established to consider divestment of their unit. They felt the decision to divest had already been made without consultation with the only people who really understood the situation. Their instinctive reaction was to fight back and protect their position.

2. The initial noncommunication was exacerbated by the reaction of the division management. They did everything possible not to cooperate with the special task force. Their resentment at the presence of the task force

was so strong, they delayed providing it with their most recent quarterly returns for over two weeks.

In short, division management surrendered a major opportunity to influence the task force's thinking by refusing to interact with it. The division's actions only served to confirm the task force's worst suspicions. The formal and informal reports tendered to corporate headquarters increasingly cast the division in a poor light.

3. However, a good portion of the fault for this lack of communication can also be placed on the shoulders of the task force.

They did not provide an opportunity for the division's management to make its case. They presumed that they could best determine what should be the fate of the division.

Moreover, the task force did not share much of its thoughts with division management. They only said that their insights would be available when they issued their report.

4. Nor did any of the members of the task force make any serious efforts to get to know division management. They expressly did not see this as part of their function; they would be there for only three or four weeks, and then they would be gone.

One consequence of the behavior of the task force and division management was a substantial deterioration in the morale of division management at all levels. Managers were no longer committed to their positions or to the corporation. Not surprisingly, within four months of the arrival of the task force, seven of the top fifteen managers in the division had left.

5. Another consequence, of course, was that when the corporation was unable to sell the division, it then found itself dealing with not only a depleted management team but one that it had very successfully ignored, belittled, and antagonized. In effect, corporate management, if it wished to develop solid working relationships with the division, would have to undo and repair much of the damage it had created in the previous twelve months.

Corporate management chose not to deal with this issue. It simply granted the division another year to get its house in order, but with very little support from corporate management to do so.

6. A major factor contributing to much of the above trauma would not be visible simply by observing the interactions among the various parties. The CSPD had made up its mind that the division ought to be divested, and then orchestrated the decision process in the following ways to help ensure that the divestment would be the decision outcome.

First, the CSPD made a presentation to corporate management, suggesting that a task force ought to be established to review this particular division's current and potential performance. Such a presentation was required before a task force would be authorized by senior corporate management.

The presentation strongly indicated that divestment was the most desirable outcome. The CSPD developed three different scenarios around "the financial numbers," and concluded that divestment was "way and afar" the most preferred outcome. A result of this presentation was that corporate management became heavily biased toward divestment.

Second, the CSPD nominated a list of individuals from whom the task force would be chosen by corporate management. This was part of the usual procedure in creating special task forces. In this case, the CSPD nominated some individuals who previously had shown themselves predisposed toward divesting complete business units.

Third, the CSPD insisted that the task force provide it with weekly summaries of its progress. Of particular interest to the CSPD was the evolution of the task force's thinking. By keeping tabs on what conclusions the task force might be moving toward, the CSPD could determine whether and to what extent it might need "to intervene."

Thus, when the corporation was unable to sell the division, the CSPD found itself confronting a division management, and perhaps more importantly, management at the group level that was well aware of its efforts to dispose of the division. This has led to further antagonism and mistrust between the two sides.

CONCLUSION

The division is now losing ground to its competitors. Division management is convinced that no matter what it does, the corporation will not be dissuaded from its intent to sell off the division.

This may be the result of a firm jumping too quickly to a conclusion—in this case, the CSPD deciding divestment was the best, if not only, course of action before it fully considered the options. It then confounded this mistake by badly managing inter-unit relations.

CHAPTER

— 10 —

THE PHASES OF
STRATEGIC DECISIONS

■

□

STRATEGIC PROBLEMS: HOW TO IDENTIFY THEM
MARJORIE A. LYLES

How do you sense a business strategy problem? How do you resolve it once identified? Many times important strategy problems go unresolved because they have not been properly identified. Witness the following three examples:

- Cummins Engine Company was surprised to realize that they had accumulated excess inventory equal to a plant's ("The Phantom Plant") inventory because Cummins could not physically locate the inventory.

- Chrysler Corporation was aware for years that consumers were buying smaller, more fuel-efficient cars but this was not considered an "important" problem.

- Johnson & Johnson was unable to relate the importance of an increase in random crime to themselves, although their President did have a premonition of the Tylenol situation.

What is common among these three examples is that all three companies had trouble sensing the existence and nature of major strategic problems. Each company had individuals within their firms proclaiming that there was a problem, but these individuals were ignored. Top management received

Strategic Planning Management, July, 1985; Commerce Communications, Inc.

confusing, diffuse, and conflicting signals that a problem might exist but its nature remained elusive.

STRATEGIC PROBLEM FORMULATION: WHAT IT IS

In the above examples, each firm had difficulty with the process by which problems are first sensed and the nature of the problem resolved.

Problem formulation is a critical process for firms that are attempting to stay on top of environmental and competitive change. In the past several years, the environment has been changing so rapidly that businesses have experienced a growing unease about the nature of the strategic problems confronting them. For example, International Harvester had many symptoms indicating that they had a critical strategic problem: decreasing sales, increasing interest rates, management turnover. It was difficult to determine the exact nature of the problem.

In the last few years, environmental change has escalated, leading to increased uncertainty within organizations regarding the nature of critical problems and to decreased abilities to identify the problems of strategic importance to the organization.

It is important to note that the way firms sense the existence of strategic problems and resolve them has a direct impact on their strategic alternatives. For example, Baker International sensed the impending oil crisis and responded not by getting out of the oil industry but by diverting its attention to the supply end.

PROBLEM SOLVING VS. PROBLEM FORMING

Businesses have spent millions of dollars to develop methods for *solving* their problems. Consider the growth in staff positions and departments that have responsibility for developing forecasts, operations research models, and control systems. Educational programs both internal and external to the organization are directed at training managers to be better problem solvers. Business schools, as well, train future employees to be action-takers and specialists.

However, my experience with over 50 firms in the Fortune 500 indicates that success in most industries today requires an organizational commitment to problem formulation as well as problem solving. The results of the 1970s suggest that most businesses have been too concerned with action-taking and problem-solving and not enough with anticipating future strategic problems and resolving the nature of them. I do not mean to imply that businesses have had their heads in the sand, but that they have not recognized the important first phase of problem solving, namely, identifying the right problem.

THE NATURE OF STRATEGIC PROBLEMS

Strategic problems have frequently been referred to as "unstructured" or "wicked" problems. They have a significant influence on the organization as a whole and are more complex and ill-defined than other problems. They are complex because there is no proven algorithm for formulating the problem, no clear relationship between problem definition and best solution, no single way to explain discrepancies in how different people understand the problem.

Occasionally, strategic problems are well structured, i.e., there is a relatively widespread consensus as to the single best definition of the problem. These are frequently problems that have been imposed on the organization, as in the case of governmental regulations or union negotiations. Most strategic problems, however, are unstructured, and there is no single "best" way for formulating the nature of the problem. In these cases, the problem formulation process becomes a critical aspect of the strategic decision-making process.

QUESTIONABLE MANAGEMENT ASSUMPTIONS

My research with organizations indicates that managers have certain key assumptions that govern their strategic problem formulation behaviors. These assumptions stem from a manager's prior training and the organization's culture and political climate. These assumptions determined whether a firm recognizes problem indicators, identifies the problem in a timely fashion, and how it responds. These assumptions include:

That problem solving is important, not problem forming.   Managers strongly agree that there should be a "rational" approach to decision-making. It should be unemotional, quantitative, and scientific. All alternatives should be considered and analyzed. However, all too often, this is impossible with problem forming. It is impossible to be unemotional. Intuitions often cannot be quantified. It is difficult to identify all alternatives.

In many firms, little emphasis is put into identifying critical problems. One vice president observed: "In our organization, we try not to identify problems. We have enough difficulty solving the ones that we have." Another manager remarked: "It is a lot easier to work on a problem that is well defined."

Other managers also noted that organizational culture is geared toward action-taking on defined problems—not reflective thought on the nature of problems. Managers are rewarded for solving problems—not for identifying them.

That problems which "rock the boat" should be avoided.   There are norms in many firms that emphasize that managers should not identify problems that pinpoint past managerial mistakes, create change, or redistribute power. Any formulation of a problem that identifies conflict or past errors in judgment is avoided or obscured. One vice president said: "People minimize failure. Their egos are involved because of the necessity to admit failures. They won't do that."

Sometimes political maneuvering results in a standoff, and the nature of the problem may never be resolved. Information regarding the nature of the problem may be distorted or withheld from others within the firm. For example, in one firm, a senior executive was left to operate without information until the day before an important meeting when he was given a late night phone call by another executive.

In another example, in order to avoid the identification of a problem, one manager purposefully misrepresented certain facts that indicated a mistake by his boss. In one insurance company, a senior executive said that he tried to tell other management people about the problem, but he was ignored. He gave up trying to bring the problem out into the open because, as he said: "I'm retiring in two years. It's not going to be my problem."

That debate is destructive.   Open debate identifying true differences in opinions makes many executives uncomfortable, and it is frequently viewed as creating ill-feelings that will continue beyond the current situation. When a strong debate occurs over the existence and cause of a problem, it may result in a lack of agreement about the nature of the problem and thus delay resolution.

The consequence appears to be that firms rely on the credibility and commitment of a manager to a particular view of the problem. If the manager is perceived as being highly credible, his/her view will be accepted. Also, if that manager's commitment to a particular view is strong, it influences the acceptance of his/her view. Debate about the problem's nature can be eliminated by the acceptance of this person's view of the problem.

Unfortunately, reliance on personal credibility and avoidance of debate can create delays and wasted efforts. As noted by one executive: "Because of the influence of one particular person, he caused several false starts because the statements he made were believed."

That if you ignore a problem, it will go away.   There is an accepted axiom within many firms that if you find a problem, it is your problem; consequently, managers ignore many problems to avoid responsibility for them. If the firm is performing well, managers are reluctant to identify potential problems. One manager acknowledged: "They were aware of a potential problem for several years, but the top management felt things shouldn't be disturbed because we had good results as things were."

Also, turnover among executives frequently leads to problems being ignored. When an executive is changed, it can result in delays, reassignments, and repetitions that may be drawn out over several years. Managers leaving a position may not be willing to acknowledge a new problem and new managers are reluctant to take on the risks immediately.

IMPROVING STRATEGIC PROBLEM FORMULATION

The dysfunctional effects of these managerial assumptions lead organizations into either initially defining the problem wrong or into avoiding it. Organizations are then forced by individuals or the problem environment into reassessing the initial conceptualization of the problem. Studies suggest that 75% of the time, organizations recycle through the problem formulation process, creating delays and lost opportunities.

The following suggestions are aimed at helping organizations to identify the nature of strategic problems.

Get hunches out early.   Do not suppress hunches even if they are unsupported by concrete evidence. One manager stressed: "You're usually aware of a potential problem—just from your background, from information that is not quantitative—from nothing that can be put into the computer. It takes ingenuity to rearrange things." Managers stress that problems do not come out of the blue but that they are usually aware of them before any formal indicators exist.

Avoid decision-making always by consensus.   Consensus frequently has the effect of creating the illusion of knowledge; just because everyone agrees does not make it the right answer. Consensus can rule out voices that present unpopular or deviant views. Yet these views may be the most accurate perceptions of reality.

Get a cross section of views.   Do not focus too early on one view of a problem. Do not supress the presentation of views even if they appear to be not relevant. More information, rather than less, is important for problem identification. What is relevant or important is very hard to determine in early stages of this process. It is better to have everyone aware of potentially relevant information.

Recognize that the credibility of individual managers will be influential in determining which view of a problem the group will support. One manager remarked: "In meetings it is possible to get a cross section of views and a higher quality of input. They are better than hearing views by individuals who will slant positions to benefit themselves. Don't silence middle to lower managers; they may be the ones to first see problems."

Identify managers good at problem forming.   Any company can begin to identify those individuals who have a sense for the *whole* rather than for details or parts. One company that was unable to do this had no one who knew what was going on overall; they were too concerned with the parts of the problem and not the whole. Avoid "experts" who claim to understand the situation better than anyone else; they tend to focus the problem too early.

Create problem-raising opportunities. The most difficult approach to improving problem formulation is development of a program for identifying problems early. A fundamental problem is that most managers try to avoid identifying problems: consequently, the culture and norms within organizations need to be changed. Assumptions should be explicitly stated and addressed, and debate should be built into the process. Most companies recognize that most strategic problems do not disappear and may cause a domino effect if ignored too long.

THE CRITICAL FIRST STEP

Recognizing the importance of strategic problem formulation as a critical skill for survival is the first step that organizations can take to improve their abilities to sense and define strategic problems. By acknowledging that dysfunctional norms exist and can impede the identification of strategic problems, managers should be able to recognize behaviors that reduce the effectiveness of problem formulation. Managing problem-rising activities is never an easy or popular task, but in the long run the organizations's health will depend on it.

□

IDENTIFYING AND GENERATING STRATEGIC ALTERNATIVES
KENNETH HATTEN AND MARY LOUISE HATTEN

Generating strategic alternatives, the strategies and actions organizations could take to exploit their opportunities or resolve their problems, is a challenging and exciting part of strategic management. The challenge is to make an organization work better and resolve its really difficult problems. Creative thinking about strategic options and participation in the definition of an organization's future can be very exciting.

GOING BEYOND PROBLEMS

Strategic alternatives are best generated with a perspective that looks toward creating opportunities rather than simply solving problems.

Very little time in our society is spent determining which problems warrant effort. Although we honor problem solvers, managers and other executives must learn to stop solving problems indiscriminately and start thinking about

Strategic Planning Management, December and January, 1985; Commerce Communications, Inc.

addressing problems selectively to create value and keep it. At its best, managing is opportunity seeking. Problems are nothing more than opportunities to act and thereby achieve our objectives.

Because management's job is not to solve problems but to define and achieve objectives, managers must select from among the problems and opportunities revealed by strategic analysis (and day to day events) those few that warrant attention. These should be problems which, if addressed, will move the company furthest toward the accomplishment of its objectives.

But before working hard to exploit these opportunities, take time to identify and evaluate your firm's strategy. What is its business? What is making the greatest contribution to its success or impeding its progress most severely? Put your effort where the payoff is likely to be greatest.

NEED FOR STRATEGIC ALTERNATIVES

Once you have developed a deep understanding of a business's current strategy, the alternatives you need will often come to mind quickly. This is natural, because strategic analysis is fundamentally a problem-finding process. With the organization's problems defined as strengths, weaknesses, opportunities, and threats, solutions develop as natural responses to each. In most instances, the alternatives that fit this natural response exploit traditional or standard strategies which are evolutionary rather than radical.

For most successful organizations, the outcomes of a strategic audit are minor changes to the existing strategy, fine tuning of operations, and limited trials of a new strategy. Successful performance implies maintaining what works.

Yet even in a world where continuity is valued highly, radical change is sometimes required. This happens when the problems or opportunities facing the organization are too large, complex, or intractable for incremental and evolutionary solutions.

GENERATING ALTERNATIVES

Strategy evaluation provides you with opportunities to understand what you do now and to do it better. It also gives you time to prepare and provide for the future; it tells what is working and what is not; it alerts you to the likely future course of events and to the need to modify objectives. Evaluation is the logical starting point as the organization seeks to generate strategic alternatives.

Either the business is working well and is properly positioned for the future, or change is needed. If change is needed, efforts to identify a response should be guided, first, by the source of the difficulty, and then by the fact that useful strategies have common characteristics.

In attempting to respond to issues coming from the evaluation process, make your moves deliberately. The least change is often the best change, and it is almost always the least costly and lowest risk. The results of small changes are easiest to monitor and control.

GENERIC STRATEGIES

The more extensive the problem, the more thought and insight seems required to solve it. Yet management need not innovate in every aspect of its strategy to succeed. Generic strategies suggest known approaches to improve performance.

Generic strategies such as performance maximizing, sales maximizing, and cost minimizing are little different from the buy low, sell high advice often heard about stock investing. Raising revenue or lowering costs both are surefire methods to increase profits.

Typically, the generic strategy's emphasis on one or two variables maximizes its visceral impact and intuitive appeal, but complicates its use. Business-level strategies by their nature are integrative; they encompass many variables. "Overall cost leadership" is a dangerously flexible strategy definition. But how could a company attain overall cost leadership? The question should provide useful thinking. Often the value of generic strategies lies more in the questions they provoke than in any simple effort to implement them independently.

Other standardized strategic options come to mind. A company might liquidate all of its assets or part only, perhaps to specialize in some particular industry role by harvesting (slowly liquidating) its activities in another. Alternatively, it might diversify. Vertical integration is another option. Growth may be by business development, emphasizing product or market expansion, and market expansion might be regional or international.

LIQUIDATION

Liquidation as a strategic alternative is often not considered until it is too late. It is also often not recognized that liquidation actually provides a number of distinct options.

One reason why liquidation is often not considered as a strategic alternative is that it is popularly seen as the result of poor business performance, rather than an active approach to improving performance. However, the liquidation strategy should imply that some activities have been found to be more attractive than others. These attractive activities warrant more of the firm's resources, which are sensibly redeployed from low return businesses to those with higher earnings. The low-return activities are sold off to other firms that see a better chance of profit opportunity. Ultimately, the liquidation strategy should improve overall corporate performance.

A harvest, or partial liquidation, strategy represents a deliberate attempt to improve performance by limiting, rather than ending, commitment to certain low-return businesses. If, as is hoped, rates of return improve when less capital is devoted to the business, the harvest strategy successfully demonstrates that resources were being used inefficiently in that area.

BACKWARD AND FORWARD INTEGRATION

Another type of strategic alternative that is often not given serious consideration is backward and forward integration. As with liquidation, it includes a number of distinct possibilities.

Integration into other components of the product-distribution chain can be an attractive alternative for managers who feel their objectives would be better served if they had more control of their suppliers or customers. Forward integration moves the firm's activities toward the consumer; for example, adding distribution to manufacturing capabilities. Backward integration involves the firm in supplier activities. Both forward and backward integration are examples of vertical integration. Horizontal integration, by contrast, refers to buying competitors at the product-distribution stage in which the firm is already operating. This strategy can be used to gain access to supply or distribution components.

Integration need not be by ownership. Contractual arrangements for input or output or for operating services can also accomplish the objectives of integration, that is, control and power, with much lower fixed cost commitments. Contracts, for example, can provide supply or distribution rights with less risk than the suppliers or distributors themselves carry. Sears and the Japanese auto makers are examples of powerful firms where contracts with suppliers give them power with less risk than the suppliers themselves carry.

To cite a complex example of vertical integration as a strategic alternative, U.S. oil companies have continuously changed positions in the chain, even jumping stages, rather than simply moving from one stage forward or backward. Changing position in the industry chain can be a valuable strategic alternative. In addition to investing in the most rewarding industry stages, an industry participant changing positions may bring valuable information and contacts from past business experience which could raise the rewards and lower the risks of entry.

DIVERSIFICATION

The product/market matrix provides a frequently overlooked framework for assessing potential markets.

The results of the interactions of markets and product technologies when a firm is serving its own supply needs include integrations and point to improvements in operations. Product development occurs when the firm serves the same customers with an expanded product line. Market development uses the current technology to service additional markets. Concentric diversification is the term used for attempts to service additional markets with expanded technology offerings. Conglomerate diversification refers to business strategies offering unrelated products to new, unrelated customers.

STRATEGY PERSPECTIVE

Identifying alternatives lies at the heart of strategy development. The perspective brought to bear upon the process of strategic alternative generation is critical: it is not simply problem-solving. Rather, it is more opportunity creation—identifying what opportunities are available to the firm and how to exploit them.

The use of generic strategy options is one useful means to systematically generate strategic options. It helps to insure that a variety of possible options will be quickly considered.

In any situation, the more alternatives that you consider, the greater likelihood you have of generating a winning strategy. If there are only a few alternatives, you often wind up operating in a stymied, non-productive situation. Consider the following range of possible alternative sources:

- Status quo. "Business as usual" is always an option.
- Generic strategies—to raise revenue and lower costs.
- Actions that may alter stockholder support and power.
- The unthinkable actions that violate conventional wisdom.

Each of these types of strategy holds a number of options for your firm. But if they are never explicitly listed, they are unlikely to be adopted—and a good approach to an opportunity or a problem may be lost.

INITIAL REQUIREMENTS

Creativity is needed to generate multiple alternatives. The objective should be to develop strategic alternatives that differentiate an organization from its competitors. Often the best alternative may integrate elements of some apparently inappropriate alternatives. Inhibiting creativity during the process of generating alternatives by committing to any one idea or evaluating it too soon will limit the number and quality of suggestions with useful characteristics.

To foster creativity, avoid hasty evaluations and judgments that induce you to discard alternatives. Rather try to rethink, rework, or combine them to make them more attractive. Discarding suggestions prematurely inhibits the creativity needed to develop alternatives.

Generating alternatives strategies also requires flexibility. As you try to employ your resources as distinctively as possible in the search for competitive advantage, remember the importance of flexibility—call it adding degrees of strategic freedom, if you like. The flexibility to see things freshly and the ability to question current practices are important skills, yet they are difficult to maintain in practice. Familiarity, pressures for action and results, and other factors lead to an inability to think flexibly and insightfully.

Timing is another variable sometimes neglected in the process of generating alternatives. Some alternatives will not work as expected without prior groundwork, and the method of staging their implementation can measurably increase the probability of success. Also, management can react more appropriately to results if those results unfold slowly rather than cataclysmically. Management needs to monitor success, and this is facilitated if timing is a managerially controlled variable. Indeed, a limited commitment early on can provide results to guide further action.

MENTAL BLOCKS

Although many of the changes managers make in their strategies and operations are clearly straightforward responses to problems found in a strategy audit, such changes are usually minor in scope and are essentially finetuning the organization's strategy and the operating systems that implement it. When larger changes are called for, generic or standardized "cookbook" strategies can often be adapted to serve the needs of the organization.

Sometimes, however, management thinking is blocked—usually experienced as a feeling before it is recognized as a fact. Nonetheless, the feeling is usually a real sign that something is wrong in the process of generating alternatives. Despite hard work and passage of time, the company has found no way to improve its position and resolve its problems.

Mental blocks typically occur when the pressure is greatest. Precisely when you need a broad perspective and flexibility, one seems most prone to narrow one's vision. Although a little pressure prompts successful effort, too much quickly becomes dysfunctional and performance tends to falter.

What are the signs? You are probably blocked when:

- You feel pressured and you are simultaneously unproductive.
- You find yourself increasingly intolerant of others' points of view and have a growing instinct to defend your point of view (a pattern, you discover, repeated by your colleagues).
- Priority is given to the loudest and most insistent voice (not necessarily yours), while you feel something is wrong, but cannot specify what it is.

To some extent, these symptoms apply whether you are working alone or with others, but in all these circumstances, management thinking tends to be inflexible.

MANAGERIAL BLOCKING

There are a number of different ways in which managerial thinking can be blocked, including:

1. "Tunnel Vision" occurs when all attention is focused on the wrong response, like a wild animal frozen by the headlights of an oncoming car.
2. "All or Nothing" is the fallacy that occurs when management defines its options as a zero to one, go/no go situation. This occurs, for example, when action against a competitive entry is defined as a success if the entry is completely prevented and as a total loss otherwise, when it might be possible to take advantage of the competing entry to grow the market while preserving a powerful market position yourself. Essentially, "all or nothing" is a perverse form of greed.
3. "Perils of Perfectionism" is an unwillingness to commit to action until even subtle and often irrelevant details are attended to. An example might be to delay market entry until a totally preemptive strategy can be developed, even though you already have a strategy that promises a relative competitive advantage.
4. "Loss of Perspective" is a fallacy that focuses on the details to the exclusion of the key factors that truly make a difference. An example is worrying about the cost details of a TV advertising campaign while your manufacturing costs substantially exceed your competitor's.
5. "Failure to Challenge Constraints" is a block that especially applies to self-imposed constraints. Consider the plight of a product manager who controls only the marketing strategy for his product and who is confronted by a corporate pressure for higher margins. Not controlling overhead or fixed or variable manufacturing costs, he feels trapped—but he does not consider price or service charges which may help sales and margins at least in the short run.

Typically, under pressure, managers are blind to opportunity. To break out of their own personal boxes, managers need to take a different point of view perhaps their boss's; perhaps their customers'. The new point of view can add new variables and flexibility to your thinking.

Recognizing that a block exists is the first step toward a breakthrough in solving the problem. Blocked problems tend to be seen as a "we can't do" situation. What's needed is a "can do" attitude, focusing on the benefits of opportunity. One way to gain perspective is to concentrate on the key factors of success and drop the less urgent details.

Essentially, blocks involve cognitive, social, and emotional factors. They develop out of a certain form of self-centeredness—for example, a focus on operations rather than on customers; a focus on divisional operations rather than on overall corporate strategy.

Breaking mental blocks requires hard work and smart thinking. More-over, you should not be content with a merely satisfactory solution. Strive for flexibility, new perspectives, and choice.

The more numerous the alternatives, the greater the opportunity for wiser and more confident choices. Having more choices means you have degrees of strategic freedom, and an ability to follow variations on strategic themes to achieve objectives.

SIDESTEPPING MENTAL BLOCKS: SOME EXAMPLES

Although most businesses begin with very tangibly defined products and services and never change, sometimes an abstract concept of the business will promote innovation.

The Bic Pen Corporation is a good example of a company whose self-concept changed. It began by making ballpoint pen refills and gradually expanded its product line to include disposable ballpoint pens, retractable pens, and porous-tip pens. Later, it added cigarette lighters, pantyhose, and disposable razors. Simultaneously, management changed its concepts of the business from "pens" to "writing instruments" and on to "manufacturers and marketers of high-quality, everyday disposable products distributed through writing instrument channels."

Bic management moved from the tangible to the abstract in the concept of its business. The test of such a concept is its productivity: Does it lead the company to new products?

Creativity such as that shown at Bic is often a mask for experience. A focus on customer, competition, and company is a three-phased checklist you can use to generate ideas. When logic does not work, try intuition to develop a new approach—intuition is your collective experience at work.

While it sometimes pays to be very detail-oriented, identifying key factors and dealing with them in a skeletal form can also be productive. When Kodak entered the instant camera business in 1976, observers rated Polaroid and Kodak on each of seven factors. Kodak was judged to have a more experienced and accomplished marketing force, with more numerous and more loyal outlets than Polaroid. Kodak also rated higher on long-term operations, financial backing, and management. Yet many felt that Polaroid, as the innovator in instant photography, had product technology as well as brand recognition on its side. Polaroid's founder, Edwin Land, was rated as a toss-up—drawing both highly positive and highly negative ratings.

In 1976, Polaroid had its SX70 operations running profitably at about 40% capacity, producing 2 million units per year. Kodak, at that point, was not yet producing instant cameras or film in commercial quantities. Kodak had broken with its traditional practice of simultaneous national and worldwide new product introduction—the company planned a phased North American rollout beginning in Canada in May, and later in Florida.

Although many felt Polaroid had a short-run advantage in its manufacturing operations, they also felt that Kodak would ultimately erode this since Kodak was about five times larger than Polaroid and so had the financial advantage.

How would you handle this situation?

Focusing on the details and attempting to develop options quickly is an overwhelming task. However, focusing on the skeletal outline of relative advantage can be quite productive. Applying the principle of strength against weakness would direct a Polaroid defense head-on with Kodak's new product, avoiding Kodak's marketing and financial strengths.

An analogy from the martial arts and self-defense would suggest ways to use Kodak's money and marketing muscle to Polaroid's advantage. A military analogy would suggest attacking when Kodak enters the instant photo market and before its presence is well-established. A fairy-tale lesson from "The Three Little Pigs" tells that wolves shouldn't climb down chimneys, but work in the open range, where their strengths give them an advantage.

What was Polaroid's range? Was it technology? Could Polaroid manufacture and supply the market in advance of Kodak's entry? Could it cut price to stimulate its own sales and Kodak's response and thereby delay Kodak's achievement of breakeven or else gain sales in a growing market stimulated by Kodak's introductory advertising?

We do not intend here to be exhaustive or detailed, nor to explicitly consider Kodak's and Polaroid's responses and reactions. The point is to demonstrate how analogy and focus on a few key factors can quickly stimulate the development of useful strategy alternatives in a tough situation.

DEALING WITH INTRACTABLE PROBLEMS

The paper industry is capital intensive and employs large scale manufacturing plants. The biggest producers, like International Paper, are vertically integrated back to the forests and even have their own fuel supplies.

How could a small company operate in this industry? How could it position its plant close to its source of materials and overcome the large companies' scale advantage?

One company, Clevepak, entered the industry as a manufacturer by using scrap paper as its source of materials. Clevepak duplicated International Paper's supply advantage by locating not in the woods but near its supply in the city. It countered cost economies due to scale with price inelasticity buttressed by service. It developed a niche by servicing not the large paper users but small specialty goods manufacturers who needed small amounts of special packaging boxes and cardboard cans. Clevepak, a small company, took every major industry characteristic and found a way to neutralize or duplicate its competitive impact.

Clevepak's strategy, systematically creating competitive capability by overcoming the rules of the game, is similar to the thinking required when a strategic problem is truly intractable and not amenable to approaches tested by experience. Sometimes problems arise which are outside the available experience. For example, you may foresee the potential development of large environmental discontinuities that would threaten the continued viability of the organization. What do you do?

When normal methods do not work, we must take a different tack and turn from logic, or vertical thinking, to what one author calls lateral thinking. Instead of proceeding to a solution step-by-step, you take a leap to where you think you want to be and then work backwards to try to fill in the intervening steps.

Such an approach to intractable problems discards the constraints that block thinking. It omits confusing details and focuses attention on the organization as a whole. The purpose is to identify new solutions or opportunities and then find the strategies that will realize their potential. By specifying an ideal and then the implicit assumptions needed to support that ideal, you may be able to develop a framework consistent both with reality and the new assumptions, and so form the basis for a feasible new strategy.

Various techniques can be used to develop a vision of a perfect world. You can simplify complexity and reduce the number of factors you have to deal with simultaneously. You can brainstorm—accept spontaneous thoughts from members of a group, even absurd ideas, and work off them in every way possible. You can use analogy, approximation, the distortion of a dominant constraint, or the bridging of apparently polarized ideas to help everyone see things differently.

Resolving intractable problems is not simply a matter of working hard and long. Rather, it is important to create a climate of trust so that people can explore their environment and their strategy, and envision a better future. Once that future is discerned, it becomes a matter of building a path back to current reality, and then reversing direction to achieve the desired future.

When apparent alternatives fail the test of evaluation and when the portents of the future are bleak, organizations need the inspiration of radical change. If management recognizes this need early, it can prepare, test alternatives, and begin conditioning the organization for change.

EVERY MANAGER CAN CONTRIBUTE

The excitement and the responsibility of generating strategic alternatives is not the exclusive province of top management. Top, middle, and functional managers all have roles to play and contributions to make. Alternative generation is an early component of strategic decision making. It is followed by evaluation, commitment, and implementation. These steps involve the resource allocation process, a process that requires the interaction of many managerial levels.

To advance through the resource allocation process, a proposal or an alternative must first be defined and then given impetus. *Definition* refers to fleshing out an alternative, giving it substantive content, and providing the technical details that differentiate it from other ideas. *Impetus* results from committed support within the organization, the process of arguing and advocating the alternative's merits to move it towards approval.

During the resource allocation process, the context of the organization will be felt, determining what is acceptable and influencing both definition and impetus. *Context* results from the culture and practices of the organization, and is affected by the way strategy is articulated; by the way work is organized, controlled, and rewarded; and by the example set by top management. Unfortunately, two primary ingredients of the organization's context, rewards and example, can thwart innovation in many large companies. It almost becomes a paradox, because anyone smart enough to innovate also is smart enough not to. The typical company rewards conservatism, not risk-taking. Risk means exactly that; the chances of success are small, and a mistake can haunt you for the rest of your career.

What are the roles of different-level managers in developing alternatives? Typically, lower level managers define the problem; middle managers provide the impetus; and top management sets context. At the lowest level, specialists and functional managers confront specific problems and use their expert knowledge to propose solutions. At the second level, middle managers integrate the work of the specialists they supervise and give impetus to alternatives by:

- Deciding which proposals will go forward for approval
- Providing liaison between senior management and specialists, clarifying corporate purpose for the specialists, and abstracting and translating technical detail for senior managers
- Accepting personal risk by staking their own reputations on proposals by underwriting them

These roles illustrate practice, but are not necessarily normative guides. In reality, managers at every level must play a part in definition, impetus, and context development—depending upon their expertise, their interest, and the strength of the management resources of the firm. In small firms, one person may take every role. In rapidly growing firms, there may be few experienced managers to give a proposal impetus; other mechanisms, including involvement of board members and consultants, will have to be used to test ideas and underwrite them.

Participation in alternative development is part of every manager's job, for it is only through the strategic alternatives it generates that the organization implements its strategy and moves from analysis to action.

☐

EVALUATING ALTERNATIVE STRATEGIES
GEORGE DAY

Any alternative strategy your firm is considering should be judged only after you have subjected it to a grid of questions. In assessing the relative appropriateness and desirability of various strategies for your firm, you need to evaluate each option on the following seven criteria:

1. Suitability—Is it based on a sustainable advantage?
2. Validity—Are the assumptions realistic?
3. Consistency—Does the strategy hang together?
4. Feasibility—Do you have the resources and commitments?
5. Vulnerability—How much risk is involved?
6. Adaptability—How flexible will you remain?
7. Financial Desirability—How attractive are the rewards?

1. SUITABILITY: IS IT BASED ON A SUSTAINABLE ADVANTAGE?

The essence of strategy formulation is the matching of competencies with threats and opportunities. An important first question is, therefore, whether a strategy makes sense in light of anticipated changes in the external environment.

But strategy is also about the pursuit of competitive advantage. Unless a strategy offers some basis for future competitive advantage or adaptation to the forces eroding the current competitive advantage, then it does not stand the test.

Here are the four key steps to follow when you subject each alternative strategy to the suitability test:

Step 1. Review the potential threats and opportunities to the business. The major sources of these threats or opportunities include:

- changes in the environment, and especially changes in customer and distribution requirements;
- the actions of present and prospective competitors;
- changes in the availability of critical skills and resources.

Strategic Planning Management, March, 1984; Commerce Communications, Inc.

Step 2. Assess each option in light of the company's capabilities. How well can the firm:

- ward off or avoid threats?
- exploit opportunities?
- enhance current advantages or provide new sources of advantages?

At this stage it is worth asking whether the strategy can work under a broad range of foreseeable environmental conditions. Some strategies are effective only when inflation is either high or low, for example. Other strategies don't travel well to new geographical markets. A robust strategy that can be readily adapted to a variety of conditions is most desirable, because frequent changes are not only costly but they disorient the organization and the market.

Step 3. Anticipate the likely competitive responses to each option. Can competitors match, offset, or "leapfrog" any advantages conferred by this option? Role playing by management teams, taking the perspective of different competitors, can be valuable in assessing competitive response. To complete this step, ask how the business would cope with the anticipated competitive actions.

Step 4. Modify or eliminate unsuitable options. If the strategy does not meet these suitability tests, it should either be modified or dropped from further consideration. This final step concludes the suitability screening test.

2. VALIDITY: ARE THE ASSUMPTIONS REALISTIC?

Choices among alternative strategies are among the least structured of all decisions that any manager must make. The manager has little hard data on which to rely. He must choose among judgments, forecasts and expectations.

At the heart of these choices lie assumptions. All those with a stake in choosing and implementing the strategy must share the key assumptions. Otherwise, the strategy will be formulated through compromise and implemented without understanding or conviction.

The difficulty lies in distinguishing sound assumptions from faulty ones. You must be constantly on the lookout for assumptions that are accepted as conventional wisdom but have either never been thoroughly examined or cannot be justified in light of probable trends. Perhaps the most common pitfalls are seen when managers assume they can derive forecasts either from the historic performance of the business or from merely their own hopes.

Furthermore, all assumptions are based on information which itself may be inaccurate, misleading, or simply out of date. You must continually ask how the data was collected, by whom, and for what purpose. These questions apply equally to internal information (such as data on costs or salesmen's calling frequency and coverage) and environmental data (on growth, market size, and price levels). Be sure to scrutinize information on changes in competitor capabilities and customer requirements with special care.

3. CONSISTENCY: DOES THE STRATEGY HANG TOGETHER?

Strategy is internally consistent if all its elements "hang together," that is, there is minimal conflict among its components. Without an "acceptable" degree of fit among the option's elements, effective coordination or implementation cannot be achieved. The consistency test is seldom pivotal, in that few strategies are rejected outright for inconsistency. But it can be very useful in improving and refining the strategy to ensure that all elements are pointing in the same direction. It may also indicate that the degree of change necessary to bring the elements into line is simply not feasible within the limitation of available resources.

4. FEASIBILITY: DO WE HAVE THE RESOURCES AND COMMITMENTS?

The feasibility test subjects each strategy to these two questions:

1. Does the business possess the necessary resources (skills, capital, and physical resources)?
2. Do the key operating managers understand the underlying premises and elements of the option, and are they likely to be committed to implementing the option?

1. Assessing resource contraints.   Financial resources (capital funds or cash-flow requirements) and physical resources are the first constraints against which the strategy option is tested. If these limitations are so constraining that undertaking a strategy would actually jeopardize competitive position, then the strategy has to be modified to overcome or live within the constraint or perhaps be rejected. Imaginative solutions may be necessary, such as innovative financing methods using sales-leaseback arrangements, tying plant mortgages to long-term contracts, or seeking cooperative marketing or manufacturing arrangements.

The next set of constraints to be tested relates to market access. Ask such questions as these:

- Do we have adequate sales force coverage?
- Is the sales force adaptable to the selling job demanded by the strategy?
- What are the cost, efficiency, and coverage of the present distribution system?

- Are the relationships with jobbers, distributors, and/or retailers sufficiently secure to adapt to the proposed new strategy?

Negative or uncertain answers to these questions should trigger a search for modifications to overcome problems, or perhaps will lead to eventual rejection of the option.

The most rigid constraints of a firm stem from the less quantifiable limitations of individuals and organizations. The basic question is whether the organization has ever shown it could muster the degree of coordinative and integrative skills necessary to carry out the change in strategy.

2. Measuring the capacity for commitment.   A broad-based commitment to successful implementation requires these two conditions:

- The premises and elements of the strategy must be readily communicable. If they are not understood, then not only will the strategy option likely be flawed, but its capacity to motivate support will be seriously compromised. A good strategy is one that can be easily understood by all functions, so they are not working at cross purposes.
- The strategy should challenge and motivate key personnel. Not only must the option have a champion who gives it enthusiastic and credible support, but it must also gain acceptance by all key operating personnel.

If managers either have serious reservations about a strategy, are not excited by its objectives and methods, or strongly support another option, the strategy must be judged infeasible.

5. VULNERABILITY: HOW MUCH RISK IS INVOLVED?

Each alternative strategy and the associated projects have a distinct risk profile. The overall level of risk reflects the vulnerability of the strategy if important assumptions are wrong or if critical tasks are not accomplished. For example, an aggressive build strategy that increases investment intensity will increase the break-even point. Thus this option is riskier, making the firm more vulnerable to shortfalls in sales forecasts than a "manage-for-current-earnings option.

The factors that contribute to the overall risk level can be either environmental or internal. The *environmental risks* stem from major uncertainties about the economic environment, competitor and market response, legislative and regulatory action, and the pace of technological change. These risks encompass such possiblities as price cutting by competitors, forward integration by suppliers, or weak market demand due to a recession.

Internal risks, on the other hand, involve uncertainties about the ability of the business to execute a critical element of the strategy and thereby jeopardize performance. A delay in design or manufacturing could be critical if it means the business will miss a market-development opportunity.

6. ADAPTABILITY: HOW FLEXIBLE WILL YOU REMAIN?

In an uncertain environment, it is important to ask whether, and at what cost, the strategy could be reversed in the future. The purpose of this questioning is to help your firm find the best ways to make fixed capital expenditures so that, if a major contingency occurs, it would not be necessary to write off the entire investment. Therefore, evaluate how each strategy offers possibilities for flexibility in design, multiple uses, or risk hedging—perhaps at a higher capital cost.

The question of adaptability applies as much to decisions about delaying changes in strategic direction as to decisions about undertaking major investment programs. The implications of a delay are difficult to assess, especially when they are buried in the implicit assumption of discounted cash-flow analysis that investments are reversible.

In capital budgeting decisions, it is typically assumed that if an investment is postponed, it can always be made later with no penalty other than that implied by the company's discount rate. But in fact, regaining this lost ground later may actually cost much more than if the company had made the investment when first proposed. If the strategic window has closed, there may be no opportunity to adapt to the new situation, and all flexibility has been lost. An inflexible strategy, therefore, may be an unattractive one.

7. FINANCIAL DESIRABILITY: HOW ATTRACTIVE ARE THE REWARDS?

The ultimate test of strategy is how attractive the forecast performance is. The most widely used benchmarks are sales growth and profitability measures, including ROS, net earnings, ROI, ROE, RONA, and cash flow. Unfortunately, they are seldom sufficient for meaningful analysis of strategy options.

Clearer signals may come from evaluating the merits of a strategy option in light of its capacity to enhance the economic value of the business or to improve competitive position.

Keep in mind that a forecast of substantial creation of economic value—or of high rates of profitability—cannot be taken as automatic indicators of the acceptability of a strategy option. Both these measures must be based on persuasive evidence of competitive advantage. Thus, further tests of the outcome require forecasts of the likelihood the option will gain or sustain an advantage.

CONCLUSION

In essence, a business strategy is an integrated set of actions in the pursuit of a competitive advantage. The seven criteria discussed in this case for evaluating an effective strategy, therefore, should both help guide your choice of a new strategy and help you assess the adequacy of your present business strategy.

CHAPTER

— 11 —

THE POLITICS OF STRATEGIC DECISION MAKING: MANAGING INTERNAL AND EXTERNAL STAKEHOLDERS

■

□

SUSTAINING YOUR POLITICAL POSITION IN STRATEGY MAKING

WARREN K. SCHILIT

The formulation and implementation of strategy is all too often presented as simply an analytical exercise. Strategy textbooks and individual managers have their own preferred mode of analysis. However, anybody who has ever been involved in strategy making knows that organizational politics can dramatically influence what strategies are chosen and how they are implemented. You, therefore, need to understand how you can create and sustain your own political position, that is, your power base vis-à-vis others in the organization. To help you do so, this article suggests six guidelines.

1. Identify the sources of your power
2. Build coalitions
3. Use multiple reference points
4. Establish goals collaboratively
5. Be flexible

Strategic Planning Management, May, 1984; Commerce Communications, Inc.

Before we discuss each of those guidelines, let us turn to two examples of politics at work.

POLITICS: TWO EXAMPLES

About five years ago, a medium-sized manufacturing company, headquartered near Washington, D.C., was considering the implementation of a new computer system. During the first planning session of that year, the Vice President of Personnel presented several good reasons for choosing a specific system for the company. His proposal, however, was rejected by the other members of the executive council.

At the next planning session, which was held less than two months later, the Vice President of Finance suggested the implementation of the identical system and gave almost the same reasons for its implementation. This time the proposal was overwhelmingly accepted.

After speaking to several members of the corporation, I learned that this turn of events was primarily due to the different political positions of these two executives. The finance division was traditionally powerful in this organization, as it controlled a very precious resource—money—whereas the personnel division was traditionally viewed as the weak link in the organization. Thus, regardless of the quality of the proposal, the Vice President of Personnel was less likely to have his ideas accepted than were executives at the same level who occupied positions that were organizationally more powerful.

In another example, the President of a large division of a multi-national firm accepted in principle a proposal by his Executive Vice President to enter a related business via acquisition. The proposal was then presented to selected members of the division's senior management team by the Executive Vice President.

The proposal met with stiff opposition from the Director of Strategic Planning and Business Development and the Product Group Manager who would assume responsibility for the new venture. They agreed that the firm should enter this business, but that it be done via internal development.

Their offer to develop a detailed strategy to enter the business through internal development was accepted by the President. In developing the proposed strategy, they worked closely with R&D, finance, and marketing personnel. Their proposed strategy was overwhelmingly accepted by the senior management team. The Executive VP grudgingly gave his support.

In this example, the opposition to the Executive VP banded together and presented a united front. Also, the Executive VP overestimated his own power: he thought that once he publicly gave a strategy option his imprimatur, it would be quickly supported by those underneath him in the organization.

1. IDENTIFY THE SOURCES OF YOUR POWER

The above two examples illustrate the importance of knowing what are the sources of your power. All of us occasionally fall into the trap of thinking that our authority (as bestowed on us by our position in the organization) is the major or only source of our power. While authority is a major source of power in organizational settings, it is not the only source.

As discovered by the Executive VP in the above example, others can use a variety of sources of power to combat your authority based power. Among these other sources of power are the following:

- expertise
- information or knowledge
- access to influential others
- control of resources
- charisma

The moral here is that as you try to influence others you need to know what is (are) the source(s) of your own power, as well as the source(s) of the power of those whom you wish to influence.

The VP of Personnel had little power in the decision context in the first example above: he did not have the authority to make the decision, he possessed no relevant expertise or knowledge (at least as perceived by others), and he controlled little resources relevant to the decision. Thus, although he developed a strong set of arguments, his opinion or preferred plan of action did not prevail.

Another important lesson is implicit here: the relevant sources of power may vary depending upon the decision or issue context. For example, in human resource matters, all of the bases of power that worked against the VP of Personnel might likely work for him. You therefore must not fall into the trap of thinking that your "power" is germane to all decision contexts. In other words, because you won one battle doesn't mean you shall win the next skirmish.

2. BUILD COALITIONS

Few individuals have the power to continually win (that is to have their recommendations accepted or their preferences implemented). Consequently, any single individual has to build a power base within the organization if his wishes or preferred course of action are to prevail. In short, the individual has to build a coalition around others who share his viewpoint, interests, or goals.

For example, the VP of Human Resources and Executive VP in the examples noted above did not create a coalition to support their proposals. Thus, neither individual received much support from others *after* they introduced their proposals. On the other hand, the Executive VP found himself confronted by a formidable coalition which evidenced solid organizational support from multiple sources for the alternate proposal.

Again, it is important to note that coalitions tend to evolve around specific decisions or issues. Thus, they often dissipate as soon as the decision or issue is resolved. Furthermore, when the next decision or issue arises, some of those who were on your side in a previous coalition may now be on the opposite side. In building a coalition, you need to ask the following questions:

- who is likely to share your viewpoint, interests, goals, etc.?
- why are they likely to be on your side?
- what can you do to induce them to join you?
- what are they likely to demand of you?

The answers to those questions will indicate who is most likely to coalesce with you and why they will do so.

3. USE MULTIPLE REFERENCE POINTS

Assessing the power base of yourself and others, and building coalitions, requires that you put yourself in the position of others. Thus, as you develop and assess strategic alternatives, and as you consider the possible problems involved in implementing a strategy, you need to consider the following questions:

- what are the "interests" of specific individuals or other groups?
- how might these interests affect your preferred alternative or proposed plan of action?
- what can you do to influence these interests?

Multiple reference points are appropriate in most strategy contexts. For example, when James McFarland became CEO of General Mills, he assembled about three dozen key executives for a three-day management retreat. After agreeing on some broad financial goals, he divided his group into units of six to eight people to answer the question, "What is a great company?" from the viewpoints of employees, stockholders, suppliers, and society as a whole. They then identified strengths and weaknesses of the company from each perspective, which served as valuable input in the development of some very successful acquisition-divestiture strategies that helped move General Mills from a very good company to a great company.

4. ESTABLISH GOALS COLLABORATIVELY

Goals provide the direction and motivation for our individual and collective actions. If goals are imposed through a blatant exercise of power, others may be directed and motivated for the wrong reasons or they may fight the imposed goals.

A good example of a misuse of power in unilaterally establishing goals recently occurred in a small electronics firm. The President established sales goals for each marketing manager without consulting them. The sales goals were based upon what the President believed he knew about the market conditions confronting each marketing manager.

Some marketing managers publicly challenged the President's facts and figures. They argued that because the President didn't know enough about the peculiarities of individual markets, he was not in a position to determine realistic sales goals. Over a series of meetings, the President was forced to conclude that he had grossly overestimated potential sales. Consequently, the sales forecasts were adjusted downward.

A major consequence of the exchange was that the President "lost face" with many of his senior marketing managers. He was seen to have little expertise and knowledge in the marketing and sales areas. His ability to influence these same managers in future exchanges was severely constrained.

5. BE FLEXIBLE

Many individuals frequently weaken their political position through their inflexibility. They choose a course of action and doggedly pursue it, or they announce their intentions or preferences and expect everybody else to follow them.

For example, the Executive VP in the second example above, committed himself much too early to his preferred choice—a strategy built around acquisitions. He then found it difficult to withdraw from his publicly stated position without forfeiting some of his political capital. In short, you should not publicly announce your goals too early, so that you can change direction if necessary.

Flexibility may also require that you invent new options in order to reach a compromise with your antagonists. Sometimes, you and your opponents may be so committed to your preferred options, that the only way out (in the absence of a forced solution) is to develop a new or alternate course of action to which all parties can subscribe. The new option creates a "win-win" situation: each party gains something from the new course of action.

This is what happened recently in a small industrial goods firm as it reassessed its strategy. Two groups of managers began to coalesce around two quite distinct strategy options. One group wanted to go for higher market share through aggressive pricing. The other group wanted to exploit the firm's current good market standing by passing through a major price increase. A compromise strategic option was eventually accepted by both groups: the firm would adopt the aggressive pricing strategy for most of its products going through specialized distribution channels, and would raise prices on its products going through its general distribution channels.

CONCLUSION

Your ability to get your way in strategy making may be more a function of your political acumen than your analytical prowess. The above guidelines should serve to strengthen and sustain your political position as you engage in the unavoidable strategy making battles.

□

BUILDING SUPPORT FOR YOUR STRATEGY BY COMMUNICATING YOUR PLANS
FRANK M. CORRADO

Businesses of all types are facing an increasing array of "demands" or "claims" from groups both internal and external to the firms. Unions, stockholders, customers, consumer and environmental groups, government agencies, community and other social interest groups are vociferously making their interests known to business managers.

Business can no longer afford to ignore these audiences. Indeed, the purpose of this article is to suggest that business managers should develop a communication program that will specifically convey the company "message" to these constituencies: its beliefs, its viewpoints, and its basic goals.

COMMUNICATIONS: A NECESSITY

Studies conducted during the last half-dozen years show that senior managers are spending more and more of their time talking to stakeholders both inside and outside of the corporation. They must deal not only with reporters, but with employees, investors, customers, legislators, and interest groups. The executives may not enjoy it, but they realize that times are changing. Management is both a science and an art—and in many ways it is becoming a *performing* art.

Executives must now face a work force that wants greater input into management decisions, a more economically savvy investor who really wants to know where the company is headed, and citizenry which sees the corporation as a public institution that affects society in everything it does. The decision to bail out Chrysler was, as we are all well aware, a public policy decision.

A company's communications program has become far more than a corporate frill. It should be an integral part of the organization's drive for profitability by developing solid relationships with stakeholders. An effective

Strategic Planning Management, April, 1984; Commerce Communications, Inc.

communications program should be designed by top executives for four distinct targets: (1) employees, (2) the marketplace, (3) the wider public (via the media), and (4) the government.

WHERE COMMUNICATION STARTS

A strategic communications program has to come from top management. The task shouldn't be delegated to the public relations department, to human resources, or to one executive vice-president. The best programs are often conceived in the boardroom, where a vision is shaped by the CEO and the board. The vision must be broad enough to cover how the company feels about its products, its employees, its customers, and maybe even society in general.

This top-down approach was well exemplified in Johnson & Johnson's remarkable handling of the Tylenol episode. Top management's approach was seen by the public as being consistent with a century-old company commitment to the health and welfare of its customers, a philosophy that had been nurtured strongly by the current CEO.

COMMUNICATIONS: AN EXAMPLE

The following example illustrates the benefits of a communications strategy. The new owner of a metal fabricating company believed he had a good product with good profit potential, but he was faced with runaway costs and a sluggish market where consolidation of competitors was increasing. He decided that his job was to emphasize cost-cutting and marketing, and to reorient the company to his new environment. In looking at his new company, he saw a management wedded to tradition, workers who viewed the company as unstable, customers who were more concerned with price than quality, and a demoralized sales force.

With the help of a consultant, the new CEO formulated a simple message—a vision of the company's future: "We are a solid company, we can be profitable, but the marketplace is changing and therefore we must change." He put together a short slide presentation illustrating these points graphically. His first step was to get the message across at an informal dinner with his management team. He then involved many of his managers in task forces to come up with marketing and cost cutting strategies and, more importantly, to get them personally involved in the change.

His next priority was to deliver that message to employees. He adapted his initial slide show and went around to each plant holding informal "stand-to's" with employees answering questions and announcing a special suggestion program to get them into the change process by coming up with their own cost-cutting suggestions.

In a meeting with the sales force, the owner outlined the new program and showed how the company was going to position itself against competitors. Finally, an advertising program was started to communicate the message of change to customers: "We are keeping quality up and cutting costs. We are competitive."

What this CEO did can be a model for many companies. He developed a strategic message and, at the same time, like any good politician, he adapted the message for different audiences: he told employees about productivity, managers about change, and customers about the product.

As illustrated in this instance, once the corporate vision is set, the message is communicated to audiences both inside and outside the corporation.

1. INTERNAL COMMUNICATION: CONVEYING STRATEGIES TO MANAGERS

The company's managers and supervisors must be kept up to date on strategic plans. At Weyerhaeuser, executives found that their most successful plants were those with the best communication networks: managers spent a lot of time walking the floor, regularly chatting with employees, and telling them how well the plant was progressing toward its production goals. When necessary, plant workers were put in direct touch with customers so that problems could be solved at the most appropriate level.

Communication to supervisors or lower-level managers is important but frequently neglected. They're often asked by their own staff to "speak" for top management, so that means that they must receive strong communication from management. At the same time, employees must understand that they work for the customer, not the supervisor. It is the responsibility of the supervisor to convey that message to his staff.

2. COMMUNICATING WITH THE MARKETPLACE

The messages a company communicates to the marketplace are critical to the customers' acceptance of the firm's products. It's important to realize that a company sends out many signals beyond its explicit communications via its advertising and public relations efforts.

Those subtle signals can be unfavorable or very positive. For example, Procter & Gamble seldom talks to the press and seems very secretive. And yet, few companies are more respected for being sensitive to their customers' needs.

Remember how fast P&G pulled "Rely" off the market when a public health question first arose? That action communicated a loud and clear message to the public about how concerned the company is about its products and customers. Contrast that incident to the acrimonious battle waged by Firestone in the late '70s to salvage the "500" radial tire.

Basically, a company should strive to be straightforward and truthful in talking about its future. Also, if a firm makes an effort to broaden its audience beyond analysts and pension-fund managers to include employees, small stockholders, customers, and brokers, the company may well reap a handsome return from that investment later when arbitragers, unfriendly suitors, and bankers start knocking on the door. A number of observers contend that such a strategy might have helped International Harvester immensely when its troubles came.

3. COMMUNICATING WITH THE GOVERNMENT

Regardless of what method a company chooses for communicating with government, the information it conveys should be consistent with the company's messages to customers. A horrendous discrepancy between these two areas developed in the 1970s as Detroit automakers faced charges for auto safety defects from government regulators while advertising "improved quality" to consumers.

Business doesn't have to roll over and play dead when it is attacked by regulators. As a matter of fact, businesses lobby aggressively for their interests, spending more than $25 million in the 1982 elections fighting for their viewpoint on voter initiatives ranging from bottle deposits to nuclear plants.

But a company must ask a key question: Are we fighting for a position that is consistent with the corporate vision and the messages that we are delivering to our constituencies?

4. COMMUNICATING WITH THE WIDER PUBLIC VIA THE MEDIA

Business is *the* hot topic of the 1980s. But you should realize that most people don't get their business news from reading thoughtful, in-depth articles in the business press. In fact, the Roper organization reports that 60% of all Americans receive their business news primarily from television.

Many companies try to ignore television as a channel for communication, even though our times clearly don't allow this anymore. But many firms still wait until a crisis occurs to upgrade their communications program hurriedly. Historically, much bad blood exists between the media (which is accustomed to challenging public officials' claims) and the business manager (who is used to having his word taken for gospel). A good number of companies have spent untold sums attempting to teach their managers how to tell their whole story in thirty seconds.

The important point here is for managers to be consistent. A company can't always control its involvement with the news media. You never know when the company may face a disaster, an emergency, or a scandal. What a company can do, however, is make sure that its approach in dealing with the media is consistent with its corporate strategy.

SOME STRATEGIC QUESTIONS ABOUT COMMUNICATIONS

In formulating a communication strategy, the following questions must be raised.

1. What is the corporate vision?
   - Has the board of directors articulated a broad vision of the corporation that addresses people, products, and markets?
   - Does the mission statement establish a clear vision of where the company is going?
   - Does the vision relate to society's changing expectations?

2. What is the corporate communications policy?
   - Has senior management identified relevant constituencies for communicating its strategic vision?
   - What channels have been selected? Are they "soft touch?"
   - Have expectations been established for communications?

3. What are the communications priorities?
   - Employees?
   - Investors?
   - Customers?

4. Is the corporation organized for effective communications?
   - Do supervisors have enough information to communicate effectively?
   - Are effective feedback systems in place?

5. Are top executives committed to the program?
   - Does top management see profit in better communications?
   - Is that communicated throughout the organization?

CONCLUSION

While the guidelines noted above will help in formulating an approach to communicating strategy, the act of executing that program must follow from an internal belief in the message and commitment to making the organization believe in the message. By devoting explicit attention to strategy communications, your company can overcome many of the problems currently facing organizations as a consequence of others misunderstanding the organization's viewpoint.

☐

APPLICATION IN STRATEGIC MANAGEMENT:
Building Support for New Ventures
LIAM FAHEY

Large corporations are frequently criticized for not being entrepreneurial. One piece of evidence often cited in these criticisms is the low volume of "new ventures" generated within large corporations.

New ventures take corporations into new terrain. They involve doing something the firm hasn't done before. Consequently they require someone who is willing and able to "champion" them. Otherwise, they may never gain the attention of the organization.

What follows is a brief description of the efforts of two individuals to champion a new venture in a large consumer goods corporation.

CREATING THE NEW VENTURE

This venture was the brain child of one division's VP of marketing. He believed that the "time was right" for the emergence of a specialized national retail chain, and that the organization had the resources to develop such a chain over a five year time period.

This new venture involved the firm moving into a "new business," the establishment of free standing, full line, retail stores to sell not only the firm's own products but also those of multiple other manufacturers. The firm previously had only minimal experience in the retail business.

The plan was to start with pilot stores in a few select areas, and, if successful, expand to several stores regionally, with the ultimate intent of going nationwide.

The concept of free standing, well stocked retail stores was not new. A number of strong regional chains were already in existence. What distinguished this new venture was its proposed scale—a national operation.

PACKAGING THE BUSINESS CONCEPT

Since the division had never previously embarked upon a venture of this magnitude, the VP in conjunction with his staff, wanted to pull together the strongest possible "package," that is, arguments to support the venture.

The major arguments in support of the proposed venture were:

1. Although the firm had no retailing experience, it did know the industry.
2. Although no other major competitor had entered retailing, a move into retailing as a form of vertical integration made strategic sense.

Strategic Planning Management, September, 1984; Commerce Communications, Inc.

3. A few large geographic areas existed where pilot stores could be tested in the absence of strong local or regional chains.

4. The capital investment required to fund two pilot stores was relatively small compared to the cost of some other projects the division was considering.

The VP pulled together a short document outlining the scope, thrust, and merits of the proposed venture.

MOBILIZING EARLY SUPPORT

Once he had the strategy developed, the VP informally presented it to the division President. The President's response was clear and emphatic. The proposed new venture did not fit with the division's mission. The division was a manufacturing entity.

However, in discussing the venture with the VP, the President agreed that it made strategic sense, that the corporation probably should be in retailing, and that the resources required were not unreasonable.

The VP then requested the division President to forward the proposed venture's documentation to the corporate President with a cover letter indicating the division President's support for the strategic direction inherent in the venture.

The corporate President responded by granting the VP an opportunity to present the proposal to the corporate staff. The intent of the presentation as stated by the corporate President was to test the idea rather than discuss the details of its implementation.

The outcome of the presentation was that the corporate President authorized further development and assessment of the proposed venture. He did not set any deadlines or make any specific requests.

The major consequence of this initial meeting, in the eyes of the VP, was that retailing as a potential corporate activity had received at least preliminary support from the corporate President's office. The VP now felt that others in the corporation for political reasons, if nothing else, would have to treat the proposed venture with some seriousness.

INSTITUTIONALIZING EARLY SUPPORT

The VP was concerned that the impetus generated by the meeting with the corporate President and staff might quickly peter out. He felt that unless somebody in the corporation—preferably at the corporate rather than divisional level—had formal authority to oversee development of the venture idea, it would fall through the corporate cracks.

It was at this point that the VP decided to deviate from the normal organizational structure and procedures. He requested and received permission from the corporation to report directly to the group Vice-President on all matters regarding the new venture.

The VP believed that the institutional support of the group VP would signal to the rest of the organization that this venture was receiving serious attention. The VP as venture champion recognized that the group VP might be able to "rock some boats" that were outside his own reach.

Another reason for the request was that the VP believed the venture was too big for his own division. To succeed it would require corporate support.

As the two VPs were building support for the project, they kept the corporate President informed of their activities. They particularly emphasized the objections to the venture and who was making them.

Their purpose in alerting the corporate President to objections to the venture was twofold. They did not want to be "sideswiped" by having others bring these to the attention of the corporate President. Also, they hoped that he might bring some pressure to bear on the objectors. They were, of course, happy to provide the corporate President with the ammunition to do so.

BUILDING AN EFFECTIVE COALITION

The VP next set about selling the venture to enough people so that it would receive corporate approval. Having the group VP as a spearhead and figurehead for the venture was not sufficient.

At this stage, the development of the actual strategy for implementing the venture was in large measure subordinate to the strategy for gaining widespread support for the venture itself within the organization. Unless the latter was achieved, the venture would not come to pass.

The VP identified the key individuals who would be instrumental in approving or rejecting the venture. Along with the group VP, he then met each of these individuals.

They presented the proposed venture in outline form and filled in details as requested. Each individual was given as much time as he required to critique the venture.

They met a second time with those individuals who had serious reservations about the venture. In these meetings, the two VPs identified each objection to the venture and then presented their own case.

WINNING VENTURE APPROVAL

To attain corporate approval for initiating the venture (i.e., funding the initial store), the venture proposal had to pass through a number of decision points in the firm's strategic planning and capital budgeting process.

To help ensure that the venture would be favorably viewed, the following are some of the key elements in the strategy adopted by the two VPs.

First, wherever possible, they involved others in presenting the proposed venture. For example, they had a member of the corporate finance staff present the financial aspects of the venture to the corporate planning group and senior corporate officers.

Second, they tried not to let discussion of the venture get bogged down in details at any stage during the approval process. They felt that because it was a truly new venture for the firm, it could be nit-picked to death.

Third, they prepared special presentations for some key phases of the decision process. They presented a financial analysis to the capital budgeting committee, a marketing analysis to the corporate marketing department, and a strategy "fit" analysis (how retailing fit the firm's present strategies) to the firm's senior officers.

Fourth, they tailored their formal presentations to meet what they believed would be the objections of those involved in each decision point. Many of these objections were noted in the largely informal interactions involved in generating early support for the venture.

The venture won corporate approval. The success of the pilot store exceeded corporate expectations. Additional stores are now being added.

CONCLUSION

Getting this new venture off the ground required a dedicated venture champion (the initiating divisional marketing VP), a venture sponsor (the group VP) and a highly visible venture supporter (the corporate President).

The two VPs developed what in effect was a political strategy to sell the project within the firm. It did not sell itself.

The political strategy entailed a number of elements:

1. They mobilized support from select individuals at each stage of the decision process.

2. They involved different individuals or sub-units at different stages of the decision process.

3. Through 1 and 2, they gradually built a wide coalition within the organization to support the venture.

4. They involved others in developing and shaping the venture. "Ownership" in the venture was thus spread, and this in turn helped to mobilize support and generate a supportive coalition.

5. They anticipated objections and developed counter-arguments. This often meant adapting the project proposal to meet the expertise and interests of individuals and groups involved in the firm's decision process. For

example, in meeting with the corporate President, they emphasized the venture as a base for major further strategy development.

6. In doing much of the above, they also used the informal side of the organization. They frequently used chance meetings with others as occasions for one-on-one selling of the venture.

7. They kept a few key individuals continually informed of what was happening with regard to the project. They also used these individuals to formally "intervene" in the decision process to build and sustain support for the venture.

Both VPs had to be willing to assume the personal risks involved in the venture. They did not want to be associated with a losing venture. Thus, they committed themselves to the project and became its figureheads.

CHAPTER

— 12 —

IMPLEMENTING STRATEGY: UNDERSTANDING THE ORGANIZATIONAL CONTEXT

■

□

PUTTING YOUR STRATEGY INTO ACTION
L. J. BOURGEOIS III AND DAVID R. BRODWIN

Most discussions of strategic planning focus on how to formulate strategy. There are several tools and techniques in wide-spread use. Management consulting firms offer strategic planning on a commodity basis, and business school programs are adorned with methodologies for choosing the "best" strategy.

By contrast, scant attention has been given to how to implement those strategies. Yet many people have recognized that problems with implementation in many companies have resulted in failed strategies and abandoned planning efforts. This reading will identify many of these implementation problems and then offer you some remedies for them.

Our discussions will provide suggestions that can help managers be more successful in three general areas:

- developing strategies that can realistically be implemented, given not only the marketplace but also the politics, culture, and competence of your firm
- putting your strategies into action and
- revising strategies continually so you can take advantage of new opportunities and respond to threats.

Strategic Planning Management, March/April/May, 1983; Commerce Communications, Inc.

FIVE WAYS COMPANIES IMPLEMENT STRATEGY

In studying the management practices of a variety of companies, we have found that their approaches to strategy implementation can be categorized into one of five basic descriptions (Table 12-1). In each one, the chief executive officer plays a somewhat different role and uses distinctive methods for developing and implementing strategies. We have given each description a title to distinguish its main characteristics.

The first two descriptions represent traditional approaches to implementation. Here the CEO formulates strategy first, and then thinks about implementation later.

1. **The Commander Approach**—The CEO concentrates on formulating the strategy, giving little thought to how the plan will be carried out. He either develops the strategy himself or supervises a team of planners. Once he's satisfied that he has the "best" strategy, he passes it along to those who are instructed to "make it happen."

2. **The Organizational Change Approach**—Once a plan has been developed, the executive puts it into effect by taking such steps as reorganizing the company structure, changing incentive compensation schemes, or hiring staff.

The next two approaches involve more recent attempts to enhance implementation by broadening the bases of participation in the planning process:

3. **The Collaborative Approach**—Rather than develop the strategy in a vacuum, the CEO enlists the help of his senior managers during the planning process in order to assure that all the key players will back the final plan.

4. **The Cultural Approach**—This is an extension of the collaborative model to involve people at middle and sometimes lower levels of the organization. It seeks to implement strategy through the development of a corporate culture throughout the organization.

The final approach takes advantage of managers' natural inclinations to develop opportunities as they are encountered.

5. **The Cresive Approach**—In this approach, the CEO addresses strategy planning and implementation simultaneously. He is not interested in planning alone, or even in leading others through a protracted planning process. Rather, he tries, through his statements and actions, to guide his managers into coming forward as champions of sound strategies.

In studying these five approaches we noticed several trends. First, the two traditional methods are gradually being supplanted by the others. Second, companies are focusing increasingly on organizational issues involved in getting

TABLE 12-1 The Five Approaches to Strategic Management

Approach	The CEO's Strategic Question	CEO's Role
I. Commander Approach	"How do I formulate the optimal strategy?"	Master Planner
II. Change Approach	"I have a strategy in mind—now how do I implement it?"	Architect of Implementation
III. Collaborative Approach	"How do I involve top management in planning so they will be committed to strategies from the start?"	Coordinator
IV. Cultural Approach	"How do I involve the whole organization in implementation?"	Coach
V. Crescive Approach	"How do I encourage managers to come forward as champions of sound strategies?"	Premise-Setter and Judge

a company to adapt to its environment and to pursue new opportunities or respond to outside threats. Finally, we see a trend toward the CEO playing an increasingly indirect and more subtle role in strategy development.

METHOD 1: THE COMMANDER

The typical scenario depicting the most traditional approach to strategy formulation and implementation is as follows: after the CEO approves the strategic plan, he calls his top managers into a conference room, presents the strategy, and tells them to implement it.

The CEO is involved only with formulating the strategy. He assumes that an exhaustive analysis must be completed before any action can be taken, so the CEO typically authorizes an extensive study of the firm's competitive opportunities. In general, focusing on the planning succeeds in at least giving the CEO a sense of direction for his firm, which helps him make difficult day-to-day decisions and also reduces uncertainty within the organization.

However, this approach can be implemented successfully only if several conditions are met. First, the CEO must wield a great deal of power so he can simply command implementation. Otherwise, unless the proposed strategy poses little threat to organizational members, implementation cannot be achieved very easily.

Second, accurate information must be available to the strategist before it becomes obsolete. Since good strategy depends on high-quality information, it is important that critical information entering the firm at lower levels is being compiled, digested, and transmitted upward quickly.

Third, the strategists must be insulated from personal biases and political influences that can impinge on the plan. Managers are likely to propose strategies favorable to their own divisions but not necessarily to the corporation as a whole.

One problem with this approach is that it often splits the firm into "thinkers" and "doers," and those charged with the doing may not feel that they are part of the game. The general manager must dispel any impression that the only acceptable strategies are those developed by himself and his planning staff, or he may find himself faced with an extremely unmotivated, un-innovative group of employees.

METHOD 2: ORGANIZATIONAL CHANGE

With this approach, the CEO makes the strategy decisions and then paves the way for implementation by redesigning the organizational structure, personnel assignments, information systems, and compensation scheme.

This method goes beyond the first one by having the CEO consider how to put the plan into action. The CEO basically uses two sets of tools: (1) changing the structure and staffing to focus attention on the firm's new priorities; and (2) revising systems for planning, performance measurement, and incentive compensation to help achieve the firm's strategic goals.

The first set of tools—changing the organizational structure and staffing—has been the traditional approach espoused in most business strategy texts. Generally, the organizational structure should reflect the diversity of the firm's strategies. For example, if a company's strategy calls for worldwide coordination of manufacturing in order to capture cost efficiencies, the CEO would implement a "functional" organization for production, while a strategy calling for selling diverse product lines to various markets would demand a divisional organization of separate profit centers.

The second set of tools involves adjusting administrative systems. Various planning, accounting, and control tools such as those governing capital and operating budgets, can be used to help achieve desired goals. For example, if the firm's strategy calls for investing certain businesses and harvesting others, or for channeling profits from one national unit into funding others, these goals should be featured prominently in the capital budgeting procedure so that business-unit managers can effectively plan their resource requests and others can effectively evaluate them.

Performance measures should be designed so that they target meaningful short-term milestones in order to monitor progress toward strategic goals. The incentive compensation scheme should then be tied into the clearcut numerical terms of the performance measures. At a minimum, the general manager must insure that the current compensation plan isn't thwarting the achievement of the strategy in ways such as rewarding short-term profitability at the expense of longer-term growth.

One company, with which the authors are familiar, clearly illustrates the problems which can arise when performance measures and administrative systems are inappropriate. This firm—a major diversified manufacturer—concluded that a steady stream of new products was the most important factor in maintaining the stock price at the desired level, yet the performance measures and management reports imposed on the division heads stressed quarterly profit above all else.

Unlike the first approach, in this method the CEO doesn't merely command his subordinates to put the plan into action. He supervises the implementation and may only reveal the strategy gradually, rather than in one bold proclamation.

However, it usually is inadequate for the CEO simply to tack "implementation" onto "strategy." This approach doesn't deal with problems of obtaining accurate information nor does it buffer the planner from political pressures. Also, as in the first approach, imposing the strategy downward from the top executives still causes motivational problems among the "doers" at lower levels.

In addition, another problem can develop when the CEO manipulates the systems and structures of the organization in support of a particular strategy. The general manager may be losing important strategic flexibility.

Some of these systems, particularly incentive compensation, take a long time to design, install, and become effective. If a dramatic change in the environment suddenly demands a major shift in the strategy, it may be very difficult to change the firm's course, since all the "levers" controlling the firm have been set firmly in support of the now-obsolete game plan.

In the interest of retaining strategic flexibility in situations where environmental uncertainty is high, it may prove more advisable in the long run to refrain from using some of the tools described above. For example, many high technology firms, which rely on the rapid development and introduction of a continuous stream of technological innovations, avoid imposing bureaucratic administrative systems which would cripple their ability to create strategic change.

Dependence upon the Commander Approach has significant limitations. Yet it is the approach to strategy implementation with which all too many line managers are familiar. Strategy implementation is most divorced from strategy formulation under this approach.

But, with a set of powerful implementation tools at his or her disposal, the executive using the Organizational Change Approach can implement more difficult strategies or plans in a wide variety of organizations.

The strategist who has used either of these two traditional approaches eventually confronts a basic dilemma: How do I make realistic strategic decisions based on accurate and unbiased information, and then set up an administrative system to put those decisions into action over the long-run? Of course, these goals should also be achieved without hurting managers' motivation, stifling creativity, or creating an inflexible bureaucracy.

METHOD 3: THE COLLABORATIVE APPROACH

In contrast to the two earlier approaches in which the chief executive makes most of the strategic and organizational decisions, the Collaborative Approach extends strategic decision-making to the organization's top management team. The purpose here is to get the top managers to help develop and support a good set of goals and strategies.

In this model, the CEO employs group dynamics and "brainstorming" techniques to get managers with different points of view to contribute to the strategic process. Our research indicates that in effective top management teams the executives will have conflicting goals and perceptions of the external environment, so the CEO will want to extract whatever "group wisdom" is inherent in these different perspectives.

The typical scenario depicting this approach should be familiar to readers: With key executives and division managers, the CEO embarks on a week-long planning retreat. At the retreat, each participant presents his own ideas of where the firm should head. Extensive discussions follow, until the group reaches a consensus around the firm's longer-range mission and near-term strategy. Upon returning to their respective offices, each participant charges ahead in the agreed-upon direction.

In relying on collaboration among top executives, this approach depends on the skillful structuring of group interaction. This can take a variety of forms. For example the consulting firm of Arthur D. Little engages in a process designed to gain team consensus on which generic strategies "fit" their particular industry situation.

We have employed another variant of the Collaborative Method which involves *teaching* analytical tools to the top management team. These variations all involve managers' participation in contrast to the typical approach used by consulting firms, in which top managers rely on outsiders to provide a final report and recommendations.

A number of corporations now use some type of Collaborative Method. General Motors formed "business teams" in 1980 which consisted of managers from different functional areas; the role of the team was simply to bring out different points of view on whatever strategic—usually product-focused—problem was identified.

The CEO of a wholly owned Exxon subsidiary informed us that *his* job was not to make and implement strategy. Instead, he was responsible for assembling a team of competent managers—most more competent than he in their respective functional fields—which could, jointly, collaborate in the formation of strategies.

The Collaborative Approach overcomes two key limitations of the previous two methods. By incorporating information from executives who are closer to the line operations and by engaging several points of view, it helps provide better information than the CEO alone would have. Also because participation breeds commitment, this method helps overcome any resistance from top managers—which improves the possibility of successful implementation.

However, what the Collaborative Approach gains in team commitment may come at the expense of "strategic perfection." That is, it results in a compromise that has been negotiated among players with different points of view. The strategy may not be as dynamic as one CEO's vision, but it will be more politically feasible.

A second criticism of the Collaborative Approach is that it is not "real" collective decision-making from an organizational standpoint, because the managers—the organizational elite—cannot or will not give up centralized control. In effect, this approach still retains the wall separating thinkers from "doers," and it fails to draw upon the resources of personnel throughout the organization.

Our fourth approach to strategy implementation overcomes that shortcoming.

METHOD 4: THE CULTURAL APPROACH

The Cultural Approach extends the benefits of collective participation into lower levels of the organization in order to get the entire organization committed to the firm's goals and strategies.

In this approach, the CEO sets the game plan and communicates the direction in which the firm should move, but he then gives individuals the responsibility of determining the details of how to execute the plan. To a large extent, the Cultural Approach represents the latest wave of management techniques promulgated to (and, in some cases, enthusiastically adopted by) American managers seeking the panacea to our current economic woes in the face of successful Japanese competition.

The implementation tools used in building a strong corporate culture range from such simple notions as publishing a company creed and singing a company song to much more complex techniques. The complex—and usually effective—involve implementing strategy by employing the concept of "third-order control."

Since implementation involves controlling the behavior of others, we can think of three levels of control. First-order control involves direct supervision. Second order control involves using rules, procedures, and organization structure to guide the behavior of others (as in the Organizational Change Approach described earlier). Third-order control is a much more subtle—and potentially more powerful—means of influencing behavior through shaping the norms, values, symbols, and beliefs that managers and employees use in making day-to-day decisions.

The key distinction between managers using the Cultural Approach and those simply engaged in "participative management," is that these executives understand that corporate culture should serve as the handmaiden to corporate strategy, rather than proselytize "power equalization" and the like for its own sake.

Some of the tools used in the Cultural Approach involve some readily identifiable personnel practices, such as long-term employment, slow promotion of employees, less-specialized career paths, and consensus decision-making. For many managers, the Cultural Approach will also lead to change in their management "style"; it will involve much more interaction where subordinates will be seen as "partners."

The Cultural Approach begins to break down the barriers between thinkers and "doers." Examples of the successful application of this model are numerous. Hewlett-Packard is a much-heralded example of a company where the employees share a strong awareness of the corporate mission. They all know that the "HP Way" encourages product innovation at every level and at every bench. Matsushita starts each day at 8:00 A.M. with 87,000 employees singing the company song and reciting its code of values.

Once an organizational culture is established that supports the firm's goals, the chief executive's implementation task is 90% done. With a cadre of committed managers and workers, the organization more or less "carries itself" through cycles of innovation in terms of new products and processes at the work bench, followed by assimilation and implementation at the lower levels.

The most visible cost of this system also yields its primary strength: the consensus decision-making and other culture inculcating activities consume enormous amounts of time. But the pay-off can be speedy execution and reduced games-manship among managers. At Westinghouse, as William Coates, executive vice president of the corporation construction group, described it, "We spend a lot of time trying to get a consensus, but once you get it, the implementation is instantaneous. We don't have to fight any negative feelings." (*Fortune*, June 15, 1981).

Based on our assessment of the nature of the companies generally held up as examples of this approach to strategic management, we have reached some tentative conclusions about the organizational characteristics for which it is best suited. The Cultural Approach works when power is decentralized, where there are shared goals between the organization and its participants, and where the organization is stable and growing.

This last point may be key: there must be sufficient organization slack (i.e. unused resources) to absorb the cost of installing and maintaining the culture. Consider some of the example firms: Hewlett-Packard, IBM, Matsushita, and Intel. These tend to be high-growth firms. As *Fortune* magazine describes Intel's experience, "To lessen the threat of change, Intel promised not to fire any permanent employee whose job was eliminated. The company's phenomenal sales growth, 29.3% in 1980 helps absorb everyone who wants to stay."

The Cultural Method has several limitations. For one, it only works with informed and intelligent people (note that most of the examples are firms in high technology industries). Second, it consumes enormous amounts of time to implement. Third, it can foster such a strong sense of organizational identity among employees that it becomes almost a handicap—that is, it can be difficult to have outsiders at top levels because the executives won't accept the infusion of alien blood.

In addition, companies with excessively strong cultures often will suppress deviance, impede attempts to change, and tend to foster homogeneity and inbreeding. The intolerance of deviance can be a problem when innovation is critical to strategic success. But a strong culture will reject inconsistency

To handle this conformist tendency, companies such as IBM, Xerox, and GM have separated their ongoing research units and their new product development efforts, sometimes placing them in physical locations far enough away to shield them from the corporation's culture.

Homogeneity can stifle creativity, encouraging non-conformists to leave for more accepting pastures and thereby robbing the firm of its innovative talent. The strongest criticism of the Cultural Approach is that it has such an overwhelming indoctrinal air about it. It smacks of faddism and may really be just another variant of the CEO-centered approaches (i.e. the previously discussed Commander and Organizational Change Approaches). As such, it runs the risk of maintaining the wall between thinkers and "doers."

Preserving that thinker/"doer" distinction may be the Cultural Approach's main appeal. It affords executives an illusion of control. But you should also realize that holding tight the reins of control (a natural tendency in turbulent times, we have observed) may result in some lost opportunities—opportunities encountered by line managers in their day-to-day routines.

How can executives capitalize on their line managers' natural inclinations to want to develop opportunities as they encounter them on the firing line? The answer to this question is contained in the fifth implementation method, the Crescive Approach.

METHOD 5: THE CRESCIVE APPROACH

Here's a scenario depicting the Crescive Approach:

> As a general manager, you have just received a proposal to pursue continued development of a new product. You evaluate the report, deflate some overly optimistic figures, and consider the manager's track record. The product offers attractive profit potential and seems to fit the general direction you envision for the firm, so you approve the proposal.

The Crescive Approach differs from others in several respects. First, instead of strategy being delivered downward by top management or a planning department, it moves upward from the "doers" (salespeople, engineers, production workers) and lower middle-level managers. Second, "strategy" becomes the sum of all the individual proposals that surface throughout the year. Third, the top management team shapes the employees' premises—that is, their notions of what would constitute strategic projects. Fourth, the chief executive functions more as a judge, evaluating the proposals that reach his desk, than as a master planner.

WHY DID THE CRESCIVE APPROACH ARISE?

At first, the Crescive Approach may sound too risky. After all, it calls for the chief executive to relinquish a lot of control over the strategy-making process, seemingly leaving to chance the major decisions which determine the long-term competitive strength of the company.

To understand why the Crescive Approach is sometimes appropriate, you need to recognize five constraints that impinge on the chief executive as he sets out to develop and implement a strategy.

1. The chief executive cannot monitor all significant opportunities and threats.   If the company is highly diversified, it is impossible for senior management to stay abreast of developments in all of the firm's different industries. Similarly, if an industry is shifting very quickly (e.g., personal computers), information collected at lower levels often becomes stale before it can be assimiliated, summarized, and passed up the ranks. Even in more stable industries, the time required to process information upward through many management levels can mean that decisions are being made based on outdated information.

As a result, in many cases the CEO must abandon the effort to plan centrally. Instead, an incentive scheme or "free-market" environment is established to encourage operating managers to make decisions that will further the long-range interests of the company.

2. The power of the chief executive is limited.   The chief executive typically enjoys substantial power derived from the ability to bestow rewards, allocate resources, and reduce the uncertainty for members of the organization. Thus, to an extent, the executive can impose his or her will on other members of the organization.

However, the chief executive is not omnipotent. Employees can always leave the firm, and key managers wield control over information and important client relationships. As a result, the CEO must often compromise on programs he wishes to implement.

Research indicates that new projects led by managers who were coerced into the leadership role fail, regardless of the intrinsic merit of the proposal. In contrast, a second-best strategy championed by a capable and determined advocate may be far more worthwhile than the optimum strategy with only lukewarm support.

3. Few executives have the freedom to plan.   Although it is often said that one of the most important jobs of an executive is to engage in thoughtful planning, research shows that few executives actually set aside time to plan. Most spend the majority of their work days attending to short-range problems.

Thus, any realistic approach to strategic planning must recognize that executives simply don't plan much. They are bombarded constantly by requests from subordinates. So they shape the company's future more through their day-to-day decisions—encouraging some projects and discouraging others—than by sweeping policy statements or written plans. This process has been described as "logical incrementalism" because it is a rational process that proceeds in small steps rather than by long leaps.

4. Tight control systems hinder the planning process.   In formulating strategies, top managers rely heavily on subordinates for up-to-date information, strategic recommendations, and approval of the operating goals.

The CEO's dependence on his subordinate managers creates a thorny control problem. In essence, if managers know they'll be accountable for plans they formulate or the information they provide, they have an incentive to bias their estimates of their division's performance.

A branch of decision science called "agency theory" suggests how this situation should be handled. First, if the CEO wants his managers to deliver unbiased estimates, he cannot hold them tightly accountable for the successful implementation of each strategic proposal. Without such accountability, he places great emphasis on commitment as a force for getting things done.

Second, in order to assess the true ability and motivation of any subordinate, the CEO must observe him over a long period of time on a number of different projects. Occasional failures should be expected, tolerated, and not penalized.

One means to promote the ongoing flow of strategic information is to establish a special venture capital fund to take advantage of promising ideas that arise after the strategic and operating plans have been completed. Like the IBM "Fellows" or the Texas Instruments "Idea" programs, this approach allows opportunities to be seized and developed by their champions within the company.

5. Strategies are produced by groups, not individuals. Strategies are rarely created by single individuals. They are usually developed by groups of people, and they incorporate different perspectives on the business. The problem with group decisions is that groups tend to avoid uncertainty and to smooth over conflicts prematurely.

To reduce the distortions that can result from group decision-making, the CEO can concentrate on three tools: first, encouraging an atmosphere that tolerates expression of different opinions; second, using organization development techniques (such as group dynamics exercises) to reduce individual defensiveness and to increase the receptivity of the group to discrepant data; and third, establish separate planning groups at the corporate level and the line organization.

HOW THE CEO CAN USE THE CRESCIVE APPROACH

As the preceding discussion indicates, the CEO of a large corporation simply cannot be solely responsible for forming and implementing strategy. The Crescive Approach suggests that the CEO can solicit and guide the involvement of lower-level managers in the planning and implementation process in five ways:

1. By keeping the organization open to new and potentially discrepant information;
2. By articulating a general strategy of superordinate goals to guide the firm's growth;

3. By carefully shaping the premises by which managers at all levels decide which strategic opportunities to pursue;
4. By manipulating systems and structures to encourage bottom-up strategy formulations; and
5. By approaching day-to-day decisions as part of strategy formulation in the "logical incrementalist" manner described above.

One of the most important and potentially elusive of these methods is the process of shaping managers' decision-making premises. The CEO can shape these premises in at least three ways. First, the CEO can emphasize a particular theme or strategic thrust ("We are in the information business") to direct strategic thinking. Second, the planning methodology endorsed by the CEO can be communicated to affect the way managers view the business. Third, the organizational structure can indicate the dimensions on which strategies should focus. A firm with a product-divisional structure will probably encourage managers to generate strategies for domination in certain product categories, whereas a firm organized around geographical territories will probably evoke strategies to secure maximum penetration of all products in particular regions.

CONCLUSION

The five approaches to developing and implementing strategy that we've discussed represent a range from which you can choose the techniques most suited to your particular situation. Through extensive interviews most managers indicated to us that one of these five approaches is predominant in their company, although often one or two of the other approaches may also play a limited role.

In the few cases where two different approaches played equally strong roles in the same company, an explanation could be found in the history and makeup of the company. For example, one company we studied was active in two distinct industries: its aerospace divisions, based in California, used a crescive strategic management process, while its automotive operation, headquartered in the Midwest, used a planning system incorporating elements of both the Commander and the Change Approaches.

Our research suggests that the Commander, Change, and Collaborative Approaches can be effective for smaller companies and firms in stable industries while the Cultural and Crescive alternatives are used by more complex corporations.

To conclude, a summary of the five approaches, the strategic question each addresses, and the CEO's role in each is given in the accompanying table. The choice of method should depend on the size of the company, the degree of diversification, the degree of geographical dispersion, the stability of the business environment and, finally, the managerial style currently embodied in the company's culture.

CHAPTER

— 13 —

IMPLEMENTING STRATEGY: MONITORING ACTION PROGRAMS

███

DECIDING IF YOU'RE ON THE RIGHT TRACK: HOW TO MONITOR YOUR STRATEGY

DONALD W. COLLIER

Carrying out strategy is like racing a yacht. You can't simply chart your course, point in the desired direction, and assume you'll beat everyone to the finish line. You've got to assess your position constantly to see whether you've been blown off course, a competitor has moved in to cut off your wind, or a threatening squall has suddenly darkened the horizon.

Once you begin implementing your strategy you need to monitor two things: first, whether the company is actually executing the plan; and second, whether those tactics are still desirable in light of changing conditions. When line managers complain that the plans are unrealistic or have become outdated, it's a sign that the company needs a better strategy monitoring system.

This case and the following one will highlight some key considerations in designing and implementing a good system for monitoring your strategy. Our discussion will focus primarily on corporate-level monitoring in multi-business firms, where the main issue facing corporate management is how to deploy the company's assets to create the greatest return for the stockholders.

Strategic Planning Management, September, 1983; Commerce Communications, Inc.

ASSESS LAST YEAR'S PERFORMANCE BEFORE APPROVING NEW BUDGETS

The simplest way to ensure that strategic plans are monitored at least once a year is to review each business unit's performance relative to its strategic plan for the past year before you make your capital budgeting decisions for the upcoming year.

In order to allocate capital efficiently among business units the corporate management must ask itself three questions about each unit's proposed plan:

1. Where does this business's plan take it and is that goal compatible with the corporation's objectives?
2. How feasible is the plan?
3. How cost-effective is this business's plan?

The best way to judge the feasibility of proposed plans is to assess how well the business units have succeeded in attaining their previous strategic goals.

Most executives heavily emphasize a business-unit manager's "batting average" before betting on him for the future. They compare previous years' actual performances with the past plans, to check how well the manager has attained the targeted goals. Also, by comparing this year's plan with last year's, they monitor how capable the manager is at forecasting environmental conditions (such as competitors' moves and market growth rates) on which the strategy was based.

As part of an ongoing strategic management effort, the corporate executives should tell all the business-unit managers the results of all of the tests made on the plans to answer the foregoing three questions. This feedback is particularly important for managers who don't receive the full allocation requested in their new plan. Such a report clearly informs the business-unit manager what the corporation's strategic standards are, so he can formulate and implement stronger annual strategic plans.

MONITORING STRATEGY VIA THE "STRATEGIC BUDGET"

The annual monitoring process we've just discussed is necessary but not sufficient for good strategic management. More frequent assessments should also be made. To make this possible, the business-unit manager must first formulate a strategy, and then outline specific tactics along with their budgetary requirements of the first year.

This "strategic budget" will differ from an ordinary budget in that it will contain strategy-sensitive indicators (such as market-share growth, quality improvements, new product development, and acquisition timetables) in addition to the usual financial forecasts. The strategic budget should also include a listing of key assumptions about the environment on which the strategy is based.

The advantage of tying strategy into the budget in this manner is that it enables the strategy to be monitored as routinely as budgetary performance: monthly by the business-unit manager, and quarterly by higher management. Then corrective action can be taken quickly if necessary.

In order to develop a truly strategic budget, the strategy formulation phase should precede and remain independent of the budgeting process.

In the strategy-formulation phase the manager shouldn't get bogged down in estimating precise projections, providing only enough data to permit comparison of the cost-effectiveness of alternate strategies. This first-stage strategic plan should contain the following elements:

1. A description of current competitive conditions (how your sales, margin, and asset turnover compare to your major competitors');
2. A projection of your future competitive position (your goal), based on your strategic analysis of future trends and your chosen strategy;
3. An estimate of how long and how much investment is required to reach your goal;
4. A clear statement of your strategy for reaching the future competitive position;
5. The key assumptions on which the strategy is based;
6. The supporting logic for why you think it will work; and
7. The contingencies which could upset this plan.

This initial plan will provide a basis for determining what tactics are necessary to support the strategy. The plan will also suggest a timetable for phasing in the programs, with specific guidelines for how much needs to be accomplished in the first year. At this point, agreement with the next higher level of management should be obtained.

Once the general strategic plan has been formulated, a detailed multi-year plan should be outlined. The first-year projection should include sufficient budgetary detail so it can be monitored as the "strategic budget." The second- and third-year plans should include precise enough projections so they can be used for allocations of future capital. The plan for subsequent years needs only as much detail as is feasible to serve as a basis for estimating total investment requirements.

This approach to strategy formulation establishes guidelines for monitoring not only the first-year strategic performance, but also the environmental assumptions on which the strategy is based. The previous year's strategy and the environmental analysis on which it was based can be assessed in light of the first year's accomplishments and any unforeseen environmental changes.

This review will indicate whether the strategy is on track and whether the original strategy should be modified. Then the second-year outline from the original strategic plan, modified if necessary, becomes the basis for developing the current year's strategic budget.

THE CEO IS THE ULTIMATE MONITOR OF STRATEGY

Remember, the chief executive officer also serves as the chief strategist for a firm. Therefore the CEO should be an active participant in monitoring strategy.

In most companies the chief executive officer concentrates on strategy (that is, determining where the company should be going) while the chief operating officer focuses on managing the internal operations necessary to implement the strategy. The CEO should actively participate in the approval of stage one strategies and in the allocation of resources. The CEO should ask the chief operating officer to monitor the strategic budget, and to alert the CEO if any deviations from the plan are substantial enough to require a change in strategy.

The CEO can also provide managers with incentives to develop and execute better strategies by establishing a compensation system that rewards successful implementation of strategic plans. In such cases, performance objectives are expanded, beyond the usual financial ones, to include objectives which most quantitatively and sensitively measure the implementation of the key strategy elements expected during the budget year.

MONITORING MANY BUSINESS UNITS

While no CEO can be expected to single handedly monitor dozens of business units, the CEO remains ultimately responsible for their overall performances. In the next case, we will examine how CEOs can keep a large set of business units on the right track.

□

STRATEGY MONITORING IN MULTI-BUSINESS COMPANIES
DONALD W. COLLIER

In the previous case, we discussed how the chief executive officer (CEO) of firms with fewer than 10 strategic business units (SBUs) should play an active role in monitoring strategy by supervising the development of a "strategic budget." If a company has many SBUs, however, the CEO cannot personally monitor the strategy of each one.

Strategic Planning Management, October, 1983; Commerce Communications, Inc.

MONITORING STRATEGY "BY EXCEPTION"

In large multi-business companies, similar SBUs are usually grouped together and put under the supervision of group or sector heads, who form the layer of line management between the chief operating officer (COO) of the corporation and the SBU general managers.

Each month, the group heads typically monitor the strategic budget of each of their SBUs, and then each quarter they meet with the corporation's COO to review their group's performance, including the progress of strategy implementation.

The CEO gets involved in the monitoring process during the annual capital budgeting procedure. At that time, the CEO reviews brief summaries of all the SBU plans. Along with these summaries, the CEO's staff should prepare an analysis aimed at answering the three questions the corporation must ask itself in making the allocations. As we discussed in the last case, these questions are: (1) Will this plan take the SBU in a direction that is compatible with the corporation's objectives?; (2) How credible is the plan?; and (3) How cost-effective is this business's plan?

In the process of analyzing business-unit plans, the CEO's staff identifies the "critical SBUs," which are the ones that will have a significant impact—positive or negative—on the corporation's overall performance or resource requirements. An SBU may also be labelled "critical" if there is a serious question about the appropriateness of its strategy.

From these "critical SBU" plans, the CEO selects a manageable number (usually 10 to 12) and designates them "strategic issues." For these plans, the CEO will withhold approval of capital allocations until he receives a detailed and persuasive defense of the strategy, including the available options by the business-unit manager.

Once a plan has been designated a strategic issue, the CEO sends the business-unit manager a "strategic issue commentary" explaining what the core of the issue is (such as the chosen direction, the size of the capital requirement, or the projected performance). The commentary also includes the CEO's specific questions that the business-unit manager should address in defending the strategy. Finally, the CEO sets a date for the presentation and specifies the person or persons responsible for preparing it.

IDENTIFYING A STRATEGIC ISSUE

To give you an example of how a CEO might identify a strategic issue, let us assume that a CEO is reviewing a plan that proposes expansion of production capacity from the SBU that is the leading producer of a versatile plastic. The plan would require a capital allocation of about 15% of the total available.

The business unit claims that this extra capacity is needed to maintain market share. However, projections of future returns are not in line with the corporation's goals.

One alternative is to accept lower margins in order to meet a competitor's price in some of the lower-performance grades, which the competitor is able to produce at lower cost. A second option is to abandon this part of the market to the competitor, and concentrate existing production capacity on the higher grades.

Neither alternative is particularly attractive. Both put the firm's position in this market in jeopardy. Neither option seems to position the firm for better strategic performance. Thus the CEO designates this plan as a strategic issue.

The CEO sends a commentary back to the unit manager, via his group head, in which the essential question underlying the issue is identified as this: Should the capital needed to expand capacity of the present process be invested?

The concerns expressed above are given as the reason for selecting this plan as a strategic issue. The questions the CEO wants the business-unit manager to address include:

1. What fraction of the market is accessible to the competitor's process?
2. How fast will this segment grow compared to the rest of the market?
3. What is the relative production cost by the competitor's process compared to ours?
4. What alternatives exist to match or better the competitor's cost for this segment?

THE BUSINESS UNIT'S PRESENTATION

The business unit's presentation provides a detailed, documented response to each of these four questions. Of course, the presentation can go well beyond these questions. Critical uncertainties, key assumptions, and the most important projections or forecasts are especially noted. This alerts corporate and group managers to particularly sensitive items or plan elements. The presentation confirms that the concerns of corporate management are valid. In responding to the set of questions, the business-unit manager proposes another alternative that the CEO ultimately selects over the other two: the unit possesses the technology to produce the lower-grade material by converting one of the existing reactors to an alternate process. This conversion will cost only 1/10 the expense of the original plan, and will provide sufficient capacity to meet the expected market demand for the next three to four years. Additionally, the unit is developing a new process that promises to reduce the cost of the alternate process below competition's.

THE CEO'S RESPONSE

The CEO would then send a written response to the unit manager (again, through the group head) that would authorize the allocation of capital for the reactor conversion. It would state that rather than undertaking the first two proposals, which risk permanently damaging the stockholders value, the corporation will temporarily sacrifice the income resulting from the lower margins in order to accelerate the new process development.

The CEO's response then lays out major milestones (e.g., time and cost targets) associated with this alternative. The business unit's presentation provides the basis for these milestones. Specific milestones might include specifying items such as these:

1. time and cost of the conversion;
2. availability and cost of materials; and
3. ability to estimate processing and plant costs reliably in one year. More comprehensive and detailed targets can also be established.

Such guidelines or milestones provide the basis for monitoring the strategy alternative on which the CEO and the business-unit management agree.

MONITORING THE STRATEGIC ISSUE

The monitoring is usually done by the chief operating officer during his regular quarterly operating reviews with each group head. He asks questions which test whether the strategy is being implemented in the way that the CEO's response directed.

In preparing these questions, the COO must be careful to phrase them so that they must be answered with objective facts rather than subjective opinions. Avoid vague questions such as "Are you on track with the new process development plan?"

In our example, the monitoring questions used at the first quarterly review with the plastics unit's group head might be as follows:

1. Has the engineering design been completed and the conversion work started?
2. In what quantity, at what price, has a contract been negotiated for materials?
3. Is the pilot plant for the new process in operation?

The third quarterly review might include such questions as:

1. Have you begun production using the newly converted reactor with the purchased materials?

2. Are the production cost targets being met?
3. Is the materials supplier delivering on time and at the specified quality?
4. Are the yields, reaction time, and utility usage targets of the new process being met?

From these two illustrations, you can see what types of questions are used to monitor implementation of the strategy, how they vary over time, and how they may lead to the identification and specification of "problems" which require the attention of the CEO and business unit management.

ACTIONS RESULTING FROM MONITORING

If the answers indicate that the strategy is being implemented in line with the response, no action is required on the part of the CEO. If the answers indicate that a deviation is occurring, the chief operating officer must first decide if it can be corrected.

This will also involve one or more "sessions" with business unit management. If it cannot, the COO brings the deviation to the attention of the CEO. At that point, the CEO decides whether to permit the deviation, change the allocation, or call for a new presentation of strategy to be followed with a new decision.

This quarterly monitoring continues until the strategy outlined in the response is fully implemented. In this manner, the strategies critical to the overall performance of the corporation are monitored at the highest level in the corporation.

□

APPLICATION IN STRATEGIC MANAGEMENT:
Testing Your Plan of Action
LIAM FAHEY

When your firm drafts its annual operations plan for implementing its long term strategy, how do you tell if that action plan is any good? Do you just run with it and hope it works?

Many organizations spend a number of months translating their longer term strategies into a one-year operational plan. But in many firms, once those

Strategic Planning Management, November/December, 1983; Commerce Communications, Inc.

plans are approved by senior management, too often they are not subjected to any serious appraisal until the results fail to live up to expectations, and/or events render the plan obsolete.

One management team had gotten burned for three years in a row by weaknesses in their operations plan. The problems developed because the plans generally were just "not well put together," and they could have done a far better job of anticipating certain actions of competitors, customers, and suppliers.

So this division of a large multidivisional firm decided to set up a process to review and assess critically its operations plan before it was used as the basis for detailed functional-area plans.

The division's senior management came together in a series of meetings to raise and discuss the following questions, not only to test the soundness of their overall operations plan, but also to begin to develop the strongest possible annual blueprints for each of the functional-areas (marketing, manufacturing, R&D, etc.).

HOW (AND WHY) DOES THE NEW PLAN DIFFER FROM THE PREVIOUS YEAR'S PLAN?

The management team begins by identifying what it considers the significant changes from the previous year's plan. They assess changes for each of the functional areas and each of the product groups.

Next, the management team tries to place a dollar value on each major change. It is a relatively straightforward process to quantify the expenditures or savings resulting from many changes (e.g., a new advertising program, the hiring of additional brand managers for a product group, restricting an R&D project, etc.). But it is much more difficult to allocate a dollar figure for other changes (e.g., refocusing sales force efforts or introducing new manufacturing procedures).

Then, the functional-area managers and/or product-group managers briefly outline the arguments supporting each change. If necessary, senior managers outline and discuss how the overall plan of action was determined. This first activity helps remind managers exactly how the new plan differs from the previous year's. More importantly, it also alerts managers—many for the first time—as to *why* those changes were made. The managers thus have an opportunity to question and find out, not only why various elements in the operations plan were adopted, but also how much resources those changes will require and what results are expected.

WHAT ASSUMPTIONS UNDERLIE THE PLAN?

Although pivotal assumptions are noted in the division's strategic (two- to five-year) plan, they receive little emphasis in the operations plan. The managers, therefore, found it a very productive exercise to identify and discuss the principle assumptions underlying the new plan of action.

Their initial discussion of assumptions is quite open-ended. Each manager is expected to identify what he or she considers the two or three most important assumptions and their implications for the plan of action.

They make an effort to categorize the assumptions in three ways: (1) by functional areas, (2) by product group, and (3) by whether they relate to the external or internal environment. This allows each manager to note the assumptions most critical to his or her area of responsibility.

In this process, they place particular emphasis on discussing the validity and implications of their assumptions about the external environment. This analysis is critical because it evaluates beliefs about events and trends outside the control of the firm.

Managers, therefore, scrutinize their assumptions about issues such as these:

- rate of market growth;
- changes in customers' purchasing criteria;
- rate of technological changes;
- introduction of new products by competitors;
- nature and extent of change in competitors' strategies;
- likely competitors' responses to changes in the firm's strategy; and
- anticipated impact of new governmental regulations

The managers also try to rank-order their assumptions in order of importance for the entire plan of action and for each product group. One benefit of this effort is that it alerts the management team to specific areas that need to be monitored, beyond merely the consequences of the action plan itself.

For example, in a previous year, this critical assumption surfaced about one product group: they believed that competitors would not introduce any new products for at least one year. However, within four months, one of their major competitors announced a significant technological breakthrough. Although the competitor said that this advancement would not affect its product line for another 15 months, the managers decided to alter their own plan in mid-course. Even though the current plan had been yielding results that exceeded expectations, the firm intensified its marketing and sales efforts so that in the longer term it would be in a stronger position to compete against the competitor's new products.

WHAT SUCCESS CRITERIA UNDERLIE THE PLAN?

Every plan or strategy contains some presumptions about what it takes to succeed in specific product-markets. The review sessions revealed that, even after the plan had been "put to bed," executives lacked a consensus about what it took to be successful within any of their major product-markets.

Thus, for each major product-market, the managers first identified what they believed to be the essential factors for competitive success, then identified differences across product-markets and discussed the bases for these differences.

For example, they listed the following success criteria for one consumer-oriented business:

- a strong brand image;
- a steady stream of product modifications flowing from internal R&D;
- well-developed relationships between the sales force and distribution channels; and
- manufacturing efficiency as a means to achieving low product prices

Once they'd identified these factors, the executives analyzed—and challenged—how each of these elements might lead to market success. In considering the importance of having a strong brand image, for example, they asked *why* was this factor required? And how might it be possible to succeed *without* a strong brand image? How is brand image related to the other success dimensions?

IS THE PLAN VULNERABLE TO EXTERNAL CONSTRAINTS?

With the benefit of hindsight, it was easy to see one reason why previous operations plans had to be changed in mid-course: they proved vulnerable to events outside the control of the firm.

Consequently, the managers attempted to identify vulnerabilities of the plan. They attempted to answer these questions: to what is our strategy vulnerable, and how can we lessen the vulnerability?

Their analysis revealed that they had been primarily hurt by competitors' actions—that is, their strategies were vulnerable to competitors' actions. Thus, for each product group, the management team first identified the possible competitive actions that would be most detrimental to their proposed strategy. Then, they assessed both the likelihood of these actions and how much impact they would each have. Here are some of the types of competitive actions they considered:

- new product developments;
- major price changes;
- distribution channel changes;
- new alignments with suppliers and customers; and
- reallocation of sales force efforts

The managers carefully "played out" the scenarios involving each of these possible actions in order to assess how vulnerable the firm was. They asked such questions as these: how could the firm respond, and how might it defend itself? They concluded that, if the firm could only respond and defend itself at high cost, it was very vulnerable.

An illustration of one vulnerability they identified was the possibility that newly emerging competitors might "go after" the firm's key distributors in one particular product-market. If the firm lost these distributors, it would not have access to major blocks of customers.

The firm concluded that competitors could lure key distributors away through a combination of potential higher volume and higher margins—which would leave the firm in a highly vulnerable position. As a result of this analysis, the firm decided to prevent these competitive moves by adopting this new strategy toward its key distributors: they offered higher margins, increased joint promotional efforts, and undertook a commitment to take back unsold products in certain circumstances.

IS THE PLAN VULNERABLE TO INTERNAL CONSTRAINTS?

Another reason why previous operations plans had to be changed in mid-course was due to lack of attention to constraints arising within the firm.

The managers thus attempted to identify actual and potential constraints which might impinge upon plan attainment, and how these constraints might be ameliorated or eliminated.

The following are some of the constraints which the management team identified and at least partially resolved:

- production bottleneck;
- insufficient inventory in some product lines;
- insufficient distribution and warehousing facilities;
- too many demands on sales force time;
- insufficient personnel and time devoted to monitoring the market and competitive environment; and
- lack of engineering personnel to test product prototypes

CONCLUSION

Asking these five questions about an action plan has helped this firm not only strengthen ties between its operating and functional plans, but also test the underlying strategies.

By using this approach, plans are no longer accepted on blind faith, but are incisively critiqued in a simple but powerful way.

CHAPTER

— 14 —

BUILDING THE STRATEGIC ORGANIZATION: INITIATING AN ORGANIZATIONAL THRUST THROUGH STRATEGIC PLANNING SYSTEMS

LAUNCHING A STRATEGIC PLANNING SYSTEM

DONNA WILLIAMSON

Strategic planning systems came into vogue in the 1970s, when many large multidivisional firms installed their own versions of a planning system. However, in the 1980s, it has become fashionable to criticize planning systems as being inflexible, requiring excessive documentation, and suppressing creativity.

Yet, if properly introduced and managed, a strategic planning system can serve many useful functions and become indispensible in formulating and implementing effective strategies.

In the first section of this reading, we'll consider the key elements in successfully introducing planning into a company. Then, in the final section, we will discuss some facets of managing the planning system.

Strategic Planning Management, April, 1984; Commerce Communications, Inc.

EXACTLY WHAT IS A PLANNING SYSTEM?

A strategic planning system has essentially three elements:

1. It establishes a *systematic and comprehensive methodology* or set of analyses for evaluating each business group and division or business unit.
2. It provides *the means to generate and communicate critical information* necessary for formulating and implementing the best possible strategies.
3. It involves designing *a set of organizational procedures* to foster the development of both the methodology and the flow of strategic information.

Putting these elements in place and attaining the desired benefits of a planning system have proved to be difficult yet rewarding tasks in many firms.

HOW A PLANNING PROCESS CAN HELP

A planning process can benefit your organization in several ways. First, a planning system can help meet top managers' need for succinct, accurate, and consistent information about the company's performance, strategic thrust, and position relative to competitors.

Second, a planning system can greatly help a company reevaluate its strategy in light of changing internal and external environments.

Third, a planning system can assist the implementation of strategy through the formulation and execution of action plans.

Finally, because it is a company-wide function, a planning system acts as an integrating device—allowing separate functions of a company to share information and coordinate their activities with the help of top management and the planning staff.

SOME MISCONCEPTIONS ABOUT PLANNING SYSTEMS

Many planning systems have recently fallen into disrepute, largely because too much was expected of them and/or they were initiated for the wrong reasons. A planning system cannot solve all your strategic problems immediately, nor can it be put in place quickly. Managers at all levels need time to learn what the planning system is and is not, and also to understand how they can both contribute to the system and benefit from it.

The development of a planning system should also not be conceived as an instrument to "shake up the company culture." In companies where an attempt is made to use it for this purpose, the planning system may never really get off the ground.

LAYING THE GROUNDWORK

A planning system cannot simply be foisted on an organization. Before the system is introduced, some groundwork must be laid.

1. A planning system can only get off the ground when there is an atmosphere of support from the CEO and top management. This does not mean that *everyone* must be gung-ho for the planning system right from the start, but rather that some of the senior managers, and particularly the CEO, must display their commitment for the system.

2. The CEO and other senior managers must "sell" the idea of the planning system to the rest of the organization, emphasizing the benefits it can provide. The CEO must also impress upon the senior management team that they must begin to integrate planning into their everyday thinking, to help managers at every level of the company approach their activities strategically.

    Be careful not to introduce the system with too much fanfare. Many planning systems begin with so much hoopla in off-site conferences that managers get the idea that planning is a special once-a-year duty.

3. A key role the CEO plays in launching a planning system is to anticipate and overcome objections of senior staff. Some staff may see the addition of a planning system as a burdensome waste of time. They will criticize it as an unnecessary and meddlesome task that is based on a theoretical notion of how their company should be run.

4. The CEO must show candor and a willingness to confront the sensitive issues, rivalries and archaic methods that may be uncovered through the planning process. Like other forms of auditing, a systematic evaluation of a company can break up sediment, expose hidden issues, and generally force the firm to face the tough questions it may have been avoiding. The CEO must set the example for fearlessly addressing whatever issues the planning system brings into the open.

In my experience at Baxter Travenol, the CEO impressed upon the senior staff the need for the company to address the rapidly changing environment for health-care products. He strongly maintained that a planning system *was* necessary in order to sustain the company's leadership positions in key markets.

INTRODUCING THE PLANNING PROCESS

The planning process can be introduced into the organization in a series of steps. At Baxter Travenol we adopted different approaches for senior management and line management.

1. *For senior management: an off-site conference.* The new system can be introduced to the senior management in a special off-site conference

as our company did. Our CEO outlined his hopes and expectations with regard to the company's future. A deliberate effort was made to identify those issues most likely to impact the company both internally and externally. Strengths and weaknesses were carefully assessed. At the conclusion of the meeting, the planning staff laid out their timetable for planning, and they discussed what the benefits and problems of a planning system might be.

The conference provided an opportunity for a systematic strategic analysis of the company operations. In this way, it was a microcosm of the planning process itself, and an effective way to introduce senior staff to how such a system could be used to good effect.

Prior to the conference, the planning staff at Baxter set up team meetings among senior managers. These meetings were focused on the topics that were on the agenda at the conference. The teams discussed strategy and future direction in areas such as investor perspectives, future markets, financial scenarios, R&D directions, anticipated human resource needs, and others. These team discussions can stimulate interest and encourage participation in the conference topics, as well as give the participants an idea of what the planning process is all about.

The ultimate goal of this type of planning conference is to establish a broad consensus among senior managers not only about the specific issues discussed, but also on the validity of a planning system as a useful method for bringing out issues in a systematic way.

This initial conference was so successful at Baxter that it has been repeated annually. The conferences have become more sophisticated in terms of the issues they address, and more efficient in terms of how the senior staff tackle and resolve them. Even though this conference for senior executives is only part of a larger process which involves the entire company, it is still a very useful method for generating fresh perspectives and renewing senior staff energies each year.

2. *For line managers: a series of workshops.* The success of a planning system depends not only on the acceptance of senior management, but also on that of the line managers—the people who will develop the fact base in the planning process. A critical task is to get line management involved in the planning system. Doing so is a very delicate process. It cannot seem like the system is being handed down arbitrarily from on high. Rather, the planning system should be presented as what it truly is: a superstructure on which line managers build and shape priorities through their inputs.

At Baxter we introduced the system to line managers in a series of workshops. Members of the planning staff, plus consultants who were helping implement the system, conducted small group meetings with line managers. In these meetings, the planning staff shared with the line managers the objectives of the system, and then asked for their thoughts on how best to carry out the process.

An effective introduction of a planning system to line managers must get across the following points:

1. "Planning" is not a new concept. It is something most line managers have been doing already: assessing their markets, competitive position, and environment in order to determine what actions to take to exploit opportunities and repel threats.
2. A planning system needs to be simple, relevant, and as free of jargon as possible. It should capture managers' best thinking and provide a means of developing their own priorities.
3. Finally, it is important to highlight the idea that a formalized planning system is as much a bottom-up process as it is a top-down one. It is directed toward sharing with top management the valuable information line managers possess about their markets, competition and environment. In this sense, the planning system is a new form of communication between senior management and line managers. Line managers should understand how their input will aid top management directly in its decision-making process.

INTRODUCING THE PLANNING CALENDAR

Another step in introducing line managers to the new planning system is to walk them through the *planning calendar,* a schedule breaking down the planning process over the course of a full year. The calendar begins with an on-site meeting of senior staff to discuss general strategy issues for the year. During the second quarter, senior staff and line managers review strategies in preparation for developing operating plans.

The second half of the calendar is devoted to preparing operating plans, looking at a multi-year time horizon. Again, the process involves preliminary discussions, preparation of specific strategies and calculations, and a formal review of these plans between line and senior managers.

The first-year projections in the plan become, after senior management's review, the next year's budget.

The use of a planning calendar demonstrates to line managers the senior staff's commitment to a planning process, and emphasizes the idea that planning is not a one-shot deal but an ongoing process.

HOW CONSULTANTS CAN—AND CAN'T—HELP

Outside consultants can offer a valuable perspective on setting up a planning process based on their experience with other clients. However, they cannot serve as a substitute for the CEO's commitment, nor should they be given the managers' responsibility for implementing a plan.

One of the most valuable functions of a consulting team is that they help educate staff and line management in the key requirement for good planning: environmental analysis and assessment of competitive strengths and weaknesses.

BUILD UPON YOUR CURRENT CULTURE AND SYSTEMS

Managers at many levels initially expressed concerns about what a planning system might mean for the way "business was conducted" within the firm. Managers were fearful that it would require learning a whole new way of doing things.

However, both the CEO and the planning staff were committed to integrating the new system with the way things operated before. One-on-one and small-group meetings had long been the popular form of communication within the firm. Our planning system took advantage of this element of company culture. As previously noted, the system was implemented through small-group meetings and small-group workshops conducted by the planning staff and consultants.

Once you have laid the proper groundwork for a planning system, managers at all levels will feel like they're part of the process, so they'll be more interested in *contributing* to the process than *fighting* it. In the next case we'll discuss some of the ways to ensure that their interest is sustained and the process remains vital.

The primary reason why some planning systems, which were introduced with much fanfare, did not deliver what their proponents promised was that not enough attention was paid to actively managing them. A planning system, like any other organizational decision making system, can not be put on "automatic pilot;" it does not manage itself.

The introduction of a planning system unavoidably involves many individuals learning a new way of doing things: developing new forms of documentation, dealing with different types of data and modified reporting relationships, etc. Individuals bring different expectations, experiences, and backgrounds to a planning system. They place different demands on the system—they want different problems solved by the system.

The planning system provides the arena within which these expectations and demands meet. If they are not managed, they can quickly evolve into head-on confrontations, bogging down the whole planning system and possibly, much worse, stalling organizational decision making.

MANAGING THE PLANNING SYSTEM

Managing a planning system involves the following key elements:

1. Managing the introduction of the corporate planning staff;
2. Managing the activities built around the planning calendar;
3. Managing the information requirements and flows which are the bedrock of any planning system;
4. Managing the outputs of the system.

Each of these elements needs to be managed to avoid some major pitfalls and to deal with problems as they arise.

MANAGING THE INTRODUCTION OF THE CORPORATE PLANNING STAFF

Managing a planning system begins before the system is formally launched. A critical ingredient of the successful launch of a planning system is the manner in which the planning staff at the corporate and/or division or business unit levels is introduced to the organization.

If you are not careful in how the planning staff is brought onboard, you may leave a very sour taste in the mouths of many of the managers with whom you will have to work.

Our initial philosophy behind the development of a corporate planning staff was to keep it as small as possible, to force line operations to do their own strategic planning. The corporate planning staff did not want to undermine the roles and responsibilities of division management.

Initially keeping the corporate staff as small as possible also allowed for phasing in staff requirements as the planning system evolved.

The corporate planning staff must provide good communication links between corporate staff and the divisions, to allow the planning process to evolve successfully. As part of our efforts to create good communication links, we wanted to develop a process in which we solicit both corporate and divisional inputs, prior to formalizing both the planning calendar and the activities during each phase. In order to do this effectively, we brought in individuals on the staff who had good conceptual thinking, a capacity for leadership, and a proven track record. No formal planning experience was—or still is—required. We find that assignment of these individuals to act as a liaison between divisions and corporate staffs helps improve communications, and increases the chance of success that the planning requirements will be understood and will lead to realistic plans that can be implemented.

MANAGING VIA THE PLANNING CALENDAR

The planning calendar facilitates management of the planning system in the following ways. First, it provides the timetable around which the major planning activities take place: three- to five-year strategy development, review and evaluation, one-year strategy development, review and evaluation, and budget determination. The sequence of these activities in the annual planning calendar constitutes the major focal points of managers' attention with regard to the ongoing aspects of the planning system.

Second, the planning calendar provides an opportunity to initiate and solidify relationships between corporate headquarters and division personnel, and frequently among personnel across divisional boundaries. It is these informal relationships which ultimately provide the glue for many of the activities involved in the planning system.

Third, the planning calendar provides a structured organizational framework within which the corporate planning staff can exercise its "teaching function." That is, the corporate planning staff, as it works with division line management through the course of the planning calendar, helps line managers on an individual basis to understand the broad purposes of the planning system, the specific requirements of individual tasks, how to tailor the planning process to meet their own unique needs, etc.

Successful management of the planning calendar requires flexibility on the part of the corporate planning staff. You must be willing to adapt the planning system to the needs, capabilities, and culture of individual business units. Any attempt to impose unbending rigidity on the system is a recipe for frustration and anxiety on the part of everybody involved.

However, adjustments to the sequencing and timing of planning system activities should be clearly explained to corporate and division personnel. Possible misinterpretations of adjustments should be avoided; these frequently lead to suspicions of favoritism and inequality in how the system is implemented.

MANAGING INFORMATION

A core function of a planning system is to facilitate the collection, assessment, and dissemination of strategy relevant information. How information related tasks and activities are handled is pivotal to generating and sustaining the interest and enthusiasm of managers at all levels for the tasks inherent in a planning system.

USE FORMATS AS GUIDES

It is probably impossible to devise an effective planning system without some sort of information collection "formats" or standardized forms. These formats represent a systematic method for division and line managers to synthesize and provide information on sales and financial trends and results, market characteristics, cost structure, competitors' strategies, and environmental conditions. However, the corporate planning staff, and others involved in managing the planning system, should take every opportunity to emphasize, to those managers and staff involved in collecting and analyzing the data, that the formats are intended to facilitate information collection and sharing. They are not intended to straightjacket managers' thinking. In other words, completing the formats should not be allowed to degenerate into a routine, dominated by a "get the planning group off our back" attitude.

DON'T ASK FOR THE IMPOSSIBLE

In managing a planning system, the temptation is high to demand too much detail in the completion of the necessary system documentation. It is easy to err on the side of asking for too much data. Worse, it is also possible to ask for data which line managers consider unattainable and/or irrelevant.

It is, therefore, important that lines of communication always remain open with those completing the documentation. They should feel free to discuss data related issues at any time. It is frequently much better to have managers think strategically using readily available or easily attainable data, than it is to force them to obtain data the validity of which they question.

MAKE USE OF EXISTING DATA

Especially in the early stages of launching a planning system, it is important to make use of the available data within the firm. Emphasizing existing data lessens the burden involved in collecting and analyzing data, and thus helps lessen managers' fears and trepidations about learning a new system.

When managers have exploited the existing data base and it has been subjected to scrutiny by the corporate staff and by the managers themselves, gaps in the firm's knowledge base usually become evident and it is then easier to push for further data collection and analysis.

MANAGING THE OUTPUTS

Managing the outputs of the planning system can be just as important as managing its processes. In many ways, the two are related. Planning systems often fail to live up to expectations because the process side is over emphasized. This sometimes happens because it is assumed that outputs of the system do not need to be managed.

MANAGING PLANS AND BUDGETS

The major outputs of the planning system are plans and budgets. These two must be managed. These outputs do not "speak for themselves." Very often, they may give rise to debate, after they have been broadly accepted by multiple levels of management. Thus, there is a vital need to ensure that open discussion about these outputs is possible, among different levels of management even after they have been "put to bed."

Different business units and functional areas may have different "cultures" with respect to the development and implementation of plans and budgets. Some may readily accept the need to develop plans, others may not. Some may readily accept the changes implied in a given plan, others may not. Thus, you need to understand the culture and past experiences of a specific business unit or functional area in order to manage the change which is frequently inherent in plans and budgets.

MANAGING ISSUES

Another key output is the identification of strategic "issues," that is, problems, opportunities, and threats that must be analyzed over some specific period of time. The following points are important in managing issues.

You must be careful in how you influence what are designated as issues. Only those things which are of major strategic importance should be titled issues. The choice of issues focuses managers' attention and consumes their resources.

You must, therefore, "negotiate" with managers as to what are the important issues, those things upon which they should focus their attention. You can not decide for them what those issues are, but you can help them to see how and why specific issues are important or unimportant, how some issues are related as well as the methodology for "attacking" the important issues.

MAINTAINING A PERSPECTIVE ON THE OUTPUTS

The outputs are not ends in themselves. A key task, therefore, is to continually remind managers and staff that the outputs represent an ongoing process. The outputs are not "the final word." As the world changes, the outputs will have to be adapted. The output can be used to heighten sensitivity in the organization to key issues, problems, and opportunities, and to integrate activities throughout all levels of the organization. In this way, the planning system plays a major role in focusing the organization's attention on those things which are truly strategically significant.

CONCLUSION

Launching a planning system can be a major undertaking. If properly introduced, it can contribute tremendously to effective strategy performance. The organizational changes unavoidably involved in getting a planning system off the ground can be managed. The successful management of these changes requires continued attention; it is not something than can be accomplished by devoting specific time periods to it.

A planning system has to gain the respect and interest of managers. However, it can do so only when it is effectively managed. Effectively managing a planning system requires attention to multiple things: the planning calendar, information, the systems outputs and, of course, the people who make up the system. If you don't manage each one of these elements, you'll likely not experience a successful strategic planning system launch.

☐

LAUNCHING STRATEGIC PLANNING IN A SMALL, CLOSELY HELD BUSINESS

JOEL A. DYSART

For a small business, developing the company's first strategic plan can loom as an awesome and expensive undertaking. Executives begin by asking such fundamental questions as "Where should we start?" and "How should we go about it?" One answer, of course, is to hire the expertise of a consultant. After all, plenty of strategic-planning purveyors are available to assist you in developing and even implementing your company's plan—you can buy the cookbook or the completed cake! But do you really need outside help to plan an effective strategy for your business? No, not really.

But, you do need to understand how planning for small, closely held firms is similar to and different from planning in large public firms.

WHAT'S DIFFERENT ABOUT PLANNING FOR SMALL FIRMS?

Of course, all effective strategic planning efforts share some common characteristics, regardless of the size of the firm. For example, any plan must talk about how to deal with competition. If a company's strategy does not explicitly define *how the firm expects to compete over the long term,* then the company does not really have a strategy.

Strategic Planning Management, November/December, 1983; Commerce Communications, Inc.

Another universal feature of planning in firms of all sizes is that a company's strategy virtually always reflects the CEO's personality. This characteristic is especially noticeable in small, closely held firms where the CEO is responsible for calling most of the shots.

In any firm, the CEO is ultimately responsible for developing, approving, and implementing strategy. The difference between CEO's in large vs. small firms is that in the big company, the CEO has a large support staff, whereas in the small, closely held firm, the CEO has fewer shoulders to lean on.

A more important distinction of closely held firms is that their individual stockholder's goals are well known and can heavily influence strategic decisions, in contrast to the diverse interests of shareholders in large, publicly held companies.

Thus, the small firm both can and must tailor the company's strategy as much as possible to the full gamut of its stockholders' objectives.

Another strategy-related issue critical to small, closely held firms relates to management succession. Often family desires and interests may have to be explicitly treated in the company's strategy development. Recruiting a new executive capable of implementing a specific strategy for the firm is not always feasible or desirable, so the issue of management succession has to be handled before the planning process gets underway.

Small businesses typically conduct their planning in a much more informal style than big corporations use. Rather than producing massive documents that will undergo multiple reviews by many management levels, small firms can keep their planning more informal because communication between managers is more frequent and intimate. The planning process can, therefore, also be less time consuming, even though it must be equally rigorous intellectually.

The final distinction of small, closely held firms is that because they tend to be much more resource-constrained than larger companies, their strategic planning is usually oriented toward a limited set of pragmatic options. Small firms will often face issues such as whether to trade off higher growth and profits in order to remain fiscally conservative, or to preserve the company's unique culture that is valued by owners and employees alike.

In summary, small, closely held companies need to recognize the distinctive characteristics that will affect their planning process. If they merely try to imitate other corporate planning systems, they will likely end up with a frustrating, costly, and unworkable strategy.

BEGIN BY IDENTIFYING YOUR CURRENT STRATEGY

All companies have a strategy. It may not be explicitly stated or even fully understood by management, but it is there. If you are starting a new business, you probably have a strategy in that you have some concept of market needs and how you want to compete, though these concepts may be difficult to articulate and may not be fully tested.

In most existing small firms, the founders of the business had a strategy—at least a vision—when they formed the company. They knew what they wanted to do: to take advantage of the under-served markets, for example, or to market a "custom" product that large firms couldn't economically deliver. But the strategy of a company usually goes beyond just the product-market emphasis.

Somewhere in the history of the business, the entrepreneur will have made one or a number of important decisions that resulted in a defensible competitive position in the marketplace. If you can isolate these decisions and their impact on the company, you are a long way toward understanding the current strategy.

For example, small businesses gain competitive advantage by means such as finding a local low-cost source of raw materials, establishing a strong distributor network, or producing technological innovations.

The combination of the company's product-market emphasis and the key decisions that resulted in a defensible competitive advantage are the essence of the company's current strategy.

Thus, the first task of strategic management in small companies is to identify and understand the competitive history of the firm and what gave rise to past success. The information needed for this task is usually readily available in the company's financial, production, and marketing records, and in the memories of key executives.

ANALYZE BEYOND YOUR CURRENT STRATEGY

Identifying current strategy does not just happen. Managers must get together to do so. The preferred method of planning in the small firm is to gather together several key managers for periodic discussions and planning sessions. All functional areas should be represented because they each bring different information and perspectives. These managers may, therefore, raise issues which any single manager may not have considered.

Keep these sessions focused on the future and on major issues facing the company—not how you'll get this week's orders out! Unless you can temporarily escape the pressing business of today, truly strategic thinking will not be possible.

To inject strategic thinking into your organization, this small group of managers will need to tackle the following issues:

1. What do you agree are the basic elements of the company's current strategy?
2. How do you define your business? Who are your current and potential competitors?
3. What are your competitive advantages (product line, price, service, quality, etc.)? In which markets do you have these advantages? What evidence suggests that these advantages really exist?

4. What are the important trends in your environment and your industry, and how do they affect your current strategy?
5. What strategic and business opportunities face you (i.e., what are your strategic options)?
6. What constraints will inhibit you from exploring these opportunities (lack of financial resources or human skills, stockholders' objectives, etc.)?
7. What are your stockholders' objectives? What implications do these objectives have for capital retention vs. dividends and for debt-to-equity structure? Do you want to remain a private company at all costs? Why?
8. Who will execute the strategic plan that you are devising? How will management succession be provided for beyond the time horizon of this particular plan?

After getting management attuned to thinking about the future, you're now ready to engage in the steps associated with determining the plan itself. In the following sections we will examine the second and third issues above: what business are you in, and what competitive advantages do you have?

WHAT BUSINESS IS YOUR FIRM IN?

Determining what business your firm is in is usually the most *troublesome* and *important* step in the strategic planning process for most small companies. Managers frequently believe and act like they are in a single business. While many small firms are really in just a single business, many others will be engaged in more than a single business.

Over time, small companies often "grow" into new businesses in an opportunistic fashion. Customers and suppliers often suggest new product ideas when a long-standing and satisfactory relationship has developed. Thus, they might expand their product line, which carries them into new markets, while they continue to serve their old customers. In addition, decisions to "make" rather than "buy" (vertical integration) may place a company against a different set of competitors.

In general, a business can be defined by the *preferences* of buyers, and the *economics* of suppliers. Buyer preferences are expressed in terms of product characteristics, such as the quantity, quality, price, and service content desired. Buyers or customer groups having different preferences can be segmented into distinct markets. Thus, industries can be sub-divided into product-market or business segments.

Suppliers, on the other hand, can be segregated along economic lines by how they choose to serve the various product-market segments in an industry. Differences between firms' costs, prices, and asset turnover delineate different competitor groups. These differences in costs, prices, and asset turnover form barriers to entry in the product-market segments that compose the business.

Thus, in identifying the business(es) you're in, you're first faced with a substantial jigsaw puzzle of products, markets, and competitors, that must be sorted out. The key elements to examine in this sorting out process are:

- who the end-user of the product or service is;
- the individual (or organization) that is responsible for specifying the characteristics of the product to be bought and the agents that influence the product's specifications;
- the pricing desired by customers and their price sensitivity;
- the volume of product demanded and the customer's willingness to concentrate that volume among suppliers; and
- the distribution chain that is required to reach the end-user of the product

Indicators that can be found "inside" the company also help you to define your business. One such indicator is the proportion of value added that is shared by all the different products produced. An obvious example is advertising. If one product is advertised on television, while another is advertised in trade magazines, you can almost bet that two different businesses exist. This concept of shared value added can also be applied in manufacturing. If specialized machinery or a group of machines is used for only one of the company's products, there is a strong possibility that the company is in two different businesses.

Knowing what business(es) you're in is vitally important because if your company is in more than one business, then no *single* strategy is likely to be optimal for all the businesses. At worst, the single strategy that is developed will be sub-optimal for *all* of the business(es) the company is in. Some of the dangers include:

- Setting the wrong strategic pricing policy may liquidate the company's market position in one business while diluting revenue generation in another.
- Cutting out a key step in the distribution chain, in a desire to reduce selling expenses, may destroy the company's market position.
- Trying to enter a market or solidify a market position where the company is not equipped to compete will waste scarce resources and may jeopardize the entire firm's viability.

WHAT COMPETITIVE ADVANTAGE DOES YOUR FIRM HAVE?

Another important step is to identify your company's competitive advantage. If your company has properly identified the businesses it is in, then your competitors are known—both current and potential. You then must examine differences between your firm and the competition in terms of costs, prices, and asset turnover.

Typically, small firms have a cost advantage over large firms—in the cost of serving the customer, not in the cost of manufacturing the product.

- Just being located closer to the customer leads to a cost advantage in selling or after-sale service.
- A technically knowledgeable sales force that focuses on a single product or product line may possess a selling cost advantage over a large sales force that sells a "bagful" of different lines including a product that competes with yours. In addition, low-volume, low-value products can't be accommodated by highly paid sales forces, leading to a selling cost advantage for some small firms.
- Lastly, small firms generally have fewer layers of management, less bureaucracy, and less overhead cost than large organizations.

In some cases, the small firm can build a competitive advantage on differences in manufacturing technology that lowers product costs as well. Having highly skilled craftsmen that can make products from rough drawings or manual machinery can be more cost effective than producing products on automated machinery after substantial investments in engineering expenses.

A small firm might also have specialized tools, jigs, or fixtures that allow for lower labor costs and capital expenses than are associated with specialized machinery. "Owner" involvement in quality control decisions can also lead to a cost advantage in that the product gets made right the first time through, eliminating the costs of rework, returns, and customer ill will.

Finally, you shouldn't discount the cost advantages associated with a non-union shop in terms of the wage scale and flexibility in manufacturing operations.

CONCLUSION

Small, closely held companies need an overall strategy just as much as their larger counterparts. But, they should not try to emulate the systems and procedures of large firms. Rather, they should ask the same fundamental strategic questions and get a number of managers intimately involved in the thinking associated with answering those strategic questions. If you get stumped, you can always call in the consultant to help you out. But, in the final analysis, management has to decide what to do.

☐

HOW THE CEO CAN HELP STRATEGIC PLANNING GET OFF THE GROUND

JOHN R. GAULDING

Whether or not strategic planning gets off the ground in a company depends largely on how involved the CEO is in its takeoff. The strategic planning officer is like a well-trained pilot who needs the proper guidance and support from the control tower. Unless the CEO gets involved and offers the right signals, the planner will remain grounded, confirming the weighty suspicions of everyone on board who doubted that the thing could ever fly.

The chief executive officer's responsibilities in the planning process are far broader than many CEOs realize. He must guide the process from the beginning, helping to introduce the process, to establish the planner as a member of the senior management team, and to voice his commitment to strategic planning repeatedly.

The seven suggestions discussed below can help you understand specific ways that the CEO can ensure that the strategic effort becomes airborne.

1. The CEO must understand his own role in strategic planning and how it relates to those given the title of "planners." Ultimate responsibility for strategic planning—that is, for charting the strategic direction of the organization—resides with the CEO, not with the strategic planning officer.

The role of the strategic planner is to use his knowledge, skills, and training to help senior managers (including the CEO) think more critically and creatively about their business. All of the planner's myriad activities should be oriented to getting senior managers to identify and appraise new strategic options and to reconsider old "answers" (such as the firm's accepted notion of what is required to succeed in its industry). In short, the planner must stimulate senior managers to go beyond the obvious and generally accepted ways of thinking.

The strategic planner who believes his job is primarily to produce a written plan will fail. For this reason, we find that many planners are actually trying to do the wrong job. They focus on producing a document rather than trying to understand and change (if necessary) how the organization thinks.

For planning to be accepted by the organization, the CEO must understand and publicly support the planner's job and know what his own planning role is. As one CEO described it, "My planner is the creator, catalyst, and broker of the conceptual future of our corporation. I am still the chief planner, and the role of my planner is to make sure I do my job."

Strategic Planning Management, March, 1983; Commerce Communications, Inc.

2. The CEO should articulate that strategic planning and strategic change are vital and continuous activities.   The CEO is fulfilling his role as the chief executive when he publicly declares his commitment to strategic planning. He must inform his managers that strategic planning should now be seen as an ongoing process in the corporation, not as a temporary phenomenon.

This commitment should be expressed not only explicitly but also indirectly through symbolic actions of the CEO. For example, the CEO should pointedly mention the importance of strategic planning at the firm's annual meeting as well as in group meetings with his senior management. He should also attend meetings at major junctures in the planning process rather than just waiting to receive the final output.

?. The CEO and the planner must both understand the organization's internal culture or environment in order to ensure that planning can be successfully implemented.   (By "culture" we mean the set of values and beliefs that shape the rules for behavior in the company or determine how things get done.)

An awareness of the culture is essential because it initially determines the planner's approach and ultimately helps indicate which values and beliefs of senior management must be shifted to allow for the strategic changes.

If the senior managers are hard-chargers with a strong orientation to the bottom line, a planner must infuse a longer-term perspective into the group. At the same time, he needs to introduce new ideas and perspectives without disrupting the working cohesiveness of the group.

On the other hand, if the top managers are a more deliberate group who spend a lot of time collaborating on long-range issues facing the firm, what may be required is a planner who can orchestrate complex analysis and infuse constructive conflict into the group.

In organizations that have little understanding of planning, the first function of the planner may be to teach other employees what planning is and is not (e.g., what kinds of analyses are required, how it could be done, when it should be done, by whom, etc.). The more teaching that is required, the more patient the CEO must be in his expectations of planning success.

4. The strategic planner should become a member of the senior management team.   This step is absolutely essential for planning success. The unusual nature of the planner's position makes it imperative for the CEO to make this move, though it will not be easy.

Unless the strategic planner reports directly to the CEO he cannot be effective. If the CEO has the planner report to a lower executive (e.g., to the chief financial officer), the CEO has abdicated his role as the ultimate strategist for the corporation—which minimizes the chance that the strategic planning function will be effective.

Another common mistake of some CEOs is that they delegate complete authority for the strategic planning process to the new director of strategic planning. Although a CEO should give the planner responsibility for day-to-day management of strategic planning activity, the CEO must also aggressively reinforce his own role in planning by explicitly proclaiming that ultimate responsibility for strategy resides in his office. If he doesn't retain this leadership role, the planner's power is sapped because other senior managers sense that the power of the CEO's office is not behind the planning process.

Once the planner is on board, the CEO must help him to become involved quickly. The planner should be included in all meetings related to strategy. He should also review current performance and major strategic issues with as many members of senior management as possible, identify critical issues, and explore what key pieces of analysis are needed.

5. The CEO needs to be sensitive to the dilemmas that confront the strategic planner in his delicate role. Strategic planning is more of a staff than a line position, so there is no evident "bottom line" by which to assess a planner's contribution. His success will be judged on the quality of his thinking and his ability to assist senior managers.

Much of the power in the strategic planner's position emanates from his relationship with the CEO. "Power is a zero-sum game," says one CEO, "and giving it to the planner means you've got to take it away from others." Thus the planner finds himself trying to influence others without having the power to command them.

A good portion of the strategic planner's effectiveness will, therefore, depend on his ability to develop strong peer relationships with the other senior managers. Yet he is in an unusual position. The strategic planner cannot compete with or even relate to other managers in traditional ways because he does not wield power and influence based on the number of people working for him and the size of his budget. His stature will depend largely on his ability to use interpersonal skills to influence his peers.

The strategic planner will also face very high levels of uncertainty stemming both from the nature of the planning task and the tenuousness of his position among the other senior managers. In addition, the strategic planner will have to relinquish much of the credit for almost everything he does because the praise for strategic planning successes will inevitably go to the CEO and the rest of the senior management team.

6. The CEO should create a "safety net" around the planner at first. This safety net is created when the CEO explicitly tells his management team that a new strategic planning function has been established, that there will be some false starts, and that—by definition—there will be no failures.

In other words, the CEO is protecting the planning process during its introductory phase. And because the planner is really the CEO's alter ego in the planning process, the CEO is also protecting himself. Thus, the CEO and the strategic planner must work in close harmony to ensure that they are on the same wavelength.

A safety net is especially warranted in those organizations where a previous attempt to introduce strategic planning resulted in failure. In these organizations, a number of individuals may harbor lingering antipathy toward both planning and planners.

In addition, the "no-one-can-fail" approach helps senior managers feel freer to think of the business in new and creative ways. Without a safety net, managers are much more likely to play by the old rules—rules that, in all likelihood, will not give rise to innovative thinking, new questions, or to the search for new answers to old questions.

The strategic planner, in effect, is the catalyst for this process. So, in a brainstorming session, for example, he can encourage the vice-president of manufacturing to toss out new creative ideas without restricting himself to his usual concerns for minimizing unit costs.

7. Many of the strategic planner's early efforts should be oriented toward developing partnerships with the CEO and each member of the senior management team. There is no magical way to create these relationships instantly. They take time to cultivate. But they must be developed before an effective strategic plan can be formulated and implemented.

An important means of developing partnerships with senior managers is to solicit an identification of the projects which they and the strategic planner could work on jointly. This gives the managers some ownership in the planning activities, and fosters an ongoing opportunity for interaction between the planner and the managers.

To help nurture these relationships, the CEO should appear to be actively involved in strategic planning activities. The CEO participation sends clear signals to other senior managers that active involvement in the process of planning is expected. However, the strategic planner must realize that managers may react differently to the requirements placed upon them by their involvement in strategic planning. They may also have different expectations as to how strategic planning will contribute to their day-to-day activities. The strategic planner, therefore, will have to develop quite distinct types of relationships or partnerships with different individuals.

To enhance these relationships, the strategic planner should resist over-formalizing the planning process during the first year. If he makes the mistake of initially emphasizing systems and procedures rather than building strong relationships he will only implant deep-seeded antagonism toward planning and planners. Therefore, a more formal planning system should only be evolved later through ongoing consultation with the CEO, senior management, and line managers.

CONCLUSION

Integrating a strategic planning process within an organization is a difficult, hazardous, and time-consuming task. Many CEOs have been disappointed by strategic planning because they didn't understand their own critical role in the process. But if the CEO understands how to introduce the strategic planner into the organization, the planning effort can be launched successfully.

APPLICATION IN STRATEGIC MANAGEMENT:
A Planning System that Went Awry:
Learning from Failure
LIAM FAHEY

Many firms have learned the hard way that the introduction of a planning system, that is, a more formal and systematic approach to strategy analysis, is paved with pitfalls. A planning system design that looks good on paper may prove impossible to implement, or it may get implemented and have little impact on organizational decision making.

However, we can learn much from failed attempts to implement planning systems. The following is an account of one such failed attempt and some lessons which can be derived from it.

A newly appointed Executive Vice-President of Business Development and Marketing, in a division of a large multidivisional firm, decided that his organization needed a planning system. He felt that he needed to infuse a strategic perspective into the organization, rather than the sales orientation which had been dominant for many years. He also saw the planning system as a means of getting more line managers and staff involved in strategy development and implementation. Also, he believed it would lead to the development of new products, something which the division had been noticeably lacking for two or three years.

INTRODUCTION OF THE PLANNING SYSTEM

As envisioned and implemented by the Vice-President, the introduction and integration of the planning system into the organization was a four-step process.

Strategic Planning Management, April, 1984; Commerce Communications, Inc.

1. Design of the planning system. The Vice-President, in conjunction with two consultants from a small consulting firm, detailed what the planning system should look like and how it should function. They developed a planning calendar, identified who should perform which functions and tasks, and created formats for data collection and plan development.

2. Initial introduction. The planning system was introduced to all the division's managers in a workshop format. The first workshop lasted four full, consecutive days. The two consultants conducted the workshop. The VP took very little active role in the proceedings.

The purpose of this initial workshop was to "sell" the benefits of a planning system, familiarize the managers with the intended planning system, and introduce each manager to his or her role in the system.

3. A training program. As a follow-up to the initial introduction, the consultants conducted a two-day workshop in each of the succeeding nine months. Each workshop was intended to deal with a different facet of strategic planning and the firm's emerging planning system.

In some of these workshops, groups of managers were given project assignments, and asked to make a presentation on them to the entire set of managers. Sample project asssignments were: identification of new product-market opportunities, assessment of competitor's strategies, identification of the firm's strengths and weaknesses, and the development of strategic and marketing plans.

4. Integration into ongoing activities. Outside of the workshops, the consultants worked with individual managers on projects related to their on-going functions. The VP determined which managers could most benefit from assistance by consultants and which projects they should collectively work on. The VP himself had little involvement in these relationships, other than to monitor their progress through frequent contact with the consultants.

THE RESULTS

As soon as the nine month series of workshops ended and the consultants were no longer involved in any formal way, the intended planning system began to disintegrate. The Vice-President was unable to keep the system functioning. The tasks required to meet the planning calendar schedule were not completed.

None of the division's managers were willing to assume a leadership role in maintaining and further developing the planning system. Indeed, some managers covertly and overtly were active in sabotaging the system: they did not attend meetings, they asked their subordinates not to complete or to delay completion of required planning system tasks, and they publicly questioned the merits of many aspects of the planning system.

Three months after the completion of the workshop series, the division president was promoted to a position in a much larger division and was replaced by an individual from a much smaller division. The new president was heavily sales oriented, and quickly indicated through his words and actions that he had little faith in planning systems. The Executive VP asked for and received an appointment in another division.

WHAT WENT WRONG?

Reflecting upon his efforts to design and develop a planning system, the Vice-President was able to identify a number of reasons why it never really got off the ground.

First, in designing and introducing the planning system, the Vice-President did not consult with the division's line and staff managers on whether a planning system was needed, what type of planning system they thought appropriate for the firm, how it should be introduced, and who should be involved in doing so.

The Vice-President simply assumed that once they understood the potential benefits of a planning system, all the firm's managers would immediately support and aid the introduction and development of the system.

However, it quickly became clear in the initial four-day introduction of the planning system that there was strong resistance to the notion of a planning system and how it was being introduced. It was clear that for most managers the system would involve a "hard sell."

Second, the Vice-President in essence disregarded the obvious resistance. He did not take any steps to surface the resistance, that is, to better understand why it was arising so that he and the consultants could deal with it. The resistance was allowed to grow into antagonism, to the point where some managers were publicly belittling the idea of a planning system, and bemoaning their involvement in it, as early as a few weeks after the initial introduction of the system.

Although these types of statements were brought to the attention of the VP, he felt that the individuals involved would be swept along in the tide of support for the planning system and, therefore, would eventually support his efforts to put in place a more formalized and organized approach to strategic management.

Third, the Vice-President misdefined his role in introducing and managing the planning system. He saw his role as passive leader rather than as an active teacher. He did not want to be put in a position of critiquing the work and contributions of others. He felt that all feedback to those involved in the system should emanate from the consultants.

A major consequence of the VP's desire to remain in the background as much as possible was that the consultants, in effect, assumed the VP's position with regard to development and management of the planning system. This was resented by some individuals who felt that many of the consultants' functions should have been performed by the VP.

Fourth, the consultants also contributed to the resistance and confusion. They were inflexible in their approach; they had one conception of a planning system, and that was what they wished to implement. They resisted the efforts of some senior managers to adapt the proposed planning to their own specific needs.

The consultants also saw it as their role to lead the planning system development effort. They believed that they had the relevant expertise and they, therefore, should lead the workshops, and work one-on-one with individual managers.

One consequence of how the consultants saw their role was that the VP was implicitly further encouraged to view his role as that of passive leader rather than as active teacher. The consultants did little, if anything, to give the VP a more visible and central role in the whole process.

Fifth, the Executive VP and consultants were primarily concerned with the outputs of the planning system (plans, programs, budgets), whereas many managers and staff were primarily focusing upon the processes involved in the planning system (data collection, meetings). The latter were preoccupied by what had to be done to achieve the outputs.

The planning system was not presented to the organization as a means of enhancing strategic thinking and as a way of learning more about competitors, markets, the environment, and the firm itself. It was presented as a set of steps or routines which had to be completed in order to realize the desired outputs.

Sixth, implicit in much of the above, is that the planning system was seen by almost all the managers and staff as something entirely new to the organization. They did not understand how it built upon what they already did. Worse, they saw it as an impediment to some of the many tasks they performed.

Again, this was in part attributable to how the planning system was introduced. The core of much of the early efforts of the VP and consultants was that a planning system would be "a new, exciting, and revolutionary way of doing things."

Finally, much of what went wrong could be attributed to miscommunication or non-communication. The VP and consultants saw the system as simple, logical, easy to understand, readily adaptable, and congruent with how the organization operated. This was the heart of the message they persistently tried to convey to the organization.

Many of the organization's members, however, saw the planning system as complex, difficult to comprehend, redundant to their functions, and poorly integrated. This perception of the planning system underlay much of their resistance and consequent behaviors.

Yet, at no stage in the introduction of the planning system was an opportunity created by the VP, consultants or managers, to expose and discuss these quite distinct perspectives. Each side *acted* as if the other had a clear understanding of what the planning system was all about.

In short, there was no review process built into the introduction of the planning system, that is, a point in time when those involved in designing, implementing and carrying out the tasks inherent in the system could take stock of what was working as planned, what wasn't, and why.

The Vice-President, by his own admission, committed a number of errors in introducing the planning system:

1. He tried to impose his own model of a planning system on the organization;
2. He did not allow those who would actually implement the system to have any involvement in its design or evolution;
3. He did not adopt a leadership or teaching role—he assumed the system would sell itself.
4. He concentrated too much upon achieving the intended outputs of the system, at the expense of attention to the processes involved in the system; and
5. He allowed the consultants to perform many of the tasks which should have been part of his responsibility.

In summary, a planning system doesn't introduce itself. Its benefits may not be obvious to those whose work routines are being upset. The things that can go wrong are many, yet they can all be managed. However, if those introducing the system do not keep their ears to the ground, they will never know how well or how badly they are doing.

CHAPTER

— 15 —

BUILDING THE STRATEGIC ORGANIZATION: MANAGING THE PLANNING PROCESS

■

□

BEFORE PLANNING, LET MANAGERS KNOW WHAT THEY'RE IN FOR

ROBERT A. VECCHIOTTI

When managers express disillusionment with a planning process, they're usually indicating that the experience didn't meet their expectations. But what *did* they expect?

Unless you make sure before you begin planning that your managers share a common—and realistic—understanding of what the process will involve, you'll quickly encounter frustration. That disillusionment will undermine the strategy formulation effort and obliterate your chances for building the line and staff commitment necessary to implement strategies effectively.

This article will outline six aspects of the planning process that managers should discuss and define before the cycle gets underway. In this way, they will all share the same general expectations about the following dimensions of their strategic planning:

1. The nature and amount of change required,
2. The degree of risk involved,
3. The time horizon,
4. Who will be involved,

Strategic Planning Management, September, 1983; Commerce Communications, Inc.

5. The degree of formality, and

6. How planning responsibilities fit into their daily routines.

1. THE NATURE AND AMOUNT OF CHANGE REQUIRED

The first pre-planning consideration is to identify what type and degree of change is required. Is the most important need to find ways to redirect the major assets of the corporation toward new ventures, for example? Or does top management want to focus on changing the marketing strategy for a product line? Perhaps the firm only seeks to make a minor change such as modifying the advertising budget. As these sample questions illustrate, different problems entail varying types and amounts of change that involve efforts ranging from a major corporate planning thrust, to market planning, to a simple operating decision.

In the early stages of the strategic planning process, managers should be asked to help identify what changes are needed. To stimulate discussion, I have found the two following questions helpful:

"What changes are necessary to help us achieve our broad objectives?"
"What changes are necessary to help us maintain or gain more market share?"

Raising these types of questions gets people involved in the thinking process sooner, which yields two benefits. First, it's a valuable source of information to help top management identify critical areas. And second, it helps everyone begin to understand the scope of the planning effort and what resources are necessary to carry out the changes.

The recent experience of a manufacturing firm illustrates the importance of raising these questions. The company was in a declining industry and had assumed for some time it needed to redirect its major assets into more profitable ventures. But not until managers began to discuss how much change was required did they begin the search for alternatives.

They identified a very promising option: to attract through new product introductions and product modifications new customers from related industries while retaining their traditional customer base. Sales people were free to choose the market area, traditional or contemporary, in which they wished to sell. The firm saved valuable time and effort by next hiring a marketing manager whose thoughts about new markets were integrated into the overall business plan.

By arriving at an early consensus of the degree of change required, managers can anticipate the effort that will be demanded of them. And, they will also be able to establish a more realistic timetable for implementation.

2. THE DEGREE OF RISK INVOLVED

A second consideration is how much risk will be involved in various strategy options and what levels of risk are acceptable. Almost any managerial action involves risk, whether hiring new people, entering a new market, spending capital, upgrading technology, or even doing nothing. In the early stages of planning, attempt to identify the different types of risks and make them visible to the key players in the organization.

Small-group discussions which draw upon individuals' perceptions of risks during the pre-planning stage can be as valuable as the more common risk-related aspects of strategy formulation and implementation, such as cost-of-capital determination, and risk management. Such discussions help integrate planning into day-to-day management actions, and lead toward more immediate and committed implementation.

By alerting managers to the risks involved before they launch a major strategic thrust, various "watchdogs" can be assigned to monitor the inherent risks from factors such as uncertainty in the economy, aggressive competition, likely changes in the marketplace, and changes in the labor pool.

The "risk-watching" departments or persons would therefore become involved early in the planning process. They could then build on their earlier perceptions of risk as they are encouraged to search for strategic information, to identify realistic alternatives if necessary, and to help anticipate risks involved throughout implementation.

3. THE TIME HORIZON

The appropriate time horizon for any planning effort depends on how much change is required, and how much risk the company will undertake.

The farther into the future we try to plan, the more uncertainty, imprecision, and risk we face. It becomes harder to identify what actions should be taken, and in what sequence. In contrast the shorter the time horizon, the easier it is to implement the plan. You'll want to choose a time horizon that is short enough for you to be able to project meaningfully, but long enough to ensure you're not short-sighted.

While an entrepreneurial start-up venture may not be able to plan more than two years, a city water-treatment facility might comfortably set a 20-year horizon. Firms more typically select a three-to-five year planning horizon. Keep in mind that changing conditions may make a different time horizon more appropriate. If your industry suddenly becomes very volatile, you'll probably want to shorten your time horizon.

4. WHO WILL BE INVOLVED?

Early in the planning process it helps to identify what levels of the organization will participate. The more risk anticipated, and the longer the time horizon, the more top-level corporate wisdom should be sought.

Systematic collection of ideas from several levels of the organization, planned in advance, and carried out early in the planning process, will help assure broader participation in the processes of planning. Dissemination and discussion of these ideas encourages involvement in various phases of planning and enhances the likelihood of the acceptance of the outputs of planning, i.e., strategic and tactical programs.

You may be amazed to discover how much information can be gathered when the right questions are asked of the right people. The best sources are people who have a good view of how the company is doing relative to the external world:

- sales people who know what customers are saying and doing,
- the legal staff who monitor new regulations,
- the financial experts seeking new investments,
- marketers studying competitive and market forces,
- purchasing agents who know what vendors are saying and doing, and
- research and development people who stay informed about the cutting edge of technology.

All of these sources are likely to appreciate being asked to share their expertise. Their participation early in the planning process not only helps ensure their cooperation later in implementation but it dramatically extends the base of relevant information.

The decision about which levels of the organization should participate in strategy development and the scope of their participation should be made very early in the planning process to identify the risks of not involving a particular group or level. Even if strategies or broad strategic plans are initiated and eventually completed at the CEO level, the steps needed to implement them will require the participation and commitment of a much broader group.

Keep in mind that at some point all levels of an organization will need to come together to hear, discuss, understand, and modify the corporate vision. If this meeting takes place early in the planning process, it may make it far easier for the subsequent steps in that process to flow naturally out of the agreed-upon vision.

5. THE DEGREE OF FORMALITY

A planning process can quickly suffocate if a mound of formal paperwork is expected to accumulate. Remember, strategic planning is not a dry paper-and-pencil exercise. It is an opportunity for organizational renewal—a time to trigger fresh ideas, not to imprison creativity within the bars of a standardized planning form.

To introduce excessive formality into a planning process only increases resistance to change, and ultimately hurts implementation. Yet some degree of formality (i.e., forms, manuals, meetings, presentations, etc.) is necessary if strategy analysis, development, and implementation is to become a shared organizational activity. Otherwise, all strategic planning is likely to take place in the heads of a few key executives, and is not likely to be evaluated and tested by others in the organization.

The CEO of a small firm wanted to know how a larger firm did its strategic planning. He was even eager to purchase their forms and manuals until he realized what would be the potential consequences to his own informal management style. He decided that his firm was small enough that he did not require a large set of forms and planning documents, but he did add some formality by establishing some planning meetings to review results, set goals, and develop strategies.

Formality has a place, but, as a rule, only introduce formality where you are convinced it is necessary. Also, continue to ask whether the degree of formality you have is necessary.

6. HOW PLANNING RESPONSIBILITIES FIT INTO THE DAILY ROUTINE

For any planning effort to succeed, the participants must integrate their planning responsibilities into their daily routine. Everyone already has more than enough meetings to attend, so rather than set up special planning sessions consider gradually introducing topics at scheduled meetings. These topics will help people learn what to plan for, what techniques to use, as well as the considerations noted above.

Invite other groups to participate in working sessions to share ideas. We have little choice but to become accustomed to sharing ideas, discussing options and consequences, choosing alternatives, and preparing action plans in groups. One-on-one sessions can be used to check individual plans and raise any concerns which can be resolved mutually before moving toward implementation.

By incorporating planning tasks into managers' daily routine, you can ensure that they will begin to consider feasibility of implementation as they formulate initial plans. Also, follow-up actions will be more easily integrated with existing policies and procedures, and changes can also be introduced more systematically with less interference in the daily routine.

CONCLUSION

If managers participate in helping define these six dimensions of the strategic planning process before the cycle begins, the firm benefits in several ways. Not only will the managers provide a rich set of insights that enhance the formulation of a strategy, but their own early involvement in the process will give them realistic expectations of and subsequent commitment to the strategy or plan they helped develop.

☐

KEEP YOUR PLANNING ALIVE
R.T. LENZ AND MARJORIE A. LYLES

Beware! Even the healthiest strategic planning efforts need to watch out for threats to their livelihood. If you're not alert, you could eventually find that your planning process has been sealed off from the rest of the company and left to suffocate. No one would even try to save you—not the line managers, who grumbled about the time they spent helping you, nor top management, who increasingly have begun to regard your plans as a piece of fiction unrelated to reality.

To ensure that your planning process stays lively, producing fresh insights that result in workable blueprints for the organization, you need to understand how to cope with the forces that can hurt the vitality of the planning process.

As your strategic planning process develops, you must be sure that walls don't grow up around it. Even as the planning process becomes more complex it does not need to become an overly formal, time consuming process that separates the planners from the rest of the company and also shuts out innovative thought and action.

THE "PLANNING PRIESTHOOD" BARRIER

One of the most common forces that builds walls around planners is when a "planning priesthood" develops, in which planners become known as an elite group with a mysterious dogma and language all their own. Every time they mention SBUs, GAP analysis, BCG matrices, and PIMS models they shut out their co-workers a little more. Also, they usually enjoy an elevated status within the organization that line workers may resent.

Whether planners construct this barrier inadvertently, in their efforts to keep the organization on the frontier of strategic analysis, or deliberately use independent data and sophisticated analytical techniques to undercut the power of line managers, their effectiveness can be markedly reduced.

Of course, we're not suggesting that frameworks for strategic analysis should be avoided. These tools are very valuable. The point is they shouldn't create a barrier between line and staff. Effective planners need a common

Strategic Planning Management, January/February, 1983; Commerce Communications, Inc.

language and shared frames of reference with line managers. Only then can they gain the perspective and insight necessary for informed strategic decision making.

Planners sometimes block themselves off from line managers when they concentrate on demonstrating their analytical competence to top executives. To avoid this situation, planners should be "mainstreamed" into the heart of the company in the following ways:

1. Planners should work directly with line managers in the early stages of strategy formulation. This approach prevents planners and managers from developing separate and usually dissimilar assessments of relevant issues and possible strategic responses.

2. Senior executives must not allow planning to become an adversary of line managers. There are enough natural forces in organizations that conspire to drive line and staff apart without top management aggravating this potential tension.

3. Planners should act as internal consultants, offering guidance and answering questions. They should help flush out strategic issues, offer independent assessments of emerging problems and trends, and counsel line managers about strategy alternatives in light of what is happening in the rest of the organization.

4. Where possible, planners should be rotated among job assignments either within the overall corporate planning staff or into a line job. This cross-fertilization ensures that planners are not insulated from the real concerns of line managers.

THE "QUANTIFY IT" COMPULSION

A second force that can set up barriers around a planning system is an emphasis on trying to quantify everything—as if assigning a number suddenly makes uncertainty disappear. As one director of international business planning put it, "In planning meetings, the guys with the numbers inevitably win—even when everyone knows the numbers aren't worth much! Let's face it: the numbers become reality."

The stress on assigning numbers can be a problem for both line managers, who supply information, and the planners themselves as they strive for detail in the corporate plan. While laboring under the misconception that more quantification somehow leads to greater certainty in decision making, they'll spend more energy searching for the "right number" than in coming up with creative approaches.

At its core, strategic planning is simply a way to ensure the long-term growth and development of an enterprise by making corporate decisions based on systematic analysis instead of seat-of-the-pants judgments. But sometimes both staff and line managers begin to believe that only quantifiable information is reliable for planning. They tend to dismiss other qualitative considerations as lacking the "hardness" or certainty required in planning.

Such convictions greatly limit the information used to plan, shutting out such intangibles as shifts in public attitudes, lifestyle changes affecting product demand, organization morale, corporate government relations, etc. These factors will prove the decisive ones in strategic decisions.

As a planning system matures, more and more details tend to build up in the analysis. This mountain of detail can actually become more of an obstruction than an illuminator of strategic issues.

For example, a planning vice-president once recounted to us the history of planning at his corporation by showing us an incredible succession of ever-fattening ring binders, each notebook containing a weightier, more detailed plan than the previous year. The current plan was dubbed "The Beast" because it devoured so much management time. For future plans, the firm was heavily investing in computers to accommodate a larger data base capable of providing more precise data!

What managers usually encounter as they build up more layers of detail is not greater certainty but more obscurity. As strategic problems are sliced into thinner and thinner pieces, they become fragmented and disjointed. What gets lost is the coherence essential for comprehensive strategic decision making.

To combat this "quantify-it," detail-oriented syndrome, senior executives must emphasize the importance of qualitative information. One very useful way some companies have found to include these considerations is to require planners to write out a narrative that focuses on conceptual issues rather than quantitative data. This description should assess competitive forces and trends, investment requirements, human resources, and other issues.

As one executive who insists on getting such a text from his planner says, "If my managers cannot tell me in words what problems they're facing and how they intend to respond, they don't have a strategy." By removing the wall of numbers and details, planners can get a much clearer view of their true competitive position.

Of course, managers may be unaccustomed to scanning the company and the environment for the significant qualitative issues. The best way to encourage such thinking is for senior executives to hold strategy review sessions in which they probe line managers about the "whys" behind their numbers. These sessions help keep both staff and line managers' attention focused outward instead of staring blankly into a wall of their own detail. A far-seeing view of emerging competitive realities helps generate fresh innovative thoughts for strategic planning.

To operate at peak effectiveness, strategic planning needs to be kept open and stimulating to those participating in it. It requires considerable vigilance, self-reflection, and collective effort to guard against the problems discussed here. But the effort is well worthwhile, for it will keep your planning process alive.

THE DRIVE FOR BUREAUCRATIC EFFICIENCY

When strategic planning is introduced to a firm, those who are involved initially view it as an exciting experiment. They contribute their energy and time enthusiastically as the process triggers a host of innovative ideas. Morale often surges as planners experience a shared sense of purpose and direction. As time passes, however, the novelty of planning wanes, and it is seen as just one more administrative burden to endure.

No organization can expect to sustain the initial flush of enthusiasm that accompanies the introduction of strategic planning. It *is* possible, however, to sustain interest, commitment, and—most important—creativity. But, you must be aware of how these vital ingredients can be lost in the inevitable clash of two opposing forces found in a planning system: the conflicting demands for innovativeness and bureaucratic efficiency.

Soon after a strategic planning system is launched, many managers attempt to improve its efficiency and predictability. They focus on developing a standardized format—even if this process will obscure strategically significant differences in product lines, markets, businesses, or technologies.

Next, they attempt to establish a planning timetable and critical data requirements. In a short time, the emphasis shifts from encouraging creativity and unconventional thinking to merely finishing the process. A rigid planning schedule, standardized procedures, and formal meetings simply do not encourage innovative thought, nor do they foster an atmosphere conducive to supporting experimentation.

Many organizations seem to move through three learning stages in developing a planning system. In the first phase, a firm begins to practice what it calls strategic planning but is actually only financial planning. This financial focus may last two or three years before management discovers that the process is insufficient to deal with many other strategic issues such as competitors' moves and market changes.

In the second stage, an expanded concept of strategic planning is introduced. Organizational attention is directed toward monitoring and understanding industry, competitive, market, and environmental trends and events.

In the third phase, the goals are to achieve efficiency and standardization in the planning process. Schedules are developed, procedures defined, formats specified. While planning certainly must be coordinated, imposing too much rigor can undermine the ultimate purposes of strategic planning. In an effort to simplify the process and meet deadlines, "planning" can be reduced to merely revising last year's forecasts. Although the process may become more efficient, much of the spontaneity, innovativeness, and richness is lost as the procedure becomes dull and routine.

When this occurs, planners will no longer be able to design strategies that creatively address forces threatening the firm. In fact, planners may not even be able to identify those threats.

This shift in the character of planning is subtle. It occurs on many fronts simultaneously. More importantly, the compulsion to formalize and bureaucraticize is almost never questioned, probably because these actions are taken in the name of efficiency. It is important to realize that a delicate balance must be maintained between bureaucratic efficiency and creativity. Once the scales tip in favor of efficiency, the vitality begins to drain from the planning process.

To avoid overemphasizing bureaucratic efficiency, you should always keep in mind that, above all, strategic planning should foster the creativity that is essential for identifying strategic alternatives. The system should be designed to encourage the expression of creativity—even if it means *not* structuring the process. Planners should be evaluated on the basis of their output, not on how well they adhere to formal guidelines.

If each department is allowed to develop its own process for strategic planning (within parameters set by corporate planners), all will develop more of a sense of participation, or "ownership," in the planning process. This system helps sustain the groups' interest and keeps the process flexible enough so that it can be tailored to the needs of specific areas.

One innovative approach used by a firm with which we have worked is to appoint a task force to review each division's plans before they are presented formally within the organization. The task force, which includes representatives from various divisions and functional areas, can offer valuable input to the plans and also check to see that the division has provided evidence that the plan is creative, oriented to the long-term, and integrated with the organization's overall strategies.

Another technique used by some firms to avoid placing too much weight on efficiency is to design the system explicitly addressing "social goals" (i.e., creativity, role clarity, and job satisfaction) as well as the efficiency-oriented "technical goals" (i.e., timetables and long-term plans). This approach requires each division to define the unique planning problems it faces and then design a system to help overcome these problems.

When this particular system is used, divisions frequently discover that their problems are social in nature, involving such issues as relationships among people or conflict of power and/or attitudes. This technique allows the division to identify and iron out its own problems so that they do not obstruct the division's ability to develop a plan which is creative and oriented to the long-term. This approach also allows each division to benefit from the planning process and subsequently adapt it to meet its own needs.

THE DESIRE FOR "ANALYTICAL UTOPIA"

In their drive to understand strategic problems and opportunities, many firms eagerly embrace a variety of forecasting techniques and sophisticated "models" (economic models, etc.), hoping these tools will catapult them into analytical utopia. The great risk involved is that the firms may begin to accept the models' outputs describing future events as blind truth. The PIMS models, the BCG portfolio matrix, and various other financial models and industry analysis techniques are now used by some companies as their main source of identifying issues and making strategic choices.

Unqualified acceptance of any analytical model can lead to one or more of the following problems:

- The only strategic issues identified are those with which the model can deal. Issues beyond the analytical scope of the model often go undetected and, as a result, planners may waste their time on less important issues.

- When statistical models based on past economic relationships are indiscriminantly used, history essentially becomes the determinant of the future. The prospect for innovation is therefore lost.

- Many strategic models overemphasize one criterion (such as cash flow) for decision making. Such models fail to deal with the complexity of strategy making, and if other factors are ignored, the corporation can be penalized in the long run. Furthermore, decision makers rarely fully consider the underlying assumptions and limitations of the particular criterion.

- Once these strategic models are used for the first time, it becomes tempting to keep inserting new numbers into the old framework. As a consequence, it gets even harder to develop innovative approaches to strategy analysis.

The desire for analytical utopia reflects a wishful attempt to predict the future with certainty or, at the very least, to identify paths that are less risky. This pitfall is the most insidious one because it ultimately eliminates debate and innovativeness in favor of "scientific precision."

To avoid overrelying on analytical models, the models should only be used in conjunction with qualitative techniques such as assumption-identification and testing or stakeholder analysis, which help identify differing points of view as well as those potential problems not built into the models. If companies such as Chrysler had forced themselves to consider the "unthinkable" in the past they might have avoided facing extinction from the unforeseen horrors of the present.

Several specific precautions can be taken. Here are six actions an organization can take to avoid developing an obsession with analytical utopia.

1. Identify all the underlying "laws" that govern a particular model. Whenever the results of a particular model are presented, the laws should be

clearly explained to the management, and the model's resulting strengths and weaknesses should be discussed.

2. Identify the fuzzy, ill-defined areas that are not incorporated into the model. For example, when using the PIMS model, environmental issues such as changes in markets and government legislation are not assessed.

3. Use techniques such as structured debates or "assumption testing" that help management understand the complexity of the situation and share different perspectives. Planners need to identify and examine the underlying beliefs about the firm, its environment, the models, and their predictions for the future.

4. Emphasize that these models are only useful tools, not answers, and that they may be interpreted in more than one way.

5. The corporate planner should be regarded as a consultant who will offer advice on how to use these techniques correctly, not as the local soothsayer who has the power to predict the future.

6. Be sure to incorporate into the planning process some exploration of alternative scenarios not suggested by the analytical models. By pushing managers to think beyond the limits of the model they can address such possibilities as natural disasters, unanticipated uses of their product by consumers, or political upheavals in foreign countries.

CONCLUSION

As firms develop strategic planning, they often try to structure it more formally in an attempt to achieve greater efficiency and control. But you need to realize that as the process becomes restricted by too many formal guidelines, the planning will become isolated from the rest of the organization, left in the dark to suffocate without the fresh air of creative ideas on which its survival depends. As your planning process is built up, the strategies we've discussed should help ensure it has enough windows to let in the light.

LESS IS MORE: HOW LESS FORMAL PLANNING CAN BE BEST

ANDREW THOMAS

The very procedures that helped establish planning in your organization may now be stifling the creativity that should lie at the heart of strategic planning. After several years, the planning function too often becomes overly

Strategic Planning Management, May, 1983; Commerce Communications, Inc.

formalized, out of tune with the company. It also tends to have been shaped by characteristics inherited from the past: personalities, planning needs, operational crises, and organizational upheavals.

When problems arise, the natural reaction is to add more procedures, schedules and structure, until the overladen system nearly collapses from its own weight.

The best way to lift the burden of over-formalization from the shoulders of the planning process is to enlist the help of operating managers.

EMPHASIZE INPUT, NOT OUTPUT

Formal planning processes have a strong tendency to focus on producing a slick presentation for the corporate officers or the board of directors. This is the kiss of death, because it places format over substance.

Formats, schedules and timetables may be necessary to force people to *act*, but they are usually not the best way to get managers to *think*. Nothing convinces an operating manager of the futility of a process quicker than having to produce scads of numbers for financial projections five years hence.

The process should emphasize what goes *into* the planning effort, not how thick and impressive the volume is that comes *out* of the effort. Top management should keep these ideas in mind:

- The CEO or the board should be more pleased with a planning process that comes up with one or two brilliant new ideas that can be expressed in two sentences than with 75 pages of disjointed action plans and unrealistic "hockey stick" growth charts.
- Unlike the annual operating plan and budget, which should produce a detailed outline of specific actions, the long-range strategic plan should be viewed as a much broader, thought-provoking exercise. Remember: a long-range strategic plan should be more open-ended than definitive; that is, it should never attempt to be the last word on any subject.
- Just because a long-range plan is written doesn't mean it is sacred. Good ideas should continue to be adopted even if they surface the day after the long-range plan is "put to bed." The long-range strategic plan is like a tour: the travel is more important than the destination.

AIM AT THE NEEDS OF OPERATING MANAGERS

It is essential to understand from the start whose thinking you want the long-range planning process to influence. The process should be directly aimed at meeting the needs of operating managers. Unless the planning process helps communicate long-range ideas that allow managers to be more effective, the planners' requests for information will be ignored, delegated, or casually performed merely to get the planners to go away.

Here are some specific suggestions for involving managers in a flexible planning process:

- Throughout the year, let the managers tell you about their planning horizons and ideas. When the planning season arrives, structure a planning process that provides them with a good, flexible vehicle to convey their concerns.

- Let them define their own formats and planning horizons, within limits. Don't worry if one group has a three-year planning horizon while another group has a ten-year horizon. If you forced them both to operate in a five-year time frame you would actually lose a very valuable piece of planning information and would arbitrarily distort the thinking of key operating people.

- Don't constrain managers into following a standardized format in supplying their information. The plan will probably have to be edited by one person anyway. It is easier for you to rewrite a set of individual plans into a unified draft than it is to try to breathe life into hollow words that were forced into an inappropriate standardized format.

- If you want top managers to give you their own responses instead of delegating the task, don't ask for a mountain of data. The simpler and more conceptual a planning method is, the less apt managers are to delegate the project to subordinates.

- From year to year, the burning issues and the planning horizons for all businesses tend to change. You can either explicitly encourage managers to adopt their own planning format, or else deliberately change the planning process somewhat each year. In either case, you'll reduce the managers' temptation to dust off last year's plan and merely update it.

AVOID BEING LOCKED IN BY THE WRITTEN WORD

While it can be valuable to record the organization's best current thinking regularly, the very act of committing ideas to paper can have a chilling effect on the free flow of creative thought that the planning process is designed to encourage.

Frequently, top executives make it known that certain sensitive topics should not be approached in the plan. But if they are reluctant to publish any long-range decisions that will clearly impact the strategy of the operating groups, then they should also discuss how withholding that information will result in an inevitable loss of integrity for the planning system as a whole.

Proponents of innovative ideas want to be able to pick their own opportunity for suggesting a brainchild, and they want to have an opportunity to lay the groundwork and line up support before they surface the new idea. Usually the preferred forum is a face-to-face brainstorming session. The long-range planning process should follow or incorporate this type of informal strategy session as its first step.

Early in the process the top executives should be encouraged to state the assumptions on which they are basing their long-range corporate plans. In this way, they will provide a context within which the operating managers can plan.

THE PLAN IS A MEANS, NOT AN END

Managers are hired to anticipate and adapt the business to changes in the environment. The formal planning process should obviously encourage this ability, but often its effect is just the opposite. The highly structured planning system has two unwanted side effects.

First, operating managers tend to assume that only the dimensions specifically addressed in the plan are important to top management. Consequently, the managers tend to guide their thinking and judge performance throughout the year in these narrowly defined terms.

Second, the planning process sometimes becomes such a traumatic annual event that the operating managers excuse themselves from thinking any strategic thoughts for the other ten months of the year. Worse still, the review and approval procedures can become so ponderous and formalized that the operating managers begin to feel that the long-range plan represents the only "approved" way of thinking about the future.

These two tendencies can work together to actually produce an anti-planning mentality among operating managers—the opposite of the intended effect. The solution to this problem is to establish informal communications with managers in several ways:

- Circulate among the operating managers throughout the year and encourage them to talk about their ideas. Take the good ideas and (with due credit to the source) bounce them off others who can add to them. People are very pleased to hear others building on their ideas.
- When the planning cycle starts, work with these managers to get their thoughts into the hopper. That way, they know that they—rather than just the planners—are doing the planning.

Another advantage of regular, informal communication with operating managers is that it is easier to check the pulse of the formal planning process to tell if it ever runs into difficulties.

TALK ABOUT "THRUSTS," NOT PROJECTS

In requesting information, you should emphasize how all the individual pieces of a strategy fit together to support strategic objectives. This emphasis requires managers to provide a clear statement of the key strategic issues that are most important to each operating unit.

The strategic plan should only contain enough details to clarify issues, illustrate the general nature of proposed responses, and provide evidence that there exists an action plan to which the operating managers are prepared to commit if the strategy is accepted.

The specifics of a project are operational details that should not be determined in the planning process. Project management is driven by practical concerns of implementation at the operating unit level.

The finished product will be shorter, containing some real planning meat, rather than being a detailed recitation of projects and operating tactics. The top executives or the board will find it much easier to discern the big-picture issues that confront each unit.

ASSESS THE COSTS OF INACTION

The planning process is an agent for change. It tends to focus on things that are new and different. Like capital budgeting proposals, plans try to focus on how much more competitive or profitable they will make the enterprise. Consequently, plans tend to highlight projects that are very clearly understandable and offer demonstrated incremental improvements that can be expressed in very hard, financial terms.

The defect in this incremental approach is that it implicitly assumes that if you don't make the change, you'll save the investment while simply losing the benefits. In reality, many less tangible projects that are designed to prevent deterioration of the existing core business do not compare well under such analysis. Therefore, if you don't make the investment or decision you not only sacrifice the benefits, but you risk sustaining very high long-term costs.

Operating managers, particularly in the "softer" functions such as marketing and product development, often have a very hard time justifying their ideas against competing projects of a shorter-term, more tangible nature. A narrow, financially oriented planning process probably won't reflect subtle external threats. Such an approach would favor a major capital investment in efficient buggy-whip machines, rather than suggest spending money on a marketing study of the impact of the horseless carriage.

A healthy dose of "zero base" thinking is the only antidote, in which a constructively skeptical analysis of the basic operating assumptions and economics of the existing business is continuously performed. This usually does not fit well into a formal planning process, and is another task better suited to off-line, face-to-face discussions with managers who can trust that the results will be discreetly and constructively employed.

GETTING BACK TO BASICS

Planners can serve as a catalyst to help firms develop ideas that will help them function more effectively. Planners basically nurture new ideas: they pose them to other managers, encourage their discussion, analyze and research them, integrate them into the larger planning framework, and make sure they get included in both formal and informal planning processes.

The planning process is therefore a means toward an end: the deliberate development of coordinated action in responding to anticipated threats and opportunities. Planning will be seen as useful for the overall organization as well as for every manager in their ongoing efforts to be more effective.

The best way to overcome the adverse side-effects of a formal planning process is to strengthen the informal planning processes that precede and support it.

In the interests of good planning, the chief planner should make a strong effort to communicate regularly with the operating managers, the customers, and the competitors. The ongoing informal dialogue with these people can be actually far more important to the planning effort than the formal planning process.

CHAPTER

— 16 —

BUILDING THE STRATEGIC ORGANIZATION: CREATING AND SUSTAINING STRATEGIC THINKING

∎

□

HOW TO AVOID BEING STRAIGHTJACKETED BY YOUR MANAGERS' FRAMES OF REFERENCE

PAUL SHRIVASTAVA

The "common knowledge," or collective assumptions, that you and your associates share about your business heavily influences the way you develop your corporate strategies. This reading will help you identify (and, if necessary, modify) your managers' collective assumptions so you can use their biases to help liberate, rather than severely restrict, your strategy analysis and strategy formulation efforts.

IDENTIFYING UNDERLYING ASSUMPTIONS

"Managerial assumptions" are simply the deep-rooted, unquestioned, taken-for-granted knowledge that managers share about their organization and its environment. For example, one of your assumptions might be that your competitors will not introduce a major new product within the next year, or you might be assuming that no changes in government regulations will affect your

Strategic Planning Management, June and August, 1983; Commerce Communications, Inc.

business in the near future. Your assumptions, therefore, represent mental constraints within which you formulate strategy.

Individuals' assumptions often become broadly shared among managers through processes of socialization, indoctrination, training, and organizational learning. These shared assumptions form a collective world view that can be thought of as an "organizational frame of reference."

To identify the assumptions that define your firm's frame of reference, you need to assess four different areas:

1. **What kind of information does the firm value?** Many companies exhibit a distinct preference for analysis in either numbers or words. While some firms seek to quantify all decision alternatives and performance measures, companies at the other extreme prefer to focus primarily on qualitative information, specifying problems and possible solutions in subjective terms.

2. **What cause-effect relationships do you assume exist?** You use your assumptions about cause-effect relationships (sometimes called your "cognitive maps") to make sense out of all the information your firm receives. For example, if you assume that an increase in advertising expenditures will boost sales, you have a way to relate advertising and sales data.

3. **How do you test the validity of decisions?** The tests by which your firm measures the validity of data and decisions reflect the company's view of reality—that is, what the managers feel is "reasonable," given their knowledge of the business.

4. **In what terms do you discuss the business?** Each organization possesses its own language. Special jargon and short-hand phrases are developed to help members to communicate with each other accurately and quickly. By examining the way ideas are expressed, you can learn how managers view the business.

In answering the preceding questions, you can begin to identify some of the most basic assumptions that determine the way managers collect, interpret, and use information for strategic decision making. As you start to understand your firm's frame of reference you can then evaluate how it influences your strategy formulation.

HOW THE FRAMES OF REFERENCE AFFECT STRATEGY

An organization's frame of reference can affect strategy formulation in several crucial ways. First, managers tend to see only the problems that lie within the scope of the reference frame, while they largely ignore other issues. A firm preoccupied by the threat of its current competitors, for example, may be unaware of the imminent arrival of new entrants.

Second, the frame of reference will bias the selection and interpretation of information used in strategic decision making. Often, one functional area, department, or group of managers dominates the rest of the organization, and their biases influence the way issues are analyzed. For example, if most of the top managers have marketing backgrounds, they will tend to focus on marketing information, setting objectives in terms of market shares, sales targets, and advertising budgets, while placing less emphasis on finance, production, and personnel issues. If strategies are narrowly conceived around one functional area, they are far more likely to fail.

Third, the dominant frame of reference in an organization will also affect how the top management team and other groups in the organization are formed. Managers often choose to work with people who share similar views. As a result, dangerously homogeneous management teams frequently bring a far too-limited perspective to analysis of strategic problems and opportunities.

Finally, if an organization gets too entrenched in its traditional views, it may not be able to respond to changes as quickly as it should. Even when companies detect changes in the market or environment, they may suppress important debate about these changes if the new developments don't fit conveniently into the traditional frame of reference. As a result, the managers reach an uninformed consensus on strategic issues.

Organizational frames of reference vary widely across companies. Although every firm has a unique frame of reference, empirical studies have identified a few distinct categories. Basically, there are four types of frames of reference (Table 16-1):

1. professional
2. political
3. entrepreneurial, and
4. bureaucratic

It is important to note that any single organization will reflect various elements of each of the four types. Each frame of reference is best suited for some specific purposes. Also, each frame of reference has its own limitations and benefits.

1. THE PROFESSIONAL FRAME OF REFERENCE

In many ways, the professional frame of reference is the optimal one for effective strategic planning. This view favors both objective data (i.e., hard numbers) *and* subjective information. The firm encourages managers to examine their "gut feels" and insights by explicitly identifying and discussing the strategic assumptions they hold.

The managers' understanding of cause-effect relationships (that is, their cognitive maps) is based on results of analysis. Decision makers conduct formal written analyses, pulling together available quantitative and qualitative

TABLE 16-1 Frames of Reference

Questions	Professional	Political	Entrepreneurial	Bureaucratic
Who were the decision makers?	Experts	Emergent groups	Single manager	Several hierarchical levels
What type of data did they use?	Scientific, objective/subjective	Subjective	Subjective	Objective
How was the data generated?	Research studies	Personal contacts and opinions	Personal opinions	Specified procedures and rules
How was it validated?	Scientific testing	Based on its usefulness to support decision	Gutfeel	Specified procedures and rules
How was the data analyzed?	Computationally, judgementally	Bargaining	Intuitively	Computationally
What kind of language was used?	Jargon	Formal, but informal within the group	Personal, informal	Official jargon

information. They draw upon the analytical frameworks used in many areas (accounting, finance, marketing, operations, planning, etc.). Information and decisions are verified by using "reality tests" that asess the extent and rigor of analysis, empirical tests, and experimentation.

The professional frame of reference tends to promote a long-range perspective on organizational problem-solving through the use of computational analysis and sophisticated information systems. Such companies typically employ highly skilled personnel who have professional training in specialized areas (MBAs, CPAs, etc.). These managers communicate by using professional jargon that is widely understood and commonly used in decision making.

2. THE POLITICAL FRAME OF REFERENCE

Companies that have a political frame of reference prefer qualitative information and subjective interpretation of numerical data. Managers base their understanding of cause-effect relationships on their gut feel more than on any analytically determined basis. The way they interpret information is highly partisan, predicated mainly on political expediency (such as an individual's own self interest).

Two types of tests are used to validate information. First, each interest group that has a stake in the decision evaluates the information for its usefulness in supporting its position. Second, if the information is found useful, it is accepted and legitimized by anchoring it in broadly shared organizational norms.

Strategy is formulated in this political setting through bargaining among dominant stakeholder groups. Each group is pursuing its own private interests, even if it is at the expense of organizational goals. Managers form coalitions around strategic issues, and interact in both formal and informal decision-making situations to negotiate a mutually acceptable strategy.

A COMPARATIVE EXAMPLE

To give you a clearer idea of the distinction between professional and political frames of reference, let us consider how an actual decision was handled by companies manifesting the two different views. In a recent study, I examined how some firms approached the process of buying a new computer system. Although two of these companies were similar in size and in their history of computer usage, the firm with the political frame of reference behaved very differently from the one with a professional perspective.

The managers with the political outlook treated the decision as an opportunity for renegotiating resource allocations between departments. The EDP/MIS department took the lead by first developing a proposal justifying a very large computer system that would enhance its own power. Then they formed a coalition with the marketing and production planning groups, after promising to develop a special forecasting package for marketing and an inventory control package for production.

They saw their goal as being to identify the computer system that would provide the lowest cost/performance ratio. Then they used a technical analysis to justify investing in a multi-million dollar mainframe computer. After the system was bought, it took them two years to develop the necessary software and begin to implement it. Even by the end of the third year, the system was still being operated at less than 60% of its capacity.

On the other hand, the company with the professional frame of reference began its analysis by identifying the firm's information requirements. After completing a detailed analysis of systems feasibility as well as information needs, the management widely circulated the findings among departments and the corporate planning group. Then they formed a committee of the in-house "experts" (including departmental representatives in addition to the personnel involved with the purchasing and financing) to develop an overall strategy for computerization and an implementation plan.

The committee considered all the major alternatives: hiring computer time, leasing hardware, and buying hardware and software in various stages. The company decided to start by experimenting with leased equipment and developing the necessary software for its applications before investing in a large distributed data processing network. After two years of experimenting with the new equipment, the firm was able to refine its requirements for the leased system and also identified which new products it wished to purchase.

Although, in the above example, the professional frame of reference led to better results than the political, you should not jump to the conclusion that the political frame of reference is all bad. Individuals' self-interest may very well be congruent with that of the organization. Indeed, a characteristic of decision making is that managers must negotiate and bargain with each other. This usually surfaces many private motives and encourages a vigorous (albeit partisan) analysis of issues.

Implications

This brief example illustrates how the decision process and results can differ sharply, depending on the company's frame of reference in tackling an issue. You, therefore, need to identify and examine whether a professional or political frame of reference tends to dominate decision making in your organization. Answering the following questions will help you do so:

1. What types of data are used?
2. What types of data are preferred by whom?
3. How are data validated?

4. How are data analyzed?

5. What kind of language is used?

THE ENTREPRENEURIAL FRAME OF REFERENCE

Companies with an entrepreneurial frame of reference rely mainly on qualitative and descriptive information generated from personal sources, such as peers, friends, and loyal subordinates. They use simple conceptual schemes and rules-of-thumb to interpret information. Decision alternatives are evaluated almost exclusively by the judgement, intuition, and beliefs of key managers (typically owner-manager or CEO).

The personal standards and subjective concerns of the top manager(s) are unquestioningly adopted by the organization as legitimate guides to action. This frame of reference is often reflected in young organizations that are led by strong personalities. It is also frequently seen in departments or units of larger corporations headed by dominating individuals. Because of the pressures on executive time, these organizations do little formal (written) strategic analysis and are always busy with "fire fighting" or ad hoc decisions.

THE BUREAUCRATIC FRAME OF REFERENCE

In companies with the bureaucratic frame of reference, all strategic decisions follow predetermined rules and operating procedures. These bureaucratic regulations jointly determine the types of information that must be collected and used for decision making, the format in which the information must be collected, and the managers to whom it must be sent.

Decision procedures and criteria to be used for evaluating strategic alternatives are explicitly described in organizational manuals. Usually only "objective," empirically verifiable, well-documented information is considered legitimate. Managers are encouraged to use quantitative decision models and to structure their analysis in explicit sequential steps.

Such frames of reference dominate many large private firms, public sector agencies, and old firms operating in stagnating industries. Bureaucratic systems pervade every aspect of organizational functioning. This "management by form filling" tends to institutionalize objectivity to such an extent that there is little room left for intuition and judgement.

IDENTIFYING YOUR FIRM'S FRAME OF REFERENCE

You have probably already recognized which of these four categories describes your organization or certain units within it. Of course, the pure types of frames of reference are quite rare. In addition, firms can also reflect different frames of reference at different times, or can even reflect more than one approach at the same time (a predominantly bureaucratic firm, for example, may occasionally become highly political as well).

But, it can still be useful for you to understand how elements of the frames of reference affect your firms's decision making. To identify the occurrence and predominance of specific frames of reference in your organization, begin by thinking about several strategic decisions your firm has made in the past couple of years. Then, for each decision, try to answer the questions in the accompanying chart.

CHANGING FRAMES OF REFERENCE

Changing your organizational frame of reference is a slow and arduous task. Any effort aimed at such a change must be supported by top management. It must be initiated by the chief executive himself, or by some other highly respected top level manager. Since most organizational managers are locked into their own frames of reference, they may be unable to objectively analyze them. Hence, it may be useful for you to seek help from outside business associates or consultants in identifying your frame of reference.

In general, you should encourage inside participation and involvement of managers from many departments and hierarchical levels. This participation will help in quickly disseminating new ideas and social norms which are inherent in changing your organization's frame of reference.

Changing the organization's frame of reference demands altering both the set of institutionalized "practices" and the mindset of individuals in the company.

Changing institutionalized practices requires reorganizing the organizational systems and procedures, and replacing current ineffective practices with new and better designed methods. Ineffective practices in this context refer to those organizational procedures which are in conflict with the organizational frame of reference that you are trying to establish. For example, if you are seeking to establish an entrepreneurial frame of reference, detailed rules and regulations, systematic procedures, and well-documented objective information may be too slow and cumbersome and, hence, dysfunctional.

You may want to develop appropriate strategic planning systems, environmental scanning systems, and other decision-support and information systems to match the preferred organizational frame of reference. These systems will vary widely for each frame of reference, from rather loosely structured and informal systems (in the entrepreneurial frame of reference) to highly structured formal systems (in the bureaucratic and professional frame of reference).

For example, you could use SAST (Strategic Assumption Surfacing and Testing) procedures for examining the assumptions that underlie your current strategic planning activities. You could then try to develop alternative plans based on a dialectically opposite set of assumptions.

Another technique you may want to consider involves "organizational learning interventions," which aim at unfreezing the organization's existing theories-in-use, educating organizational members to self-reflective double-loop learning, and establishing a learning system which encourages dialectical reasoning in decision making.

REVITALIZING A BUREAUCRACY: A CASE HISTORY

A case example will help illustrate one way to change the frame of reference in your organization.

A very large and long-established private hospital/health service organization realized that it had such a bureaucratic frame of reference that it had begun to stagnate, and no longer could deliver its services effectively to patients. The trustees and owners realized that they needed to make a dramatic change to revitalize the firm.

The organization got an ideal opportunity to embark upon a frame of reference change effort when the current CEO retired. He was replaced by a young administratively trained physician, who had been with the organization for a few years, and was respected and liked by other staff members. So the new CEO launched a threefold strategy for changing the organization's frame of reference.

His first objective was to discard unnecessary regulations. Each department was asked to review all their major rules (which had accumulated over the past 80 years), and assess each one on three criteria:

- Is the rule in conflict with other existing rules?
- Is the rule anachronistic (outdated) and, hence, not necessary?
- Is the rule in conflict with the organization's primary objective of client-centered service?

As a result, many regulations were dropped, modified, or combined. Over the years, the organization had accumulated a set of rules and regulations that contradicted each other and led to confusion in executing routine activities.

These criteria are commonsensical and generalizable to most organizations. In many business firms, I have found anachronistic rules and procedures which were needed at the time of their institution, but had lost their relevance under current circumstances. You should periodically evaluate the current relevance of even simple rules pertaining to, for example, the circulation of information, report completion and dissemination, access to premises, interaction with customers or suppliers, etc.

The CEO's second objective was to reorganize decision-making practices. The rule-bound, bureaucratic process was replaced by an "active participation" philosophy. All major decisions were now made by committees organized around specific programs, and each project had its own "program champion" (like a product champion) to push for prompt action.

Finally, the CEO communicated a clear message (through news letters, memos, annual reports, committee meetings, posters, and notices) that the organization was adopting a new focus on an innovative client orientation. Slogans expressing this message were prominently displayed and repeated among managers. Top management supported this cultural renewal by constantly reminding their staff members of the client orientation.

This three-fold effort was supported by an active recruitment and training program. Consequently, the organization was eventually successful in changing its frame of reference from a bureaucratic to a professional one.

CONCLUSION

The issues and problems we've examined are widespread among organizations today. Perhaps your central challenge as a manager in the 1980s is to make your organization a self-reflective entity, one that constantly questions and evaluates its own assumptions and thus avoids getting straightjacketed by them. Self-reflectiveness is critical for promoting innovative behavior in your organization. If innovativeness is important to you, you will find the time-consuming task of assessing and changing your organization's frame of reference rewarding.

□

TECHNIQUES FOR IMAGINATIVE STRATEGIC THINKING
JAMES F. BANDROWSKI

Although creativity should play a central role in business strategy development, most strategic planning texts completely ignore the subject. While creativity plays some part in all aspects of planning, the most logical point for a concentrated dose of imaginative thinking is immediately after situation analysis and just before the final selection of the strategy.

When creativity is mentioned, most people think of brainstorming. Brainstorming involves withholding judgment for a period of time, so that all ideas and points of view can be presented. This unleashes management's imagination because the fear of ridicule is removed. Evaluation of the ideas comes later. This separation of creativity and criticism, which allows both to function more effectively, can be performed with a group or in isolation with one's own

Strategic Planning Management, July/August, 1984; Commerce Communications, Inc.

thoughts. However, brainstorming does nothing more than liberate the creativity that already resides in the management team. And that may not be enough in these tough times of strategy development.

How can you help management to be even more creative? The answer is: Creative Planning Techniques. Here are 20 techniques strategic planners can use, grouped in the three generic ways in which top executives give birth to strategic ideas: insights, leaps, and connections.

INSIGHTS: UNDERSTANDING THE STRATEGIC SITUATION

Once the strategic fact base for a business has been developed (analyses of the competition, markets, the general environment, technologies, manufacturing, financials, etc.), one or more of the following techniques can be used to get to the heart of the strategic situation. These strategic insight techniques are based on two principles: (1) breaking the problem down into its solvable component parts (much like market segmentation), and (2) using varying degrees of *negative* thinking to sort the facts from the fluff.

1. *Company blocks.* List all the obstacles that prevent your company from achieving a specific objective. (If your company is attaining its goals, list the impediments that keep it from becoming spectacularly successful.)

   Federal banking laws, for example, prevent banks from selling securities and other services. To overcome this block, many banks are making regulatory end runs by renting space in their lobbies to insurance companies, investment brokers, and real estate companies.

2. *Break tradition.* The essence of this technique is to challenge each and every tradition under which your company or industry currently operates.

   IBM's handling of the development and introduction of the Personal Computer is an excellent illustration. IBM set up a separate venture group, purchased components from the outside, and used distributor based sales channels, just to name a few breaks from the company's traditional policies.

3. *Pet peeves.* List every complaint made by your company's management, customers, retailers, distributors, salespersons, reps, suppliers, etc. Each pet peeve, real or perceived, represents a symptom of a need.

   An example of an outstanding product success that responded to a common complaint—the bad aftertaste of saccharin—is G.D. Searle's Nutrasweet. The aspartame-based product accounted for 25% of the company's sales in 1983, just one year after its introduction.

4. *Issues and challenges.* The purpose here is to compile all areas in the company that need decisions, ideas, or answers to questions. This is more of a problem-finding exercise than a problem-solving one. But it provides the kindling for further discussion. Also, it insures that the planning effort focuses on the high priority areas facing the company.

5. *Sales sequence.* The purpose of this technique is to fragment your customer's purchase decision into its components. Then, ideas for improving volume and profit can be focused on each critical step of the decision-making process.

   Most consumers, for example, go through seven distinctive steps in the process of buying an expensive item: (1) determine need, (2) specify features, (3) look for advertisements, (4) decide brand, (5) decide price, (6) choose store, and (7) make purchase. A retailer or manufacturer that can assist the consumer with more of these steps than its competitors stands a better chance of getting the consumer's dollar. The sales sequence for industrial products operates much in the same way.

6. *Trends and events.* Prepare a master list of all developments and isolated events occurring in or tangential to your industry that could impact the business. This list could uncover potential threats as well as fertile areas of opportunity.

   One example of a potential opportunity is the Hispanic market. Hispanics are the fastest growing ethnic group in the U.S., and some demographers say Hispanics will outnumber blacks within 15 years.

7. *Change viewpoints.* Altering the way you look at your strategic situation can offer many insights. Role playing is an effective way to bring about the switch. Which role? Your customer's, of course—the view from the marketplace. Another good role to assume is your competitors'. Other valuable roles could include those of your distributors, retailers, or OEMs. When you are inside the frame, it's difficult to see the picture.

LEAPS: MOVING TOWARD SOLUTIONS

While the above insight-development techniques define and probe the strategic issue or problem from many aspects, "leaps" move you toward the definition of solutions. Rather than trying to improve upon the old, it is often beneficial to start all over and design what could be or what should be. Grapple with how to get there later during the judgment step of the planning process (i.e., evaluation of strategic options).

1. *Success formula.* Describe the keys to both success and failure for dealing with each market segment, product line, competitor, etc. Then rank the keys so that the true success formula emerges. This can help you prioritize your strategic programs.

   You must be sure to reassess your success formula from time to time. For example, technological leadership was formerly the most important success factor in microcomputers. While it is still important, marketing ability now ranks number one.

2. *Year 2000.* The purpose here is to have your company's management team describe the industry far into the future. Ask them to visualize the industry as specifically as possible. The value is not in trying to transmute your management into futurologists, but in stretching their minds beyond the constraints of today. Many thoughts will be of little use, but some ideas usually turn out to be not so ridiculous, perhaps even brilliant.

   One such vision is that of Seiyu, a large Japanese food retailer that built a supermarket operated almost entirely by robots. Twelve robot systems monitor the parking lot, slice meats, sort foods, and staff a vertical warehouse. Since the supermarket's opening in October 1983, operations have reportedly "run without a hitch."

3. *Ideal company.* Describe in detail the consummate company in your industry—its organization, market focus, etc. One company president replayed the question as: "If I could start all over again, I'd . . ."

   In banking, the race is on to construct the ideal company—a nationwide one. As federal banking regulations have progressively loosened over the last few years, such large banks as Citicorp, Manufacturers Hanover Corp. and Bank of America have been rapidly expanding across the nation by acquisition.

4. *Ideal product.* Describe in detail what the ideal product (line) might look like. This provocative question can be used with equal success with customers and distributors, as well as with management.

   At Proctor & Gamble, a woman told a market researcher that the ideal detergent would "fly out of the box" into the washing machine. This would be ideal, she explained, because she had problems measuring the powders. This comment opened up a new viewpoint and resulted in P&G's introduction of "Salvo," a successful detergent tablet.

5. *Ideal package.* Similar to the above technique, describe alternative ideal packages for your products.

   In canned foods, the new retort pouch is relatively ideal because of its light weight, flexible nature, and supposed better quality than canned foods. In juices and drinks, aseptic boxes such as "Combiblocs," "Tetrapaks," and "Composite Cans" are ideal because they are less expensive than cans and bottles. Their other attributes include ease of opening, durability and, most importantly, the improved flavor of the beverages they contain (because of the shorter cooking time for the purposes of sterility).

6. *Ideal service.* How can your product(s) be improved by additional service? Many companies have dramatically enhanced their product support strategies by wrapping services around their offerings.

   Service can be as simple as a bicycle manufacturer including a throw-away wrench in the packet of nuts and bolts, or a drug wholesaler putting a computer in each drug store to enable 24-hour delivery of pharmaceuticals. In both instances, goodwill for the supplier is established by taking care of the customer's needs.

CONNECTIONS: BUILDING BRIDGES

Connections constitute the classic definition of creativity—the bringing together of previously unassociated things to form something worth more than the sum of the parts. The acquisition synergy slogan of "one plus one equals three" is an example. (Unfortunately, where acquisitions are concerned, one plus one sometimes equals one or even less.) Alternatively, connections are a playing off of what already exists, such as concentric expansion into new market segments. Here are some techniques that can inspire connections:

1. *Fill gaps.* Product proliferation aside, product or service opportunities exist frequently *between* two existing opportunities. One excellent example is TWA's Ambassador Class seating, which provides seats between first class and coach in terms of service, seat-size, food quality, and ticket price. Many other airlines are offering their own versions of "business class" seating, indicating that the concept has merit.

2. *Push extremes.* The inverse of filling gaps is looking to the ends of the product or service spectrum to uncover opportunities. How can a service be stripped down to its essentials, thereby offering a cost savings to the customer? Self-service gasoline currently accounts for over 70% of all gasoline sales. At the other extreme, what embellishments can be made to attract the high, and often lucrative, end of the market? American Express' new "Platinum Card," with an annual fee of $250, is targeted at affluentials who have needs in excess of American Express' upscale "Gold Card" introduced in 1966.

3. *Opposites.* Sometimes thinking in terms of the opposite of what exists opens opportunities. This is a particularly good technique for forcing fresh viewpoints (see Insights).

   Phillip Morris' recent introduction of "Players" cigarettes is one such success story. Packaged in a black box, in contrast to the normal white toned cigarette boxes, Players is promoted for active athletic people with advertisements in such magazines as *Tennis* (a contradiction in itself).

4. *Old ideas.* Try resurrecting ideas that were successes at one time, but lost their luster due to changing demands.

   Most of the time a new twist is needed, but sometimes old ideas can be recycled, as food retailers recently did with bulk food bins. The market for bulk foods exploded in 1983, based on the consumers' desire for specific quantities, their dissatisfaction with packaged products, and the natural food phenomenon. However, bulk foods may possess more elements of a fad than a bona fide trend.

5. *Rejected ideas.* Reevaluating previously rejected ideas is another great source of options. Frequently, a good idea fails because the timing wasn't right ("It was ahead of its time"), it was poorly researched, it was improperly implemented, or it was rejected due to political reasons, such as the "not invented here" (NIH) syndrome.

   Complementary metal oxide semiconductors (CMOS) serve as an example. More than a decade ago, most U.S. firms rejected them in favor of negative metal oxide semiconductors (NMOS) because NMOS were faster and more economical. It took the Japanese and a number of new Silicon Valley companies to eliminate the drawbacks of CMOS and to exploit their strengths—low power consumption, immunity to electromagnetic interference (EMI), and the ability to operate over a wide temperature range. This year, CMOS chips will account for 10% of the $15 billion sales of the world's semiconductor markets, and their share is rapidly increasing.

6. *Collect ideas.* You may find it surprisingly easy to locate useful ideas. Many good ideas are sitting out there asking to be gleaned. A division head of a major high-tech company stated in a speech: "We have a philosophy of borrowing ideas from anyone inside the company (other divisions) or outside of it. Entrepreneurs don't have the NIH problem. We think this is very important." Researchers in McDonald's constantly scan grocery store shelves and new cookbooks for ideas.

7. *Apply concepts.* The strategic planner with wide industry exposure can make a major impact with this last technique. Try applying viable business approaches from other industries to your company. Many times these approaches need to be adapted to your specific situation, but the essence is the same.

   Apple Computer hired John Sculley from Pepsico to inject a consumer marketing culture into the computer company. Apple is spending $20 million in advertising to introduce the IIc. The final game score is not in, but on the day of its debut, Apple took orders for 50,000 IIc machines.

Each of the techniques discussed above can help you to overcome "blinders" that may exist in your organization. Unfortunately, in all too many organizations, these "blinders" are never exposed, yet they shape strategic decisions in multiple ways.

BENEFITS AND CAUTIONS

The value of having many creative strategic planning techniques is that each provides a slightly different entry into the problem. As a result, many more ideas can be developed, compared with the use of just conventional brainstorming. Also, different managers relate to different modes of thinking. Being able to offer a variety of modes increases the chances that each member of the company's management team will make a creative contribution.

By emphasizing the need for increased creativity in planning, this article in no way denigrates the other planning disciplines—comprehensive market, competitor, and technology analysis; tough evaluation of final options; contingency planning; action planning; and monitoring of the roll out. All of these are essential for a productive planning effort. It is the union of creativity and hardnosed evaluation and planning that should be the planner's ultimate objective.

☐

SCENARIOS: A MEANS TO AVOIDING STRATEGIC "GROUPTHINK"

SAMUEL M. FELTON, ROBERT E. KELLEY, AND IAN H. WILSON

A common lament among many senior executives is that something has gone wrong with their strategic planning process. The essence of their concern centers around their increasing difficulty in coming to grips with the uncertainty inherent in the future. Yet strategic decision making unavoidably must confront the challenge of understanding and anticipating future events and trends, if it is to contribute to improving organizational performance.

This article contends that a major reason why strategic analysis so often does not lead to real insight may be due to "Groupthink" among senior managers. To combat this problem, which we'll describe in depth, we recommend using a method that focuses on consideration of alternative scenarios.

GROUPTHINK: WHAT IS IT?

Groupthink is a term coined by Irving L. Janis in his book, *Groupthink: Psychological Studies of Policy Decisions and Fiascos,* (Houghton Mifflin Co., Boston, 1983). He uses the term to describe the way people in a cohesive "in-group" begin to think, as their desire to reach a consensus overrides their motivation to appraise all realistic alternatives.

According to Janis, "the more amiability and esprit de corps among the policy-making in-group, the greater is the danger that independent critical thinking will be replaced by Groupthink." We have also observed that the higher one goes in an organization, and the more confidential or important the

Strategic Planning Management, July/August, 1983; Commerce Communications, Inc.

issues being discussed are, the more likely that the conditions of Groupthink exist.

THE HAZARDS OF GROUPTHINK: THREE CASES

At first glance, Groupthink may seem to be contributing to a harmonious managerial atmosphere in which agreement on decisions can be reached quickly. But it doesn't take long for Groupthink to result in disaster, as the following three case examples illustrate.

In the first case, the CEO of a large manufacturing company had decided to move into a new product line. He sold the idea to his executive team, who set the wheels in motion. Then, when the engineers and sales representatives began to tell their bosses that the new products were running into design problems and market resistance, the first-line supervisors did not want to obstruct the big boss' pet project. So, rather than displease him and risk their job security, they minimized the bad news and played up the good. This process filtered up the chain of command and led the CEO to believe the project was succeeding—when, in fact, millions of dollars were being lost.

In a second case, an aluminum company's management team convinced its CEO that the energy crisis would force automakers to add more aluminum to cars for greater fuel efficiency. They dismissed the possibility that automakers might return to using lower cost steel, assuming that such a move would be met by disapproval. But not only did automakers return to steel, they made smaller cars and added more plastic. Groupthink led to misreading the market.

In the third case, a firm's marketing VP anticipated the last recession and recommended to the CEO that they base the next year's business plan on sharply reduced demand for the kind of capital equipment the firm made. The CEO rejected the VP's recommendation, saying that the VP's job was to tell the senior management team how they could increase unit volume by at least the 10% level targeted in the firm's long-term strategic plan. The result: the VP left, and now the firm is stuck with a very substantial, high-cost inventory that it can neither move nor afford to carry. It is facing large write-downs and may have to call in its lenders to restructure its debt.

As these cases help indicate, Groupthink can perniciously lead a company astray, while seemingly helping to build a healthy team spirit among top managers.

Strong group norms can unrealistically bolster the group's faith in its own judgment. In time, as the above examples show, the group will misperceive the external environment, especially potential or real threats. These misperceptions will persist because Groupthink does not allow contrary views to emerge. Consequently, the company will make decisions based on faulty logic or incomplete information—which ultimately could be costly or even ruinous.

In Janis' book, he blames Groupthink for contributing to the Bay of Pigs fiasco under President Kennedy, where the politically disastrous decisions were all made by a closely knit, highly intelligent, capable, dedicated group of people.

SCENARIOS: ONE WAY OF HANDLING GROUPTHINK

Groupthink makes it easy to handle uncertainty about the future: it is largely avoided. Since so few executives like to deal with uncertainty or surprises, groupthink can easily become a way of life. Indeed, most managers are exhorted to manage their businesses to avoid surprises.

The process of developing and examining scenarios can force executives to confront uncertainty and the possibility of surprises to consider alternatives (particularly innovative ones), and to make explicit their assumptions about the future. Effective use of scenarios can give those who use them a distinct competitive edge over those who do not. However, the process only succeeds under the direction of strong, confident leadership that is willing to consider even the most dismal scenario if it is a realistic one. This is a critical point.

WHAT ARE SCENARIOS?

Scenarios are narratives of alternative *plausible* futures in which a business may have to operate. Scenarios represent different interpretations of how the interplay between political, economic, technological, and social forces will affect the company's business. The heart of a scenario is an explicit description of how a particular future will develop, which incorporates the set of critical assumptions that show the logic of change.

Scenarios are *not* predictions of the future, for no one scenario is likely to occur exactly as written. But collectively the set of scenarios is intended to cover the "envelope of uncertainty" within which management must make their decisions. This linkage to decisions is critical; otherwise, scenarios are interesting but irrelevant.

Because the scenario process does not force managers to arrive at a consensus on a single view of the future, but rather encourages them to consider alternative possibilities, it minimizes the danger of Groupthink and maximizes the surfacing of diverse views. At the very least, as the following examples illustrate, this process ensures that strategies tested against a set of diverse scenarios have a greater chance of being resilient enough to adapt to the changes they will encounter. At best, new strategic insights can be generated.

SCENARIOS IN ACTION: TWO CASES

Just as we used some case examples to illustrate the dangers of Groupthink, we'd like to offer two cases to demonstrate the effectiveness of using scenarios.

In the first case, the planning team at a major manufacturing corporation was convinced, after the 1973–74 oil crisis, that the demand for electricity would soon revert to its previous pattern of doubling every decade. Their whole planning culture accepted this assumption as an article of faith. But, when they developed a strong set of scenarios, they were forced to admit that the future might be different from the past. Scenarios helped them consider much larger effects on price elasticity (the effect of price on demand), and to recognize that a strategy based on assumptions about greatly increased conservation might prove to be the most resilient one in the long run.

In another case, a diversified manufacturer of industrial products had been relying on one long-term economic forecasting service as a basis for its five-year strategic plan. When economic storm clouds began to gather in the early 1970s, an economist serving on the strategic planning committee began to feel that perhaps the committee shouldn't complacently accept the conventional economic wisdom of the day.

Accordingly, he presented an economic scenario for the next ten years that suggested the possibilities of one or more recessions. He depicted increasingly sharper and wider business cycles, which would be driven more by politics than by conventional economic forces, mounting federal spending, and deficits that would not be matched by productivity gains. He then translated these factors into higher inflation, interest rate peaks, and a stop-and-go approach to monetary policy.

Although, that year, the strategic planning committee continued to base their plan on the conventional forecast, they agreed to track some of the benchmarks suggested by the economist's bleak scenario. As it turned out, some of his early benchmarks were reached within a year, thus confirming his underlying logic. The committee reconvened and, after much debate, accepted the recession scenario as the basis for their planning.

As a result, in examining divisional plans it became clear that some mature, capital-intensive, cyclical businesses would fall quite far off the mark under recessionary conditions. Over a few years, these businesses were divested (one was sold to its own management), and the proceeds were primarily reinvested in a less capital-intensive, higher technology area offering better growth opportunities. Thus, the use of just one scenario contributed significantly to a large and successful corporate restructuring.

We typically advocate the use of an even number of scenarios, with four being used most frequently. Where three are used, there is too much temptation to accept the middle one.

USING SCENARIOS TO IDENTIFY STRATEGIC OPTIONS

Scenarios can also be used to identify and evaluate a range of strategic options. Take the example of a leading grass seed company, whose founder/CEO was dedicated to being "the foremost grass seed company in the U.S." The marketing VP felt that this focus was too restrictive. But he found the CEO unreceptive to recommendations to diversify.

So, the VP developed two scenarios: one describing the firm's most optimistic prospects as a grass seed company, and the other outlining the firm's future as a leading lawn-care company. The status quo scenario would result in an eventual decline in profits, while the lawn-care approach identified a profitable range of related products and services that would offer substantial growth possibilities. This course became of more interest when contrasted to the status quo option and the underlying logic as to why it would eventually lead to a decline in revenues.

After considerable discussion, the firm tested the lawn-care concept and later adopted it as its long-range strategic mission. The use of scenarios had brought a fuzzy picture of the vague future into focus as a realistic sequence of events that could lead to a well-defined market position.

CONCLUSION

Thus, there are several benefits to the use of scenarios in setting or modifying strategic direction. They can lead to an insightful understanding of the range of strategic options that are available at a time when too many companies consider only one. They can help break the insidious grip of Groupthink, where it exits, but only if the CEO is truly willing to prove for "the truth." And they can introduce a needed element of flexibility into the strategic management process, an element that has eluded most companies.

If laid out properly, with appropriate benchmarks, alternative scenarios can provide an early warning system that can alert management to the possibility that a scenario other than the one selected is the one to guide the firm's strategic and tactical plans.

CHAPTER

— 17 —

SUSTAINING THE STRATEGIC ORGANIZATION: IDENTIFYING AND MANAGING ISSUES

■

ISSUES MANAGEMENT: THE ISSUE OF DEFINITION

JOHN MAHON

Organizations today are facing greater and more varied pressures from external groups than ever before. Many of these are involved with environmental concerns. Only one problem can lead to additional public examination and pressure. Witness, for example, the scrutiny that Union Carbide has received since its Bhopal disaster.

These external stakeholders, often operating with a narrowly conceived strategy and goal, may effect changes on an organization without regard to economic consequences. Such challenges to organizations can arise from any sphere of corporate action, but frequently occur in the political and legal arenas.

In response to these challenges, a new function, most generally known as issues management, has arisen within corporations to deal with such external threats and problems. As part of this new function, new techniques have been developed to identify and assess future areas of contention and to determine what positions key stakeholders might take on these problems.

Strategic Planning Management, November, 1986; Commerce Communications, Inc.

Issues management has received a great deal of attention recently both in the popular press and in academic publications and research. The term itself is actually a misnomer as firms and organizations rarely manage issues. They manage and attempt to influence people and other organizations in reacting to issues.

However, issues management is helpful in identifying issues of significance that potentially could arise in the future and have an impact on the organization. Their role is to lay out what the probable stakeholder positions will be on a given issue. Then attempts can be planned to direct stakeholders on an issue to a position of the company's choice.

There are two key themes in this approach:

1. The definition of an issue is critical to success. Success is defined as the achievement of desired organizational outcomes. Defining the issue affects the positioning and involvement of stakeholders.
2. If an issue can be defined and redefined, then it is necessary to determine who is controlling the definition at any given point during the process.

ISSUES AND DEFINITIONS

Before proceeding further, we need to understand what is meant by issues and why definitions of a given issue are so important.

As I define it, an issue is a conflict between at least two clearly identified organizations or groups over the process and/or content of how resources, rewards, and positions will be distributed. A recent tax debate in Congress, attempting to shift the responsibility for tax cuts away from Congress and to the Comptroller's office illustrates this definition. Several different proposals were made and in each case, various stakeholders attempted to alter the balance of support/opposition by redefining the issue in such a way as to better support their position. The same activity is likely to occur with the newest revision of the tax law.

Another example demonstrates that the dynamics of issue management can be complex and volatile. In 1965, Caesar Chavez organized California grape workers into a group to put pressure on farm operators for higher wages. This was not the first strike against the farmers, but it was the first time that the issue was redefined as being not just another labor dispute, but an issue of civil rights. The picture projected was that of a poor group fighting the rich and powerful for basic human dignities.

Figure 17-1 attempts to display the complexity of issue definition, noting key stakeholders and motivations in a given issue management situation. Personal stakes are frequently ignored when a firm or organization enters into a specific issue battle. Some of the participants may be interested in the issue from a deep personal perspective and will not easily compromise or give up

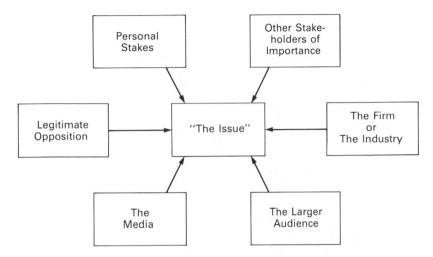

Figure 17-1   The dimensions of issue management in the public arena

even in the face of concrete evidence that clearly refutes their position. The extreme situation is the idealogue, who is willing to die for the position seen as right.

A less extreme position is that taken by those with personal attachments to a product or issue. For example, a firm may decide to make a competitive thrust against another firm's weak product. The attacked firm responds with an unexpected fury and commitment of resources. Further investigation reveals that the chief executive officer of the weaker firm was the champion of the attacked product.

WHO CONTROLS THE DEFINITION?

A position on a given issue should be undertaken with an appreciation of its effects on other stakeholders—both in other arenas and other issues. For example, given Union Carbide's experience with Bhopal, it would be difficult for them to speak credibly to environmentalists and governmental agencies on plant safety and environmental issues.

Also, there is a block called "legitimate opposition." There may also be other parties to an issue that seek their own private ends that have very little to do with the problem at hand; these stakeholders have been called "kibitzers." Finally the role of media in shaping opinions and bringing an issue to a larger audience should be obvious to any manager or company leader.

The definition of "issues" operates at both the real and perceived levels. There are real, substantive issues that an organization must deal with, and there are perceived issues—problems that are less substantive and revolve around misunderstanding, rumor, and misbelief.

Proposed Organizational Action

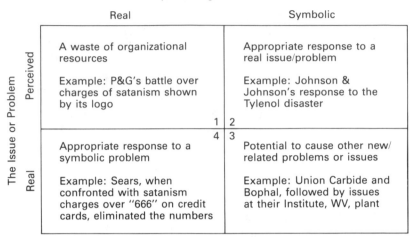

Figure 17-2   Who controls the issue

Figure 17-2 lays out the various types of issues/problems and the possible organization responses. Cell 1 illustrates the case of a perceived problem dealt with in a real fashion. Procter & Gamble's response to the charges that their logo was linked to satanism is an example of an inappropriate response to a problem. P&G spent several years trying to kill the rumor, even resorting to taking to court people who had spread the rumor, all with little to moderate success. All the activity cost P&G time, money, legal staff, and distracted them from other activities. Finally, the firm decided to drop the logo from their products—a difficult decision, but less costly than constantly fighting a rumor.

Contrast the P&G case with Sears, Roebuck's response to similar charges that their credit cards, beginning with the number "666," reflected their link with the Church of Satan (cell 2). Sears promptly decided to eliminate the "666" number and replace it with a different numerical sequence. This ended the rumors at little cost to the firm. This type of response I term symbolic, as it deals with the perceived problem or issue quickly, with little cost or distraction of the firm's resources and efforts.

Cells 3 and 4 deal with real problems. Johnson & Johnson's prompt recall of all Tylenol capsules after several deaths were linked with the product is an example of an organization dealing with a real problem by taking "real" and necessary action. Another example is Boeing's handling of a Japan Air Lines crash in Japan. Boeing quickly admitted that they were at fault in failing to provide adequate door maintenance, and established a fund to help compensate victims and their families. As a consequence, Boeing received favorable recognition and news of the crash quickly disappeared from both the popular media and the airline trade press.

In a final approach (cell 4), an organization can attempt to take symbolic action to deal with real issues. Union Carbide offers an example of this tactic. Warren Anderson, the company's chairman, flew to India shortly after the tragedy at its Bhopal plant and vowed to insure that victims were treated responsibly. Later, Anderson told stockholders: "The corporation did nothing that caused or contributed to the accident and, if it comes to litigation, we will vigorously defend our position." Then, Union Carbide offered a $100 million settlement that would pay the families of the deceased the equivalent of more than 100 years of annual income, using $127 as the annual income for an Indian.

Later, Union Carbide would run into serious gas leaks at its plant in Institute, WV, and be fined the largest amount in history for safety violations. The Institute plant made the same deadly product as Bhopal. Union Carbide's response to the Bhopal incident is termed symbolic because the company followed up its earlier statements with continuous legal action and denial of responsibility, and failed to assess the impact of Bhopal on their U.S. operations, particularly at Institute.

It should be clear that issue management is future-oriented in its ability to aid in the positioning of stakeholders on a given issue. It is also of significant importance in determining how an issue is handled at a given moment, as an awareness of the way in which a given issue can be defined and redefined can provide an organization with an advantage vis-a-vis other stakeholders involved with the issue.

A REDEFINITION THAT FAILED

In 1979, after 10 years of expanding governmental intrusion and regulation, the chemical industry was faced with yet another legislative initiative at the federal level. The legacy of Love Canal led the Carter Administration to propose a new federal fund for the clean-up of toxic wastes—quickly dubbed "Superfund" by the chemical industry. As part of the legislation, it was proposed that the oil and chemical industries bear the major burden of the cost of cleanup efforts through a tax on feedstocks.

The issue came at a key time for the chemical industry as their trade association, the Chemical Manufacturers Assn. (CMA), had recently been revitalized under the new leadership of Robert Roland. In addition, dues and requirements for membership were increased, the legal and technical staff increased in size and capability, and the organization underwent a major shift in attitude. The CMA's general counsel, Edmund Frost, announced: "CMA will bring no frivolous cases and it will not move out of spite. It will not fight for the sake of a fight, but neither will it hesitate when it thinks the general interests of the chemical industry are damaged and there is a chance of winning in court."

William Stover, CMA vice president, also noted that the Superfund legislation represented the "first time that the CMA was used vigorously as the industry's representative and voice in Congress."

In a key move, the administration proposed the same liability rules for Superfund that the oil industry was requesting in its proposal for an oil hazardous spill bill. This action split the natural alliance that would ordinarily exist between the oil and chemical industries on Superfund. The oil industry, with many of its members owning chemical subsidiaries, could not oppose Superfund and be for the oil spill legislation.

The chemical industry responded in numerous ways, one of which was a nearly continuous attempt to redefine the issue. The industry first argued that since the scope of the problem was not known, legislation with incomplete facts would be hasty and ill-conceived.

When that argument failed, the industry then argued on the grounds of equity. Why should today's firms pay for the mistakes of the past? The government should pick up the full cost of any cleanup.

When that argument failed, the CMA argued that the issue was a societal one. All of society benefited from the advances in quality of life made possible by chemicals; therefore, all society should pay for correcting the problem. In short, the federal government should pick up the full costs and not require an industry contribution.

Finally, the industry argued that the issue was not hazardous waste sites, but *abandoned* or *orphaned* hazardous waste sites—those for which no owner or responsible party could be found. In that instance, the industry would help contribute to the fund, but the overwhelming bulk of funds would come from the federal government. In addition, the number of abandoned or orphaned sites was far smaller than those encompassed by the Administration's broader bill. This issue redefinition also failed.

The industry made several attempts to redefine the issue and offered symbolic responses that were inappropriate to the situation. Love Canal and other hazardous waste sites had frightened the public at large, and the media kept up constant pressure and attention. Throughout the debate, the EPA and the Administration maintained control of the issue definition. The legislation passed in 1980.

A MISSED OPPORTUNITY

On Sunday, Sept. 21, 1980, Procter & Gamble convened a special task force in the office of chief executive officer Edward G. Harness to decide the fate of Rely tampons. The Rely tampon had been associated with toxic shock syndrome in menstruating women; in some cases, the syndrome caused death. The issue was a particularly painful one for P&G because Rely marked its first entrance into the feminine hygiene products market. In addition, the situation called into question P&G's strengths in research and development, marketing, and consumer contact.

Rely's development had begun in the 1950s with the goal of producing a superior product in terms of safety, price, and absorbency. It was finally introduced into test markets in 1974. Harkness rose to the top management ranks at P&G partly because of his leadership efforts in the development of Rely.

In 1980, medical data began to accumulate concerning a new disease, toxic shock syndrome. Although cases were reported in men, women, and children, the great majority of the cases seemed to involve menstruating women. The Centers for Disease Control began receiving reports about possible links between toxic shock and tampon usage and asked for information from tampon manufacturers about their products. Mounting data seemed to support the link between toxic shock and Rely, and in August 1980 the first lawsuits were filed against P&G. In September, the Centers for Disease Control summoned P&G officials to Washington and gave the firm a week to prove Rely's safety; otherwise, a recall would be required.

During this entire period, the Food & Drug Administration kept up intense media pressure on P&G. As noted by Wayne Pines, a public affairs officer for the FDA: "Throughout the series of events, we made sure the press was notified so as to keep the story alive. We wanted to saturate the market with information on Rely. We deliberately delayed issuing press releases for a day to maximize media impact. There was quite a concerted and deliberate effort to keep a steady flow of information before the public."

As a consequence of both the data and the media pressure, P&G signed a consent decree on Sept. 26 and had all the product recalled by Oct. 13. The way in which P&G handled the recall earned them praise from all quarters. In addition, P&G has put up substantial sums of money for research into toxic shock syndrome.

Rely was the first product recall in P&G's history. Note the personal stakes involved in this issue for Harkness and for P&G. For Harkness, not only would he preside over the first recall in P&G's history, but he also was deeply involved in the development of feminine hygiene products. For P&G, the recall raised questions both about the company's marketing prowess and about its skills in staying close to their customers.

The handling of this issue is termed a missed opportunity because P&G lost control of the issue early on to the media and the FDA, at the expense of an issue definition that would not only benefit P&G, but tampon users as well. Throughout the situation, P&G's product showed apparently higher links with toxic shock than those products of its competitors. However, P&G made only a super-absorbent tampon while its competitors had full lines of tampon products. When Rely was withdrawn from the market, the incidence of toxic shock related to competitors' products shot up by as much as 400%.

More research has now indicated that the problem was not with Rely, per se, but with super-absorbent tampons in general. During the course of the toxic shock problem, the issue was defined as Rely causes toxic shock, whereas the better and more accurate issue would be super-absorbent tampons cause the disease.

P&G was never able to seize control of the issue and redefine it more broadly and accurately. As a consequence, Rely became closely associated with toxic shock, while the problem continued with other super-absorbent tampons. It was not until April 1985 that Tambrands and Playtex stopped selling tampons that were linked with toxic shock.

SUCCESSFUL REDEFINITION

In the summer of 1982, a tumultuous conflict over containing health care costs faced the Massachusetts Senate. The issue pitted the state's hospitals, Blue Cross, and commercial insurance companies against one another. Also involved in the conflict were the Massachusetts Business Roundtable, the elderly, the Massachusetts Medical Society, and the state Rate Setting Commission. The outcome would determine billions in health care expenditures, and have a major impact on the state's economic climate.

Health care in Massachusetts has always been big business. In 1980, total expenditures were $7.5 billion, and amounted to nearly 12% of the state's gross product. Concern mounted, however, over the rapid rise in the cost of health care, the length of stay in the hospital, and the number of hospital beds per employee.

The Massachusetts Legislature had been dominated by Democrats for the previous 20 years. Concerned with the issue, Senate Majority Leader Dan Foley decided to introduce legislation to control health care costs and to introduce more competitiveness in hospital insurance costs.

Foley, as the heir apparent to the Senate presidency, was not someone to be taken lightly, and he diligently went around to his colleagues and solicited their support for his proposed legislation. The proposal would have a severe impact on Blue Cross. It would eliminate the rate differential they had over the commercial insurers, put pressure on the whole system (hospitals and insurers) to control costs, and significantly beef up the powers of the Rate Setting Commission.

Blue Cross realized the strong support that existed for controlling health care costs across the range of key stakeholders—business, government, and society at large. Yet the Foley bill was viewed as a disaster for the organization. The problem was how to oppose the legislation, the Democratic leadership, and other major business interests without alienating them and the citizens of Massachusetts.

After careful consideration of the impact of the legislation, Blue Cross realized that it would force cuts in service or premiums for the Medex program. Medex was the subsidies provided from operations for the elderly, small businesses, and individuals. Over 300,000 elderly received subsidized services from Blue Cross in Massachusetts, and the organization had complete computer records on each of these individuals.

Within a week, Blue Cross had divided up its elderly subscribers into the 40 state Senate districts and began to telephone each one, telling them of the impact of the legislation on their rates and services, and providing them with the name and address of their State Senator. In less than a week, Senators who had made commitments to Foley offered their apologies and withdrew their support for the bill. The legislation died.

What had Blue Cross done? Even after the legislation had been placed on the legislative agenda with strong support, Blue Cross had adroitly redefined the issue from health care cost containment to erosion of the benefits for the elderly. The redefinition and energizing of an active and vocal set of stakeholders effectively killed the bill. Blue Cross seized control of the issue definition from Foley and his supporters to the organization's own direct benefit.

ISSUES MANAGEMENT: TWO APPROACHES
LIAM FAHEY

Issues management is now in vogue in large U.S. corporations. Many firms now have "issues managers" and some firms possess well-staffed issues management departments or units. An Issues Management Association, with a membership that exceeds over 500 individuals, has sprung into being in the last three years.

Issues management as a management discipline or area of expertise is still clearly in search of its own identity. This is evidenced in the two quite distinct approaches to issues management that have evolved. For shorthand purposes, we shall label these the conventional approach and the strategic management approach.

THE CONVENTIONAL APPROACH

What might be referred to as the conventional approach to issues management has a number of characteristics:

- Issues management falls within the domain of public policy or public affairs management.

Strategic Planning Management, November, 1986; Commerce Communications, Inc.

- Issues typically have a public policy/public affairs orientation or flavor.
- The operative definition of issues is any trend, event, controversy, or public policy development that might affect the corporation.

The dominant emphasis in this approach to issues management is the anticipation of impacts upon the organization that originate in the public sector; that is, the social/political/regulatory/judicial milieu, and their management to the benefit of the corporation. This may require active involvement in the public policy process, both within and outside the legislative arena.

However, this conventional issues management model tends to downplay the importance of identifying emerging issues. Perhaps the major reason why issue identification typically receives such short shrift is that conventional issues managers fall back on the notion that the legislative or public policy process is reasonably predictable.

THE STRATEGIC MANAGEMENT APPROACH

A much different approach to issues management has evolved in a small number of companies: the strategic management approach.

This approach to issues management is typified by the following characteristics:

- Issues management is typically the responsibility of senior line management or strategic planning personnel. It is no longer the preserve of the public policy or public affairs department.
- A much broader conception of issues is evident. Issues may be organization or industry specific. They are no longer primarily sourced in the public policy domain.
- The process of issues identification is deemed of much greater importance.

A central theme in this perspective on issues management is that challenges to the company's strategies, plans, and assumptions may emanate from changes external or internal to the organization. Issues management is thus seen as a means to anticipate and manage these challenges.

ISSUE IDENTIFICATION

Issue identification lies at the heart of the strategic management approach to issues management. The challenge, however, is to identify issues before they have crystallized and become manifestly evident.

Everybody involved in issues management recognizes that issue identification is not an easy task. Indeed, it seems safe to suggest that it is usually the most troublesome analytical aspect of issues management for most organizations. Yet, when it is well executed, the early identification of issues exemplifies the merits of engaging in issues management.

A number of elements combine to make issue identification so difficult:

- Issues are not self-evident. Good issues, that is, issues that truly have significant implications for the corporation and that correctly capture or articulate the problem or opportunity facing the organization, are most frequently the product of considerable reflection and analysis.

- Good issues are a consequence of the integration of what may at first sight appear to be discordant, unrelated, and even contradictory bits and pieces of data. Good issues don't just fall like manna from heaven into the laps of issues managers. Rather, they are the outcome of a critical thought process.

- Different individuals within an organization may recognize issues quite differently. Some may see an issue given only a few bits and pieces of data. Others may require an issue "to be in black-and-white" before they will see it.

ISSUE IDENTIFICATION: AN EXAMPLE

A large manufacturing company had created for itself a rather unenviable environmental pollution record: in a six-year period, it had been charged with a number of violations of laws and regulations pertaining to a dumping of toxic wastes and pollution control. It had been found criminally negligent in two cases.

The firm suddenly found itself on the verge of another major environmental problem involving lengthy litigation and its attendant extensive adverse publicity.

Senior management was aware that their environmental pollution problems constituted an issue (and maybe even a complex of issues), but they were unclear as to what the issue was—they were unable to articulate the issue, at least in a way that was able to attract consensus from most members of the management team.

Various conceptions of the issue were suggested: the organization's inability to adhere to regulatory prescriptions; the harshness and unreasonableness of environmental pollution regulations; the continual changes wrought in regulations; the difficulties experienced by the industry in developing guidelines for its member companies; and the apparent inability of the company to manage environmental pollution, i.e., to preempt the problems rather than continually responding to them under crisis conditions.

As the various members of the management team began to "wallow in the data," that is, to identify what problems had arisen, why they had arisen, what causes seemed to be at work, how the company had handled the problems, what "demands" were placed on the company by outside stakeholders such as the regulatory agencies, local community groups, and other governmental institutions, a number of factors began to emerge:

1. The company had never put together a policy or set of guidelines regarding the management of environmental pollution and control.
2. As a consequence, the company had no standards or criteria by which to judge how well or badly they were managing the whole environmental pollution and control domain.
3. There was no consensus among the management team as to how to manage environmental pollution.

In short, the whole issue of environmental pollution management had not received any management attention or consideration.

As the management team discussed the company's track record in dealing with environmental pollution matters and the problems they were now facing, they gravitated toward the following conception of the issue: What should our company's policies be with regard to environmental pollution control and how do we develop support for these policies across all levels within the organization?

Thus, they determined the real issue resided within the organization rather than outside it. The issue was not changing regulations or the uneven or heavy-handed implementation of regulations. The issue was how the company should manage environmental pollution control—in other words, its own actions or inactions had greatly contributed to the series of problems it had encountered.

Once agreement was reached that the core of the environmental pollution control issue confronting the firm was the absence of strongly supported company policies, the management team entered into a consensus building exercise, with the aid of an outside consultant, to establish a set of acceptable policies. This process took over six months to complete.

The issue as ultimately identified was significantly distinct from the initial perceptions of the management team. The process of issue identification took a number of months and required the contributions of a diverse set of managers.

INTEGRATING ISSUES MANAGEMENT INTO STRATEGIC MANAGEMENT

Conventional and strategic management approaches to issues management are both marked by strengths and weaknesses. But there are a number of ways to integrate the benefits of both approaches, while limiting their deficiencies.

Issues managers and analysts following the conventional approach need to work more closely with line management and others who are intimately involved in the day-to-day running of the business. In some organizations, it is still not uncommon for issues managers to choose to remain "above the fray";

that is, not to participate in day-to-day decision-making activity unless they are asked to do so.

More specifically, conventional issues managers should create opportunities to test "issues" with line management and others in the organization before they commit significant amounts of time to studying and documenting the importance of an issue, its implications for the organization, and possible organizational responses.

Working closely with line management not only helps conventional issues managers to "sell" issues, it also allows them to understand better what makes issues "strategic" from the perspective of operating management. "Strategic" is often merely another label for issues that originate in the industry or competitive and operating domain. Working closely with line management enables conventional issues managers to integrate elements of the strategic management approach into their long-established approach to issues management.

□

APPLICATION IN STRATEGIC MANAGEMENT:
Issues Management: How One Firm Does It
LIAM FAHEY

The previous two readings on issues management do not explicitly deal with the question of how a firm organizes or structures itself to execute issues management. Yet the comprehensiveness and scope of the issues management process suggests that firms could develop many distinct options in the way they might organize to integrate issues management into ongoing organizational decision making.

What follows is how one large single industry firm has structured itself to implement issues management. This approach to managing issues management has evolved over the past five years.

ISSUES MANAGEMENT SUBUNIT

This unit is headed by the Manager of Issues Management. It has a staff of three people; each has the title of issues analyst. The subunit reports directly to the Vice President for Strategic Planning. The principle functions of the issues management subunit are:

Strategic Planning Management, November, 1986; Commerce Communications, Inc.

- To bring to the surface the key changes taking place in the firm's environment. The public policy environment receives the most attention, although the industry itself may sometimes be subjected to intense scrutiny.
- To identify current and potential key issues.
- To develop a preliminary analysis of these issues, with emphasis upon specifying the implications for the firm.
- For those issues identified as important by the steering commitee and the issues management committee, to develop alternative scenarios around different evolutions of the issues and different organizational responses. In this phase of its activities, the subunit may work very closely with others, both inside and outside the firm.

STEERING COMMITTEE

The steering committee is composed of middle-level managers from different functions across the firm. It is sometimes chaired by the Manager of Issues Management. The principle functions of the steering committee are:

- To discuss, review, and assess the issues uncovered by the issues management subunit. In most cases, this discussion leads to many insights pertaining to the issues because of the variety of perspectives brought to bear upon them by committee members.
- To pinpoint organizational implications of those issues considered by the committee as most important.
- To put priorities on the key issues as viewed from the perspective of the committee. This often leads to further refinement of the issues and often requires a more thorough investigation of the consequences of certain issues for the organization.
- To make action recommendations to the issues management commitee on the most important issues. Action recommendations may take many forms:
  - Development of a detailed policy statement
  - Specification of a firm-wide action plan
  - Request for more information (what type of information is required, why, who should be involved in producing or procuring it, etc.)

ISSUES MANAGEMENT COMMITTEE

The issues management committee consists of top-level executives. It includes the CEO and most of the heads of the functional areas. This committee serves as the major planning and control arm of issues management. Its principal functions include:

- To review and refine all the outputs of the steering committee. In particular, it considers in some detail each of the issues denoted as top priority by the steering committee.
- To assess the strategic implications for the firm of all the issues collectively and individually. In this part of its activity, the committee is looking for general patterns in the issues and long-term concerns that should direct the firm's strategic planning efforts.
- To specify strategic options with regard to the key issues and assessment of the most desirable responses. Here, the committee may look to the steering committee for further analysis and/or to other units within the organization.
- To sanction specific action plans—the firm's responses to individual issues or a collection of issues.

There is continuous flow of information, requests, and directives among the three groups. For example, the issues management committee can direct the steering committee and the issues management subunit to explore the nature and implications of an issue that arises within the committee.

Individuals within each level also often participate in the proceedings of the other levels. This interaction may occur formally or informally. For example, the manager of issues management frequently discusses specific issues on an informal basis with members of the issues management committee. This allows him to get a "reading" on key issues from senior management.

□

APPLICATION IN STRATEGIC MANAGEMENT:
Resolve Strategic Issues via
Your Own Planning Conference
LIAM FAHEY

Even if your firm has managed to identify the most critical issues it faces, chances are great that you've wished you had a more effective way of grappling with those issues. Companies are usually much better at *raising* strategic issues than *resolving* them.

An innovative system for tackling strategic issues has been devised by one large multi-business firm, which has found that holding its own internal planning conferences is the best way to evaluate the most critical issues.

Strategic Planning Management, October, 1983; Commerce Communications, Inc.

The following 12 steps used by the corporation for its two- to five-day off-site conferences will offer you guidance in developing your own planning conference.

STEP 1: ASK MANAGERS WHICH ISSUES ARE KEY

All corporate or division managers are invited to recommend an issue to be the focus of a planning conference. The "sponsor" of an issue must document in writing why the issue requires the special attention of a planning conference. The proposal should include a statement of why the issue is of critical importance to the corporation, why it cannot be handled within ongoing strategic planning processes, why multiple perspectives (of individuals, business units, and functional areas) need to be brought to bear upon the issue, and why it (the issue) cannot simply be resolved by division management.

Keep in mind that not only problems but also opportunities can be issues worthy of scrutiny.

STEP 2: SELECT THE ISSUES

The recommended issues are carefully screened by a five-person committee at corporate headquarters, chaired by the corporate director of strategic planning. They seriously consider only the issues that the committee deems of "utmost importance" to the corporation.

To ensure that the issues will be analyzed intensively, the committee authorizes no more than three issues per year for planning conferences. The final choice of issues is approved by senior corporate management.

Conferences typically address one of four general categories of issues:

1. divisional or group conferences for broad strategy reviews, including opportunity or problem analysis;
2. functional area issues, such as production control, purchasing, R&D management;
3. broad topic conferences, which cut across divisional and functional boundaries, such as the introduction of a new technology; and
4. specific issues such as an acquisition.

STEP 3: ASSIGN A CONFERENCE DIRECTOR

Appoint one of the members of the corporate strategic planning department to serve as the director for setting up the conference. These responsibilities include selecting the site, developing the conference agenda, collecting background data, and preparing an "issue report" (i.e., a summary analysis of the issue prior to the planning conference).

STEP 4: COLLECT THE BACKGROUND DATA

A wealth of illuminating information is embedded in all the data and many perspectives on the issues that are strewn within and outside the organization. A team, composed mainly of staff members from the corporate strategic planning department, can collect and organize this data into a preliminary "background report" for use in the planning conference.

The team typically interviews between 30 and 100 managers and other personnel, who are asked which elements of the issue should be featured at the planning conference, and why they consider these elements important. They are also asked to provide any pertinent background information.

When appropriate, the data-collection team also taps sources outside the firm (i.e., suppliers, customers, regulatory agencies, or industry specialists) for their insights.

These background interviews serve an important purpose beyond merely providing a basis for the issue report. They give corporate management a feel for many "soft" but critical aspects of the issue:

- the degree of individuals' commitment to alternatives or solutions;
- the political ramifications of the issue; and
- the skills (analytical or technical) of potential conference participants, as well as their insight into significant cause/effect relationships.

Understanding these forces can lead to better management of issues before, during, and after the planning conference.

STEP 5: PREPARE A PRELIMINARY ISSUE REPORT

Next, the staff draws upon their internal interviews and external research to prepare a report of the issue(s). The report includes basically four items:

1. a brief history of the issue;
2. different definitions or conceptions of the issue;
3. several alternative ways the firm might resolve the issue; and
4. the sequence of events leading to the planning conference.

The report is used by corporate and division management to assess whether the issue is a strategic one, and, if it is, whether it merits being featured in a planning conference. The appraisal of the issue's significance helps guard against one group of divisional managers overplaying an issue's importance.

The report also serves another important function: it communicates broad perspective on the issue to all conference participants. By emphasizing different sides of the issue right from the beginning, the report helps encourage participants to think *strategically* before coming to the planning conference.

In this way, participants will begin to test and critique their own opinions and assumptions, and to raise fundamental questions about the issue, before rushing to their own conclusion prematurely.

STEP 6: SELECT THE CONFERENCE PARTICIPANTS

Corporate and division staff select 20 to 50 participants for the planning conference based on the manager's area of responsibility or issue-related expertise. Each participant reviews a copy of the background report before the conference, and is encouraged to think about the strategic implications of the issue.

STEP 7: FORM ISSUE-ANALYSIS TEAMS

Prior to the planning conference, the corporate strategic planning department and division management divide the participants into three to five teams of seven to ten members. Every effort is made to balance the teams to achieve a cross-section of responsibility levels, functional-area expertise, work locations, and various perspectives on the issue (as perceived through the interview process).

Team selection is critical. It affords an opportunity to manage some of the "soft" inputs. The balance of expertise, power, and opposing viewpoints adds to the probability that a thorough analysis will be performed, and that diverse opinions and perspectives will be aired.

STEP 8: AGREE UPON BACKGROUND ASSUMPTIONS

The first session at the conference should be a 1- to 2½-hour meeting of the entire group to review the purpose(s) of the planning conference, approve the working agenda, and make any additions or corrections to the initial report.

The introductory session is followed by another 1- to 2½-hour session for the full group, this one designed to identify and reach some consensus on what broad environmental and background assumptions underlie the issue. This session surfaces key assumptions about the economic, regulatory, social, and technological climate, as well as the available resources and the beliefs and goals that serve as aids or constraints to resolution of the issue.

By identifying important assumptions early in the conference, it allows the participants to address fundamental points of difference as soon as possible. It also forces teams to discuss alternatives on their explicit merits, while taking into account opposing sets of assumptions.

STEP 9: TEAMS MEET AND PREPARE INTERIM REPORTS

By the end of the first two sessions, the group has outlined a program of action to attack the issue. It consists of a sequence of analytical tasks performed under strict deadlines.

The analytical tasks will obviously vary from issue to issue. In one conference, where the issue revolved around a new market opportunity stemming from a major technological advance by the firm's R&D group, the following sequence of tasks was completed: an appraisal of why the new technology was superior to the old, potential customer acceptance of new technology, likely competitor responses to the new product introduction, possible future developments in this technological area, alternative ways of marketing the new product, and linkages to the firm's current marketing programs.

The teams meet for a series of 1½- to 4-hour sessions for each task. During each time period all the teams are addressing the same aspect of the issue. Between these sessions each team gives a report on their analysis, conclusions, and unresolved questions to the entire group. During these reporting sessions, every team is expected to critique, question, and challenge each other's presentation.

These interim reports are an important part of the process. They force teams to use their time effectively by focusing on a short-term deliverable task. They also help disseminate new information, ideas, or directions for further analysis.

This sharing of information is essential to gaining broad-based understanding and political support for whatever conclusions or recommendations ultimately emanate from the planning conference.

STEP 10: PREPARE AND PRESENT THE FINAL REPORTS

Each team prepares a brief, final, written report and oral presentation on their conclusions. They are asked to indicate their conclusions and recommendations clearly and concisely, using the strongest possible arguments in support of them.

The requirement of having to prepare a written report helps motivate the teams to take the process more seriously, because their conclusions will be going "on record." It also more clearly focuses attention on the areas of disagreement that would be barriers to reaching a final consensus.

STEP 11: A REVIEW BOARD PREPARES FINAL CONCLUSIONS

A review board, consisting of corporate-level executives, assesses the written and oral presentations after questioning or challenging any part of them. It then makes a recommendation for resolving the issue, which is based largely upon the consensus or near-consensus of the teams.

The review board presents a written summary and analysis to the executive(s) responsible for the issue or decision. The executive can accept or reject the board's analysis and recommendations.

If the executive wishes to reject the board's findings, a written critique and rationale for doing so must be developed. A series of meetings between corporate and division management are then held to resolve the differences.

The appraisal and summary by the review board helps crystallize, for those responsible for managing the issue, how much support different plans of action or strategies will have within the organization. The review board's conclusions are also a good barometer of the need for further study and analysis of the possible options.

STEP 12: PLAN FOR RESOLVING THE ISSUE

If a specific strategy or program of action for resolving the issue is adopted, it must be integrated into the next strategic and operational (one-year) plan. Action teams are assigned as quickly as possible to help implement the changes needed to resolve the issue.

By organizing planning conferences similar to the ones developed by this corporation, your firm can gain the capability to face and resolve strategic issues squarely rather than merely living in fear of them.

CHAPTER

— 18 —

STRATEGY AND R&D

■

☐

ADAPTING YOUR R&D STRATEGIES
TO THE "PRODUCT LIFE-CYCLE"

H. KURT CHRISTENSEN

When a new type of product emerges in any industry, it evolves through several distinct stages that parallel a life-cycle: from introduction (its birth) through rapid growth and shake-out to maturity and finally decline.

Unlike people, products spend widely varying amounts of time in any one stage of the life-cycle. For example, the semiconductor industry stayed in the rapid growth stage for many years, while the hula hoop industry passed through it in just a few weeks.

In each stage of the life-cycle, firms face a different competitive environment which requires them to adjust their research and development (R&D) strategy. If you understand which phase of the life-cycle a product line has entered, as well as the key R&D issues during that stage, you can identify the firm's critical R&D priorities and assess the logic of its strategic plan.

BIRTH: THE INTRODUCTORY STAGE

This stage begins when a company first introduces a new class of product (such as the first hand-held calculator) to the marketplace, and it lasts until sales begin to increase rapidly.

Most product innovations are market-oriented, resulting from an effort to

Strategic Planning Management, February, 1983; Commerce Communications, Inc.

meet an actual or potential need of customers. However, some developments are more technology-driven; innovations such as the transistor and semiconductor emerged more directly from the R&D laboratory.

During this stage your R&D efforts should focus almost entirely on improving product performance to a level where it will both attract and satisfy the needs of some customers. At this point, products tend to be quite crude (remember how leaky the first ball-point pens were?), and they generally satisfy only a very small segment of the existing market better than the old technology does.

If you introduced a product that used a new technology (such as the electronic calculator), you would face two sets of competitors: those who still use the old technology (such as adding machine makers) and those who are trying to establish a position in the new technology.

It is those other new-technology firms that pose the greatest threat to your product. In this stage, when no dominant product design has yet emerged, model changes will be frequent so production runs should be fairly short. Your firm must stay flexible so it can respond very quickly to competitors' initiatives. For this reason, you must scrupulously monitor all of your competitors' products, strategies and tactics.

During the introductory stage, the firm shouldn't spend time refining the manufacturing process. Because the product's characteristics are changing frequently, it would be uneconomical to purchase specialized manufacturing equipment. By using basically a "job-shop" approach, with general purpose equipment and low production levels, the process will be inefficient but will provide you with the flexibility critical to your competitive survival.

Eventually, one dominant product design will emerge in the industry, and this occurrence will substantially alter your R&D strategy, as well as your manufacturing and marketing methods. This event usually occurs as the product moves from infancy into its "youth"—the rapid-growth stage.

YOUTH: THE RAPID-GROWTH STAGE

This stage begins when sales growth increases rapidly, and it lasts until sales growth slows and excess capacity starts to exist in the industry.

Now that there is a dominant design for the product, your R&D efforts should begin to focus on streamlining the production process. The greater your sales volume, the less feasible and more costly the "job-shop" approach becomes.

At this point, you will probably want to invest in some specialized manufacturing equipment. However, be aware that each piece of specialized equipment you buy, at least to some degree, will lock you into a particular product design. You'll still be able to make some modifications, but they'll become increasingly costly. As you gain efficiency, you'll be giving up some of your flexibility.

If you try to stabilize your firm's design prematurely—before your competitors have standardized theirs—the penalties could be severe. You could find yourself locked into a design that is poorly received by the market. So, before settling on a dominant design and purchasing the specialized equipment to produce it, you must analyze the market with great care.

Once the dominant design has emerged, the rate at which the firm moves to special-purpose equipment depends on economic factors. What rate of return will be generated by a given equipment purchase? How rapidly are your key competitors changing to special-purpose equipment? How rapidly do you have to decrease your costs in order to sell your products competitively?

If you're in a market where firms are producing fast enough to meet the increasing customer demand, it is more likely that price will be a factor in how they compete. To remain competitive in such an environment, you have three choices: (1) reduce your unit cost by investing in more efficient, specialized equipment; (2) find a less price-sensitive niche; or (3) withdraw from the market.

On the other hand, if you're in a market that's growing faster than firms can meet the demand, price-based competition is less likely to develop or will at least be less aggressive. You and your competitors will still have an economic incentive to buy special-purpose equipment; however, in a growing industry, equipment suppliers often develop long backlogs—which may mean delays in delivery of your special-purpose equipment.

During the rapid-growth stage, when R&D efforts are first applied to streamlining the production process, they should also continue to be directed to product development. In fact, your product-R&D costs will probably still exceed your process-R&D costs during this stage. In the rapid-growth phase, even after the basic product design has stabilized, you may need to modify the product *within* its basic design—by improving its quality or adding new features that will extend its attractiveness to new customers.

Although firms hope they can sustain rapid growth as long as possible, market growth will eventually begin to slow and the industry will enter the turbulent shake-out phase.

ADOLESCENCE: THE SHAKE-OUT PHASE

When growth rates begin to slow, you'll probably find over-capacity in the industry. It's a tumultuous time, as price competition heats up, margins erode, and many firms simply can't afford to stay in the market. In fact, the withdrawal of a high percentage of firms from the market in a relatively short period of time is the distinguishing characteristic of the shake-out stage.

In this rugged period you will not only face sharp price cuts but you'll need to consider offering better incentives to distributors and developing more distinctive product features as well.

During shake-out, you need to focus your attention on two R&D issues. First, can your firm improve the product? Coming up with an improved mouse-trap is one of the best ways to hold your own position in the market and persuade customers to make their purchase decision less on the basis of price. You should keep in mind, however, that it is *customers' perceptions of improvement* that count—not what you regard as improvements. If a change won't influence the customer's purchase decision, it's not worth doing.

The second issue concerns how much your R&D should be directed to reducing production costs. This effort becomes more important to the extent that product differentiation opportunities are limited or nonexistent. Companies that have been slow to reduce their production costs during the rapid growth stage are at a real disadvantage during shake-out. They must either make up for lost time or be shaken out.

The survivors fall into two categories: those who have remained competitive in cost and other areas critical for success in the market, and those who have been successful in identifying a less price-sensitive niche and establishing themselves in it.

When sales growth has almost stopped, the product has reached maturity.

ADULTHOOD: THE MATURE STAGE

In maturity, which is usually the longest phase of a product's life, products in the industry tend to become more alike and therefore compete increasingly on the basis of price. Thus, cost reduction continues to be important and process-R&D (to reduce manufacturing costs) continues to have high priority.

On the other hand, in most cases, don't direct much more of your R&D effort to altering your product. It will become increasingly expensive to make major changes, and genuine opportunities for product differentiation will be limited.

Of course, there are some cases where it does pay to differentiate a mature product. If it is really possible to improve your product's quality, features, or style enough to distinguish it significantly from competitors' products, it's generally worth the R&D effort. For example, the U.S. auto manufacturers have been highly successful in constantly developing new styles and accessory options that differentiate their products.

But in allocating your R&D resources wisely, you must ask how feasible it is to change the product further. It may be more desirable to focus on distinguishing your product exclusively by the way it is marketed (such as repositioning the brand or modifying the marketing mix).

During the mature phase, you should watch the environment for the emergence of possible substitutes for your product, particularly as a result of new technologies. For example, many companies now use aluminum, plastic, or fiberglass to make the tin cans and auto parts that were formerly made of steel.

Watch carefully here! When these substitutes are first introduced they may not seem like potential competitors for your product. However, after several years of product improvement and cost reduction, the new technology may result in products that are both cheaper and better. The diesel locomotive was initially considered terribly inefficient and hardly a threat to the steam engine. But it soon became preferable for short hauls, then for commuter-length trips, and finally for all uses.

One of the most common pitfalls in the mature stage, then, is that many firms either overlook or inaccurately assess the potential threats of emerging technologies. This serious problem usually results when firms have slipped into a complacent inertia in managing a mature product, particularly one that has been successful. Also, R&D managers who lack skill in the new technology may also discount its importance.

While more R&D funds may actually be needed to protect a product's position, they might be put to better use developing other products. Therefore, it's particularly difficult to manage R&D efforts during a product's mature phase because you could make a serious mistake by either over- or under-budgeting.

OLD AGE: THE DECLINE STAGE

Many product lines eventually reach a stage where sales will continue to decline over an extended period of time. Once your company decides to withdraw a product from the market, you can immediately stop all related R&D activities.

Even if your company elects to remain in the market, its need for R&D is substantially reduced. There will be virtually no opportunities for significant product modification, and the prospect of continued sales declines hardly make it worthwhile to invest in more efficient equipment—particularly if the industry has already reached overcapacity:

CONCLUSION

In the low-growth environment of the 1980s, effective strategic management of your R&D activity will become increasingly important. By developing and testing your R&D strategy against the key issues in each stage of its life-cycle, you can help ensure that your product not only survives but thrives in the market.

CHAPTER

— 19 —

STRATEGY AND MANUFACTURING

■

□

MAKING OPERATING DECISIONS STRATEGIC

ELWOOD S. BUFFA

Many studies have pointed up embarrassing contrasts between U.S. and Japanese capabilities to produce excellent quality with good productivity at the same time. It is difficult to believe that the Americans cannot do it too, but perhaps we do not incorporate these operating issues into manufacturing strategy in a meaningful way. It seems obvious that the Japanese do consider these dimensions of performance to be important in their manufacturing strategy, for high quality and low cost are important elements in their market strategies.

MAKING OPERATIONS STRATEGIC: THE JIT CAUSE-EFFECT CHAIN

If quality is poor, can it be improved best by increasing the size of the quality control staff, or would an examination of the responsibility for quality be more fruitful? If raw material and in-process inventories are high, ruthless inventory chopping is a common response, but what strategic objectives might achieve inventory reduction that would be permanent?

What kind of worker system would improve the links between productivity, quality, and inventory, in a reenforcing system? If you could improve

Strategic Planning Management, September, 1984; Commerce Communications, Inc.

these links and produce a permanent productivity and quality improvement, would that be of strategic value? The Japanese JIT (Just-In-Time) system at the worker level produces these effects. Gaining insight into how it works illustrates the benefits of thinking strategically about operations.

When the Japanese advantage in producing high-quality manufactured goods at low cost surfaced, we credited their culture and its strong work ethic. Then we looked for the secret in their personnel practices including lifelong employment for about 30% of their employees, training multifunctioned workers, collective decision-making, implicit control mechanisms, supportive government policy, and so on. But finally, we examined what they were actually doing on the factory floor. There is where operations were found to be strategic.

REDUCE LOT SIZES

The economic lot size (EOQ) is simply the number of units produced at one time which balances the annual costs of set-up and inventory. The annual inventory costs (capital tied up in the product, storage costs, and so on) increase linearly as production lot sizes increase, and the annual set-up costs decrease as production lot sizes increase. The sum of the two costs represents a tradeoff between them, and will have a minimum, if annual set-up and inventory costs are equal, defined as the economic lot size. Thus, for a given inventory cost, smaller set-up costs result in a smaller EOQ. In practice, smaller set-up costs justify smaller lot sizes and greater flexibility to changeover from one product to another.

This simple logic has formed the basis for many inventory control methods in both the U.S. and Japan. The difference in practice, however, is that the Japanese do not accept the set-up costs as given. Instead, they expend every possible effort toward reducing the set-up costs through tool designs, quick clamping devices, carefully worked out procedures, and so on.

The Japanese objective is to reduce set-up costs to the point that EOQ = 1 unit. Of course, if EOQ = 1 unit, the immediate and obvious benefits are that in-process inventories are reduced, and the flexibility to change over production from one product to another is maximized. However, reduction in production lot sizes triggers a chain of events involving improved motivation, a focus on "just in time," and finally a focus on scrap and quality control.

ENHANCE MOTIVATIONAL EFFECTS AND FEEDBACK

The "driver" of the entire system begins with a concentrated effort to reduce set-up time leading to a reduction in the production lot size. The immediate benefit of smaller in-process inventories is obvious. But of even greater significance are the motivational effects, and the effect on scrap quality. The reason for the quality improvement is not in any system of quality control; rather it is in the human behavior that results.

If a worker produces a single part and passes it directly to the next worker, the second worker will report a defect almost immediately. On hearing that the part is defective, the first worker is motivated to discover the cause and correct it before large quantities of scrap are produced. The smaller the production lot size, the more immediate will be the discovery of defects. *Each pair of operations in the sequence is closely linked,* and the awareness of the interdependence of the two operations, and particularly the two workers, is enhanced.

If the same part were produced in large lots and placed in storage, to be withdrawn as needed, this linkage is destroyed. When a defective part is discovered it is simply disposed of, perhaps with some grumbling. In many instances we might not even know which worker produced it to provide the feedback to correct future defects. The system takes advantage of one of the simplest principles of learning, that is, knowledge of results. The fast feedback leads to a heightened awareness of what probably caused the defect, producing ideas for controlling defectives in the future.

Three kinds of responses are triggered by the worker's heightened awareness of problems and causes. The workers, their supervisors, and staff become involved in generating ideas for controlling defectives, ideas for improving JIT delivery performance, and additional ideas for further reducing set-up times and therefore lot sizes.

CREATE RESPONSIBILITY EFFECTS

When lots are large, workers are prone to simply dispose of the few defective parts and continue assembling, since there are plenty of good items. The reverse psychology is in effect when lots are small. The close dependency between operations that results from reducing lot sizes places responsibility directly on each worker. A smaller number of defective parts reduces downstream problems immediately. The obvious need to avoid further defectives is apparent, leading naturally to teamwork.

The close linking of workers, and the feeling of responsibility that is engendered, creates committed workers. Committed workers carry their concerns about all aspects of job performance home with them and to social situations that involve coworkers.

WITHDRAW BUFFER INVENTORY

One of the simplest, yet most important, principles of systems is that if something in the environment changes, for example, a change in demand, then something in the system must be allowed to change or vary, in order to compensate.

You cannot change just one thing. Buffer inventories perform this function of absorbing variations in flow rates in production systems.

One of the direct effects of reducing lot sizes for JIT production is lower in-process inventories in the system. But there is another inventory effect resulting from management intervention to withdraw buffer inventories deliberately. We have, in effect, a "hand to mouth" system of supply between operations. The buffer stocks of work in process between stations exist to absorb variations in flow—the larger the variations the more buffer inventory required to insulate each operation in the sequence from the effects of lack of material supply. The Japanese recognize the function of buffer inventories, but deal with it rather differently in practice than is the norm in the U.S.

By systematically removing a portion of the buffer stocks, Japanese managers expose workers to the problems that cause variations in flow. The exposure of these problems provides goals for problem solution. When the problems that caused variation have been solved, Japanese managers remove more of the insulating buffer stock, revealing the next set of problems that cause variations in flow.

The workers are never allowed to become complacent; they are faced with continually perfecting the process. Inventories in the aggregate are reduced, and productivity is improved. This in turn leads to smoother output rates resulting from fewer interruptions due to quality problems, reducing the need for buffer stock. The improved scrap/quality control that results from lot size reductions and JIT production also results in smoother output rates, because there are fewer interruptions in flow than might otherwise occur because of poor quality.

By contrast, U.S. managers often use buffer inventories to solve their problems of flow. Indeed, the function of buffer inventories is to act as an "absorber" of the variations in demand between operations, but at the cost of additional inventories.

THE RESULT: PRODUCTIVITY IMPROVEMENT

The productivity effects of the system are quite pervasive. The close linking between workers producing the heightened awareness of problems and their causes, coupled with management's intervention to reduce buffer inventories, combine to produce the following productivity effects:

- smaller lot size inventories
- smaller buffer inventories
- less scrap
- less direct labor wasted on re-work
- less indirect cost of inventories
- less equipment to handle inventories

- less inventory accounting
- less physical inventory control effect

These productivity improvements result from workers' efforts as a part of a closely linked system. Since most of the system is run by workers and foremen, the costs of administration are low, and managers are freed to deal with strategic issues.

A BYPRODUCT: ENHANCED MARKETING

While the system leads to productivity improvements, the reduction in delays and scrap also improve market response. Production lead times are reduced because of the low cost of changeover, so that marketing can promise better delivery dates, changing the product mix and quantities quickly as demand and forecasts of demand change. Even forecasting is improved because of the shorter lead times.

THE GOAL: TOTAL QUALITY CONTROL

While quality control is obviously involved in the process just described, it is only a part of the Japanese concept of total quality control. All plant personnel are inculcated with the view that scrap/quality control is an end in itself. "Quality at the source" is the slogan. It means that error, if any, should be caught and corrected at the workplace.

This is in contrast to the widespread U.S. practice of inspection by sampling after the lot has been produced. In U.S. practice, quality is controlled by inspectors from a quality control department. But Japanese workers and foremen have the primary responsibility for quality. With quality control as the source, there is fast feedback concerning defects, all resulting in fewer rework labor hours and less material waste, in addition to the other benefits previously discussed.

The key to the Japanese practice is that "the responsibility for quality rests with the makers of the part." The workers and the foremen bear this responsibility rather than a staff department called quality control. A strategic move by U.S. manufacturers would be to transfer primary responsibility for quality from the QC department to production.

MANUFACTURING IN JAPANESE STRATEGY

The constantly repeating cycle of improvement that is such a clear part of Japanese manufacturing strategy "grinds" away at productivity and quality improvement. Obviously they have steep experience curves with which they can couple low margins to obtain initial market positions through aggressive pricing, knowing that they will gain market share and future large total profits with high volume.

The Japanese do not think of the work force, quality control, and inventory control as solely operational decisions. They are an integral part of manufacturing strategy which cannot be implemented without them. Indeed, to make operating decisions independently could easily put them at odds with the central strategy. The approach is to integrate the functions related to on-the-job performance within a largely line organization. The highly developed staff units in the U.S. tend to segment the organization, and disconnect the doers from their responsibilities.

OPERATIONS AS STRATEGY

We in the U.S. have made a distinction between long-term strategic issues and short-term operating issues. There is usually little argument that questions of capacity, process technology, and labor costs have strategic significance. But there tends to be a dismissal of the inventory, quality, and other factory-floor issues, as if "operations" had no long-term importance. At the same time, there is an understanding that quality, cost, and product delivery are important in the basic strategy of the firm. We need to erase that imaginary line, and think of all the issues as potentially being strategic.

Can systems that make a manufacturer more cost and quality competitive be anything but strategic?

□

POSITIONING THE PRODUCTION SYSTEM—A KEY ELEMENT IN MANUFACTURING STRATEGY
ELWOOD S. BUFFA

If production is not made a part of business strategy, then the likelihood of a mismatch between production system and markets is high. This mismatch usually results in conflicts between marketing and production. A firm without a unified strategy that includes the manufacturing function is likely to expect low cost, high quality, product availability, and flexibility/service from its production system, all at the same time.

Firms often act as if they did not realize that you cannot maximize all these dimensions simultaneously—that there are tradeoffs between them. A firm

Strategic Planning Management, July/August, 1984; Commerce Communications, Inc.

that attempts to be "all things" in its production system is likely to compromise all four dimensions of production competence noted above and end up "stuck in the middle," with low margins.

FIRST EXAMINE PRODUCT STRATEGIES

The public tends to focus its attention on high-volume standardized products, but these products do not encompass the full span with which managers must be concerned. At one extreme, we might have custom products especially designed to the specifications and needs of the customer. Examples are job printing, a prototype spacecraft, or many producer goods.

A custom product is not available from inventory because it is one of a kind. The emphasis in the custom product strategy is on uniqueness, dependability of delivery on time, quality, and flexibility to change the production process in accordance with changing customer preferences. Cost or price is a lesser consideration. Part of the business and production strategy is to obtain the high profit margins that typically are available for custom designs.

At the other extreme are highly standardized products. Products of this type are usually available from inventory. They are "off-the-shelf," because each unit is identical and the nature of demand is such that availability and cost are important elements of competitive strategy. There is very little product differentiation, and there is limited variety in the products. The most important managerial concerns for highly standardized products are for dependability of supply and low cost.

Between the extremes of custom design and high standardization of products, there are mixed strategies that are sensitive to variety, some flexibility, moderate cost, and dependability of supply. In these situations, quality of product is an important but not overwhelming criterion. In this middle ground, we have multiple products available, possibly from inventory, or on the basis of order, depending on enterprise strategy and the balance of costs. Also, in the middle ground, some of the products are available in fairly low volume but some, such as automobiles, are available in high volume.

The great majority of products available today are in the middle category. Most consumer products are available from inventory. Most producer goods are available by order and may be subject to some special design modifications to meet individual needs, though the basic designs are quite standard.

The product life cycle concept unifies the range of product strategies. If we look at the possibilities at an instant of time, we see the array of low-volume custom products; low-volume multiple model, partially standardized products; large-volume partially standardized products; and high-volume standardized commodities.

But, if we traced the development of a product, now available in high volume in highly standardized form, from its original introduction, we would find it had gone through phases. These phases are introduction at low volume and custom design, growth in sales during which variety became more limited, maturity during which the product variety is even more limited and it becomes basically a commodity, and finally decline as substitutions become available that may be superior in terms of function, quality, cost, or availability.

BE AWARE OF THE PRODUCTIVE SYSTEM TYPES

The basic managerial strategies adopted for the productive system must be related to the product strategies. Obviously, it would be inappropriate to use a continuous process capable of producing millions of gallons to produce a few gallons of an experimental chemical. Again, you need to think in terms of alternate strategies for the extremes, as well as a middle ground.

1. Process-Focused Systems

A production system for custom products must be flexible. It must have the ability to process according to customers' specifications. For example, an aerospace manufacturer must fabricate special component parts designs. The equipment and personnel must be capable of meeting the individual component specifications, and of assembling the components in the special configurations of the custom product. The nature of the requirements placed on the production system results in intermittent demand for the use of the facilities, and each component flows from one process to the next intermittently. Physical facilities are organized around the nature of processes, and personnel are specialized by generic process type, thus the name process-focused. For example, in a machine shop we might expect to find milling machine departments, lathe departments, drill departments, and so on.

The flow of the item being processed in these systems is dictated by the individual product requirements, so the routes through the production system are variable. Thus, the process-focused system must be flexible, as required by the custom product, and each generic department and its facilities are used intermittently, as needed by the custom orders.

Because attention is on the individual job being manufactured, process-focused systems for custom products are commonly called job shops. But the process-focused concept applies to a much broader spectrum of situations, where flexibility is needed and capacity needs do not justify facilities dedicated entirely to a single product.

2. Product-Focused Systems

By contrast, the nature of the demand on the production system that produces highly standardized products results in continuous use. Also, the material flow may be continuous, as in petroleum refining, or approaches continuous flow, as with automobile fabrication and assembly.

Because of the very high volume requirements of such systems, special processing equipment and special entire producing systems can be justified as a productive system strategy. Processing is adapted completely to the product, thus the name product-focused system. Individual processes are physically arranged in the sequence required and the entire system is integrated for the single purpose, like a giant machine. Under these extreme conditions of very high demand for standardized products, the production process is integrated and makes use of mechanization and automation to achieve standardization and low cost. Inventories of standardized products may be an important element of production as well as marketing strategy.

3. A Middle Ground of Productive Systems

Between the two extremes of intermittent demand (process-focused) and continuous demand (product-focused) systems, there is a middle ground of productive systems that must deal with low volume multiple products, and relatively high-volume multiple products. The low volume multiple product situation usually involves a process-focused system, but products are produced in *batches,* thereby achieving certain economies of scale compared with the job shop system designed to deal with custom products, but the flexibility of the process-focused system is retained.

It is estimated that 50–75% of the parts manufactured in the U.S. today are produced in batches of 50 units or less. It is also worth noting that the Japanese commonly produce a much narrower line of a given product. This policy has an important impact on the system inventories, and on the resultant part costs. The marketing emphasis in U.S. firms on product-line diversity has important implications for cost competitiveness. Coordinating marketing and manufacturing policy in an integrated overall strategy is a necessity.

The high-volume multiple product situation is likely to employ a mixed production strategy that combines both the process-focused and product-focused systems. In manufacturing, it is often true that parts fabrication is organized on a batch-intermittent basis, with final assembly organized on a line or continuous basis. Because parts fabrication output volume may be substantial, but not large enough to justify continuous use of facilities, parts are produced in economical batches. The inventories resulting from batching again provide an important producing strategy. On the other hand, the nature of assembly makes possible continuous lines dedicated to certain products.

WHEN TO PRODUCE TO-STOCK OR TO-ORDER

Now, let us consider only those products that could be produced to-stock; that is, a decision is possible. In such situations, we might decide to produce only to-order for a variety of important reasons, even though it would be possible to produce to-stock. The possible reasons for a to-order policy might be to offer product design flexibility to customers, to minimize the risk associated with carrying inventories, to control quality more closely, and so on.

On the other hand, we might decide to adopt a to-stock policy for the same type of product for good and compelling reasons; for example, to offer better service in terms of availability, to reduce variable costs, and to increase market share by making items available off-the-shelf when customers have the urge to buy.

The choice between a to-order or to-stock inventory policy is not necessarily made by whether or not a product- or process-focused physical system has been adopted. For example, one might think that the auto industry, which has adopted a product-focused system, would certainly be a to-stock producer. But this has not been the case. Therefore, we have the possibility of two types of systems, product- or process-focused, in combination with two possible finished goods inventory policies, to-stock or to-order, as shown in Table 19-1 together with examples. Some types of products, such as electronic components, may occur in more than one classification.

A reason for emphasizing the to-stock/to-order inventory policy, at this point, is that the management systems for planning and controlling production, scheduling, and inventory policy are very different, depending on the positioning decision. A to-stock policy results in each item being indistinguishable from the others, so planning and controls can deal with all like items in the same way.

On the other hand, a to-order policy means that each order must be controlled separately in a much more complex way; we must be able to respond

TABLE 19-1   **Examples of the Two Dimensions of Positioning**

Type of System	Finished Goods Inventory Policy	
	Make To-Stock	Make To-Order
Product-Focused	Product-Focused/To-Stock Office copiers TV sets Calculators Gasoline	Product-Focused/To-Order Construction equipment Buses, trucks Experimental chemicals Textiles Wire and cable Electronic components
Process-Focused	Process-Focused/To-Stock Medical instruments Test equipment Electronic components Some steel products Molded plastic parts Spare parts	Process-Focused/To-Order Machine tools Nuclear pressure vessels Electronic components Space shuttle Ships Construction projects

to individual customers concerning the progress of an order, to quote delivery dates, and to control the progress of each order through the plant.

In practice, the positioning policy allows a combination of both to-stock and to-order operations, because many organizations actually engage in a mixture of product-market situations. Consequently, it is important for managers to realize that even though outputs may appear similar on the surface, very different managerial procedures are usually necessary because of the different policy contexts in which the products are produced.

It is often emphasized that business units need careful definition in relation to chosen strategies. Here we see why this is so important—the nature of the production system should be very different for each of these situations.

HOW TO SELECT JOINT STRATEGIES

When we examine the product demand situation and production system types jointly, it is useful to think of the product volume as the independent variable and the productive system type as the dependent variable, as represented by Figure 19-1.

As the product develops through its life cycle, the productive system goes through a life cycle of its own, from a job shop system (process-focused, to-order) when the product is in its initial stages, through intermediate stages. The intermediate stages are likely to be a process-focused system that produces in batches, but to-order; a process-focused system producing in larger batches to-stock; and a product-focused system that time-shares facilities on a cycling basis, to-stock.

Cycling of a product-focused to-stock system makes possible better facilities utilization, while retaining a degree of flexibility for producing a variety of types and sizes of a product line. In the middle range, it would be common to use combinations of process- and product-focused systems to obtain good facility utilization. The progression culminates in a continuous system (product-focused, to-stock) when the product is demanded in large volume.

In the above discussion, we have therefore identified five distinct variations in the nature of the production system that can be adopted to position the system to match appropriately with the market situation:

1. High-volume, product-focused to-stock systems
2. Large-volume, multiple product to-stock, where the multiple products are cycled on time-shared facilities. Such systems are often mixed product- and process-focused
3. Moderate-volume, process-focused to-order/to-stock, multiple product batch systems
4. Low-volume, process-focused to-order, multiple product batch systems
5. Custom-products, process-focused to-order

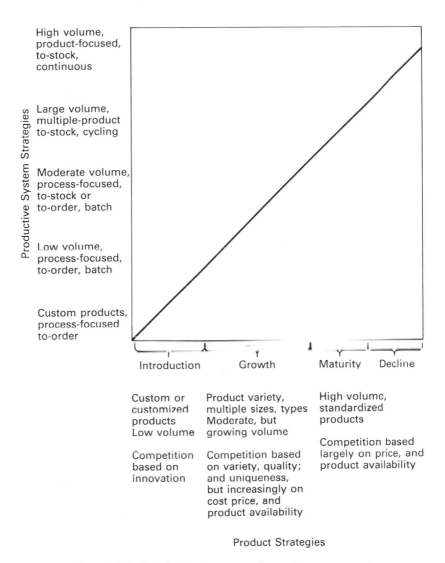

Figure 19-1   Relationship between product and process strategies

These stages of product and production system development are inter-dependent and feed on each other. There is the obvious dependence of the appropriate type of productive system on the volume of product that is sold, and the nature of the market. But in addition, the volume of product sold is dependent in part on costs, product availability, and the price-quality competitive position which is dependent on the use of the appropriate productive system.

But would a firm always follow the strategy implied by the diagonal line of Figure 19-1? As we noted in the previous discussion of productive system types,

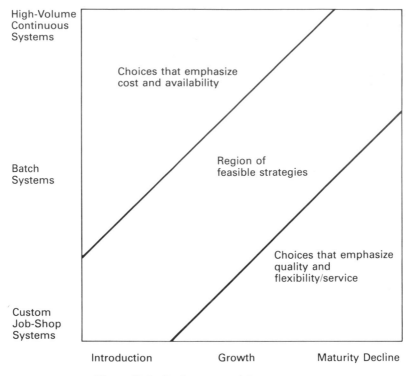

Figure 19-2   Product-process joint strategy map

process-focused systems provide flexibility and are somewhat more adaptable to product variety and to high-quality production.

Thus, where the strategy is focused on providing service, high quality, and meeting customers' individual needs, combinations between product volume and productive system types that are below the line in Figure 19-1 may be more appropriate, probably combined with production "to-order."

On the other hand, if the strategy is focused on price and off-the-shelf availability, combinations above the line in Figure 19-1 may be more appropriate, combined with a production "to-stock" system. Thus, we have a situation where Figure 19-1 may provide a general relationship that should be observed, but actual strategies are better defined by a band or range as shown in Figure 19-2.

POSITIONING IS KEY

While all the elements of manufacturing strategy are important and all need to be woven together to form a coordinated strategy, if the positioning of the system is wrong, the manufacturing strategy will be ineffective. It should be an integral part of the overall business strategy, and include both the system type, and the "to-stock/to-order" decision.

One of the most common mistakes in the positioning strategy is to attempt the production of products with fundamentally different market requirements within the same basic production system. The result is that the match between market requirements and the production system is out of sync for some of the products, and costs may be out of line, quality may not receive the required emphasis, or delivery times may not meet requirements. Another common mistake is the failure to recognize the dynamics of the production process life cycle—to change the basic design of the production system as the product goes through its life cycle.

CHAPTER

— 20 —

STRATEGY AND MARKETING

■

☐

STRATEGY AND MARKETING:
DESIGN AS COMPETITIVE ADVANTAGE

PHILIP KOTLER AND G. ALEXANDER ROTH

A great many industries are characterized by intense service and/or price competition that succeeds only in driving down everyone's profits to an unhealthy level. One of the few hopes companies have to "stand out from the crowd" is to link business strategy and marketing activities more skillfully.

In seeking to integrate strategy and marketing more tightly, many companies are searching for ways to add competitive distinctiveness to their products and images in the hope of protecting or improving their marketing positions. One way companies can "stand out from the crowd," in the form of distinct and sustainable competitive advantages, is to produce superiorly designed products and to effect carefully designed corporate images for their target markets.

Thus, in this article, we want to assert that marketing can make a major contribution to competitive strategy through design, where we use the term design as a shorthand for product design and corporate identity design.

Strategic Planning Management, November/December, 1984; Commerce Communications, Inc.

DESIGN AS COMPETITIVE ADVANTAGE

A few companies stand out for their capacity to forge competitive advantage through superior design, notably IBM in computers, Herman Miller in modern furniture, Olivetti in office machines, and so on.

But most companies lack a "design touch." Their products are prosaically styled, their packaging is unexciting, their information brochures are tedious. Their marketers pay considerable attention to product functioning, pricing, distribution, personal selling, and advertising, and much less attention to product, environment, information, and corporate identity design. Many companies have staff designers or buy design services, but the design often fails to achieve identity in the marketplace.

One only has to look at current U.S. products in many product categories—kitchen appliances, office supplies, air conditioners, bicycles, automobiles, and so on—to acknowledge the lack of good design. Yet its potential rewards are great. Consider the dramatic breakthroughs that some companies have achieved with outstanding design:

- In the stereo equipment market, where several hundred companies battle for market share, the small Danish company of Bang & Olufsen won an important niche in the high end of the market through designing a superbly handsome stereo system noted for its clean lines and heat-sensitive volume controls.
- In the sportscar market, Datsun endeared itself by designing the handsome 240Z. For most buyers before 1976, the 240Z was a dream car at an affordable price, around $4000–$6000. The latest copy is by Mazda, which coupled innovative pricing with the 240Z design, capturing a large share of the sportscar market with its first offering, the RX7.
- In the hosiery market, Hanes achieved a dramatic breakthrough in a mature market by using creative packaging design and modern packaged goods marketing techniques, catapulting the L'eggs division to the position of market leader. The L'eggs boutique (in-store display) used information design effectively, pulling consumers from other stores and brands. Design was a key component in the marketing strategy and created instant product recognition for the brand.

Well-managed, high quality design offers the company several benefits. It can create corporate distinctiveness in an otherwise product and image surfeited marketplace. It can create a personality for a newly launched product so that it stands out from its more prosaic competitors. It can be used to reinvigorate product interest for products in the mature stage of their life cycles. It communicates value to the consumer, makes selection easier, informs, and entertains. Design management can lead to heightened visual impact, greater information efficiency, and considerable consumer satisfaction.

CREATING EFFECTIVE DESIGN

Thus, the objective of design is to create high satisfaction for the target consumers and profits for the enterprise. In order to succeed, the designers seek to creatively blend the major elements of the design mix, namely, performance, quality, durability, appearance, and cost.

These elements can be illustrated in the problem of designing, say, a new toaster.

Performance.   First, the designer must get a clear sense of the functions that the target consumers want in the new product. Here is where marketing research comes in. If target consumers want a toaster that heats up rapidly and cleans easily, then the designer's job is to arrange the features of the toaster in a way that facilitates the achievement of these customer objectives.

Quality.   The designer faces many choices in the quality of materials and workmanship. The materials and workmanship will be visible to the consumers and communicate to them a certain quality level. The designer does not aim for optimal quality, but affordable quality for that target market.

Durability.   Buyers will expect the toaster to perform well over a certain time period, with a minimum number of breakdowns. Durability will be affected by the product's performance and quality characteristics. Many buyers also want some degree of visual durability, in that the product doesn't start looking "old-hat" or "out-of-date" long before its physical wearout.

Appearance.   Many buyers want the product to exhibit a distinctive or pleasing "look." Achieving distinctive style or form is a major way in which designed products, environment, and information can stand out from competition. At the same time, design is much more than style. Some well-styled products fail to satisfy the owners because they are deficient in performance characteristics. Most designers honor the principle that "form follows function." They seek forms that facilitate and enhance the functions of the object, rather than form for its own sake.

Cost.   Designers must work within budget constraints. The final product must carry a price within a certain range (depending on whether it is aimed at the high or low end of the market) and designers must limit themselves to what is possible in this cost range.

Consumers will form an image of the product's design value in relation to its price, and favor those products offering the highest value for the money. Effective design calls for a creative balancing of performance, quality, durability, and appearance variables at a price that the target market can afford.

PRODUCT DESIGN

Product design is a central source of competitive advantage. Yet it often fails to result in competitive advantage because of conflicts among functional groups.

For example, engineers and production people have responsibility for product performance while marketing people often seek changes in styling and features. The result is a battle over the relative role that styling versus technical performance design should play in product development—a battle that has gone on in several industries, most notably in automobiles.

Yet, styling and technical performance design need not be in conflict. Companies can and do design the whole product to serve and please the consumer. Consider the following example:

> John Deere & Co. of Iowa hired John Dreyfuss, a leading product designer, to develop a full line of 19 tractors. The collaboration lasted five years and Dreyfuss' design firm was involved from product concept through production, including supervising the tool and die makers to insure the end result. Dreyfuss designed the prototype tractor to be comfortable and pleasing to the farmer-operator. Through human engineering studies, he determined the best form for the machine so that farmers could manage it easily. Client-sponsored research was one of the first books on human design specifications: *The Measurement of Man*, later used extensively by both the automotive industry and NASA. Dreyfuss also took an approach leading to tractors that had a cohesive visual appearance. John Deere has kept up its philosophy of good design through the years, and commissioned Eero Saarinen to design its corporate headquarters.

Design is also a strong factor in cosmetics, particularly on the packaging side. Jovan, the Chicago based manufacturer, spends as much or more time and money on packaging as on scent development. The interlocking His and Hers perfumes is one example of their work. Jovan is organized to encourage and reward good design work, and the company views design as a fundamental tool of marketing management.

The most exciting recent development in product design is the growing use of Computer Aided Design and Computer Aided Manufacture known as CAD/CAM. The gradual drift to robot manufacturing is resulting in a new breed of managers and product designers who possess computer and engineering skills. Products and their components are being designed to be handled by robot arms rather than human fingers.

The imaginative and successful use of product design by such firms as John Deere, Jovan, and a handful of other companies is gradually spreading the recognition among competitors of the great potentialities of good product design as a marketing tool.

CORPORATE IDENTITY DESIGN

Companies are becoming increasingly conscious of the impact of their corporate image on their sales, profits, and stock prices. IBM is credited with systematically applying the idea of a *corporate identity program* in the United States. Developed in 1957 by Paul Rand, the IBM program's main purpose was to create an image of product excellence, complete corporate trustworthiness, and personalized service. It also specified use of good architecture, product design, and brochures to reinforce the corporate image.

Whether or not the corporation has a corporate identity program, it will have an image with its various publics—customers, employees, the media, stockholders, financial analysts, the community, and others. The image is generated by the company's employees, products, buildings, and communications as they reach various publics. In most cases, the image is not planned but simply results from the thousands of encounters between company materials and various publics.

Designing a corporate identity can range from creating a new logo and stationery, on the one hand, to a multi-faceted, comprehensive, million dollar communication program on the other. In the latter case, the identity tools include product packaging, information brochures, signage, office environments, car and truck decals, uniforms, advertising, employee communications, business cards, and so on.

Currently, corporate identity planners use one logo on all company media. This leads to a standardized presentation, ignoring the differences in audiences and market segments. The unidimensional corporate identity may have been sufficient a few years ago, but the proliferation of audience segments is forcing corporate identity managers to rethink their strategies.

During the 1970s, many corporations harnessed corporate identity design to lay a foundation for competitive advantage. Here is one example:

> Allegheny Airlines of Pittsburgh grew to become the sixth largest air carrier in terms of passengers served, but it suffered from a small-time, regional image. Research by corporate identity consultants showed that in the case of air carriers consumers felt "bigger is better." The consultants' job was to reposition Allegheny Airlines as a big-time, national carrier. Corporate identity planning led to changing the airline's name to USAir. To reinforce the identity change, planes, ground vehicles, and terminal stations were painted bright colors. The environmental design was supplemented with new advertising, saying, "It takes a big airline to fly more flights than TWA. . . ."

CONCLUSION

Design provides a major basis to differentiate a firm and its product offerings from competitors. Managing design can and should be one of marketing's greatest contributions to the enterprise's overall strategy.

□

DEVELOPING PRICING STRATEGIES IN AN UNCERTAIN ENVIRONMENT
DAN NIMER

No one in marketing management today—or in corporate management, for that matter—has ever before had to make critical marketing decisions in an environment such as we have today. No customer for consumer goods, industrial products, or services has ever before had to make critical buying decisions under such uncertainty. Never before has the marketplace been so chaotic and unpredictable, and never before have the traditional price "setting" and price "selling" techniques been so inappropriate. Yet the primary role of price—to capture the value of the product or service in the mind of the buyer—has remained unchanged.

PRICING: A CENTRAL MARKETING ELEMENT

When we look at the elements of the marketing mix—price, product, promotion, and distribution—as manageable strategic variables, the tactical options become quickly obvious:

1. Price versus product
2. Price versus promotion
3. Price versus distribution

It should also be obvious that although pricing tactics—meeting or initiating price changes in the marketplace—have the shortest lead time to implement, they also have the shortest competitive lead time. Developing and acting on non-price tactics in the current environment may take longer, but they also provide a longer-term competitive shield.

One must also look at the tactical options in terms of reversibility. If the marketing manager tries and exhausts his non-price options to meet a

Strategic Planning Management, February, 1986; Commerce Communications, Inc.

competitive threat and they don't solve the problem, he still has the alternative of a price reduction. However, once the price has been cut as the first tactic, the subsequent loss of profitability, however measured, will make it difficult, if not impossible, to get management acquiescence to additional marketing expenditures that can only erode profitability even more.

But before going into the strategic and tactical use of price, the firm must establish its objectives. Yet, my own experience and work in the pricing area has convinced me that:

1. Most companies do not have any meaningful pricing objectives.
2. When they do, the objectives are not communicated in a meaningful way to all involved in the pricing decision.
3. There are few in-company mechanisms for effectively measuring objective trade-offs and modifying objectives as the environment changes.

ALTERNATIVE PRICING OBJECTIVES

In general, there are four alternative pricing objectives:

1. Market share
2. Return on sales/investment
3. Price level stability
4. Meeting the competition

PRICING TO ATTAIN MARKET SHARE

Market share pricing usually is based on the assumption that if the firm lowers its price, the competitor will refrain from doing so, and the market will bestow additional volume on the lower-priced supplier. Since this result does not normally work out in practice, can market share pricing ever be a realistic objective? Yes, but only under certain conditions.

1. *Where the market is in fact price sensitive,* i.e., when a given percentage price reduction will result in a more than proportionate increase in volume. Price sensitivity is a function of a number of factors, some of which are:
   a. Availability of substitutes. The more substitutes available, the greater the price sensitivity.
   b. Frequency of purchase. The greater the purchase frequency, the greater the price sensitivity.
   c. Cost impact. The more significant the expenditure as a part of the total budget, the greater the price sensitivity.

2. *Where the firm has a small market share and is competing against companies with significantly larger market shares.* Consider company A with an annual volume of $5 million competing against companies B and C, each with an annual volume of $75 to $85 million in the relevant market. Should A decide to increase market share by reducing its price by 10%, it is doubtful whether B or C could afford to meet the price cut, or whether they would want to.

3. *Where the firm has a lower cost than its competitors.* Low-cost suppliers to an industry have more pricing options open to them—e.g., to come in under the price umbrella established by the high-cost producer or to be below them and capture market share. Here the trade-offs between profitability and market share are obvious. Should the high-cost producer decide to meet the lower price, he would experience a more severe loss of profits.

4. *Where there is a strong and "captive" aftermarket.* The objective is to price the initial sale for market share and recover profits in the aftermarket. Numerous examples exist in today's markets—the automotive industry, while offering rebates on new car purchases, increases spare parts prices; razor blade manufacturers give away razors so they can get their customers "by the blades"; the pricing practices of many heavy industrial equipment manufacturers are cases in point.

5. *Where the firm is in a strong financial position vis-a-vis its competitors.* In an illiquid financial environment, with the high costs of carrying inventories and receivables, the firm with adequate funds can strive to increase its market share on an "ability to pay" basis, while its financially strapped competitors cannot finance growth.

6. *Where the sale of the product or service is more sensitive to price than to income or promotion.* Few firms have looked at the trade-offs within the marketing mix in terms of reducing advertising rather than increasing price where the market is more price than promotion sensitive.

PRICING TO ATTAIN RETURN ON SALES/INVESTMENT

Return on sales or return on investment is the basis on which nearly 80% of most corporations price. One of the most significant reasons for establishing a cost-plus approach to pricing is that it requires little knowledge of the marketplace—and *little* knowledge is what a *lot* of companies have! What alternatives does a firm have when it doesn't:

- Know its customers
- Know its competitors
- Know itself

Understanding of the above factors requires extensive market research and feedback from the sales organization. Understandably, those firms who cling to "mark-up" pricing also reduce these activities as a means of improving profit—a true case of current-day "marketing myopia."

Yet, without profits, there can be no long-term viability for the organization. One then must consciously make the decision to give up market share for the sake of profits. But among the many logical reasons for *not* establishing a mark-up pricing objective are:

1. The uncertainty of future costs and sales forecast accuracy, both of which strongly affect the cost base.
2. Return on sales/investment may be more of a measuring device than an objective.
3. The wrong investment criteria are often used. Rather than return on total assets, a more realistic yardstick would be return on manageable assets, or return on incremental investment, basically inventories and receivables net of payables. If a manager's pricing performance is to be judged financially, it should be on the basis of assets that can be controlled rather than on an historical base.

PRICING TO ATTAIN PRICE LEVEL STABILITY

Price level stability seems to have gone by the boards to be supplemented by what I believe to be a totally inappropriate approach from a marketing standpoint—price at time of delivery. Yet what most customers really want is price level certainty. If they can't have stability, "at least *tell me* what the price is going to be, even if it is higher."

PRICING TO MEET THE COMPETITION

Meeting the competition has never been appropriate as a pricing objective. When a market or product manager tells me that he must "meet the competition," I question his judgment if not his sanity. The only circumstance under which this objective is appropriate is when you are offering the market absolutely nothing different in your product—and if this is true, why are you in the market?

PERCEIVED VALUE

There is only one valid pricing objective that cuts across all demarcation lines—to ask the customer to pay for the "perceived value" of what he is buying.

The true measurement of whether this is being achieved is change in market share and the relative buildup or decline in backlog vis-a-vis the competition.

Now, the true trade-off is between market share and profitability. Should the firm decide to increase market share at the expense of profitability, it need only price *below* the perceived value of its product in the marketplace; should it decide to harvest its market share to improve profit margins and recover higher costs, it will set a price above the customer's perceived value and allow the competitor to pick up market share.

In those cases where costs decline significantly with volume, it may be possible to pick up both market share and profit through the appropriate pricing strategies.

CREATING AND CAPTURING PERCEIVED VALUE

How does one affect or control perceived value? It is done through the use of non-price variables in the marketing mix: advertising, sales promotion, distribution, and the nature of the product itself. Price is then used as the variable to recover those costs from the buyers.

Let us consider three different scenarios to illustrate the point.

1. Company A is competing with company B in the marketplace. A's product is perceived as being worth 50% more than B's. A's price is also 50% higher. In this case, the perceived value of A's product compared with its price is equal to that of B. Under these conditions, there will be no change in A's market share over time with respect to B.

2. A's product still has a 50% higher perceived value, but its price is only 30% higher. Thus the perceived value vis-a-vis price is higher for A than B. A is able to take market share away from B, but at the expense of profitability. A then has the option of raising price to shut off market share growth and improve margin or retain the status quo.

3. Once again, A's product has the 50% perceived value edge, but is priced 70% above B's offering. This may be due to A's higher costs or a desire to earn larger profits than B. With this relationship, A will be losing market share to B, but may be making greater short-term profits. Its options are to lower price and regain market share or increase the perceived value of its product through the use of non-price variables—providing more product; more and better advertising or sales promotion; and utilizing the sales force more effectively in selling "perceived value" rather than price to the customers. Logically, in an economy where many firms are selling to markets that are not price-sensitive, it makes more sense strategically to enrich the offering and sell perceived value rather than reducing price.

SELLING THE PRICE

Once prices have been set on a perceived value basis, the next step is to "sell" the price. This is the role of sales management. It requires an understanding of the marketplace by the selling arm of the company. How many organizations are content with the sales person's knowledge of:

- The customer
- The customer's needs and wants
- The competition
- The firm's position in the marketplace

Corporate management has, in the main, failed to provide its sales force with the requisite ammunition, preferring instead to cut market research, advertising, promotion, and all other expenditures that facilitate the selling of the price to the market.

The role of price in making a profitable sale has never been more important; the perceived value must not be overlooked; yet they must be measured against their ability to meet corporate short-term and long-term objectives. Until this has been done—and the proper positions taken by marketing and finance—then proper pricing will be impossible task.

CHAPTER

— 21 —

STRATEGY AND FINANCE

∎

□

PLANNING "RIGHT ON THE MONEY":
CAPITAL BUDGETING THAT PAYS OFF

FRANCES E. BAIRD

CAPITAL ALLOCATIONS AS UNFULFILLED PROMISES

Corporations routinely commit huge amounts of capital to a bewildering array of projects, businesses, or strategies in hopes of producing superior returns. But often performance is sub-par or worse, and somehow the expected big payoff never materializes. This problem is most common in businesses where the funds must be committed long before any results will be visible.

To evaluate why projects frequently fall short of their expected returns, a firm needs to answer some critical questions about the projects for which managers are requesting funds:

- How can a business unit expect to achieve returns, on a single project, that are far higher than the overall returns of the company?

- Why do overall returns remain stable, or even decline, after a corporation has committed capital to projects with such high expected returns?

Strategic Planning Management, February, 1984; Commerce Communications, Inc.

WHY PROJECTS FAIL TO DELIVER

Capital is not cheap or plentiful and most companies have an overabundance of "good" investment opportunities. But in a period of capital scarcity, the inability to discriminate between good and bad projects is deadly. Despite the expectation of high returns, inadequate returns will persist. Barring luck, the consequence of failing to deal with this problem is to lock in low returns forever.

Actual performance falls short of forecasted project returns for more reasons than merely sloppy project analysis, on which firms often initially place the blame.

The problem also cannot be resolved simply by improving the mechanics of the capital budgeting process. The approach of allocating capital on the basis of which projects will exceed the cost of capital is conceptually sound, because it seeks to identify the key elements of value creation, cash flow, and risk.

Yet, although this method is technically correct, this form of conventional capital allocation analysis often fails in practice (i.e., returns do not materialize or get any better). It simply is very hard to forecast accurately the risk and the actual cash flows that will be generated by a new project. And, after all, any forecast is only as good as the assumptions that go into it. However, it *is* possible to identify several circumstances that lead to unfulfilled investment expectations. In most cases, the root of the problem lies in the fact that the returns were misestimated in the first place.

Here are six major pitfalls in capital budgeting.

1. *Forecasts ignore competitive and environmental factors.* Individual projects or capital requests rarely consider important factors such as environment and market conditions or competitor responses.

   As a result, it is nearly impossible to calculate cash flows properly or forecast returns accurately. Thus, the return calculated for the project does not reflect the actual economic return to the business and, more often than not, expected returns are deceptively high.

   This phenomenon occurs most frequently when we are faced with a "good" project proposed by a "bad" business. For instance, a business unit may claim that a cost-reduction project will generate savings that would yield a very high return, say 50%, on a discounted cash-flow basis. On its face, the return is excellent.

   If, however, the investment is made in a price-cutting environment, it will only help *maintain* margins, not *improve* them. In other words, if the expected price reduction is incorporated into the sales-revenues forecast, the projected cash flows will be unrealistically high—and the firm will forever await the big returns in vain.

   Admittedly, it is difficult to quantify the impact on cash flow of competitor response or market conditions. But these factors greatly affect your sales volume and profitability, and to ignore them usually results in inflated projections and misallocations of capital.

2. *Additional funding requests aren't evaluated for their strategic compatibility.* Unbudgeted projects are not inherently bad. However, when business units submit capital requests outside the scope of either a plan or capital budget, the requests are not usually accompanied by any strategic justification. Too often they are evaluated without any regard for whether they are consistent with the strategic objectives or capital programs contained in the plan and budget documents. Accepting a project without assessing its strategic merits could unintentionally take the company in a new—and not always good—strategic direction. It may also close off a more attractive option.

3. *No clear standards exist for what constitutes an attractive opportunity.* Strategic plans often fail to provide specific targets for growth, anticipated returns, and investment options. Without this information, managers can't assess the overall attractiveness of a project or determine appropriate investment strategies.

   Ideally, a strategic plan should be able to serve as the cornerstone of the capital allocation process, fostering decisions about whether returns are adequate, how a business should be run, and how capital should be invested. Unfortunately, plans often do not function in this way. All too often they contain lofty earnings projections and understated investment programs, without the data necessary to assess their credibility. They do not demonstrate whether that forecasted growth, at a proposed investment level of working and fixed capital, will yield adequate returns. In addition, they may not show how different growth and investment scenarios might alter the incremental return.

4. *Alternative options aren't adequately explored.* Failure to probe alternative strategies or investment programs sufficiently can lead to the acceptance of projects with unrealistically high expected returns. This tendency is confounded by the fact that plans rarely suggest that a given business unit be "merely" maintained, harvested, or divested. If every business unit consistently requests funds to allow aggressive investment in its product lines, some less flashy but more realistic alternatives (such as eliminating unprofitable products) will never even be considered.

   Furthermore, if investment plans aren't discussed in detail or linked to specific strategic objectives, plans become in large measure merely technical descriptions of the project and the dollar amounts required in each year of the plan. Apart from intuition, there is no way of determining whether the planned capital program is appropriate to strategic objectives or if it will achieve the desired result at the lowest cost.

5. *No guidelines exist to indicate how investments should relate to objectives.* The more separate your firm's strategic planning and capital budgeting processes are, the more likely it is that no one will know how they should be relaxed. To the extent that those processes are integrated, any project description in a capital budget should indicate how it supports one or

more of the strategic objectives outlined in the strategic plan. But the first step is to develop a consistent set of objectives, or else investment programs will be disjointed and inconsistent.

6. *Capital budgets are not prepared with conservation of capital in mind.* Every business unit should be encouraged to pursue any investment opportunity that might yield superior returns. Accordingly, some corporations do not impose spending ceilings on their business units.

An unfortunate consequence of this policy is that businesses may develop capital budgets with utterly no sense of capital conservation in mind. In fact, a dominant attitude in business-unit budgeting is that "the more you ask for, the more you'll get."

SELECTING PROJECTS THAT WILL DELIVER THEIR PROMISED RETURNS

First of all, managers must be asked—and given incentives—to propose projects that are consistent with strategic objectives and that are accompanied by realistic forecasts. The ideal "strategic manager" will design the lowest-cost, highest-yielding, capital programs that facilitate the firm's strategic objectives. Unfortunately, even hiring the best managers is not sufficient to ensure better allocation of capital, because it will not resolve the issues which give rise to the problem.

Next, it can also help to tinker with the mechanics of the allocation process by improving the content of individual capital requests and the corporate review procedures. This process involves such steps as these:

- request managers to describe specifically how their projects relate to strategic goals and the capital programs outlined in the strategic plans and the budgets;
- discuss the continued validity of those programs and the underlying strategic objectives; and
- realistically assess the projects' incremental effect on the overall returns of the business.

This alternative is cumbersome and will only yield limited improvements. It would impose on the capital budgeting group a duty to reach conclusions about the propriety of business strategies and investment programs—issues traditionally outside their responsibility.

The only way to overcome the problems endemic to the capital allocation process is to meet them at their origin: that is, you must develop better strategic and operational planning supported by consistent capital budgets and complementary capital requests.

Better planning requires an awareness that value-creation is all-important, and that growth, investment, and return are the determinants of value.

Better planning should lead to the following results:

1. A strategic plan should be developed that recognizes and analyzes realistic growth and investment alternatives, and selects the alternatives which yield the highest return.

   To achieve this goal, each strategic plan should explicitly address the following issues:

   - What financial and market results can be expected for each business segment under the current strategy?

   - What growth and investment alternatives are available in each business segment? What effect will they have on expected returns?

   - Given the highest value strategic alternative for each business segment, will the business as a whole earn an adequate return?

   Such a plan will make an unambiguous statement about how a business will be managed. Furthermore, it will provide a solid groundwork for the capital budget project requests which follow.

2. Business units should be required to follow a uniform approach for measuring returns. This consistency establishes a basis for comparing returns of one unit to another and deciding where the corporation should invest, divest, or merely maintain its operations.

3. Strategic planning meetings between corporate and business-unit personnel should not be allowed to degenerate into battles over numbers. Instead, the emphasis should be upon a more qualitative discussion.

   One key focus should be the attractiveness of the business: market, competitive, and environmental trends. This provides the corporate staff with the necessary content within which to understand and assess business-unit plans and capital allocation requests.

4. Linking capital requests to strategic plan investment programs will streamline the project authorization process. Capital budgeting departments should continue to review cash-flow computations and determine if the project is cost-effective. However, they need not be concerned with the strategic merits of any individual project, but only whether the project follows the objectives and programs outlined in the plans and budgets.

In conclusion, by combining more thorough project analysis with more realistic forecasting and a tighter integration between strategic and operating goals, a firm can ensure that it not only *selects* high-yielding projects but that it actually *achieves* the promised payoffs.

CHAPTER

— 22 —

STRATEGY AND
INFORMATION SYSTEMS

□

INFORMATION SYSTEMS FOR COMPETITIVE
ADVANTAGE: PLANNING IMPLEMENTATION
NICK RACKOFF, WALTER A. ULLRICH, AND CHARLES WISEMAN

The principal role that information systems have performed in the past has been one of operational and management support. But recently companies have begun using information systems strategically to reap significant competitive advantage.

American Hospital Supply, being the first to install online order entry terminals in hospitals, now dominates the medical supply business. Merrill Lynch, with its Cash Management Account, dependent on database and laser printing technology, preempted the market with its innovative product. American and United Airlines, through their computerized reservation systems, Sabre and Apollo, established an edge that other air carriers have found impossible to overcome.

The significance of these computer-based products and services lies neither in their technological sophistication nor in the format of the reports they produce. Rather, it is found by examining the role they play in their firm's quest

Strategic Planning Management, November, 1985; Commerce Communications, Inc.

Reprinted by permission from MIS Quarterly, Vol. 9, No. 4, December 1985. Copyright 1985 by the Society for Information Management and the MIS Research Center.

for competitive advantage. The cases just mentioned are instances of strategic information systems (SIS)—information systems used to support or shape an organization's competitive strategy, its plan for gaining and/or maintaining advantage.

Although the use of information systems may not always lead to industry domination, it can serve as an important weapon in a firm's strategic arsenal. Up to now, companies have uncovered SIS in an ad hoc fashion, without the benefit of a planning methodology designed specifically for the purpose. But as the pace of competition accelerates in the '80s, competitive leaders must develop a more systematic approach for identifying SIS opportunities.

This reading presents the approach developed and implemented at GTE. It is a comprehensive method for generating a multitude of SIS ideas and selecting the most promising prospects for yielding substantial competitive advantage.

FROM CONVENTIONAL TO STRATEGIC

The dominant view on information systems planning has for decades focused exclusively on the internal functions of the business. But this conventional perspective, powerful as it is for some purposes, cannot account for the SIS examples cited above in which information technology was used to gain competitive advantage. To understand why the conventional perspective is unsuited for identifying SIS, we need first to examine its theoretical underpinnings.

In the conventional view, the targets for information system applications are the organization's planning and control processes. These processes comprise: strategic planning (processes related to the organization's objectives, resource allocation policies, etc.); management control (processes related to assuring that strategic objectives are attained); and operational control (i.e., processes related to assuring that tasks are executed efficiently.

While the conventional perspective has served well to identify opportunities to improve internal business functions, it does not lead directly to the discovery of competitive uses of information technology.

To uncover SIS opportunities, we need a new foundation for information systems planning, a foundation based in the world of competitive strategy, rather than in the arena of planning and control. This new foundation draws on some of the concepts developed by Michael Porter.

Porter views business as being pressed by five competitive forces: the threat of new entrants, the intensity of rivalry among existing firms, the pressures from substitute products, the bargaining power of buyers, and the bargaining power of suppliers. He further proposes three generic strategies with which to combat these forces: differentiation (distinguish your company's products and services from others in all market segments), cost (become the low-cost producer in all market segments), and focus (concentrate on a particular market segment and then either differentiate or become the low-cost producer in that segment).

While Porter's model is helpful in thinking about the firm's competitive environment and the generic strategies a firm may follow, we have found it necessary to develop a more comprehensive framework for identifying SIS opportunities, which we call the theory of strategic thrusts.

Strategic thrusts are major competitive moves (offensive or defensive) made by a firm. Most such moves reduce to five basic thrusts.

- *Differentiation:* Achieve advantage by distinguishing your company's products and services from competitors, or by reducing the differentiation advantage of rivals.

- *Cost:* Achieve advantage by reducing your firm's costs, supplier's costs, or customer's costs, or by raising the costs of your competitors.

- *Innovation:* Achieve advantage by introducing a product or process change that results in a fundamental transformation in the way business is conducted in the industry.

- *Growth:* Achieve advantage by volume or geographical expansion, backward or forward integration, product-line or entry diversification.

- *Alliance:* Achieve advantage by forging market agreements, forming joint ventures, or making acquisitions related to the thrusts of differentiation, cost, innovation, or growth.

Information technology can be used to support or shape the firm's competitive strategy by supporting or shaping strategic thrusts. Strategic thrusts, therefore, constitute the mechanisms for connecting business strategy and information technology.

These thrusts strike at three classes of strategic targets.

- *Supplier targets:* organizations providing what the firm needs to make its product—materials, capital, labor, services, and the like.

- *Customer targets:* end users as well as organizations (e.g., middlemen, physical distributors, financial institutions, etc.) purchasing the firm's product for its own use or for sale to end users.

- *Competitor targets:* organizations selling (or potentially selling) products judged by customers to be the same as, similar to, or substitutable for the firm's products.

DESCRIPTION OF GTE

GTE, a diversified, international telecommunications and electronics company with 185,000 employees and revenues over $14 billion, provides local telephone service in 31 states, two Canadian provinces, and the Dominican Republic. GTE Sprint operates the third largest long-distance telephone system in the U.S. and GTE Telnet runs a nationwide, packet-switched data communication network. In addition, GTE manufactures and markets a complete line of communication equipment, systems, and services, more than 6,000 types of Sylvania lamps and other lighting products, and precision metal, plastic, and ceramic materials used in electrical and electronic devices.

The largest business division, domestic telephone operations (TELOPS), contributes revenues of more than $9 billion, almost 90% of GTE's income. It consists of a corporate group, seven telephone companies, and a data services organization—GTE Data Services (GTEDS)—which provides information systems and services to the TELOPS units. Headquartered in Tampa, GTEDS has its own president who is also a TELOPS corporate vice president.

SIS PLANNING PROCESS

GTEDS information management planning staff realized the importance of the strategic perspective on information systems and took the challenge of developing and implementing a planning process based on this point of view. They saw the task as two-fold:

1. Introduce management to this new perspective and secure its support.
2. Create a mechanism for generating and evaluating SIS proposals.

To accomplish these ends, they designed a five-phase SIS planning process (see Table 22-1) that moved from an initial dissemination of SIS ideas and identification of opportunities to a final acceptance by members of the TELOPS senior management team. The last step in the process resulted in a portfolio of SIS applications ear-marked for implementation.

In Phase A, the head of TELOPS' information management planning function introduced GTEDS president to the SIS concept through a series of informal meetings and memoranda on the subject. The purpose here was to win top-level support for the project and approval for the next two phases.

In phases B and C, GTEDS information management planning staff ran offsite idea-generation meetings aimed at developing the strategic perspective on information systems and identifying SIS opportunities. These sessions involved two groups of information systems professionals. In Phase B, participants were drawn from the data processing company's cadre of middle managers; in Phase C, attendees were the top information management executives within the local telephone companies and GTEDS.

The successful completion of Phases A–C led to a meeting (in Phase D) between GTEDS president and TELOPS top business executive. The latter was introduced to the SIS concept and told of the opportunities already discovered at the previous two brainstorming sessions. This meeting set the stage for Phase E, an SIS idea-generation meeting with TELOPS corporate business planners, those responsible for initiating the business' strategic thrusts.

The idea-generation meetings, which occurred at Phases B, C, and E of the SIS planning process, consisted of seven explicit steps designed to introduce the strategic perspective on information systems, stimulate the systematic

TABLE 22-1   SIS Planning Process

Phase	Activity	Content	Purpose
A	Introduce Chief Executive to SIS Concepts	Overview of SIS concepts; cases of SIS applications in other companies	Gain approval to proceed with SIS idea-generation meeting
B	Conduct SIS Idea-Generation Meeting for Middle Management	Execute SIS idea-generation methodology; evaluate SIS ideas	Test SIS idea-generation methodology; identify significant SIS ideas for executive consideration
C	Conduct SIS Idea-Generation Meeting for Executives	Execute SIS idea-generation methodology; evaluate SIS ideas	Identify SIS ideas and evaluate these together with ideas from previous meeting
D	Introduce Top Business Executives to SIS Concept	Overview of SIS concepts and some candidate SIS ideas for the business	Gain approval to proceed with SIS idea-generation meeting for business planners
E	Conduct SIS Idea-Generation Meeting for Corp. Business Planners	Execute SIS idea-generation methodology; evaluate SIS ideas	Identify SIS ideas and evaluate these together with ideas from previous meetings

search for SIS opportunities, and evaluate and select a set of projects expected to secure the greatest competitive advantage for the firm.

Step 1: Present Tutorial

The tutorial was led by a consultant expert on the theory of strategic information systems. The tutorial emphasized the concepts of strategic targets and strategic thrusts and covered the role of information systems in supporting or shaping the competitive strategy of the firm. More importantly, it provided attendees with an analytical framework to identify SIS opportunities and threats.

Step 2: Apply SIS Concepts to Cases

Following the tutorial, participants solidified their understanding of the concepts presented by analyzing a set of actual SIS microcases drawn from a variety of industries. Working through about 20 examples selected from a prepared list of 50, they learned how to identify strategic targets and thrusts.

Step 3: Review Competitive Position

This step acquainted participants with the competitive realities facing the business. It was presented by the information management planning staff and covered such topics as markets, products, customers, suppliers, competitors, strengths, weaknesses, and business strategies. By understanding these elements, one is in a position to consider the question: How can information technology be used to support or shape strategic thrusts aimed at the firm's strategic targets?

Step 4: Brainstorm for Opportunities

In this step the group divided into teams of five to eight participants and each brainstormed for different kinds of SIS opportunities. Some teams focused on leveraging existing information management assets, while others explored the possibility of creating new assets. Some concentrated on opportunities related to suppliers (providers of raw materials, capital, or labor) by addressing such questions as:

1. Can we use information systems to gain leverage over our suppliers?
   - Improve our bargaining power?
   - Reduce the supplier's bargaining power?
2. Can we use information systems to reduce buying costs?
   - Reduce our labor costs?
   - Reduce our supplier's costs?
3. Can we use information systems to identify alternative sources?
   - To locate substitute products and services?
   - To make versus to buy?
4. Can we use information systems to improve the quality of products and services we receive from our suppliers?

Other teams looked for SIS opportunities related to customers (those who retail, wholesale, warehouse, distribute, or use the firm's products) by responding to such questions as:

1. Can we use information systems to reduce our customer's telecommunications costs?
2. Can we use information systems to increase a customer's switching costs (make it difficult for the customer to change suppliers)?
3. Can we make our databases available to our customers?
4. Can we provide administrative support to our customers? (billing, collection, inventory management, etc.)
5. Can we use information systems to learn more about our customers and/or discover possible market niches?

6. Can we use information systems to help our customers increase their revenues?

And still other teams searched for SIS opportunities related to competitors by answering such questions as:

1. Can we use information systems to raise the entry cost of competitors into our markets?
2. Can we use information systems to differentiate our products and services?
3. Can we use information systems to make a preemptive strike (e.g., to offer something they can't because we have the data) against our competitors?
4. Can we use information systems to provide substitutes before the competition does?
5. Can we use information systems to improve or reduce distribution costs?
6. Can we use information systems to form joint ventures to allow entry into new markets?
7. Can we use information systems to match an existing competitor's offering?
8. Can we use new information technology to establish a new market niche?
9. Can we use our knowledge of the information industry and markets to find new markets or better ways of doing business?

To aid in the development of an SIS idea, each team completed a short form describing the idea, the intended strategic target, the basic strategic thrust, and the specific competitive advantage. The main ground rule in these SIS idea-generation sessions is that criticism or evaluation of ideas must be suppressed so that creativity is not inhibited or stifled in any way.

Step 5: Discuss Opportunities

Each team reported its SIS ideas to the entire group and a scribe posted them on a flip chart for all to see. Group discussion encouraged clarification, elimination of duplicate proposals, or identification of overlapping suggestions. But again, as in the previous step, criticism was prohibited.

Step 6: Evaluate Opportunities

The purpose here was to rate and rank each of the SIS proposals generated. Participants were to apply the following evaluative criteria when making their judgments:

- Degree of competitive advantage
- Cost to develop and install
- Feasibility (from technical and resource points of view)

- Risk (understood as the probability of reaping or sustaining the competitive advantage promised by the SIS idea)

Applying these criteria, SIS proposals were classed into four categories:

- Blockbuster (potential for strategic dominance)
- Very high potential (but not blockbuster)
- Moderate potential (worthy of further consideration)
- Low potential (not worthy of further consideration)

Step 7: Detail Blockbusters

Here the group concentrated on refining and recording the SIS blockbuster ideas. This refinement details the technology employed, customer benefits, competitive advantage, responsibilities, and implementation concerns that aid in the process of transforming the idea into reality.

The SIS idea-generation meetings lasted for two full days. Each step took about two hours, with the exception of the tutorial and the exercise (Steps 1 and 2), which together needed about five hours from an outside consultant to convey the concepts.

RESULTS

Each of the three brainstorming meetings generated over 100 SIS ideas. At each meeting about 10 were considered real winners. Many proposals overlapped across meetings, and there was consensus on the blockbuster suggestions. This consensus was fortunate since it validated the top ideas and built support and commitment for them from a variety of constituencies: corporate management, information management, and local telephone companies.

The SIS opportunities discovered by each group were combined after the final idea-generation meeting. Of the top 11 proposals, six were rated as blockbusters and five were classed as having very high potential. When one considers that most stories about the strategic use of information systems concern only one primary SIS idea, the process at GTE was prolific indeed. We would have scored our process a success had we uncovered one or two top ideas in this first pass, but instead we uncovered 11 worthy of implementation.

The development of a strategic perspective on information systems and the specific ideas generated in the SIS planning process resulted in several major managerial changes at TELOPS:

1. For the first time, members of top management focused their attention on SIS opportunities. They now believe that information systems can play a critical role in shaping business strategy. Proof of this comes in management's immediate allocation of resources to implement the three best blockbuster ideas.

2. To insure that their new strategic vision about the role of information systems is made part of the fabric of the organization and not just a passing fancy, top management elevated the information management function in the corporate hierarchy. It created senior information systems positions at headquarters and at the telephone operating companies. These senior positions now report directly to the chief operating officers of these units instead of to the chief financial officers as they had done in the past. Information management has finally become an equal partner in setting the strategic direction of the company.

3. Executives at GTE's local telephone companies agreed to implement similar SIS planning processes in their operating units. These will address the unique competitive environments, threats, and opportunities confronting each. These units also agreed to champion one of the original 11 SIS ideas.

4. To emphasize the importance TELOPS attaches to the strategic perspective on information systems, TELOPS information management function formally added a new SIS strategy to its long-range plan, which previously focused only on operational improvements.

TELOPS, GTE's largest division, was the first to implement the SIS planning process outlined above. Its success prompted other GTE units, in widely different competitive environments, to initiate similar projects.

CHAPTER

— 23 —

STRATEGY AND
HUMAN RESOURCES

■

□

LINKING STRATEGIC PLANNING
AND HUMAN RESOURCE PLANNING

DAVID ULRICH

A colleague and I recently visited a Fortune 500 company which had spent many months drafting a strategic plan. At the conclusion of this extended work, expectations were high that the plan would inform managerial decisions and help the company succeed.

In our visit a few months later, we observed one of the challenges many companies face with strategic planning. We labeled this challenge SPOTS— Strategic Plans On the Top Shelf. While the plan was technically correct, it did not address the process whereby it could be implemented.

For planning processes to work, plans must be more than blueprints of the future. The plans must identify the specific building specifications through which they can become a reality. Perhaps the key element in these specifications is the human resources necessary to implement the plan.

Some companies have done an excellent job at linking human resources into strategic planning. In these companies, plans are not completed until the human resource demands of the plans are considered and acted upon.

Strategic Planning Management, November, 1985; Commerce Communications, Inc.

Considering such human resource concerns helps these companies shape and focus their planning process.

At IBM, the human resource function has the opportunity and responsibility to "non-concur" with the strategic plan. Non-concurrence by human resources means that the people demands implied by the plan exceed the company's capability.

In one division, the preliminary strategic plan projected a 20% growth for the following year. However, after the human resource concerns were reviewed in light of this objective, the plans were modified since it was clear that hiring 20% more people to reach the objectives was inconsistent with the division's human resource capabilities.

LINKING STRATEGY AND HUMAN RESOURCE REQUIREMENTS

Making the link between strategy plans and human resource requirements, while intuitively a good thing to do, is often more difficult than many firms first anticipate. We have found that creating this link necessitates the following requirements:

1. Rethinking traditional personnel functions as strategic human resource activities. This implies thinking about the long-term impact of human resource practices. For example, are the people hired today not only going to meet the immediate company needs, but fit with the long term direction of the company?

2. Upgrading the human resource department's understanding of and commitment to company strategy. All too often, human resource personnel are not well tuned into the strategic context of their organizations. In one company working to link human resources and strategy, we asked the top 20 human resource management (HRM) executives how much money the company grossed in sales in the previous year. We found 20 different responses.

    For HRM professionals to become more strategic, they must be challenged and stimulated to learn more about their company's strategies and goals. We have called this process one of becoming a strategic partner, a partner being one who can be trusted to help run the business because of the partner's knowledge, skills and complementary expertise. HRM executives must become strategic partners.

3. Coordinating work between general managers, strategic planning staffs, and HRM staffs. General managers have primary responsibility for making strategy work through people, but often they receive mixed messages from strategic planning and HRM support staffs. These mixed messages need to be translated into a clear, cohesive approach to making strategy work through effective management of people. The information provided

by the staff support groups should provide the general manager with specific information on what human resource decisions can be made to make strategy happen.

Given these requirements, we have found the following three-step approach extremely useful in specifying how managers can move from strategic plans to human resource activities.

1. Decide on strategic objectives.
2. Do organization planning to reach the strategic objectives.
3. Design human resource systems to reach the strategic objectives.

What follows is a brief description of the second and third steps.

ORGANIZATION PLANNING

Once a strategic objective has been identified, efforts must be made to plan how the organization will be designed to reach the objective. In organization planning, four concerns need to be addressed:

1. What roles should be established in the organization? Roles refers to how the organization is structured, who reports to whom, and reporting relationships.

    You should ask the following questions:

    - Do some jobs need to be redesigned in order to meet the strategic objective?
    - Is there a need to clarify the roles expected of some key individuals?
    - Can different work tasks be combined into one job assignment?
    - Can some jobs be recombined to give individuals more responsibility for accomplishing work towards the task?

2. What rules should be established in the organization? Rules refers to the means of coordinating work. Work may be coordinated through procedures and policies, common culture, or rigorous information systems.

    You should ask the following questions:

    - Are liaison roles required, that is, individuals who will have specific organizational responsibilities to coordinate work?
    - Are short-term or long-term task forces required to coordinate specific projects or activities?
    - Are information system modifications required to effect better management and flow of information throughout the organization?

3. Who has responsibility for making key decisions? Responsibility can be centralized or decentralized, in one function or another, or shared. Delineation of responsibility, then adherence to accountability, are central to organization planning.

You should ask the following questions:

- Are the individuals with responsibility for making the key decisions at the right level in the organization? Do they have enough visibility to get these decisions made and implemented?
- Are these individuals reporting through the right chain of command?
- Do these individuals have the political clout to sustain enough organizational commitment to get the necessary tasks accomplished?

4. How does the system maintain responsiveness? Paradoxically, as an organization is settled, it must also be unsettled to respond to changing environmental demands. Building innovating subunits becomes a part of the organization plan.

You should ask the following questions:

- What new sub-units may be required to create and sustain innovativeness?
- What can be done to infuse innovativeness into current subunits?

General managers constantly make decisions about organization plans in each of these areas. As these decisions are linked with strategic plans, the strategic plans are more likely to occur.

HUMAN RESOURCE PLANS

Just as the organization needs to be planned, so also do the human resource practices within the organization if a strategy is likely to occur. In making human resource plans which link to strategic objectives, four areas of human resource management can be considered.

Selection/Succession Systems

Selection refers to who is brought into the organization, succession to who is moved up the organization. Ensuring the right person is in the right position at the right time is critical for success. Making strategy work through people means seriously considering what skills are required to make the strategy work, and what individuals have those required skills.

If the entire cost of hiring a professional employee (including benefits, training, moves, etc.) is totaled over a 30-year period, assuming 5% inflation, each hiring decision costs about $5 million. Unfortunately, many companies make such decisions with little foresight about whether the new hire will fit culturally in the company, or if the new hire will have the right skills for the company's future. Hiring and promoting decisions can be excellent tools for making a strategy work.

Development Systems

Often, to reach a strategic objective, new skills are required. To help employees gain the needed skills, training programs can be designed which are linked to a company's strategy. In addition, development programs of cross-training, job rotation, individual counseling, etc., can be used to ensure that key individuals have the necessary skills to make a strategy happen. For General Motors' strategic objective of automation to occur, many employees will have to be retrained.

Key questions to consider are:

- What development programs are required to build the necessary new skills into the organization?
- What employees should be involved in these programs?
- What changes are required in current training programs?

Reward Systems

Financial and non-financial reward systems should be designed to fit with strategic objectives. Companies with growth strategies need to design compensation systems which encourage risk and innovation. Non-financial rewards such as status, recognition, autonomy, etc., also can be used to ensure that individual efforts focus on reaching strategic goals.

Appraisal Systems

If parents only gave their children annual performance reviews, they would not be doing a good job as parents. Performance appraisal, or feedback on performance, should occur continually. The process of performance reviews should facilitate the goal that individual performance standards be consistent with the strategic objectives.

Key questions to consider are:

- Are key individuals provided with adequate feedback to link their own performances to the attainment of the strategic objective?
- Are formal appraisals held frequently enough?
- Are the appraisals based on a variety of data sources?

In each of these four areas, human resource practices can be modified to make strategies happen. While modifying human resource practices is not sufficient to guarantee that strategies will go from formulation to implementation, not considering the above human resource issues will ensure that SPOTS will persist.

CONCLUSION

Companies which have been successful at making strategy work carefully consider human resource practices as key elements in strategic planning. This reading provides a brief description of some of these key linkages between strategic planning and human resource planning.

INDEX

Abell, Derek, 15
Acquisitions, 79, 162, 216–218
  See also Acquisitive diversification
Acquisitive diversification, 207, 208–210, 211–213, 215–216, 217, 219, 220
Adaptability strategy, 254
Administration, evaluating competitor's, 72
Advertisements, 80–81
Amit, Raphael, 173
Analysis center, 126
"Analytical utopia," 330–331
Appraisal systems, 425
Asset-reduction strategies, 169, 170
Assumptions, 54
Audits, 84
  See also Market audits

Backward integration, 242
Baird, Frances E., 407
Batch production, 390
Benefits and cautions, 351–352
Blue Cross, 364–365
Board of directors, 79–80
Bourgeois, L.J., III, 270
Brand identity, 152
Brodwin, David R., 270
Budget, 284–285
  See Capital budgeting
Buffa, Elwood S., 382, 387
Buffer inventories, 384–385
Bureaucratic efficiency, 328–329
Bureaucratic frame of reference, 340, 343
Burnett, Stephen, 12
Business definition, 12–18
Business intelligence, 3
Business strategies, 78, 305–310
Business turnarounds, 164, 165–172
Businesses, stagnant
  See Stagnant businesses
Bypass strategy, 91, 180, 189–190, 191–193, 201–205

CAD/CAM, 399
Camerer, Colin, 32
Capital budgeting, 407, 408–411
Cash flow, 74–76, 119, 121

Chemical Manufacturers Association (CMA), 361–362
Chief executive officer (CEO), 286–289, 297, 306, 311–315
Chrisman, James J., 206, 214
Christensen, H. Kurt, 113, 377
Coalitions, 257–258
Collaborative approach to strategy implementation, 271, 272, 275–276
Collier, Donald W., 283
Combination strategies, 169, 170
Commander approach to strategy implementation, 271–273
Communications, 80–81, 261–263, 334
Company ownership, 79
Competition strategies, 178–193, 194–205
Competitive advantages, 18–19, 20–26, 29–30, 113–118, 309–310, 397
Competitive analysis, 52–56, 57–85, 90–112, 130–132, 133–135, 159–160, 161
Competitive differentiation strategies, 152–153
Competitor analysis system, 136–141
Competitors, 57–61, 68–72, 76–81, 107, 129, 133, 178–181
Conferences, 298, 371–376
Connections, 350–351
Consistency, strategy, 252
Consultant, 132
Consumer preferences, 30–31
Contract management, 163
Contracts, 92
Controllable factors, 25–26
Corporate culture, 4
Corporate identity design, 400
Corporate structure, 4–5
Corrado, Frank M., 260
Cost analysis strategies, 118–123
Cost leadership, 173–174, 175–176, 177
Cost planning, 122–123
Cost-cutting strategies, 169–170
Crescive approach to strategy implementation, 271, 272, 279–282
Cross-market retaliation, 34
Cultural approach to strategy implementation, 271, 272, 277–279

Customer analysis, 81–85, 86–90
Customer groups, 121–122
Customers, 87–89, 96–100, 101–102

Daily routine, 324
Data, 142, 143–144
Data collection, 141–144
Day, George, 250
Debt/equity ratio, 74
Decision support systems, 109
Decreasing returns to scale, 176
Defects, 383–384
Definition, business.
  See Business definition
Demography, 157
Design, 127, 396–400
Differentiation, 151–153
Differentiation thrust, 109
Discretionary operating costs, 119
Disposable products, 154–155
Distinctive competences, 113, 114–115,
  116–118
Distribution, 71, 149–150, 155
Distribution agreements, 57
Distribution channel analysis, 160–161
Diversification, 215–216, 217, 219, 220, 242–243
  See also Acquisitive diversification
Divestiture, 79, 221–226, 227–228, 229–233
Dysart, Joel A., 145

Economic lot size, 383
Economic signals, 32.
  See also Strategic signals
Emerging markets, 156–157, 158–161,
  162–164
Employee policies, 80
Encirclement strategy, 185–187, 188–189
Entrepreneurial frame of reference, 340, 343
Entry flanking, 184
Entry strategy, 156–164.
  See also Emerging markets
Environmental analysis, 38.
  See also Macroenvironmental analysis
Environmental analysis center, 126
Environmental change, 47–51
Environmental factors, control over, 26
Environmental risks, 253
Executive training programs, 209
Expected net cash flow, 74–75
Experience curve, 173–176

Fahey, Liam, 18, 38, 43, 57, 86, 95, 113, 136, 141,
  178, 181, 185, 189, 194, 197, 201, 229, 290,
  315, 365, 369
Feasibility, strategy, 252–253
Felton, Samuel M., 352
Fershtman, Chaim, 173
Fifer, Robert M., 68, 72, 76
Finance drivers, 67
Financial analysis, 72–76
Financial desirability, 254
Financial ratio analysis, 73–74
Financial systems evaluation, 72
Flanking strategy, 181–182, 183–184, 185, 189,
  197–201
Foley, Dan, 364

Form 10-K, 79
Forward integration, 242
Frame of reference, 338, 339–342, 343,
  344–346
Franchise, 163–164
Freehill, Michael, 81
Frontal attack, 178–179, 180–181
Functional strategies, 68–72
Funding sources for new product development,
  65–66

Gaulding, John R., 311
Generic strategies, 241
Geographical flanking, 183
Globalization, 104
Government, 65–66, 105, 263
Groupthink, 127, 352–354
Growth differentiation strategies, 151–152
GTE, 414–415, 419–420
Guerrilla strategy, 194–196, 197

Hambrick, Don, 26
Hatten, Kenneth, 239
Hatten, Mary Louise, 239
Health care industry, 158–160, 162
Herring, Jan, 102
Heublein, 211, 212, 214
Hofer, Charles W., 206, 214
Horizontal integration, 106, 242
Human resource planning, 421–426

Implementation, 4
Industry, 52–56, 57–61
Industry assumptions, 54
Industry boundaries, 48
Industry entrants, 57–61
Industry forces, 47–51
Information systems, 108–112, 412–414
Innovation thrust, 109–112
Inside directors, 79
Inside-out approach, 115
Insight techniques, 347–348
Integration, 106, 148–150, 242
Internal communication, 262
Internal risks, 253
Inventory policy, 390–392
Investment banker, 228–229
Investment history, 77–78
Isenman, Albert W., 90
Issues, 40, 41–42, 366–367
Issues management, 2–3, 357–358, 359–376

Janis, Irving L., 352, 354
Japanese strategy techniques, 3, 188, 382–387
Joint ventures, 59, 66, 112, 162–163
Just-in-time system (JIT), 383, 385

Kelley, Robert E., 352
Key contingencies, 200–201
Kibitzers, 359
Kotler, Philip, 396

Land, Edwin, 13–14
Leaps, 348–350
Learning curve, 175
Legal factors, 59

Legitimate opposition, 359
Lenz, R.T., 325
Levitt, Theodore, 13
Lifecycles, 39, 378-381, 388
Lifestyle, 39, 40, 41
Line responsibility, 3
Linkage process, 126, 128
Liquidation, 241-242
Long-range planning, 7-8
Louden, Teri, 156
Luck forces, 55
Lyles, Marjorie A., 234, 325

McCaffrey, Lynn, 23
McFarland, James, 258
MacMillan, Ian, 23
Macroenvironment, 39, 43-44
Macroenvironmental analysis, 38-42, 43-51, 124-128
Macroenvironmental analyst, 127
Macroenvironmental assumptions, 54
Mahon, John, 357
Mail-order business, 148
Make-or-buy decision, 91
Management, 77, 226-227, 320-325, 333
Management information systems, 109
Management leveraged buyouts, 223-224
Managerial blocking, 245
Managerial process considerations, 127-128
Managers, 80
Manufacturing processes, 69, 70
Map of industry, 57-58
Market access, 107
Market assumptions, 54
Market audits, 81-82, 83-84, 85
Market communications, 80-81
Market definition, 19, 27-28
Market encirclement, 186-187
Market entry, 156-164
Market response, 386
Market segment, 158-159
Market share, 27, 28-31, 402-403
Market-focused guerrilla strategy, 194-195.
    See also Guerrilla strategy
Market drivers, 67
Marketing plan, 70
Marketplace, 262-263
Markets, emerging.
    See Emerging markets
Markus, Robert, 6
Massachusetts legislature, 364-365
Mature markets, 151-155
Media, 263
Mental blocks, 244-247
Mergers, 59
Moore, Craig W., 129
Motivational effect, 383-384
Multi-industry strategic management.
    See Acquisitive diversification

Narayanan, V.K., 27, 47, 124
Negotiations, divestiture, 225, 227-228
Net-to-gross fixed ratio, 74
New products, 58-59, 106, 190-192
New ventures, 265-268
Nimer, Dan, 401

Non-market-focused guerrilla strategy, 194-195.
    See also guerrilla strategy

Operating costs, 119, 123
Operating health assessment, 167-168
Operations decisions, 382-387
Organization levels, 322-323
Organizational change approach to strategy implementation, 271, 273-275
Organizational learning interventions, 345
Organizational politics, 255, 256, 257-259, 260-264, 265-269
Outside directors, 79-80
Outside-in approach, 115-116
Ownership of company, 79, 162

Paine, Frank T., 118
Paperwork, 323-324
Pensions, 228
Perceived value, 404-405
Perelman, Lewis J., 1
Pines, Wayne, 363
Planning calendar, 229-302
"Planning priesthood" barrier, 325-326
Planning process, 320-321, 322-324, 325-336
Polaroid, 13-15
Political frame of reference, 340-342
Politics.
    See Organizational politics
Porter, Michael, 133, 413
Positioning strategy, 394-395
Positive-sum game, 184
Predatory pricing, 33
Price-based frontal attack, 180
Pricing, 33, 401-402, 403-405
Problem formulation, 235, 238-239
Process research and development, 69
Process strategies, 392-394
Proctor & Gamble, 362-363
Produce drivers, 67
Produce to-order, 390-392
Produce to-stock, 390-392
Product, 19, 97, 154-155
Product design, 396, 397, 398-400
Product development, 64-66
Product encirclement, 186-187
Product forms, 152
Product life cycle, 377-381, 388
Product position, 62-64
Product research and development, 68-69
Product strategy, 67-68, 388-389, 392-394
Product strategy evaluation, 61, 62-68
Product substitution, 49
Production drivers, 67
Production systems, 388-391, 392-395
Productivity improvement, 385-386
Product-line costs, 118-121
Products, new, 58-59
Professional frame of reference, 339-342
Projections, 42
Purchasing strategy, 69-70, 94-95

Quality circles, 5
Quality control, 386
"Quantify it" syndrome, 326-328

R & D.
  See Research and development
R & D-based frontal attack, 180
Rackoff, Nick, 412
Ratio analysis, 73–74
Rely tampon, 362–364
Research and development, 65, 68–69, 192
Research and development strategy, 377–381
Resource allocation, 6, 249
Resource analysis, 161
Resources, 54–55
Response lag, 24–25
Results measurement, 7
Retail distribution, 71
Retention rate, 74
Return on assets, 73
Return on equity, 74
Return on investment, 403–404
Return on sales, 73, 403–404
Revenue-increasing strategies, 169, 170
Reward systems, 425
Risk levels, 253, 321–322
Roth, Alexander, 396
Rothschild, William E., 52

SAST (Strategic Assumption Surfacing and Testing), 344
Scenarios, 42, 354–356
Schilit, Warren K., 255
Segment analysis, 158
Segmentation, 151
Segmented flanking, 183–184
Selectivity, 66–67
Self-audit, 84
Sensitivity analysis, 75
Sequential negotiations, 225
Service level, 71
Short-range planning, 7
Shrivastava, Paul, 337
Signals, 32.
  See also Strategic signals
Simultaneous negotiations, 225
SIS alliances, 110–112
Sloane, Alfred, 54
Slow-follow position, 63
Small firms, 305–310
Small-share firms in mature markets, 151–155
Stagnant businesses, 146–150
Stasch, Stanley F., 151
Stevenson, Howard, 211
Stock market performance, 73
Stover, William, 361–362
Straddle products, 154–155
Strategic alliances, 102–103, 104–112
Strategic alternatives, 239–240, 241–244, 245–246, 247–254
  See also Strategic problems
Strategic analysis, 46–47, 141–144
Strategic budget, 284–285
Strategic circles, 5
Strategic costs, 119
Strategic data base, 123
Strategic driver concept, 67
Strategic groups, 49–50
Strategic health assessment, 168

Strategic information systems (SIS), 109, 413, 415–420
Strategic insight techniques, 347–348
Strategic management, 57–61, 368–369.
  See Acquisitive diversification
Strategic management process, 6–7
Strategic organization, 4–5, 10–11
Strategic planning, 2, 6, 7–9, 305–310, 421–426.
  See also Strategy implementation monitoring
Strategic planning system, 296–300, 301–305, 315–319
Strategic problems, 2, 234–235, 236, 238–250.
  See also Strategic alternatives
Strategic signals, 32, 33–37
Strategic thinking, 5, 8, 337–356
Strategic thrusts, 109, 414
Strategic turnaround, 170–172
Strategy, 1–2, 8–9, 156–173, 250–253, 271–282
Strategy implementation methods, 271–282
Strategy implementation monitoring, 283, 284–285, 286–289, 290–294, 299
Structural mechanisms, 125–126
Suitability, strategy, 250–251
Superfund, 361–362
Suppliers, 48, 90–102
Supply assumptions, 54

Teams, 132
Teamwork, 3
Technology, 157
Technology assumptions, 54
Telematics, 3–4
Thomas, Andrew, 331
Thorelli, Hans, 15
Time horizon, 322
Timex Corp., 182–183
Tischler, Leonard J., 118
Top-down audit method, 84
Trends, 39, 40, 41–42
Turnaround process.
  See Business turnarounds
Turnover rate (financial), 74

Ullrich, Walter A., 412
Ulrich, David, 421
Uncontrollable factors, 25–26

Validity, strategy, 251–252
VanWijk, Giles, 23
Vecchiotti, Robert A., 320
Vertical integration, 106, 148–150, 242
Vulnerability, strategy, 253

Ward, John L., 151
Warranty issues, 228
"What if" approach to cost planning, 122–123
Wholesale distribution, 71
Williamson, Donna, 295
Wilson, Ian H., 352
Wiseman, Charles, 108, 412
Workshops, 298–299
Worldwide marketing, 106

Zero-sum game, 184